DAVID BUSCH'S PENTAX™ K200D

GUIDE TO DIGITAL SLR PHOTOGRAPHY

David D. Busch | Matthew Bamberg

Course Technology PTR
A part of Cengage Learning

COURSE TECHNOLOGY
CENGAGE Learning™

Australia, Brazil, Japan, Korea, Mexico, Singapore, Spain, United Kingdom, United States

COURSE TECHNOLOGY
CENGAGE Learning™

David Busch's Pentax K200D Guide to Digital SLR Photography
David D. Busch | Matthew Bamberg

Publisher and General Manager, Course Technology PTR:
Stacy L. Hiquet

Associate Director of Marketing:
Sarah Panella

Manager of Editorial Services:
Heather Talbot

Marketing Manager:
Jordan Casey

Executive Editor:
Kevin Harreld

Project Editor:
Jenny Davidson

Technical Reviewer:
Michael D. Sullivan

PTR Editorial Services Coordinator:
Jennifer Blaney

Interior Layout Tech:
Bill Hartman

Cover Designer:
Mike Tanamachi

Indexer:
Katherine Stimson

Proofreader:
Sara Gullion

For product information and technology assistance, contact us at
Cengage Learning Customer & Sales Support Center, 1-800-354-9706

For permission to use material from this text or product,
submit all requests online at **cengage.com/permissions**
Further permissions questions can be emailed to
permissionrequest@cengage.com

Library of Congress Control Number: 2008929217

ISBN-13: 978-1-59863-802-8

ISBN-10: 1-59863-802-5

Course Technology, a part of Cengage Learning
20 Channel Center Street
Boston, MA 02210
USA

Cengage Learning is a leading provider of customized learning solutions with office locations around the globe, including Singapore, the United Kingdom, Australia, Mexico, Brazil, and Japan. Locate your local office at: **international.cengage.com/region**

Cengage Learning products are represented in Canada by Nelson Education, Ltd.

For your lifelong learning solutions, visit **courseptr.com**

Visit our corporate website at **cengage.com**

Printed in the United States of America
1 2 3 4 5 6 7 11 10 09

For Cathy

Acknowledgments

Once again, thanks to the folks at Course Technology PTR, who have pioneered publishing digital imaging books in full color at a price anyone can afford. Special thanks to executive editor Kevin Harreld, who always gives me the freedom to let my imagination run free with a topic, as well as my veteran production team including project editor Jenny Davidson and technical editor Mike Sullivan. Also thanks to Bill Hartman, layout; Katherine Stimson, indexing; Sara Gullion, proofreading; Mike Tanamachi, cover design; and my agent, Carole McClendon, who has the amazing ability to keep both publishers and authors happy.

About the Authors

With more than a million books in print, **David D. Busch** is one of the best-selling authors of books on digital photography and imaging technology, and the originator of popular series like *David Busch's Pro Secrets* and *David Busch's Quick Snap Guides.* He has written thirteen hugely successful guidebooks for Pentax and other digital SLR models, including the all-time #1 best-seller for the Canon EOS 40D, additional user guides for other camera models, as well as many popular books devoted to dSLRs, including *Mastering Digital SLR Photography, Second Edition* and *Digital SLR Pro Secrets.* As a roving photojournalist for more than 20 years, he illustrated his books, magazine articles, and newspaper reports with award-winning images. He's operated his own commercial studio, suffocated in formal dress while shooting weddings-for-hire, and shot sports for a daily newspaper and upstate New York college. His photos have been published in magazines as diverse as *Scientific American* and *Petersen's PhotoGraphic*, and his articles have appeared in *Popular Photography & Imaging, The Rangefinder, The Professional Photographer*, and hundreds of other publications. He's also reviewed dozens of digital cameras for CNet and *Computer Shopper.*

When About.com named its top five books on Beginning Digital Photography, debuting at the #1 and #2 slots were Busch's *Digital Photography All-In-One Desk Reference for Dummies* and *Mastering Digital Photography.* During the past year, he's had as many as five of his books listed in the Top 20 of Amazon.com's Digital Photography Bestseller list—simultaneously! Busch's 100-plus other books published since 1983 include best-sellers like *David Busch's Quick Snap Guide to Digital SLR Lenses.*

Busch is a member of the Cleveland Photographic Society (www.clevelandphoto.org), which has operated continuously since 1887, and can be located at http://www.clevelandphoto.org. Visit his website at http://www.dslrguides.com.

Matt Bamberg is a photographer and writer based in Palm Springs, California. He began his career in the arts as a graduate student at San Francisco State University in 1992. His work in the visual and media arts included video production and software applications. He completed his MA in Creative Arts in 1997.

After being a public school teacher for 14 years, Bamberg became a photographer and writer. He began to photograph for the articles he was writing while working for the *Desert Sun* and *Palm Springs Life* magazine. Bamberg has authored two other photography books: *Digital Art Photography for Dummies* and *50 Greatest Photo Opportunities in San Francisco.*

Contents

Chapter 2
Pentax K200D Roadmap 25

Chapter 3
Setting Up Your Pentax K200D 67

Chapter 5
Advanced Techniques for Your Pentax K200D 159

Chapter 6
Working with Lenses 199

Chapter 8 Downloading and Editing Your Images 255

Chapter 9 Pentax K200D: Troubleshooting and Prevention 271

Glossary 293

Index 305

Preface

You don't want good pictures from your new Pentax K200D digital SLR camera—you demand *outstanding* photos. After all, this Pentax model is quite advanced for an entry-level camera, with 10 megapixels of resolution, blazing fast automatic focus, and cool new features like the anti-shake technology that steadies your camera to help eliminate blurry pictures. But your gateway to pixel proficiency is dragged down by the slim little book included in the box as a manual. You know that everything you need to know is in there, somewhere, but you don't know where to start. In addition, the camera manual doesn't offer much information on photography or digital photography. Nor are you interested in spending hours or days studying a comprehensive book on digital SLR photography that doesn't necessarily apply directly to your Pentax.

What you need is a guide that explains the purpose and function of the Pentax K200D's basic controls, how you should use them, and *why*. Ideally, there should be information about file formats, resolution, aperture/priority exposure, and special autofocus modes available, but you'd prefer to read about those topics only after you've had the chance to go out and take a few hundred great pictures with your new camera. Why isn't there a book that summarizes the most important information in its first two or three chapters, with lots of illustrations showing what your results will look like when you use this setting or that?

Now there is such a book. If you want a quick introduction to the Pentax's focus controls, flash synchronization options, how to choose lenses, or which exposure modes are best, this book is for you. If you can't decide on what basic settings to use with your camera because you can't figure out how changing ISO or white balance or focus defaults will affect your pictures, you need this guide.

Introduction

The glorious Pentax name lives on, in a robust line of digital SLR cameras for photographers of all proficiency levels, including those, like you, looking for a powerful camera at an entry-level price. Indeed, the Pentax K200D has features that belie its economical cost. What other low-priced dSLR has a dust-proof, weather-resistant body with 60 seals to protect its components from moisture and dust? What other camera in this price range lets you store photos in *two* different "RAW" formats, including Pentax's own PEF format and Adobe's nascent industry standard DNG?

Pentax has packaged up some of the most alluring features of advanced digital SLRs and stuffed them into this compact, highly affordable body. You'll find your new camera is loaded with capabilities that few would have expected to find in such a reasonably-priced dSLR. Indeed, the Pentax retains the ease of use that smoothes the transition for those new to digital photography. For those just dipping their toes into the digital pond, the experience is warm and inviting. The Pentax K200D isn't a snapshot camera—it's a point-and-shoot (if you want to use it in that mode) intended for the thinking photographer.

Nor will you easily outgrow this camera. Pentax must love fledgling photographers, because it seems to work extra hard to give them incredible value for their money. That's been true for as long as I've used Pentax cameras, dating back to my first Pentax Spotmatic, through my "upgrade" to a Honeywell Pentax 6 x 7 medium format film camera, to more recent times when I first got my hands on a Pentax *ist digital model while reviewing cameras for *Computer Shopper* and CNet Networks.

Of course, once your camera is out of the box and you've confirmed that you made a wise purchase, the question comes up, *how do I use this thing?* All those cool features can be mind-numbing to learn, if all you have as a guide is the manual furnished with the camera. Help is on the way. I sincerely believe that this book is your best bet for learning how to use your new camera, and for learning how to use it well.

If you're a Pentax dSLR owner who's looking to learn more about how to use this great camera, you've probably already explored your options. There are DVDs and online tutorials—but who can learn how to use a camera by sitting in front of a television or computer screen? Do you want to watch a movie or click on HTML links, or do you want to go out and take photos with your camera? Videos are fun, but not the best answer.

There's always the manual furnished with the Pentax. It's compact and filled with information, but there's really very little about *why* you should use particular settings or features, and its organization may make it difficult to find what you need. Multiple cross-references may send you flipping back and forth between two or three sections of the book to find what you want to know. The basic manual is also hobbled by black-and-white line drawings and tiny monochrome pictures that aren't very good examples of what you can do.

Also available are third-party guides to the Pentax, like this one. I haven't been happy with some of these guidebooks, which is why I wrote this book. The existing books range from skimpy and illustrated by black-and-white photos to lushly illustrated in full color but too generic to do much good. Photography instruction is useful, but it needs to be related directly to the Pentax dSLR as much as possible.

I've tried to make *David Busch's Pentax K200D Guide to Digital SLR Photography* different from your other Pentax learn-up options. The roadmap sections use larger, color pictures to show you where all the buttons and dials are, and the explanations of what they do are longer and more comprehensive. I've tried to avoid overly general advice, including the two-page checklists on how to take a "sports picture" or a "portrait picture" or a "travel picture." Instead, you'll find tips and techniques for using all the features of your Pentax dSLR to take *any kind of picture* you want. If you want to know where you should stand to take a picture of a quarterback dropping back to unleash a pass, there are plenty of books that will tell you that. This one concentrates on teaching you how to select the best autofocus mode, shutter speed, f/stop, or flash capability to take, say, a great sports picture under any conditions.

This book is not a lame rewriting of the manual that came with the camera. Some folks spend five minutes with a book like this one, spot some information that also appears in the original manual, and decide "Rehash!" without really understanding the differences. Yes, you'll find information here that is also in the owner's manual, such as the parameters you can enter when changing your Pentax's operation in the various menus. Basic descriptions—before I dig in and start providing in-depth tips and information—may also be vaguely similar. There are only so many ways you can say, for example, "Hold the shutter release down halfway to lock in exposure." Not *everything* in the manual is included in this book. But if you need advice on when and how to use the most important functions, you'll find the information here.

David Busch's Pentax K200D Guide to Digital Photography is aimed at both Pentax dSLR veterans as well as newcomers to digital photography and digital SLRs. Both groups can be overwhelmed by the options the Pentax offers, while underwhelmed by the explanations they receive in their user's manual. The manuals are great if you already know what you don't know, and you can find an answer somewhere in a booklet arranged by menu listings and written by a camera vendor employee who last threw together instructions on how to operate a camcorder.

Once you've read this book and are ready to learn more, I hope you pick up one of my other guides to digital SLR photography. Five of them are offered by Course Technology PTR, each approaching the topic from a different perspective. They include:

Quick Snap Guide to Digital SLR Photography
Consider this a prequel to the book you're holding in your hands. It might make a good gift for a spouse or friend who may be using your Pentax, but who lacks even basic knowledge about digital photography, digital SLR photography, and Pentax photography. It serves as an introduction that summarizes the basic features of digital SLR cameras in general (not just the Pentax), and what settings to use and when, such as continuous autofocus/single autofocus, aperture/shutter priority, EV settings, and so forth. The guide also includes recipes for shooting the most common kinds of pictures, with step-by-step instructions for capturing effective sports photos, portraits, landscapes, and other types of images.

David Busch's Quick Snap Guide to Digital SLR Lenses
A bit overwhelmed by the features and controls of digital SLR lenses, and not quite sure when to use each type? This book explains lenses, their use, and lens technology in easy-to-access two- and four-page spreads, each devoted to a different topic, such as depth-of-field, lens aberrations, or using zoom lenses. If you have a friend or significant other who is less versed in photography, but who wants to borrow and use your Pentax dSLR from time to time, this book can save you a ton of explanation.

David Busch's Quick Snap Guide to Lighting
This book tells you everything you need to know about using light to create the kind of images you'll be proud of. It's not Pentax-specific, and it doesn't include any details on using any of the three Pentax-dedicated flash units, but the information you'll find applies to any digital SLR photography.

Mastering Digital SLR Photography, Second Edition
This book is an introduction to digital SLR photography, with nuts-and-bolts explanations of the technology, more in-depth coverage of settings, and whole chapters on the most common types of photography. While not specific to the Pentax, this book can show you how to get more from its capabilities.

Digital SLR Pro Secrets
This is my more advanced guide to dSLR photography with greater depth and detail about the topics you're most interested in. If you've already mastered the basics in *Mastering Digital SLR Photography*, this book will take you to the next level.

Why the Pentax K200D Needs Special Coverage

There are many general digital photography books on the market. Why do I concentrate on books about specific digital SLRs like the Pentax K200D? One reason is that I feel dSLRs are the wave of the future for serious photographers, and those who join the ranks of digital photographers with single lens reflex cameras deserve books tailored to their equipment.

When I started writing digital photography books in 1995, digital SLRs cost $30,000 and few people other than certain professionals could justify purchasing them. Most of my readers a dozen years ago were stuck using the point-and-shoot low-resolution digital cameras of the time—even if they were advanced photographers. I took tons of digital pictures with an Epson digital camera with 1024×768 (less than 1 megapixel!) resolution, and which cost $500.

As recently as 2003 (years before the original Pentax *ist and later models were introduced), the lowest-cost dSLRs were priced at $3,000 or more. Today, around $800 buys you a sophisticated model like the Pentax K200D, and anyone with around $600 can afford its "junior" sibling the K2000D (with lens). The digital SLR is no longer the exclusive bailiwick of the professional, the wealthy, or the serious photography addict willing to scrimp and save to acquire a dream camera. Digital SLRs have become the favored camera for anyone who wants to go beyond point-and-shoot capabilities. And Pentax cameras have enjoyed a favored position among digital SLRs because of Pentax's innovation in introducing affordable cameras with interesting features, such as Anti-Shake image stabilization, and outstanding performance.

You've selected your camera of choice, and you belong in the Pentax camp if you fall into one of the following categories:

- Individuals who want to get better pictures, or perhaps transform their growing interest in photography into a full-fledged hobby or artistic outlet with a Pentax and advanced techniques.
- Those who want to produce more professional-looking images for their personal or business website, and feel that the Pentax will give them more control and capabilities.
- Small business owners with more advanced graphics capabilities who want to use the Pentax to document or promote their business.
- Corporate workers who may or may not have photographic skills in their job descriptions, but who work regularly with graphics and need to learn how to use digital images taken with a Pentax dSLR for reports, presentations, or other applications.

- Professional webmasters with strong skills in programming (including Java, JavaScript, HTML, Perl, etc.) but little background in photography, but who realize that the Pentax can be used for sophisticated photography.
- Graphic artists and others who may be adept in image editing with Photoshop or another program, and who may already be using a film SLR, but who need to learn more about digital photography and the special capabilities of the Pentax dSLR.

Who Am I?

After spending years as the world's most successful unknown author, I've become slightly less obscure in the past few years, thanks to a horde of camera guidebooks and other photographically-oriented tomes I've written. You may have seen my photography articles in *Popular Photography & Imaging* magazine. I've also written about 2,000 articles for magazines like *Petersen's PhotoGraphic* (which is now defunct through no fault of my own), plus *The Rangefinder*, *Professional Photographer*, and dozens of other photographic publications. But, first, and foremost, I'm a photojournalist and made my living in the field until I began devoting most of my time to writing books.

Although I love writing, I'm happiest when I'm out taking pictures, which is why I invariably spend several days each week photographing landscapes, people, close-up subjects, and other things. I spend a month or two each year traveling to events, such as Native American "powwows", Civil War re-enactments, county fairs, ballet, and sports (baseball, basketball, football, and soccer are favorites). A few months ago, I took 14 days for a solo visit to Europe, strictly to shoot photographs of the people, landscapes, and monuments that I've grown to love. I can offer you my personal advice on how to take photos under a variety of conditions because I've had to meet those challenges myself on an ongoing basis.

Like all my digital photography books, this one was written by someone with an incurable photography bug. As I mentioned earlier, one of my first SLRs was a Pentax Spotmatic, and I've used a variety of newer Pentax models since then. I've worked as a sports photographer for an Ohio newspaper and for an upstate New York college. I've operated my own commercial studio and photo lab, cranking out product shots on demand and then printing a few hundred glossy 8 × 10s on a tight deadline for a press kit. I've served as a photo-posing instructor for a modeling agency. People have actually paid me to shoot their weddings and immortalize them with portraits. I even prepared press kits and articles on photography as a PR consultant for a large Rochester, N.Y., company, which shall remain nameless. My trials and travails with imaging and computer technology have made their way into print in book form an alarming number of times, including a few dozen on scanners and photography.

Like you, I love photography for its own merits, and I view technology as just another tool to help me get the images I see in my mind's eye. But, also like you, I had to master this technology before I could apply it to my work. This book is the result of what I've learned, and I hope it will help you master your Pentax digital SLR, too.

As I write this, I'm currently in the throes of upgrading my website, which you can find at www.dslrguides.com, adding tutorials and information about my other books. There's some information about the Pentax models right now, but I'll be adding more tips and recommendations (including a list of equipment and accessories that I can't live without) in the next few months. I hope you'll stop by for a visit.

1

Shooting Your First Pentax K200D Picture

I'm going to divide my introduction to the Pentax K200D into three easy-to-understand pieces. First, I'm going to show you just what you absolutely *need* to know to get started using the camera (you'll find that information in this chapter). Then, I move on to a more comprehensive look at what you *should* know about the camera and its controls to use its features effectively (that'll be found in Chapter 2). Finally, you'll learn how to make key settings using the menu system, so you'll be able to fine-tune and tweak the K200D to operate exactly the way you want, in Chapter 3.

If you've previously used a Pentax digital SLR of recent vintage, such as the Pentax K100D or even K10D, you may be able to skim through this chapter quickly, and move on to the two that follow. If you used an older model, such as the *ist D, DL, or DS cameras, you'll want to slow down and read carefully, because a lot has changed.

The next few pages are designed to get your camera fired up and ready for shooting as quickly as possible. Of course, I recognize that anyone who purchases a full-featured camera like the K200D probably hasn't the inclination—or patience—to sit down with a book and slog through basic instructions before snapping off a few—or maybe a few hundred—photos using nothing more than intuition and a general familiarity with digital SLRs. I understand the urge, because my own response to buying a new camera is usually to take a few pictures of the guy in the camera store who sold me my latest treasure. I generally bring along a memory card and a suitable lens (if purchasing a body) when I sidle in to pick up the camera. Assuming there's enough of a residual charge in my new camera's battery to power up the device, I'm off and shooting as soon as the shop's door slaps my behind on the way out. The K200D has an advantage over some of the other cameras I use: it operates using ordinary AA cells, either the rechargeable type or the long-lasting (but not rechargeable) lithium batteries supplied in the box. So, in this case, I was able to drop the batteries inside and begin shooting immediately.

Now that you've got that initial creative burst out of your system, you'll want to take a more considered approach to operating the camera. After all, this Pentax dSLR is not a point-and-shoot camera, although you can easily set it up in a semi-automated mode using Program exposure or Auto Picture modes and a basic autofocus setting for easy capture of grab shots. There is also a nice selection of "Scene mode" options with icons on a handy dial representing a person (for portraits), flower (close-ups), mountain scene (landscapes), or runner (sports activity), with additional scene types located in a menu. So I'm going to provide a basic pre-flight checklist that you need to complete before you really spread your wings and take off. You won't find a lot of detail in this chapter. Indeed, I'm going to tell you just what you absolutely *must* understand, accompanied by some interesting tidbits that will help you become acclimated to your K200D. I'll go into more depth and even repeat some of what I explain here in later chapters, so you don't have to memorize everything you see. Just relax, follow a few easy steps, and then go out and begin taking your best shots—ever.

Unboxing Your K200D

The Pentax K200D comes in a black box filled with the items that most new things shipped from factories come with—the manuals, connecting cords, software, and paperwork. The most important components to get the camera up and running are the camera and "kit" lens, the lithium batteries, and neck strap. You'll need an SD memory card, too, as one is not included. If you purchased your camera at a full service camera shop, they probably went through the initial setup with you. If you shopped at a "big box" store, they probably told you what extras you might need to get the camera working right away. (The only extra you really need is a Secure Digital memory card.) If you ordered your camera on the Internet, they left you on your own to figure everything out after you clicked through all the steps to make your purchase final. Internet shoppers will also have to buy a Secure Digital Flash memory card either online or on the ground.

While you might think that missing items in the box couldn't possibly be a problem, think about who may have been inside the box before you. No matter where the camera came from, it's not uncommon for those who sold it to have used it in a demonstration, forgetting to replace all the parts. It's best to know right away if something is missing, rather than discovering two months down the line that the video cable you thought you'd never use was never in the box. If you look closely on the box your camera came in, you'll find a list of contents (in several languages, mind you). It's a good idea to check the contents in the box with that listed on the box. Inside the box you'll find:

- **Pentax K200D camera body.** Make sure the camera hasn't been physically damaged in shipment. Pay particular attention to the LCD to ensure that it has no cracks or scratches. Neither is very likely, but you want to double-check now.
- **Kit lens.** (If purchased in a kit with a lens included.) The Pentax 18-55mm II lens is the most common lens sold with this camera.
- **Hot shoe cover FR.** This small piece of plastic protects the contacts of the accessory shoe (*hot shoe*) on top of the camera from moisture or accidental short-circuits caused by touching metal items. In practice, the likelihood of both types of damage ranges from implausible to rare, so you can safely leave this cover off your camera for long periods. That's especially true if you frequently use accessories like external flash units or radio triggers, as the cover can be inconvenient to mount and remove, and may be easily lost.
- **Eyecup FP.** (Installed on the camera.) This soft rubber cup lets you nestle your eye up to the viewfinder, and also protects your eyeglasses (if you wear them) from the scratching that the hard material of the viewfinder bezel might cause.
- **ME viewfinder cap.** This is another easy-to-lose and largely superfluous component. It fits over the viewfinder when taking photos without your eye glued to the window, to prevent extraneous light from leaking inside and affecting exposure. When I'm shooting under these conditions (say, when the Pentax is mounted on a tripod), I just shade the viewfinder with my hand.
- **Body mount cover.** The body cap is fitted on the camera when no lens is mounted, to protect the delicate innards (such as the flip-up mirror) and to help keep dust from infiltrating inside and finding its way to your sensor.
- **USB cable I-USB17.** This cable links your K200D to your computer when transferring photos directly.
- **Video cable I-VC28.** Use this cable to view images on an external monitor or television.
- **Software CD S-SW74.** This CD contains software, such as the Pentax Photo Browser and Photo Laboratory applications discussed in Chapter 8.
- **Strap O-ST53.** The neckstrap is what keeps your camera from crashing to the ground when you let go of it with both hands. You might prefer a more sophisticated strap from Op-Tech (www.optechusa.com) or Upstrap (www.upstrap-pro.com).

- **Lithium batteries.** These are non-rechargeable batteries that last about seven times as long as alkaline cells, or, for about 1,100 shots (more or less, depending on how much you use the Pentax's built-in electronic flash). You can buy them virtually anywhere, which is a big plus when you're using your K200D and find yourself in need of more juice. I'll discuss batteries in more detail in the next section.
- **Operating manual.** Even if you have this book, you'll probably want to check the user's guide that Pentax provides, if only to check the actual nomenclature for some obscure accessory, or to double-check an error code. Google "Pentax K200D manual PDF" to find a downloadable version that you can store on your laptop, a CD-ROM, or other media in case you want to access this reference when the paper version isn't handy. If you have an old SD card that's too small to be usable on a modern dSLR (I still have some 128MB and 256MB cards), you can store the PDF on that. But an even better choice is to put the manual on a low-capacity USB "thumb" drive, which you can buy for less than $10. You'll then be able to access the reference anywhere you are, because you can always find someone with a computer that has a USB port and Adobe Acrobat Reader available. You might not be lucky enough to locate a computer with an SD card reader.
- **Quick Guide.** This fast-start booklet has some of the same information you'll find in this chapter, but not in enough detail to be useful.
- **Pentax software manuals.** You'll learn how to use Pentax Photo Browser and Pentax Photo Laboratory from these guides. I don't pad out my books with software instructions, so you'll want to study the Pentax manuals if you choose to use their software instead of some of the alternatives, such as Adobe Photoshop Elements and Adobe Photoshop.
- **Warranty and registration card.** Don't lose these! You'll want to register your Pentax K200D for those times when you need Pentax service or support.

Initial Setup

The initial setup of your Pentax K200D takes no more than a few minutes. You just need to attach the neckstrap, insert the batteries and SD card, mount the lens, and, *voila,* you're ready to shoot. I'll provide step-by-step instructions for putting your camera together in case you need some assistance. If you already know how to do this, feel free to skip this section.

Batteries Included

When you open the box to your K200D, you'll see caps, cables, batteries, and other accessories for your camera, as listed above. The most important items are the camera body, the lens, and the batteries. There won't be a battery charger because unlike most other cameras the K200D takes AA batteries, which are supplied in the box. The batteries shipped with the camera are lithium cells, which last much longer than alkaline batteries. Pentax doesn't recommend that you use alkaline batteries as they don't have enough juice to operate with all camera functions. There are other battery options, described next.

To open up the battery compartment, slide and hold the battery lock that's recessed into the battery cover with your thumb, then push it toward the outside edge of the camera, and then slide the door towards the front of the camera. Insert the batteries in the orientation shown inside (see Figure 1.1). (Despite what comic Steven Wright says, the battery-insertion diagram was *not* invented by the comic's uncle, who got rich from the patent. However, I suspect there *was* a genius at work at Pentax, which thoughtfully used legible black-on-yellow stickers instead of the usual impossible-to-read black-on-black molded guides most cameras have.)

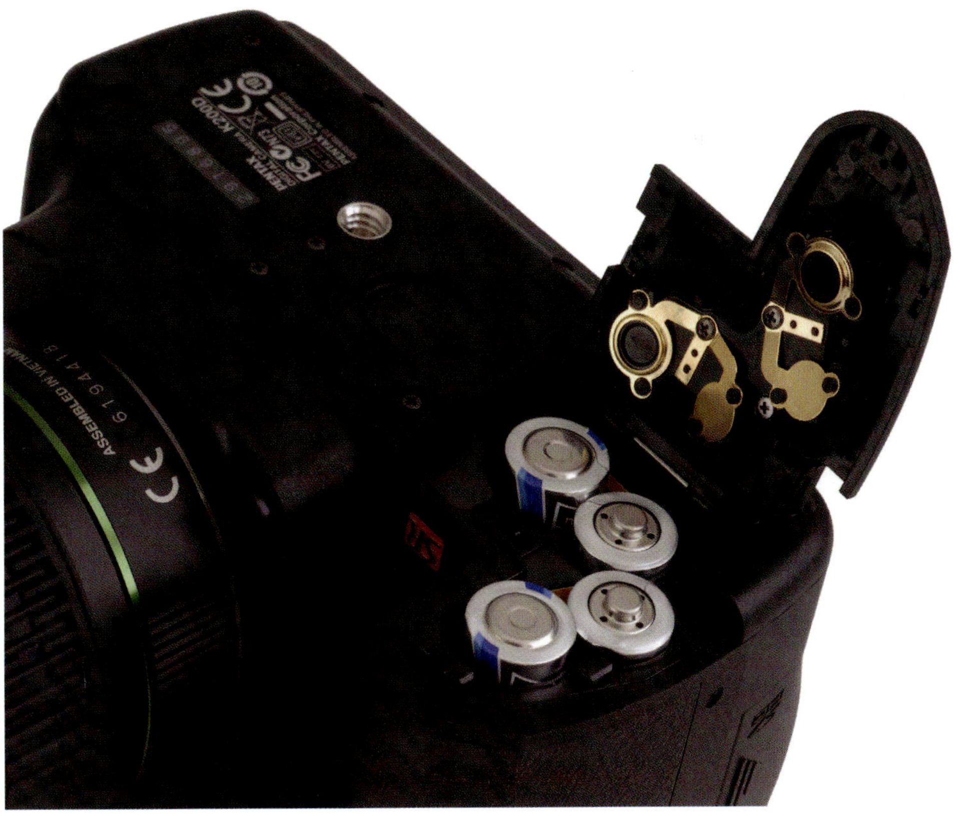

Figure 1.1
Insert the batteries in the camera in the configuration shown.

Using Lithium Cells

Always have some extra lithium batteries in your camera bag, even if you normally use rechargeable cells. Replacement lithium batteries can be purchased at the major drugstore chains for about $5 for a set. There are many situations in which you'll be glad you kept some handy:

- **Remote locales.** If you like to backpack and will often be far from a source of electricity, rechargeable cells won't be convenient. They tend to lose some of their charge daily, even if not used, and will quickly become depleted as you use them. You'll have no way to recharge the cells, lacking a solar-powered charger that might not be a top priority for your backpacking kit. Lithium cells can retain their power for years when stored in a cool, dry environment, and they will typically last a lot longer than a single set of rechargeable cells. When they are dead, just pop in a fresh set.
- **Unexpected needs.** Perhaps you planned to shoot landscapes one weekend, and then are given free front-row tickets to a Major League Soccer game. Instead of a few dozen pictures of trees and lakes, you find yourself shooting hundreds of images of David Beckham and company, which may be beyond the capacity of the one or two sets of rechargeable cells you own. If you have a spare set of lithium cells, you're in good shape.
- **Unexpected failures.** I've charged up batteries and then discovered that they didn't work when called upon, usually because the rechargeable cells had passed their useful life, the charger didn't work, or because of human error. (I *thought* I'd charged them!) That's one reason why I always carry three or four times as many batteries as I think I will need. But, if you're not as paranoid as I am, a set of lithium cells can provide the same protection with less bulk and weight.
- **Long shooting session.** I use lithium cells, despite their extra cost, when I expect to be shooting for longer periods and don't want to change batteries during that span. Perhaps your niece is getting married, and you want to photograph the ceremony, receiving line, and reception without filling the pockets of your outfit with extra rechargeable batteries. A good set of lithium batteries should be able to see you through the longest shooting session.

Rechargeable Options

There are two types of common rechargeable cells in use these days, with one species more common than the other. You may find *nickel manganese* (NiMn) AA cells offered in some stores. Pentax does not recommend using these, as their voltage characteristics might cause the K200D to malfunction. I see the word "malfunction" and that's enough to convince me.

The second common type is the more popular *nickel metal hydride* (NiMH) cells, which Pentax does recommend. They are sold in capacities up to nearly 3,000mAh (milliAmpere hour). You'll need a minimum of four, plus a charger, preferably either the one supplied by the battery manufacturer or a sophisticated unit from Maha (www.mahaenergy.com). Maha also sells batteries, and they work great. Beware of quick-chargers that can recharge your cells in 10-15 minutes, while overheating them and reducing battery life. (This happens even with quick chargers that have built-in fans.) I own one, and use it *only* when I really do need to recharge some batteries in 10 minutes. More often, I'd rather use an overnight charger, or Maha's intelligent charger that takes 100 minutes, but doesn't fry your cells.

Accessory Options

There are several other power options for your Pentax K200D. The Pentax Battery Grip BG3 grip is an add-on battery pack/vertical grip that attaches to the underside of the camera using the tripod socket to secure it firmly. It holds an additional four AA batteries to effectively double the number of exposures you can take with your camera, up to about 2,200 shots when using lithium AA batteries. The grip has a shutter release button that is easier to access when you rotate the camera to shoot vertical photographs, as the button is oriented on what becomes the "top" edge of the camera.

You can also run your camera for long periods using AC power, which can be useful when making a series of long exposures, or if you're shooting in "studio" type environments and taking lots of pictures. The Pentax AC Adapter Kit K-AC76U includes an AC adapter and AC power cord that connects the adapter to a power outlet.

Setting the Time and Date

The first time you use the Pentax K200D, it will ask you to enter the time and date. Just press the Menu button, at top to the immediate left of the LCD, press the right four-way controller button (located to the right of the LCD) until the Set-up menu (with the wrench icon) screen appears, then the down four way controller button to select Date Adjust. Press the right button again to view the Date Adjust screen.

There, you'll be given the option to select the Date Style, Date, and Time, as shown in Figure 1.2. Use the up/down buttons to select the information you want to modify, then the right button to activate that information field:

- **Date style.** You can select mm/dd/yy, yy/mm/dd, dd/mm/yy, and either 12-hour or 24-hour time displays. Use the up/down buttons to make your selection, then press the left button to return to the list of Time/Date choices.
- **Date.** Press the right button to highlight the Date field you want to change, then the up/down buttons to modify the setting. Press the left button to return to the list of Time/Date choices.
- **Time.** Press the right button to highlight the Time field you want to change, then the up/down buttons to modify the setting. Press the left button to return to the list of Time/Date choices.

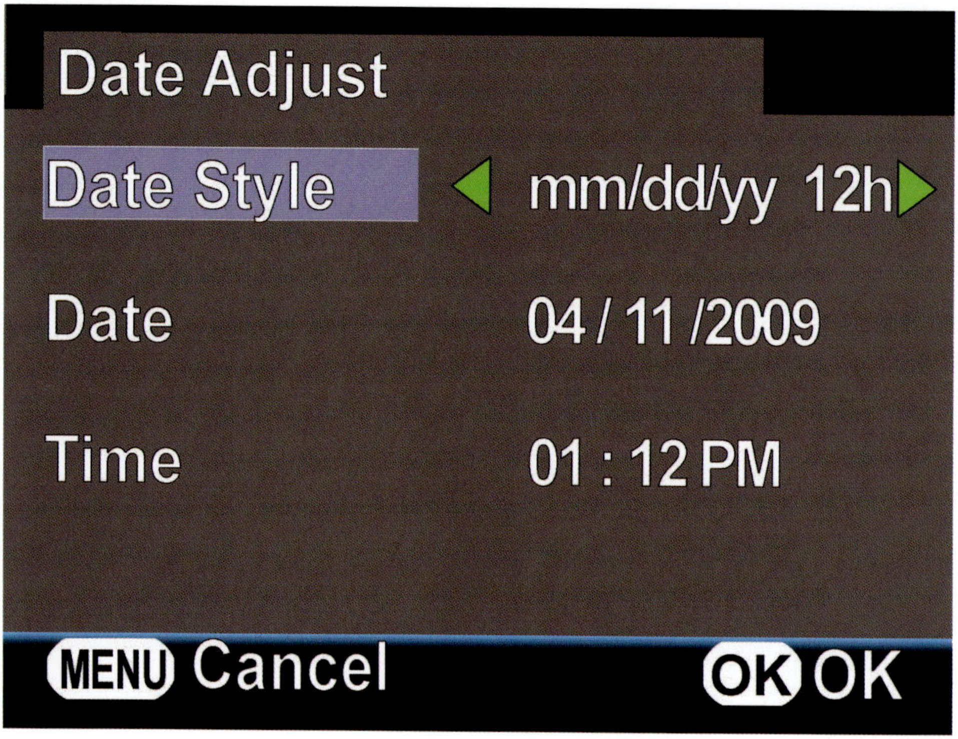

Figure 1.2
Adjust the date format and enter the current date and time.

When finished setting the date and time, press the four way controller's center button to confirm your changes and exit.

Final Steps

After the batteries are loaded and locked, you might as well attach the neckstrap (no instructions needed, although the process can initially be as befuddling as refolding a highway roadmap), mount the lens, insert the SD card, and adjust the viewfinder's diopter correction for your vision.

Mounting the Lens

The most important thing you want to remember when mounting a lens is to prevent extraneous material such as dust or lint from getting inside your camera or on the rear element of your lens.

Unless the helpful folks at the retailer mounted it for you, your K200D doesn't have a lens attached. Select the lens you want to use and loosen the rear lens cap. I place the lens I'm planning to mount vertically with the front side face down with front lens cap still attached, so that it's protected but ready to pick up quickly. When you are ready to move the lens onto the camera, you can quickly take off the rear cap to facilitate the switchover.

Next, check to see that the camera is turned off. The main switch, located concentrically with the shutter release on the top of the handgrip at top right, turns the camera on and off. To turn the camera on or off, rotate the main switch. To remove the body cap, press the lens release button located on the front of the camera between the lens and the handgrip, and gently turn it counterclockwise towards the handgrip until it lifts off. You should always mount the body cap when there is no lens on the camera to keep dust and dirt off the mirror, focusing screen, mirror box, and sensor. The body cap also protects the mirror from intruding objects.

Once the body cap has been removed, remove the rear lens cap from the lens and set it aside. Then mount the lens on the camera, aligning the red dot on the camera's lens mount with the red dot on the lens barrel. Secure the lens to the body of the camera by turning the lens clockwise until it clicks (see Figure 1.3).

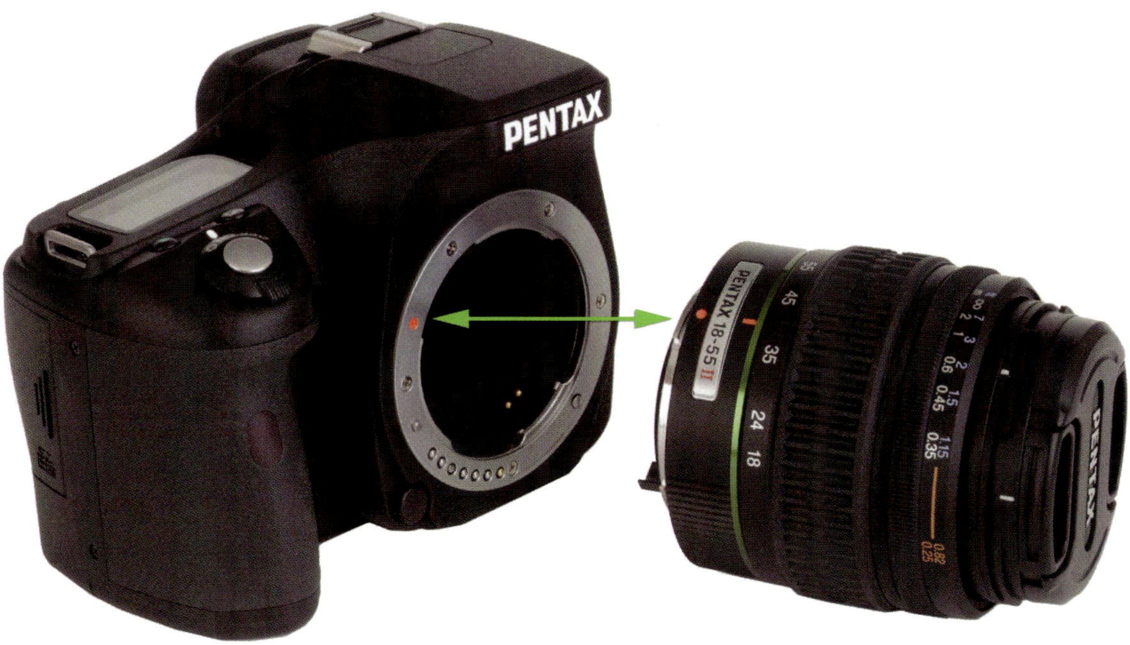

Figure 1.3 Match the red dot on the lens barrel with the red dot on the camera mount to align them.

Set the focus mode switch on the camera to AF (autofocus). The focus mode switch is directly below the K200 label on the camera body. If you're using a lens furnished with a lens hood, and it is bayoneted on the lens in the reversed position (which makes the lens/hood combination more compact for transport), twist it off and remount with the "petals" facing outward (see Figure 1.4). A lens hood protects the front of the lens from accidental bumps and reduces flare caused by light striking the front element of the lens from outside the picture area.

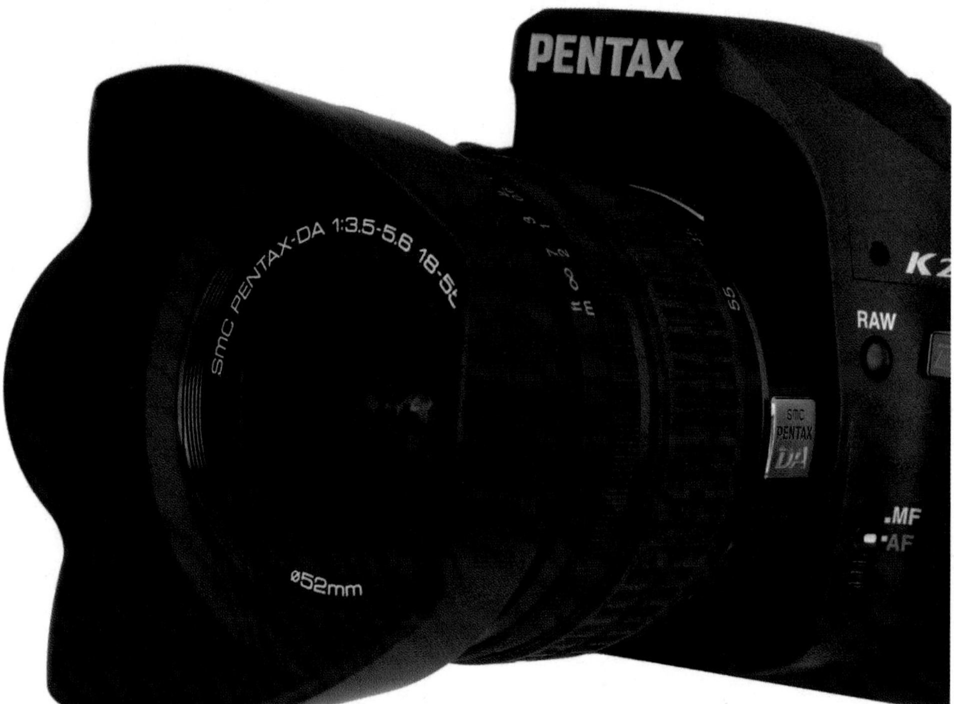

Figure 1.4
A lens hood protects the lens from extraneous light and accidental bumps.

Adjusting Diopter Correction

If you wear glasses or contact lenses and want to use the Pentax K200D without them, or if your normal or corrected vision requires a bit of fine-tuning when you're peering through the viewfinder, you can modify the camera's built-in diopter adjustment. The diopter slider provides from -2.5 to +1.5 correction. To fine-tune for your eyesight, tap the shutter release to activate the viewfinder readouts. Locate the diopter adjustment, which is just above the viewfinder (see Figure 1.5). Slide the lever back and forth slowly until what you see in the viewfinder is in sharp focus (use the autofocus indicator lines for best results). If you can't get the diopter adjusted to suit your vision, Pentax offers eight different Series M correction lenses for the viewfinder window.

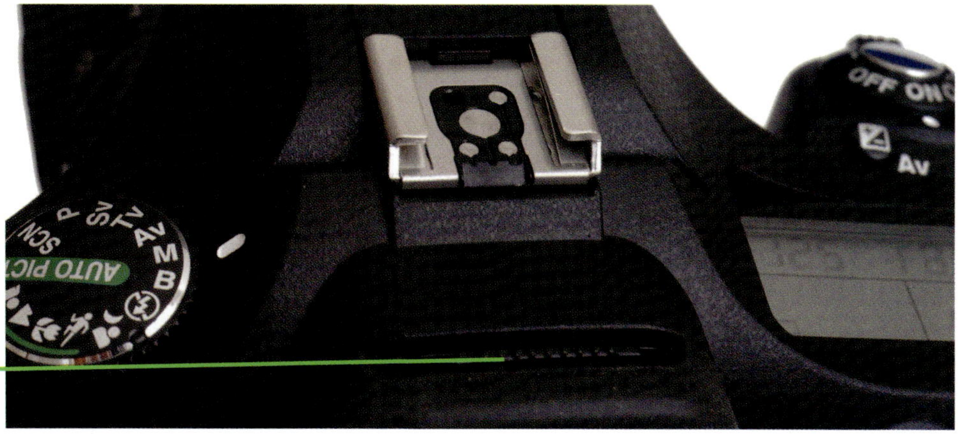

Figure 1.5
Adjust the diopter to suit your eyesight.

Inserting a Secure Digital Memory Card

You need an SD memory card in your camera to store the photos that you take. (Although, the K200D will operate without one.) Before you insert the memory card, turn off the camera. To insert the SD memory card, slide the card cover door on the right side of the body (the side where the shutter release button is) in the direction of the arrow (toward the back of the camera) to release the cover, and then open it. (The camera will automatically shut off if you accidentally left it on while opening the SD memory card door.)

Insert the memory card with the label facing the back of the camera, as shown in Figure 1.6, oriented so that the row of metallic contacts faces the front of the camera and goes

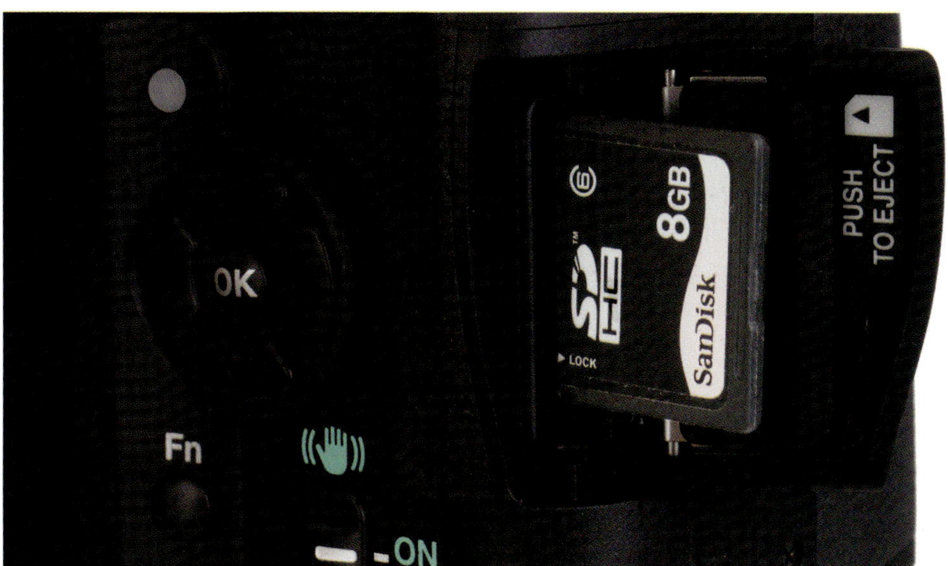

Figure 1.6
The SD memory card is inserted with the label facing the back of the camera.

into the slot first. Close the door. To remove the memory card, push on it once to pop it out, and then pull it out from its sides.

Now you have everything set up to take your first shots. Remember to take off your lens cap before you start!

Selecting a Scene Mode

There are seven basic Scene modes available on the Mode dial, located on the top-left edge of the Pentax K200D. One of the Scene mode settings, the Scene mode (SCN), lets you choose eight additional shooting scenes, so that the total number of Scene mode options is 15. That's a lot of choices, more than you'll find in most other digital SLRs! You'll find a complete description of both Scene and Exposure modes (described next) as well as Camera User Settings in Chapter 4.

Now you need to decide which Scene mode you are going to use. If you're very new to digital photography, you might want to set the camera to Auto (the green area on the Mode dial that says AUTO PICT) or P (Program mode) and start snapping away. Either mode will make all the appropriate settings for you for many shooting situations. If you have a specific type of picture you want to shoot, you can try out the basic Scene mode settings indicated on the Mode dial, as shown in Figure 1.7.

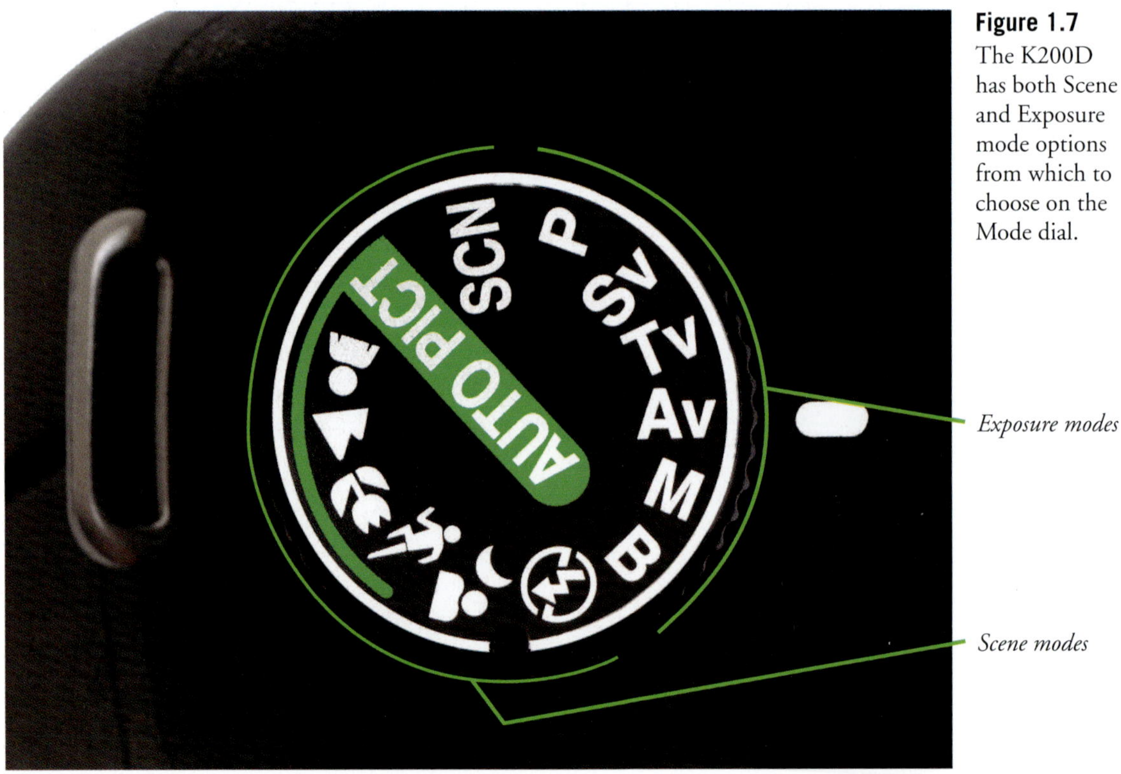

Figure 1.7
The K200D has both Scene and Exposure mode options from which to choose on the Mode dial.

You can also choose from other Scene modes available on the monitor screen when the Mode dial is set to SCN mode. If you want to control your exposures and you know a few things about f/stops and shutter speeds, then you'll want to use the Exposure modes, which are explained in Chapter 4. But beginners will find that Scene modes are, to start, a quick-and-easy solution to everyday photography. The seven basic Scene modes, found on the Mode dial, are as follows:

- **Auto Pict.** The K200D makes all the decisions for you. It will choose from one of four modes (Portrait, Landscape, Macro, and Moving Object, indicated by the green line under them on the Mode dial), or choose other settings to take the picture you have framed.
- **Portrait.** The K200D recognizes human subjects, and adjusts its settings accordingly. (More on this and other Scene modes in Chapter 4.)
- **Landscape.** The K200D attempts to put the entire frame in clear focus, both background and foreground.
- **Macro.** The K200D focuses on the closest subject in the frame, even those only a few inches from the camera. This setting is especially good for objects like flowers and bugs.
- **Moving Object.** In this Sports mode, whether you are moving (say, while in a car) or your subject is in motion, your K200D will use a faster shutter speed to freeze the action.
- **Night Scene Portrait.** Camera detects people in the night. You might want to use a tripod here as the camera may leave the shutter open long enough to cause blur from camera shake.
- **SCN.** Camera lets you decide among eight more shooting scenes that you choose from the monitor screen.

There are eight additional Scene modes available from the SCN position on the Mode dial:

- **Night Scene.** Use a tripod to shoot the view from skyscrapers at night, or other typical night scenes that don't include people.
- **Surf & Snow.** The camera will compensate for bright backgrounds such as white sand beaches or snowy mountains.
- **Food.** Produces vivid, saturated colors that makes food look especially tasty.
- **Sunset.** Increases the contrast for more vivid sunset and sunrise colors.
- **Kids.** The camera focuses continually to keep active kids sharp, and adjusts the color for good skin tones.

- **Pet.** Like the Kids setting, this one follows fast-moving subjects, but balances the color for fur instead of skin!
- **Candlelight.** The K200D focuses properly on bright areas of light in a dark scene.
- **Museum.** Disables the flash and increases the sensor's sensitivity, as museums often ban flash photography.

To choose one of these additional Scene modes, just follow these steps:

1. Set the Mode dial to SCN.
2. Press the Fn (Function) button.
3. Press the OK button to view the Mode Palette, shown in Figure 1.8.

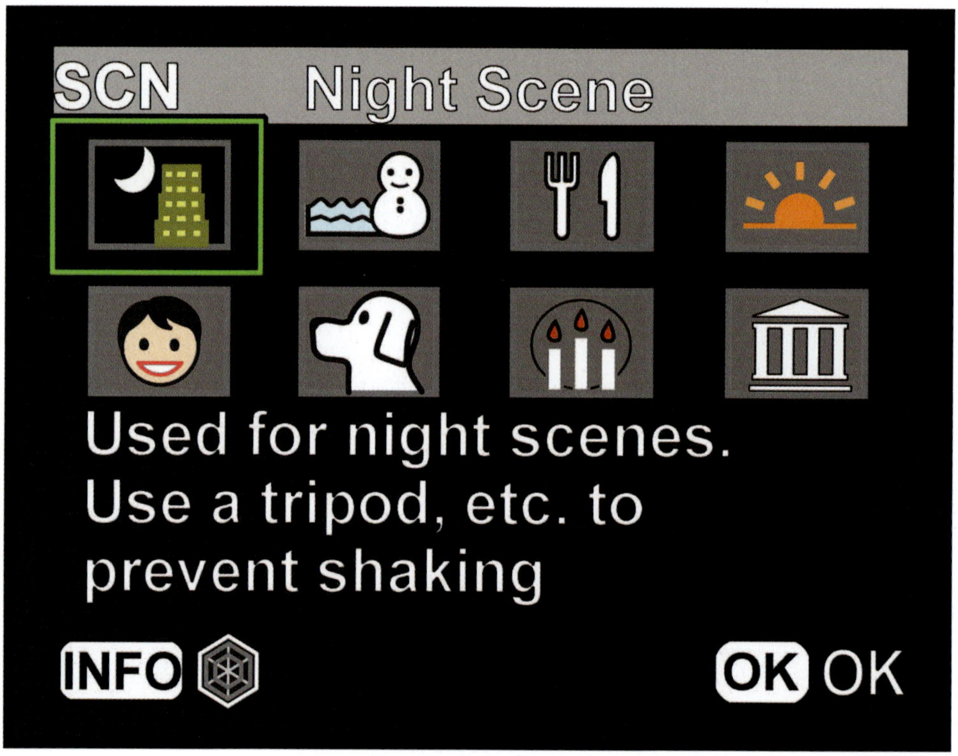

Figure 1.8 Additional Scene modes are available when you set the Mode dial to the SCN setting.

4. Use the four-way controller to choose one of the Scene modes.
5. When the Scene mode is highlighted by a green box, press the OK button again to confirm your choice. Note that while selecting one of these Scene modes, you can press the Info button to produce a screen of additional options. For now, keep things simple and use the unadorned Scene modes. I'll explain how to change the options in Chapter 4.

Selecting an Exposure Mode

If you have enough experience and find Scene modes to be kids' stuff, you can select one of the more advanced Exposure modes. I'll explain them in more detail and tell you why you might want to use or not use each in Chapter 4:

- **P: Program.** The K200D automatically sets shutter speed and aperture, but you can select other options such as sensor sensitivity (ISO) and exposure value compensation (EV), or select a different combination of shutter speed and aperture settings that will produce the same equivalent exposure.
- **Sv: Sensitivity Value Priority.** You determine the ISO setting (sensor sensitivity) and the camera selects an appropriate shutter speed and aperture to produce the correct exposure.
- **Tv: Time Value (Shutter) Priority.** You select the shutter speed and the K200D will calculate the appropriate aperture setting.
- **Av: Aperture Value Priority.** Aperture priority works the other way around—you determine the f/stop (aperture) and the camera selects the right shutter speed for the correct exposure.
- **M: Manual.** You set both shutter speed and aperture, but can follow or ignore the camera's metering indicator.
- **B: Bulb.** This isn't really an exposure metering mode, but Pentax includes it on the Mode dial grouped with the "true" Exposure modes. Most cameras use Bulb as one of the available shutter speeds, after the longest timed setting (usually 30 seconds). Bulb leaves the shutter open as long as you have the shutter release pressed down all the way. Needless to say, you'll want to use a tripod with this setting, unless you're trying for some weird or artistic "moving camera" images.

Metering Methods

The metering mode you select determines how the Pentax K200D calculates exposure. You might want to select a particular metering mode for your first shots, although the default Multi-Segment metering is probably the best choice as you get to know your camera. I'll explain when and how to use each of the three metering modes later. To change metering modes, follow these steps:

1. Press the Menu button, which is the top button to the left of the LCD, to produce the menu screen, with its four tabbed menus. If you press the Menu button after the camera's been idle awhile and the camera doesn't respond, press the Info button first (it's the second from the bottom to the left of the LCD).
2. The Rec. Mode tab will be in front, as you can see in Figure 1.9. Press the controller down key to select AE Metering.

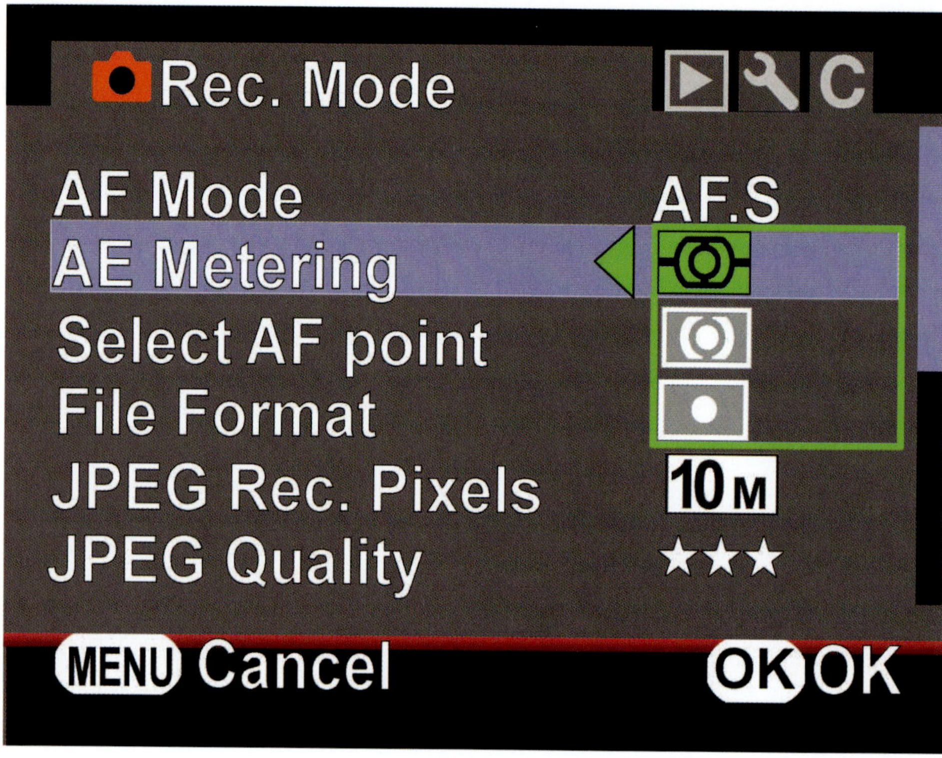

Figure 1.9
The drop-down list on the Menu screen shows three metering methods—Multi-Segment, Center-Weighted, and Spot.

3. Press the controller right key when AE Metering is highlighted, and a drop-down menu with three metering mode icons will appear. The icons represent, from top to bottom, Multi-Segment, Center-Weighted, and Spot metering. (I'll describe them next.)
4. Press the up/down key to select the mode you want.
5. Press the OK button to confirm your choice, then the Menu button to exit the menu system.

For right now, all you need to know about the three metering modes is listed here:

- **Multi-Segment metering.** Exposure is based on readings from 16 parts of the frame, which the K200D uses to make some intelligent guesses about what kind of photo you're taking based on the distribution of light and dark values (landscape, portrait, and so forth).
- **Center-Weighted metering.** Exposure is based on the entire frame, but with emphasis on subject matter placed in the center.
- **Spot metering.** Exposure is calculated based only on what's in the center of the frame within the round brackets shown in the viewfinder.

Choosing a Focus Mode

The Pentax K200D has both manual and auto focus, which means you can focus the camera yourself by turning the focus ring on the lens, or you can allow the camera to determine correct focus. Switch from manual to automatic focus (and back again) by sliding the MF/AF focus switch on the right front side of the camera. To tell the camera to initiate focus, press the shutter release halfway down. In Chapter 3, I'll show you how to redefine the OK button so that it starts the focus process instead.

You can choose from two different autofocus modes when the K200D is using one of the Exposure mode settings. (When using any of the Scene settings, the camera selects a focus mode for you, as I'll outline in Chapter 5.)

To choose a focus mode, follow these steps:

1. Press the Menu button to produce the menu screen with the Recording Mode tab active.
2. Press the controller down key to select AF Mode.
3. Press the controller right key when AF Mode is highlighted in blue, and a drop-down menu with two choices, AF.S and AF.C, will appear, as shown in Figure 1.10. (I'll describe them next.)

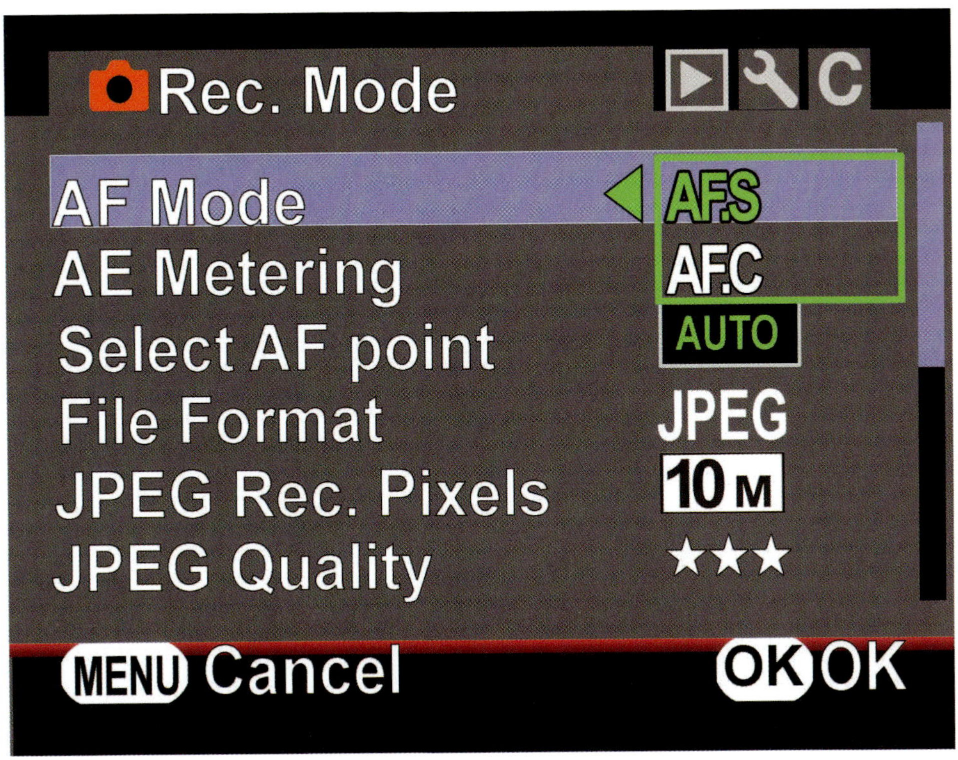

Figure 1.10 You can navigate to a drop-down menu bar to change autofocus modes to either Single Mode (AF.S) or Continuous Mode (AF.C).

4. Press the up/down key to select the mode you want.
5. Press the OK button to confirm your choice, then the Menu button to exit the menu system.

The two autofocus modes are as follows:

- **AF.S: Single Mode.** This mode, sometimes called Single Autofocus, locks in a focus point when the shutter release button is pressed halfway down. You'll see a red square in the viewfinder that illuminates to indicate the focus point selected, a green octagonal focus confirmation indicator is shown at the bottom of the viewfinder, and the camera will emit a beep when the K200D has focused (unless you've disabled the beep, as I'll describe in Chapter 3). The focus locks until you either release the button or press it all the way down to take the picture. If the K200D isn't able to focus, the green octagon in the viewfinder will blink and the shutter release will be locked. This mode is best when your subject isn't moving. All the Scene modes use this focus exclusively, except the Moving Object, Kids, and Pet modes.
- **AF.C: Continuous Mode.** While the shutter release button is pressed halfway down, the focus locks on your subject, but the camera will refocus as required if the subject is moving. If the subject is slightly out of focus, as indicated by the flashing green octagon, the shutter button is not locked and the K200D can still take a picture when the shutter release is pressed all the way down. The Moving Object, Kids, and Pet Scene modes use this focus method exclusively. In order for the K200D to continually focus, you have to keep the shutter release button pressed halfway down.

Selecting a Focus Point

The Pentax K200D allows you to specify which locations on the screen are used to calculate focus, or to let the camera determine the focus point automatically. The options include Auto, Select, and Center. Here's how the camera operates when you're in each mode:

- **Auto.** The K200D chooses the best AF point from among 11 zones distributed throughout the center area of the frame (as shown in Figure 1.11). Your subject does not have to be centered for the camera to locate it.
- **Select.** You select one of those 11 focus points for more control of what you want in focus, using the controller's up/down/left/right keys. The center point is the default option unless you change it with the controller keys. Note: the focus points don't "wrap around" left to right/right to left/ or up/down. When you reach the farthest focus point in any direction, the point movement stops.
- **Center.** The K200D uses the focus point in the center of your frame.

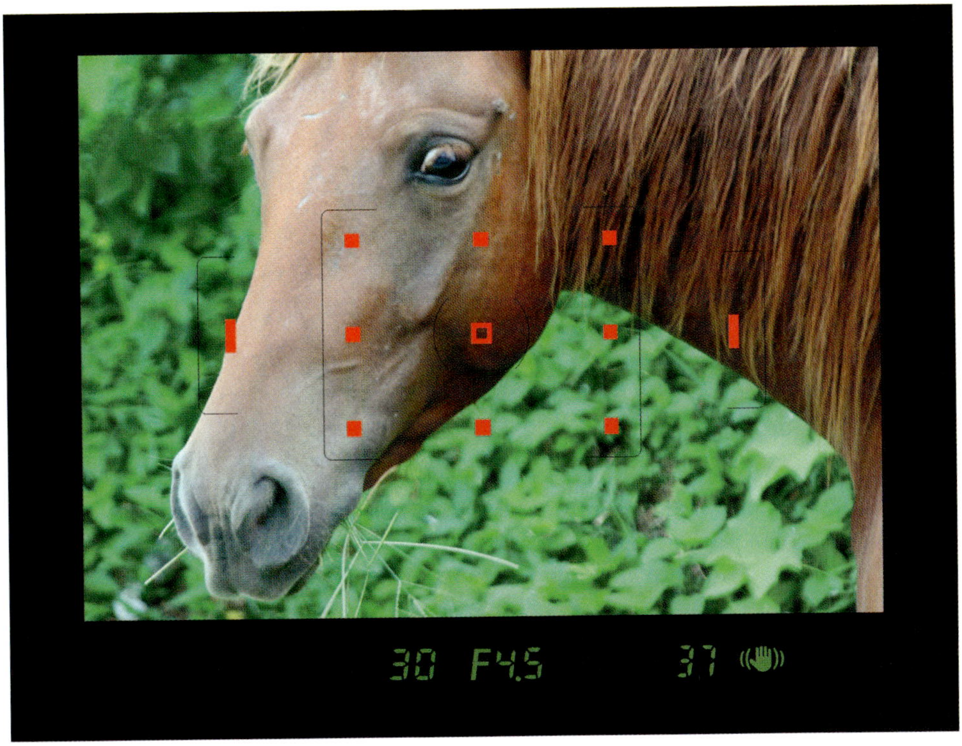

Figure 1.11
The Pentax K200D uses 11 different focus points or zones (highlighted in red).

To choose a focus point, follow these steps:

1. Press the Menu button to produce the menu screen.
2. Press the controller down key to choose the Select AF point entry.
3. Press the controller right key when the Select AF point option is highlighted in blue, and a drop-down menu appears with three choices, Auto, Select (a grid of 11 rectangles), and Center (a single rectangle) as shown from left to right in Figure 1.12.

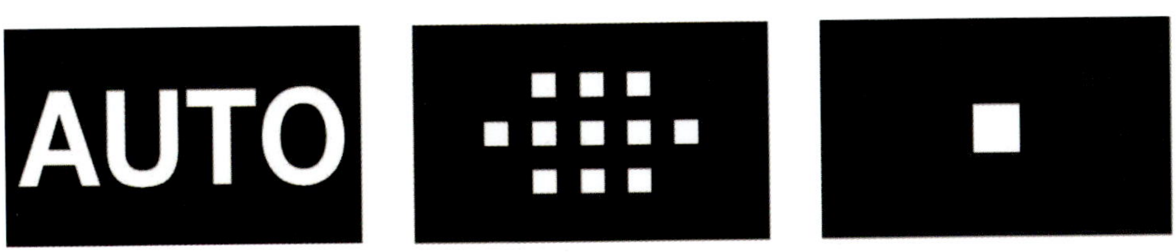

Figure 1.12
Auto, Select, and Center (left to right) selections for focusing area.

4. Press the up/down key to select the mode you want.
5. Press the OK button to confirm your choice, then the Menu button to exit the menu system.

Other Settings

There are a few other basic options that you might want to explore during your first foray with your new Pentax K200D. For example, you can change white balance to adjust the color relationships in your image, adjust the ISO setting to make the sensor more or less sensitive to light, or flip up the built-in flash if there is not enough light to properly expose your subject. I'll explain all these in more detail later in this book, but if you're chomping at the bit, here's all you need to know for now.

White Balance and ISO

The K200D has lots of choices for ISO sensitivity settings and for White Balance (WB). I recommend just setting the WB to Auto at first. But, if you like, you can change it to one of the preset values (Daylight, Shade, Cloudy, Fluorescent Light, Tungsten Light, Flash) or Manual. Press the Fn button to the lower right of the LCD screen on the back of the camera, then press the left controller key to produce the White Balance menu. Use the up/down buttons to choose one setting, then press the OK button to confirm. These too-brief instructions will get you started, but you'll find more complete information in Chapter 4.

For ISO, you can choose Auto, 100, 200, 400, 800, or 1600. As with White Balance, Auto mode will work fine for most situations. But you can set the sensitivity yourself by pressing the Fn button, followed by the right controller key, then a few presses of the up/down keys to choose from the available ISO values. Press OK to confirm your choice. ISO 100 or 200 is sufficient for daylight photos and ISO 400 to ISO 800 should be good for most pictures in dimmer light. In Auto mode, the camera will use ISO settings from 100-400, unless you change that range using a custom menu choice I'll show you in Chapter 3. Note also that you cannot change sensitivity settings when the camera is in Sv mode (Sensitivity Priority mode).

Setting the Self-Timer

If you're using a tripod and don't want the camera to shake when you're pressing the shutter release button, you can use the self-timer. When set, you'll get a 2- or 12-second pause after you press the shutter release before the camera takes a picture.

To activate the self-timer, press on the Fn button, then push the up arrow once to access the Drive mode screen (more on the Drive modes in Chapter 3). Highlight the Self-Timer icon (it looks like a clock with a sweep second hand) and press the down button to reveal the 12-second and 2-second options. The left/right controller buttons will let you highlight one of these. Then press OK to confirm your choice.

When you press the shutter release after the 2-second timer has been activated, you'll first hear a click then a quick series of beeps, which remain on until just before the K200D takes a picture. If you selected the 12-second timer icon, the beeper will sound at a slower cadence, until the final two seconds (when it beeps faster).

Reviewing Your Images

The K200D has a variety of playback options. You can read about all of them in Chapters 2 and 3. In this section I'll cover the basics. Listed below is all you need to know at this point. Fig. 1.13 shows the buttons on the camera that control playback options.

- **See last image taken.** Press the Playback button (the bottom-most button to the left of the LCD, marked with a blue right-pointing triangle) to display the most recent image on the screen.
- **Change information shown.** After pressing the Playback button, press the Info button to change the information display. The information display changes each time you press the Info button in the following repeating cycle: Standard (basic information about shot), histogram display, No information display, and detailed information display. I'll cover all these in the next chapter.

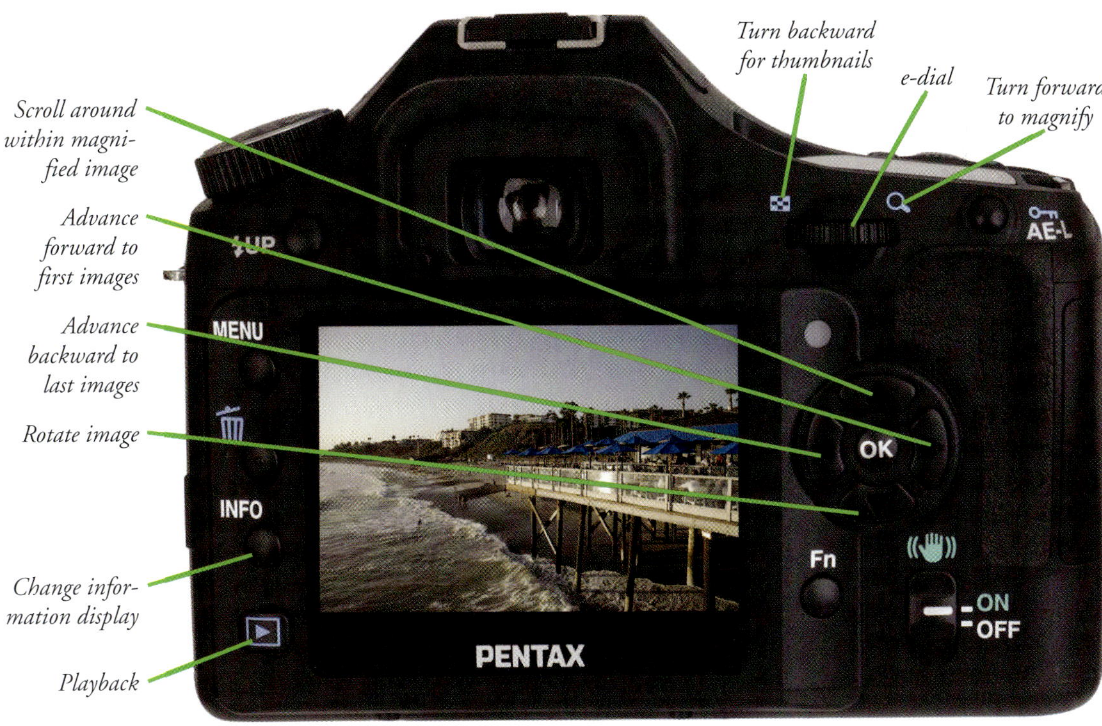

Figure 1.13 Review your images.

- **Browse through images.** Push the right arrow to start with the first image on the SD memory card and cycle forward to the newest. Push the left arrow to review images from the most recently taken to the oldest.
- **Rotate an image.** After pressing the Playback button, you can press the down arrow on the four-way controller to rotate an image. The image is rotated 90-degrees counterclockwise each time the button is pressed.
- **Zoom in and out.** After pressing the Playback button, you can magnify your image by turning the e-dial (located at the top right backside of your camera). Turn it towards the right to zoom in (up to 16X), and towards the left to zoom out, and to change from full screen to thumbnail view. To move around within a magnified image, use the four-way controller buttons. Press the Playback button twice to exit a magnified display.

You'll find more about thumbnails and folders for images, comparing images, slideshows, and other options in Chapter 3.

Deleting an Image

All of us make goofs, and when that happens, one of the most valuable features of any digital camera is the ability to delete images that are really bad before someone else sees them and your reputation is trashed. To delete an image, press the Trash Can button when an image is on view during playback. The choices Delete and Cancel will appear on the screen. Select the option you want, and press the OK button to delete that image or cancel the deletion. But be careful: press the Trash Can button again at this time, and the K200D will assume you want to delete *all* the images on the memory card. Don't panic! You'll be shown another confirmation screen that asks if you *really* want to remove all the images on the memory card. You'll have to choose Delete All, then press OK to do that. Otherwise, with Cancel highlighted, pressing OK backs out of the delete screens. Pressing Menu at this point takes you back to the original single-image delete screen. Whew!

Using Your Flash

I've got an entire chapter on working with light, which includes electronic flash. Check out Chapter 7 if you want to know the details. But, as you get started using your Pentax K200D, you may find a need for your camera's built-in flash, but not much need to learn everything there is to know about it. In a nutshell, here's all you need to understand to get started:

- **Auto flash Popup.** If you're using Auto Pict, Portrait, Close-Up, Motion Object, or Night Portrait Scene modes, the built-in flash will pop up automatically when needed as you press the shutter release down halfway. This is called Auto Discharge mode.

- **No Pop.** The flash will not pop up automatically if you're using Night Scene, Sunset, Candlelight, or Museum modes, found in the SCN mode dial position.
- **Enabling/Disabling Popup.** Press the Fn button, then the down controller key to view the Flash Mode menu. Use the left/right controller keys to choose Auto to enable Auto Discharge, or Flash On to disable Auto Discharge. Press OK to confirm your choice.
- **Pop-it-Yourself.** When Auto Discharge is disabled, or you're using one of the Exposure modes rather than Scene modes, you can elevate the flash yourself by pressing the Flash Up button in the upper-left corner of the back of the camera.
- **Auto exposure.** The K200D will calculate flash exposure for you automatically. You can learn about your other flash exposure and synchronization options in Chapter 7.

Transferring Photos to Your Computer

The last step of your initial photo shoots will be to transfer your pictures from your camera to your computer. From there you can upload them to your blog or webpage, send them to friends via e-mail, or print them out. The K200D lets you print to PictBridge-compatible printers, too. You can also order photo prints by taking the SD card out and bringing it to a photo department at any of the chain stores. The K200D lets you print the date and request how many copies of the photos you want. I'll cover all these output options in Chapter 3.

To transfer your photos to your computer, you can either connect the camera to your computer using a USB cable or you can purchase a memory card reader that connects to your computer that will read the SD memory card on which your K200D has recorded the images. You'll find more detailed instructions on transferring photos in Chapter 8.

To transfer images from the camera to a Mac or PC, just follow these steps:

1. Turn off your camera.
2. Open the port door (see Figure 1.14) where the USB port nestles inside. Plug the USB cable furnished with the K200D into the port. The smaller end (called a 4-pin connection) goes into the camera.
3. Connect the other end of the USB cable to a USB port on your computer. The other end is the larger end (called a Type A connection).
4. Turn the camera on. The installed software on your computer usually detects the camera and a window will pop up on your computer asking you if you want to download the images, or the camera appears on your desktop as a mass storage device, enabling you to click and drag the files to your computer.

To transfer images from an SD card to the computer using a card reader follow these steps:

1. Turn off your camera.
2. Open the SD card door on the right side of the camera, and remove the card by pushing gently on it, and then pulling it out.
3. Insert the SD card into your memory card reader. The installed software on your computer usually detects the camera and a window will pop up on your computer asking you if you want to download the images, or the camera appears on your desktop as a mass storage device, enabling you to click and drag the files to your computer.

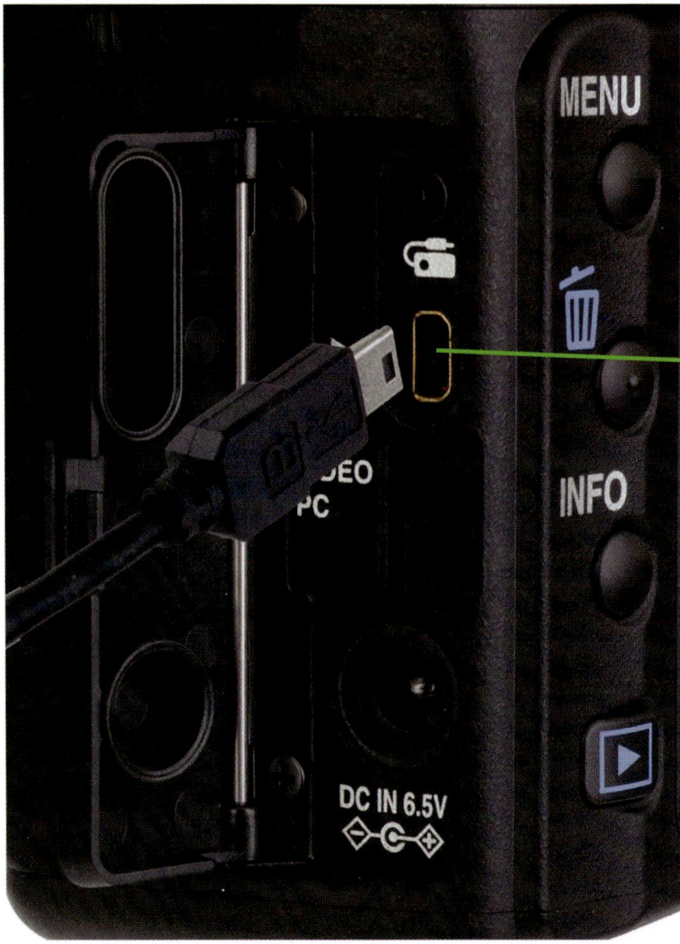

Figure 1.14
Images can be transferred to your computer using a USB cable.

2

Pentax K200D Roadmap

On first glance, the controls, dials, and buttons on the Pentax K200D appear, to the typical user, as complicated as the cockpit of a Boeing 767. In practice, however, your Pentax camera is marginally easier to "fly." Once you've gone through the pre-flight checklist (Chapter 1) and set the camera on autopilot (Auto Pict, Program, or perhaps one of the Scene modes), it can take off and land by itself and capture many great pictures along the way. With 15 or so automatic modes you can shoot just about anything you like without having to think about f/stops, shutter speeds, or focus modes.

But, when you decide to depart from the flight plan and do some creative sight-seeing, there are all those controls to deal with. Whether you are a digital SLR newbie or a seasoned veteran photographer who is just unfamiliar with the latest Pentax cameras, the available options can be confusing. The manual Pentax supplies is not much help. It provides you with a series of tiny line drawings with three views of the camera that are repeated, and then divided into Camera, Capture Mode, and Playback. The label for each control is accompanied by a series of cross-references that point you to the pages deep within the book that contain the information you really want to know. Learning to operate your K200D can be more of a scavenger hunt than a learning process.

For my camera books and field guides, I originated a more useful approach, which provides you with a street-level map rather than a satellite view, featuring large, close-up, full-color photographs of the camera from several angles. Each camera "zone" has a smaller number of labels that point clearly to each individual feature. And, I don't force you to flip back and forth among dozens of pages to find out what a particular component does. Each photo is accompanied by a brief description that summarizes the control, so you can begin using it right away. Only when a particular feature deserves a lengthy explanation do I direct you to a more detailed write-up later in the book. For example, in this chapter I'll show you how to use the Exposure Compensation button to change the exposure the camera calculates when you want to make your picture darker or lighter. If you want to learn more about exposure, I'll point you to the discussion in Chapter 4.

By the time you finish this chapter, you'll have a basic understanding of every control and what it does. I'm not going to delve into the main menu functions here—you'll find a discussion of your Recording, Playback, Setup, and Custom Setting menu options in Chapter 3. I will, however, explain the Function menus, because they directly control shooting and playback features. Overall, everything here is devoted to the button pusher and dial twirler in you.

Front View

The front of the K200D (see Figure 2.1) is what your subjects see when you ask them to smile when they're looking at the camera. This is the "face" of the camera, the view shown on the box and the front of the camera manual. But, oddly enough, the business end is on the reverse side, where the LCD is located and most of the controls reside. For the

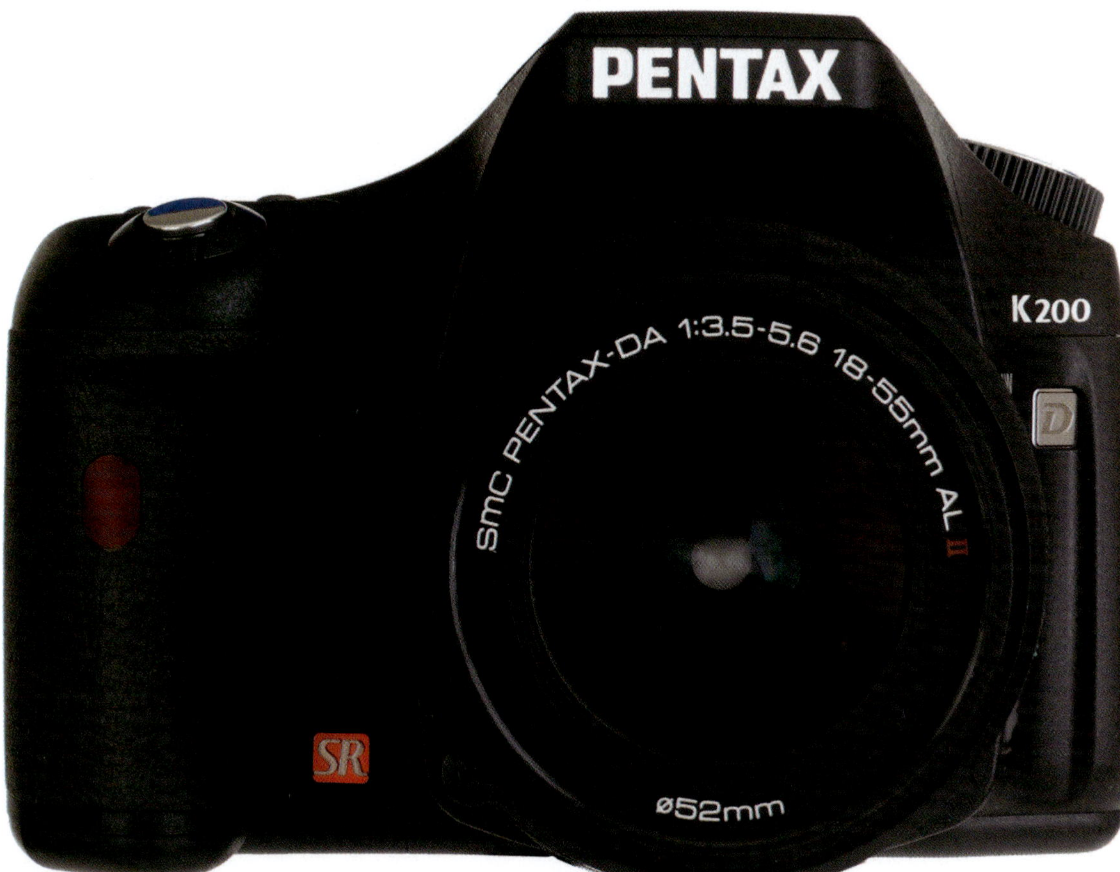

Figure 2.1

photographer, the front of the camera is little more than the surface your fingers curl around as you hold the camera up to your eye while looking through the viewfinder. But, even so, there are several important controls on the front, as you can see in Figure 2.2.

- **Main Switch (On/Off).** This switch, located concentrically with the shutter release button, has two functions. To use the power function, rotate the dial one click clockwise to turn the camera on, and rotate it back to turn it off again. The K200D will automatically "go to sleep" after a period of non-use during a given shooting session, so it is not necessary to physically turn the camera on or off to save battery power while you're actively using it. Power down the camera only when you plan not to take any pictures for a lengthy period of time (say, 30 minutes or longer).
- **Main Switch (Digital Preview/Optical Preview).** Rotate the switch another click to view either a traditional *optical preview* or clever *digital preview* of your image. The preview appears in the viewfinder (optical) or on the back panel LCD (digital), and can be used to evaluate composition, and focus. You can save the digital preview image to your memory card, if you like. See the sidebar, "Using the Digital and Optical Preview" for more information.

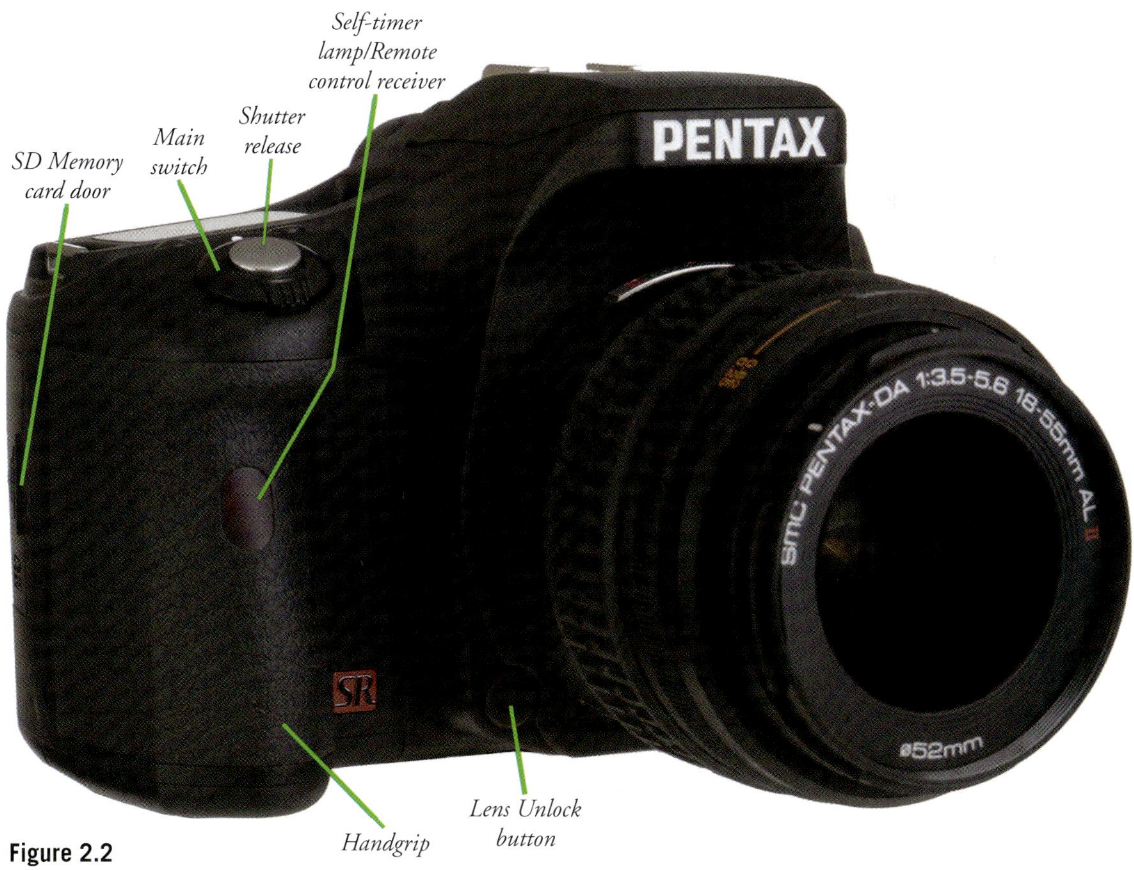

Figure 2.2

USING DIGITAL AND OPTICAL PREVIEW

Single lens reflex (SLR) cameras (of both the film and digital variety) have traditionally included a feature called *depth-of-field* preview, which closes down the lens aperture (otherwise kept wide open until the moment of exposure to improve viewing brightness) to the f/stop that will actually be used to take the picture. The Pentax K200D offers this kind of preview when you set the Preview Method to Optical Preview in Custom Setting #18, as explained in Chapter 3. This conventional depth-of-field preview offers a darker image (because the lens opening is usually reduced in size) that may actually make it *more* difficult to evaluate the image. The Pentax K200D includes as a default method a novel *digital* preview that serves the same function, but in a new way (see Figure 2.3).

When the exposure meter is active (tap the shutter release to activate if it is not), and you rotate the Main Switch all the way clockwise, the camera actually takes a picture, which is displayed on the K200D's LCD. Unless the light levels in the environment where you're shooting are very high, it can be easier to evaluate this big, bright image. (In Chapter 3, I'll show you how to enable two more aids for digital preview mode, *histograms* and *bright/dark areas* ["blinkies"]). Once the preview appears, you can do one of several things:

- Rotate the e-dial (located just to the right of the viewfinder window) to zoom in and out of the preview image, with up to 16X magnification. Use the four-way controller keys to move the viewing window around in the zoomed image.
- Press the Fn button to save the image as a new file. A screen pops up. Choose Save as or Cancel with the up/down keys and press OK to confirm your choice. If you choose neither, after a few seconds, the message (and your preview image) disappears.
- Press the shutter release halfway. The preview image vanishes from the LCD, and you can continue shooting in the normal way.

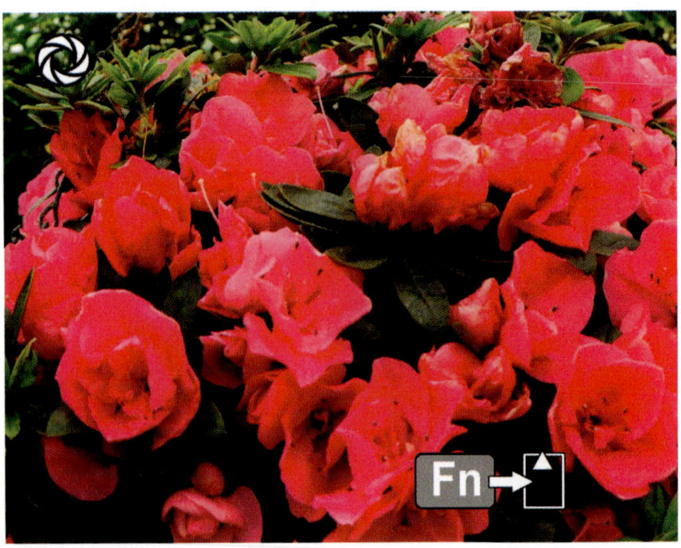

Figure 2.3
Digital Preview lets you check focus, composition, and exposure, and save your "test" shot to your memory card if you want.

- **Shutter release.** Angled on top of the handgrip is the shutter release button. Press this button down halfway to lock exposure and focus (in AF-S mode). The K200D assumes that when you tap or depress the shutter release, you are ready to take a picture, so the release can be tapped to activate the exposure meter or to exit from most menus.
- **Self-timer lamp/Remote control sensor.** The LED behind this window flashes to mark the countdown until the photo is taken. There is also a sensor that receives signals from the optional infrared Pentax Remote Control F (about $20). In Chapter 3, I'll show you how to set the K200D to either take the picture immediately when the remote's button is pressed or after a three-second delay. Note that the sensor is on the hand grip and thus would be blocked if you happened to be holding the K200D when trying to take a picture. In practice, of course, the camera will be mounted on a tripod or supported in some other way when using the remote control. The remote control generally must be used from in front of the camera and within about 15 feet for the sensor to detect its signal.
- **Hand grip.** This provides a comfortable handhold, and also contains the K200D's battery.
- **SD Memory card cover.** Use your thumb to push the door toward the back side of the camera to open the compartment. Press on the memory card inside, and it will pop up so you can extract it.
- **Lens Unlock button.** Press this button to release the lens so it can be rotated towards the shutter release to remove it from the camera.

There are more controls on the other side of the K200D as shown in Figure 2.4.

- **RAW button.** Press this button to override the file format settings you've specified in the Recording Menu's File Format option, such as JPEG, RAW, or RAW+, either temporarily or permanently. I'll explain this process (which isn't as complicated as it appears on first glance), in Chapter 3. The sidebar that follows, "Making Sense of the RAW Button" offers a quick introduction to what you need to know.
- **Focus Mode lever.** The switch to change from autofocus to manual focus and back. I'll explain more about choosing focus modes in Chapter 5.
- **Port cover.** This plastic door protects the optional wired remote release cable connector, the USB/Video output terminal, and the DC input terminal.

MAKING SENSE OF THE RAW BUTTON

The RAW button is your friend. Honest. But its use can seem complicated at first. Basically, what this button does is override the file format setting you've made in the Recording menu. You might have selected JPEG (only), RAW (only), or RAW+ (RAW and JPEG shot simultaneously). (You'll find tips on choosing the right format in Chapter 3.) As you shoot, you may decide you'd like to quickly switch to another format. The K200D allows you to *specify ahead of time* what format to switch to when you press the RAW button. You can choose an alternate format to use instead of the current format, and specify which format is to be used instead. You can do this for each of the three basic formats. For example:

- If you're using JPEG when you press the RAW button, the camera can switch from JPEG to RAW (only), RAW+ (RAW+JPEG), or JPEG (in other words, don't switch at all).
- If you're using RAW when you press the RAW button, the camera can switch to JPEG (only), RAW+ (RAW+JPEG), or do nothing at all.
- If you're using RAW+ when you press the RAW button, the camera can switch to JPEG (only), RAW (only), or do nothing at all.

The menu entry for this option can also be set to cancel your format switch after one picture is taken, or to remain in force until the RAW button is pressed again, or until any of four other actions (all described in Chapter 3) are performed. So, the RAW button's effects can be temporary, or permanent, for that shooting session.

When you open the port protector door on the side of the Pentax K200D, you'll find three connectors, shown in Figure 2.5.

- **Cable switch terminal.** This is a port for the Pentax CS-205 Cable Switch, a wired remote control that triggers the shutter release when its button is pressed.
- **USB/Video port.** Plug in the I-USB17 cable furnished with your K200D and connect the other end to a USB port in your computer to transfer photos. This same port is used with the camera's IVC28 video cable to direct video output to a television monitor, VCR, or other device.
- **DC Input terminal.** Plug in the optional Pentax D-AC76 AC adapter to power your camera with AC power. You might find this capability especially useful when displaying your camera's output on a TV monitor in Slideshow mode (described in Chapter 3).

Figure 2.4

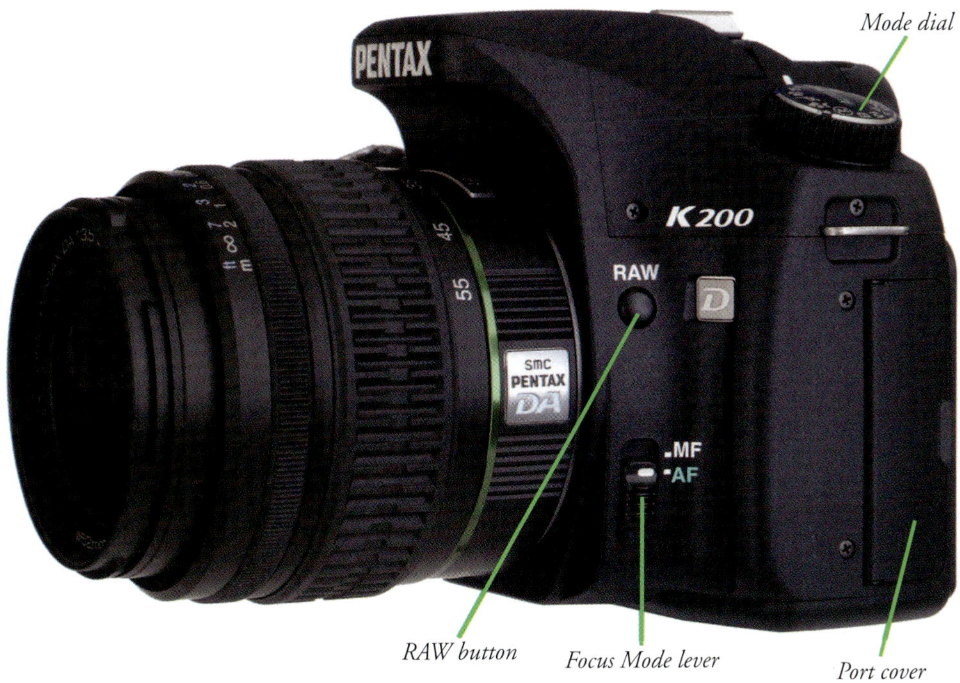

Figure 2.5

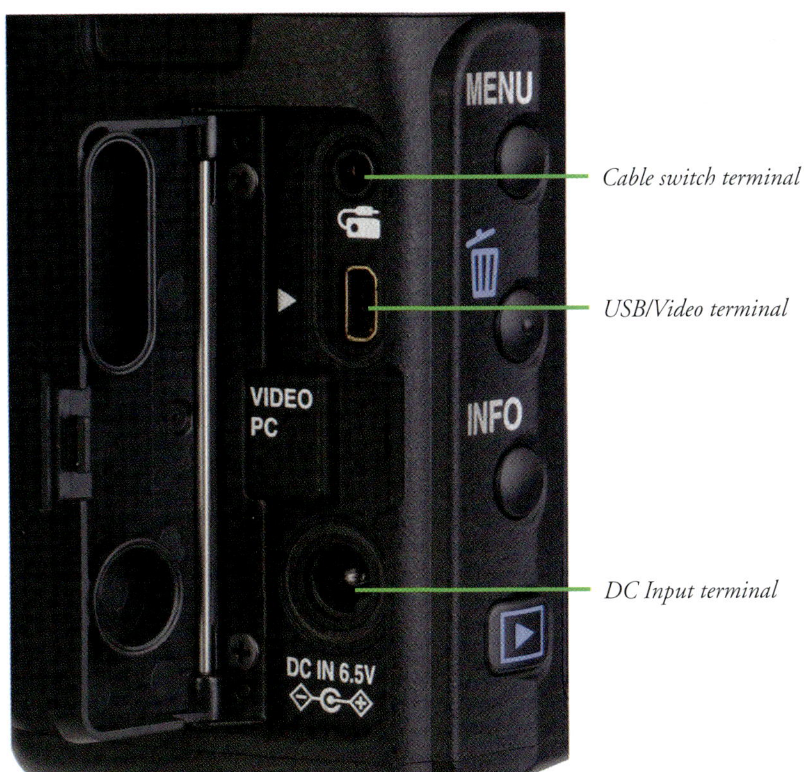

Investigating the Back Panel

Controls, buttons, and knobs cover the back of your K200D like sprinkles on a Krispy Kreme donut, as you can see in Figure 2.6. You'll also find the camera's LCD screen and viewfinder there. This is truly the "business end" of your camera. I'm going to divvy up the controls into two sections, left and right, concentrating on the left side first, where there are fewer buttons to worry about. That side is shown in Figure 2.7.

- **Pop-up Flash button.** The button releases the built-in flash so it can flip up (see Figure 2.8) and start the charging process. If you decide you don't want to use the flash, you can turn it off by pressing the flash head back down.
- **Menu button.** Summons/exits the menu displayed on the monitor screen of the K200D. The menu's divided into four submenus: Rec. Mode, Playback, Set-up, and Custom Setting. Navigate among the menu tabs using the left/right keys of the four-way controller. Select a menu item within a tab using the up/down keys. Once a menu entry has been highlighted, select from its options using the left/right/up/down keys. Press OK to confirm your choice.

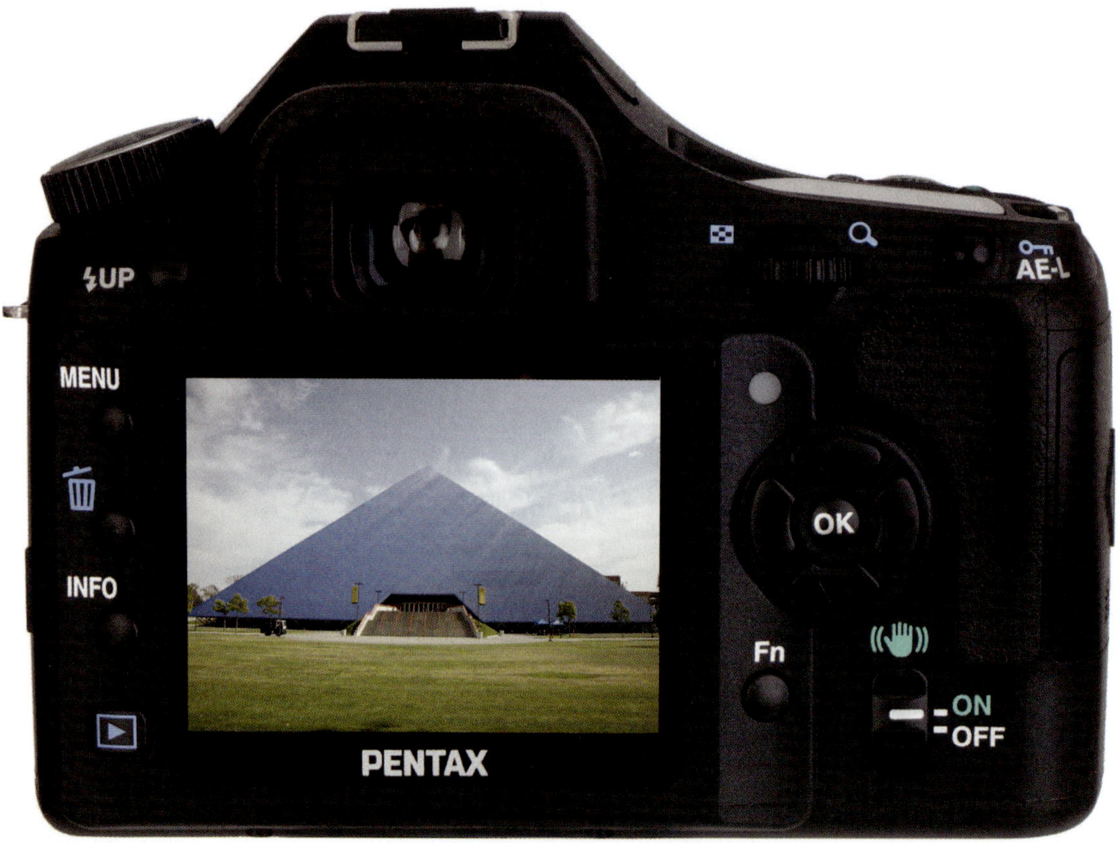

Figure 2.6

Figure 2.7

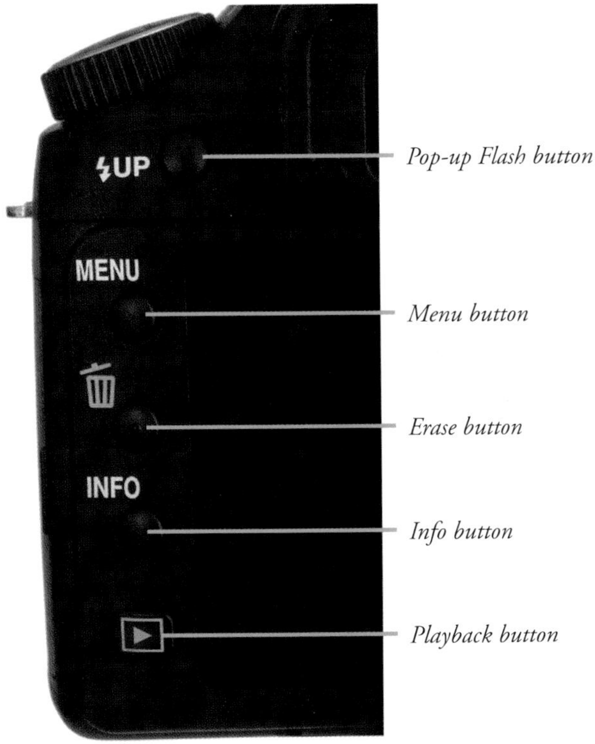

Figure 2.8

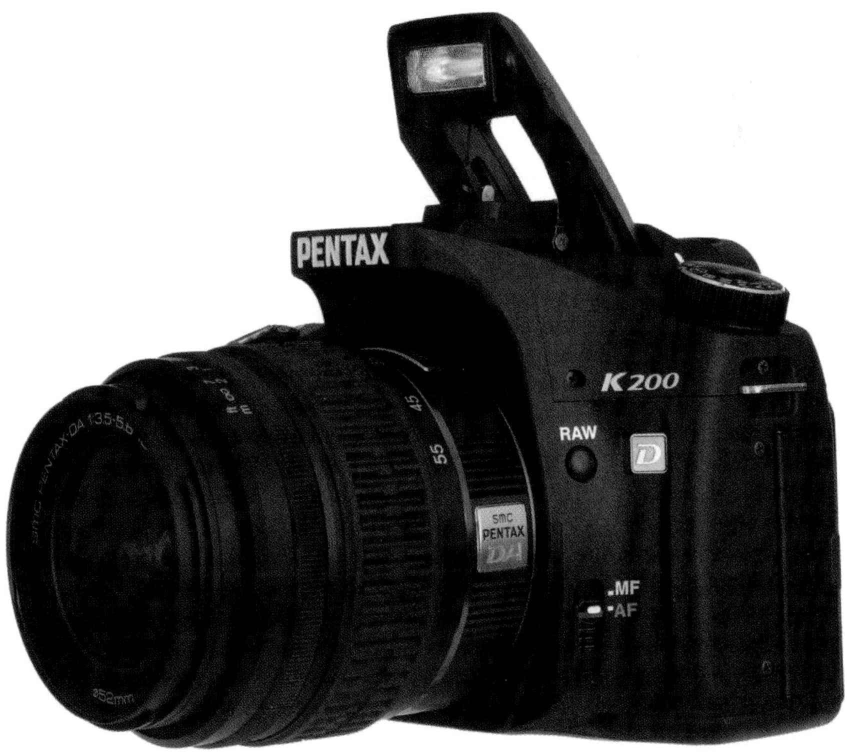

- **Erase button.** Press this button to delete the displayed photo during playback. A screen will pop up (see Figure 2.9) giving you the option to delete the image, cancel the process, or delete all images. Select Delete or Cancel with the up/down buttons, then press OK, or press the Delete button again to produce a screen that asks you if you really want to delete all the images on the card.

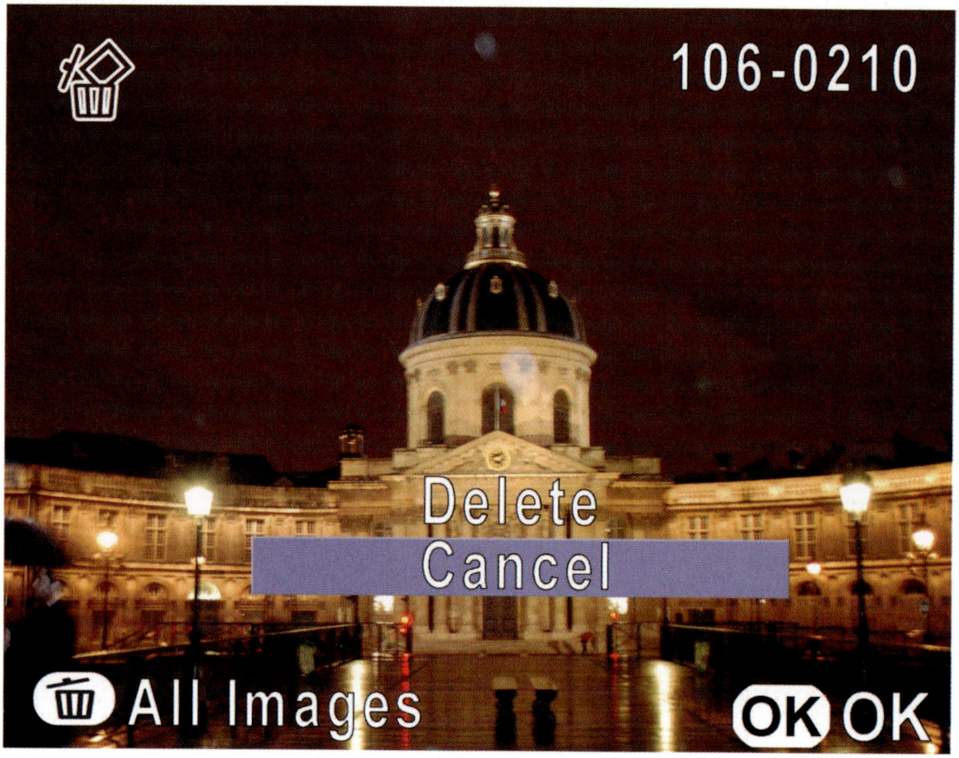

Figure 2.9
You can delete the image displayed, all images on the card, or cancel the process.

- **Info button.** When you're in Capture mode and you press the Info button, you'll get detailed shooting information on the monitor screen. This information, while more detailed, includes some of the same information (f/stop and shutter speed settings, for example) as in the LCD panel at the top of the camera. If you can't see the LCD panel, say, at night, you can press the Info button to find out your shooting info. When you press the Info button in Playback mode, the camera changes the screen display to one of two other choices. It cycles among Standard Display with the image in the background overlaid with basic parameters in each of the four corners of the monitor display; to Histogram Display with a brightness histogram; to Detailed Info Display with a thumbnail of the image, shooting parameters, and settings; to No Info Display. When the K200D displays the brightness histogram, you have the option to see the red, green, and blue channels by pressing the up or down arrow on the four-way controller.

- **Playback button.** Displays the last picture taken. You can move back and forth among the available images by pressing the buttons with the right and left arrows on the four-way controller. The K200D exits Playback mode when you press the shutter.

There are more buttons on the right side of the K200D (see Figure 2.10). By now, you probably know what some of them do from Chapter 1. I'm going to go over them again and map them out for reference.

- **E-dial.** This multi-purpose dial serves a number of functions, depending on whether you are in Capture (shooting), Playback, or menu navigation modes. While shooting, use the e-dial to set shutter speed, aperture, ISO sensitivity, and exposure compensation (EV) values, as described later in this chapter. During playback, rotate to the right to zoom in for up to 16X enlargement; rotate to the left to zoom out to full image frame, and then to thumbnail mode. See the section on Playback later in this chapter for more details. In menu navigation mode, the e-dial serves the same function as the left/right controller keys.

Figure 2.10

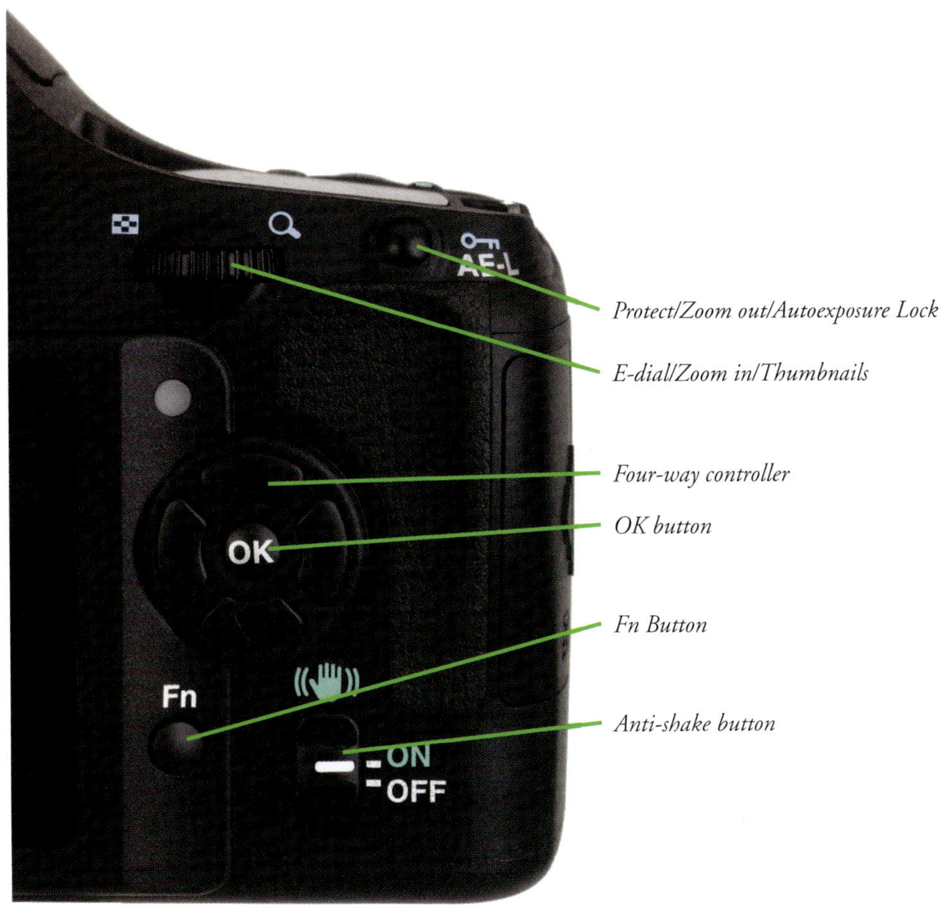

- **AE-L/Protect/Zoom Out.** In Recording mode, this button serves as an autoexposure lock, so you can reframe the picture, if you like, while keeping the current setting. You can read more about the use of the AE-L button in Chapter 3. In Playback mode, if an image has been zoomed in, pressing this button zooms the display back out one increment, until you reach 1.2X (another press at that point won't return the image to the 1X, full-screen mode). This function almost duplicates the function of spinning the e-dial to the left when viewing a zoomed image. If an image is not zoomed when you press this button, the Protect feature is activated, instead, and a screen with choices including Protect, Unprotect, and Protect All appears.
- **Four-way controller.** The up, down, right, and left arrow buttons of the four-way controller can be used to move the cursor and select items in menus, during image playback, and when using the Fn menu.
- **OK button.** This button is used to confirm your choices during menu navigation and playback, and to activate the second set of Scene modes when the Mode dial is set to SCN and you first press the Fn button.
- **Anti-Shake Switch.** Turns the Pentax K200D's shake reduction on or off. You can safely leave this feature turned on, except when the camera is mounted on a tripod; when you are shooting close-ups (because the shaking in such situations may be too much for the camera to counter—use a tripod instead); and when you want to save the power that the anti-shake feature consumes. Keep in mind that the effectiveness of this feature varies, depending on the lens' focal length (see the sidebar that follows), and the shooting distance (the closer you are, the more camera shake affects your image).
- **Fn button.** This button serves different functions, depending on the camera's current mode. In Capture mode or when navigating menus, the Fn button activates the Function Recording menu. In Playback mode, the Function Playback menu appears. Both are described next.

ANTI-SHAKE AND FOCAL LENGTH

The Anti-Shake feature needs to know the current focal length setting of your lens in order to calculate shake reduction appropriately. (Lenses with longer focal lengths require more aggressive anti-shake compensation because they magnify vibration.) Most newer lenses supply this information to the K200D automatically. Older lenses which are otherwise compatible with the camera don't communicate this information. In addition, lenses that have an aperture ring need to be set to the A (automatic) position for anti-shake features to work. When the camera can't acquire focal length information, an Input Focal Length screen appears, and you must use e-dial to specify the focal length you want to use, as shown in Figure 2.11. Press the controller center (OK) button to confirm your choice. I'll discuss using older lenses in more detail in Chapter 6.

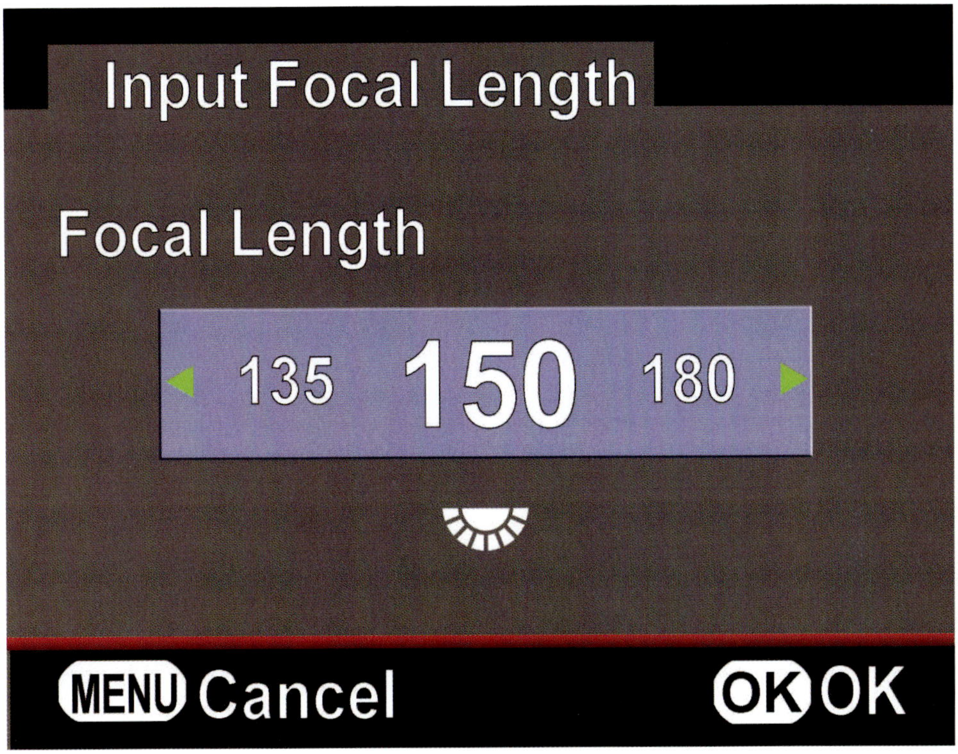

Figure 2.11 Input Focal Length screen.

Using the Function Menus

Pressing the Fn button activates either of two menus, depending on whether the Pentax K200D is in Capture or Playback modes. In addition, when an image is zoomed in, pressing the Fn button takes you directly to one of the Function menu playback options. The Function menus make selecting and modifying certain features quick and easy, so I'm going to take some time to explain them in detail.

Function Menu While Shooting

In Capture mode, when the exposure meter is active (tap the shutter release to activate it, if it is not), pressing the Fn button produces the screen like the one shown in Figure 2.12. (The icons in the Custom Image box will vary, depending on what Exposure mode you have selected.) The screen shows an image of the four-way controller, with labels representing the functions you can activate by pressing the controller's keys. They are as follows:

- **Up button.** Activates the Drive mode options. You can select from Single Shot, Continuous Shooting, Self-Timer, Remote Control, or Auto Bracket shooting. I'll explain how to use the Drive modes in Chapter 5.

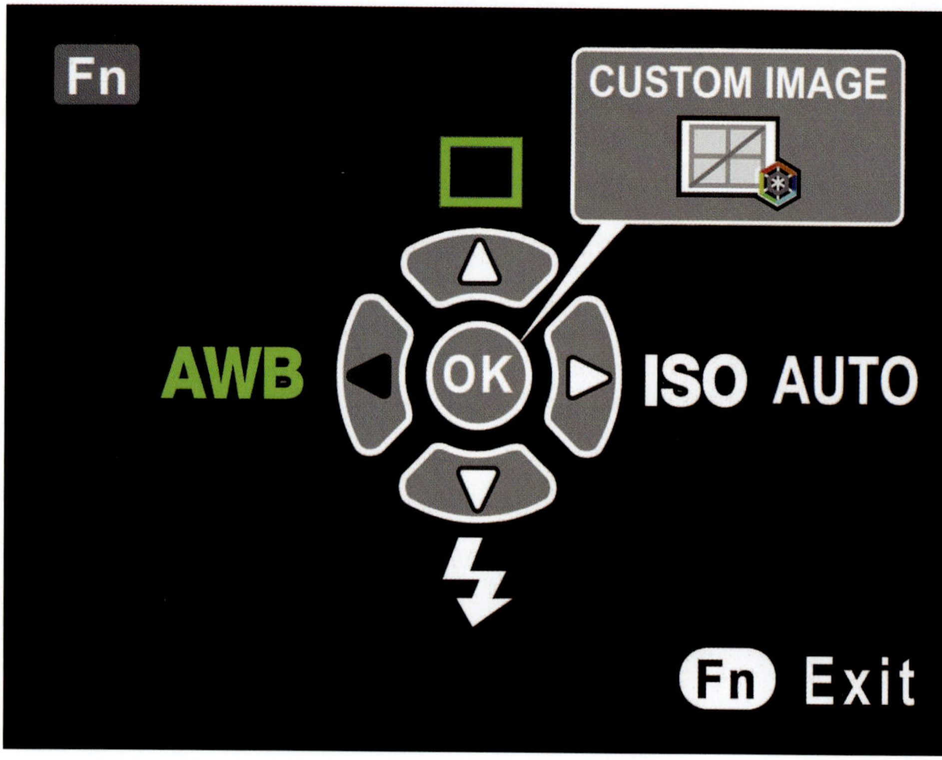

Figure 2.12
In Capture mode, the Function menu offers a choice of shooting settings for White Balance, Drive options, ISO sensitivity, and Flash settings.

- **Down button.** Produces a screen that lets you select the electronic flash modes, including Auto Discharge, Flash On, Auto Flash+Red-eye, Flash On+Red-eye, and Wireless mode. I'll explain these options in detail in Chapter 7.
- **Left button.** Pops up the White Balance screen, which I'll explain in Chapter 4. Your choices are Automatic White Balance (AWB), Daylight, Shade, Cloudy, three varieties of Fluorescent lighting, Tungsten, Flash, and Manual (a custom setting for special lighting conditions).
- **Right button.** Reveals a screen that allows you to choose ISO sensitivity, either Auto (using a range you select) or individual ISO settings from ISO 100 to ISO 1600. You can learn more about choosing the increments between ISO values in Chapter 3, and more about selecting an ISO setting in Chapter 4.
- **OK button.** This Custom Image button is used to select Image Processing options that allow you to adjust the saturation, hue, contrast, sharpness, image tone, and filter effects. I'll explain these options in Chapter 5.

Function Menu During Playback

In Playback mode, pressing the Fn button produces the screen like the one shown in Figure 2.13. The screen shows an image of the four-way controller, with labels representing the functions you can activate by pressing the controller's keys. They are as follows:

- **Up button.** Produces the DPOF (Digital Print Order Format) screen, which allows you to specify the number of copies you'd like to print of the image displayed, and whether or not you want the date printed with the image. You can also apply your print order information to all the images on the card in one step. You'd use this option if you planned to print directly from your memory card, using a PictBridge-compatible printer, a retailer's self-service printing kiosk, or a retailer's digital minilab. I'll explain DPOF in more detail in Chapter 3.
- **Down button.** This option is available only when you are shooting RAW images. It allows you to save the current RAW image as a JPEG file. When activated, you're given the opportunity to choose White Balance, Saturation, Hue, Contrast, Sharpness, Image Size and Quality, and Sensitivity before the new JPEG file is stored on your memory card. I'll explain this process in Chapter 4.
- **Left button.** Produces a screen that allows you to choose from a series of filter effects, such as Black & White, Sepia, 18 different color filters, three levels of softness, and a pencil effect. You can learn more about these filters in Chapter 3.

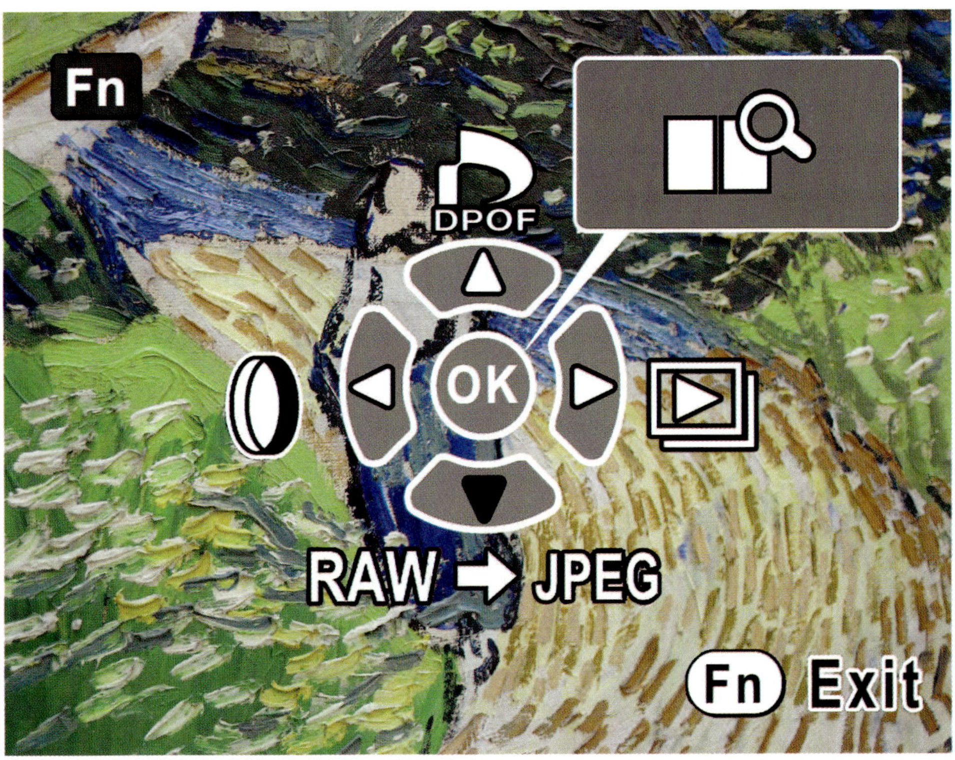

Figure 2.13 In Playback mode, you can specify a print order, view a slide show, convert a RAW file to JPEG, apply filter effects, and compare two images side by side.

- **Right button.** Plays back the images on your memory card one after another in a slide show displayed on your LCD screen, or on a connected television monitor.
- **OK button.** Activates a feature that shows two images side by side, and zooms in on either or both to compare them. I'll explain how to use this great feature later in this chapter under Playback Options.

Going Topside

The top surface of the Pentax K200D (see Figure 2.14) has its own set of frequently accessed controls.

- **Mode dial.** Rotating this dial chooses the basic selection of Screen modes, with eight more Screen modes available when the dial is set to the SCN position. You can also choose any of the six Exposure modes, Sv (Sensitivity Value/Priority), Tv (Time Value/Shutter Priority), Av (Aperture Value/Priority), Manual, and Bulb. I introduced all the Scene and Exposure modes in Chapter 1, and I will describe them in more detail in Chapter 4.
- **LCD panel.** This is a monochrome readout that shows shooting information including shutter speed and aperture settings, exposure compensation, battery status, and other information. (For even more detailed information about your camera's settings, press the Info button and view the data presented on the LCD monitor screen.) I discuss the available LCD information later in this chapter.
- **Flash Hot Shoe/Cover.** The Pentax's accessory shoe accepts external flash units and other gadgets, such as clip-on radio controls. The contacts of the hot shoe are protected by a plastic cover that you slide off when you want to attach an accessory.
- **Diopter correction lever.** As described in Chapter 1, this is the adjustment available for those who wear glasses or contact lenses and want to use the Pentax K200D without them, or those with normal or corrected vision who want some visual fine-tuning while peering through the viewfinder. The slider adjusts from –2.5 to +1.5 correction. Tap the shutter release to activate the viewfinder readouts. Slide the lever back and forth slowly until what you see in the viewfinder is in sharp focus. Pentax offers eight different Series M correction lenses for the viewfinder window if you need additional correction.

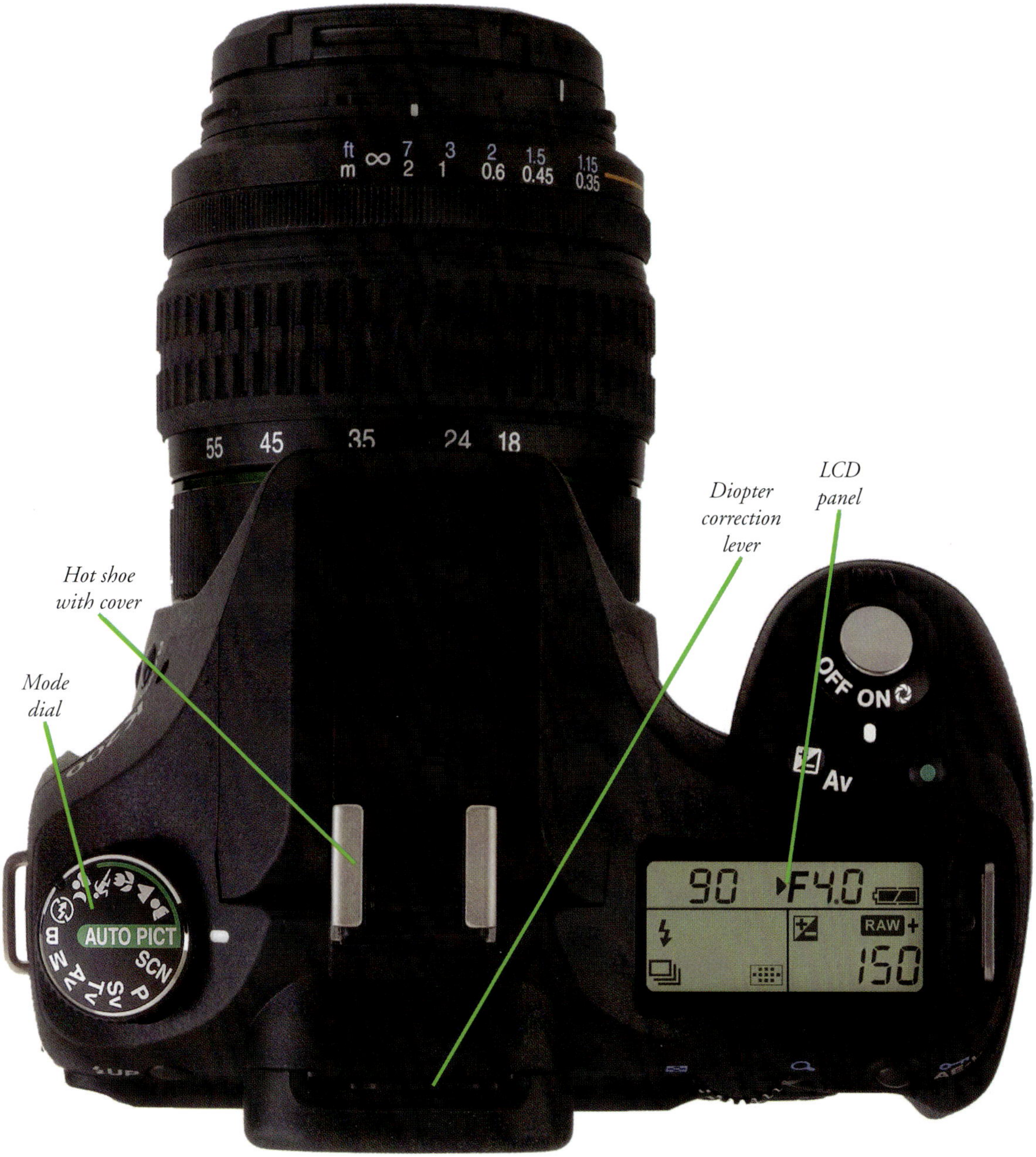
LCD panel
Diopter correction lever
Hot shoe with cover
Mode dial
AUTO PICT
SCN
OFF ON
Av
RAW

Figure 2.14

The functions of the controls on the top surface of the Pentax K200D's handgrip deserve a close-up look, and are illustrated in Figure 2.15:

- **Main Switch (On/Off).** As described earlier, this switch turns the camera's power on and off, and activates either Digital Preview or Optical Preview when rotated all the way clockwise. Review "Using the Digital and Optical Preview" earlier in this chapter for more information.
- **Shutter release.** Press this button down halfway to lock exposure and focus (in AF-S mode). The release can also be tapped to activate the exposure meter or to exit from most menus.
- **Green button.** There are lots of uses for this button, and the detailed explanations of each of them can be found in Chapter 3. But, in brief, this button serves as an exposure "reset" button when using Program Shift exposure mode; returns the K200D to Program mode when using Tv (Shutter Priority) or Av (Aperture Priority) modes, and disables further exposure changes with the e-dial when using Program mode; tells the camera to calculate aperture and shutter speed for correct

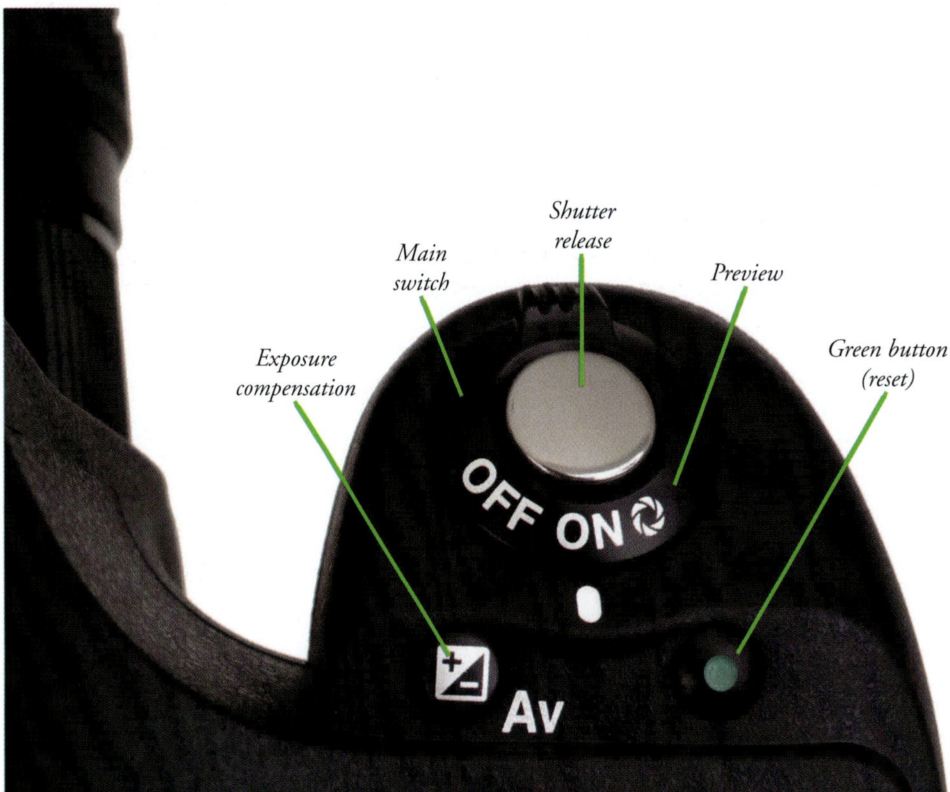

Figure 2.15

exposure in Manual mode; resets EV compensation to 0 when the AV button is also pressed; and resets Flash exposure compensation. Whew! For setting the adjustments using Green button in the menus, see Chapter 3.

- **Exposure Compensation (EV)/Aperture Value (AV)/Zoom in button.** In Capture mode, press this button while rotating the e-dial to add or subtract exposure in any Scene or Exposure mode except Manual and Bulb. Turn to the right to add exposure (make your picture lighter) or to the left to subtract exposure (make your picture darker). In Manual mode, hold this button while rotating the e-dial to change the f/stop. Press the button alone to display the current exposure value (EV) changes on the monochrome LCD. In Playback mode, pressing this button zooms in further on an image that is already magnified (1.2X or more), partially duplicating the function of the e-dial when rotated to the right.

Monochrome LCD Panel Readouts

Monochrome LCD panels on the top surface of digital SLRs are a dying breed among small, compact cameras, with most models relegating the information they display to the color LCD on the back of the camera instead. The Pentax K200D gives you the best of both worlds, with a status screen on top, visible any time, with a similar display on the color LCD that appears when you press the Info button. The top panel LCD may be more convenient when you are looking down at the camera (e.g., when the K200D is hanging around your neck), while the back panel LCD is usually easier to read under dark conditions and when the camera is held up to your eye. The basic display with some of the possible settings is shown in Figure 2.16. Not all of these will appear on the LCD at one time. For example, only one of the Drive mode settings clustered at lower left will appear at any given time.

Figure 2.16

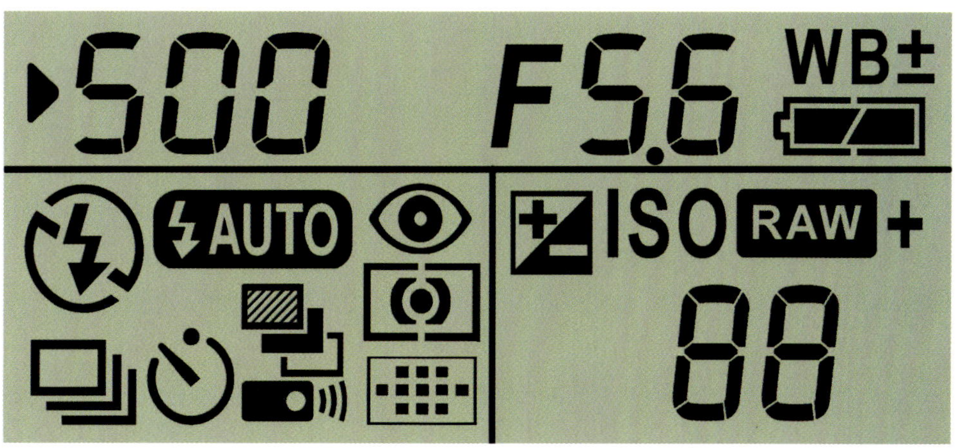

I've color coded the various settings for easy reference in Figure 2.17.

- **Shutter speed.** Displays the current shutter speed, from 30 seconds to 1/4,000th second, plus bu when using the Bulb exposure setting on the Mode dial.
- **Aperture.** Shows the current f/stop.
- **White Balance.** If white balance is set to Auto, nothing is displayed in this area. Otherwise, the WB indicator appears. If you've adjusted one of the WB presets to bias the color in the green/magenta or amber/blue directions, a plus sign appears.
- **Battery level.** This indicator shows how much life remains in the K200D's batteries.
- **Flash mode.** The lightning-bolt symbol blinks when the shutter release is depressed halfway and flash should be used. When the flash is elevated and the lightning-bolt symbol shows steadily, the flash is charged and ready for use. When the symbol has the circle with slash (meaning "No"), then Flash Off is activated. The Auto Discharge and Red-Eye Reduction symbols appear when the autoflash and red-eye prevention features, respectively, are enabled.
- **Drive mode.** One of the indicators highlighted in pink will appear, depending on the Drive mode you've selected. The icons represent Single Shot/Continuous Shooting; Self-Timer; Bracketing (top); and Remote Control (bottom).

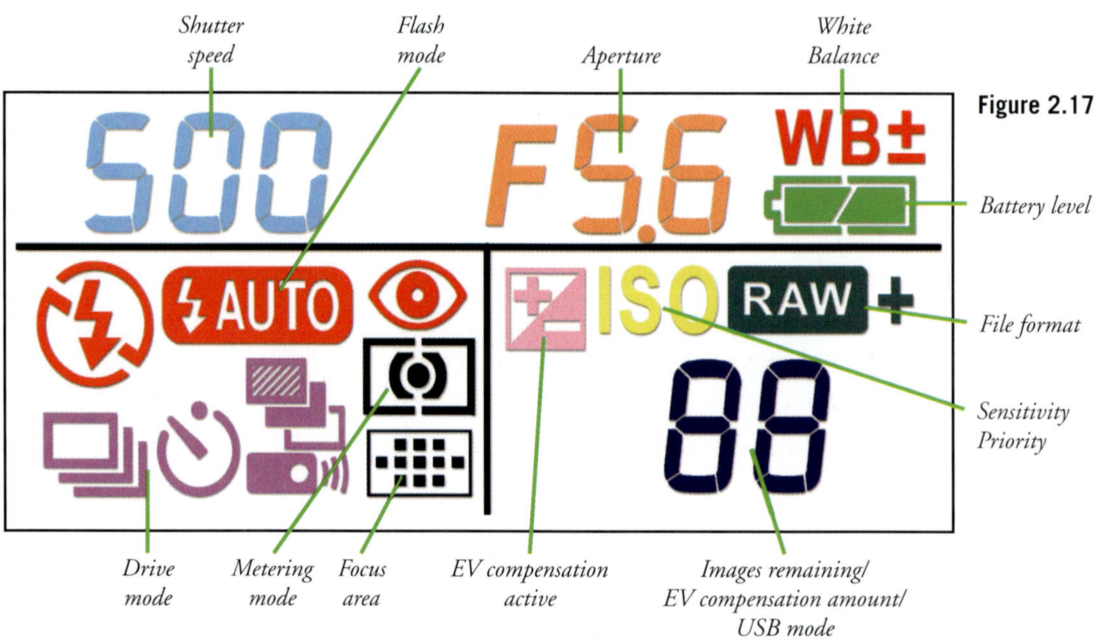

Figure 2.17

- **Focus area.** This section of the display shows which focus mode is in use. If Auto is chosen (the camera selects the focus zone), no icon appears; if the icon shown in the figure is visible, then Select autofocus is active (you choose which of the 11 focus zones should be used); if Center autofocus is selected (only the center focus point is active), the icon shows only a focus area in the middle. You can learn more about autofocus options in Chapter 5.
- **Metering mode.** If no icon is shown, then Multi-Segment metering is enabled; the icon shown in the figure represents Center-Weighted metering; if Spot metering is active, only a center spot appears within the icon indicator.
- **Images remaining/EV compensation/ISO/PC mode/PictBridge.** This area of the display shows the number of images remaining on your memory card, or the selected ISO sensitivity, depending on how you have CS #12 set in the Custom Setting menu, as described in Chapter 3. When you press the EV/AV button on the top of the camera, it shows the amount of exposure compensation that has been dialed in. When the K200D is attached to a computer through the USB cable, this area shows whether PC or PictBridge USB modes have been selected. I'll explain exposure compensation in Chapter 4. You can read more about USB modes in Chapter 3.
- **EV compensation active.** Whenever exposure compensation is being applied, this plus/minus icon appears.
- **Sensitivity Priority.** The ISO indicator appears whenever Sensitivity Priority Exposure mode is active.
- **File format.** If no indicator is shown, the camera is set for JPEG capture. Otherwise, either RAW or RAW+ will be shown. You can learn more about file formats in Chapter 3.

Color LCD Readouts

When you turn on the Pentax K200D, or change to a different Scene or Exposure mode using the Mode dial, a Guide Display appears on the color LCD for three seconds, unless you've selected a longer display of 10 or 30 seconds or disabled the Guide Display entirely in the Set-Up menu (as I'll describe in Chapter 3). The Guide Display shows only basic information about the current Scene or Exposure mode.

More useful is the full shooting information screen shown on the back panel color LCD when you press the Info button. This screen shows the same basic information found in the Guide Display, and much more. I've divided the main Capture mode information screen into two sections to avoid having to cram a couple dozen labels into a single figure. The upper half of the Capture mode screen is annotated in Figure 2.18. (I'll explain the Playback information screen later in this chapter.) Not all this

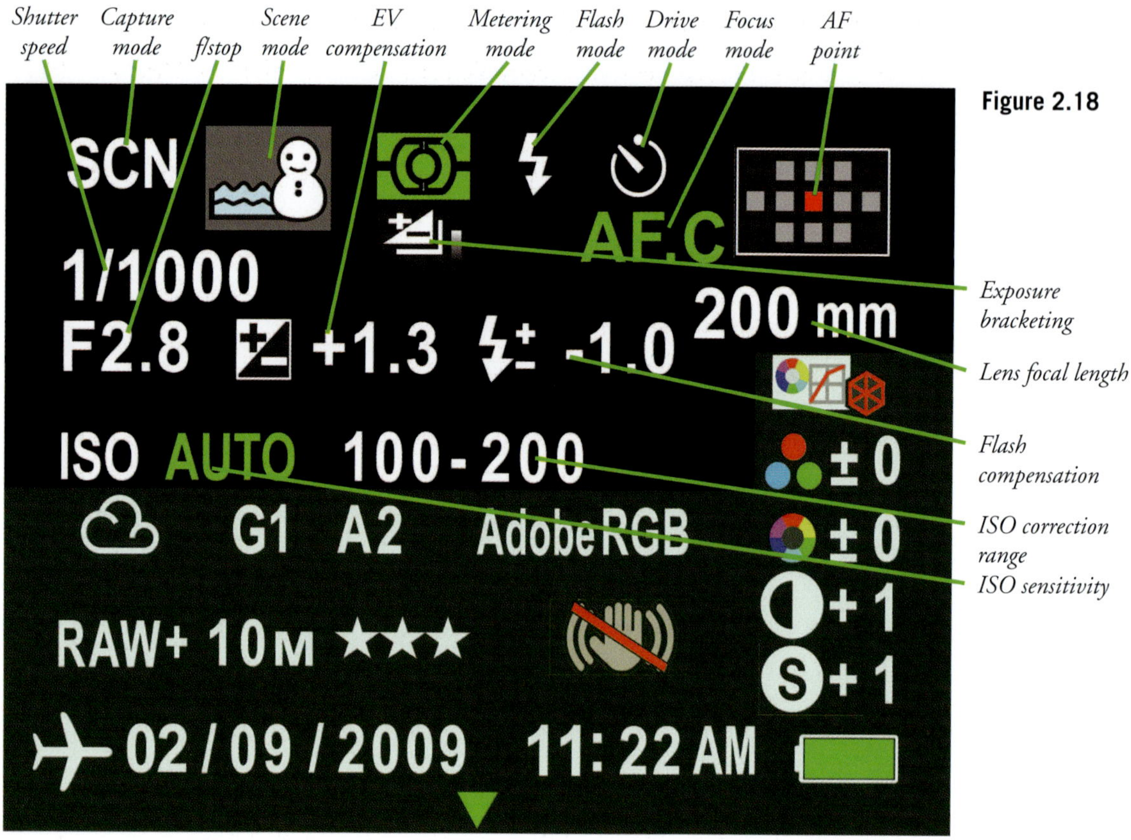

Figure 2.18

information is displayed at once; only the relevant displays for a particular Capture mode will be shown. You can find more information about each of these settings in the chapter indicated.

- **Capture mode.** Indicates which Scene mode (Auto Pict, Portrait, Landscape, Macro, Moving Object, Night Scene Portrait, Flash Off, or SCN) or Exposure mode (Program, Sensitivity Priority, Shutter Priority, Aperture Priority, Manual, or Bulb) setting is in use. (Chapter 4.)
- **SCN Scene mode.** If a Scene mode selected from the SCN Mode dial position is active, an icon representing that mode is shown here. The SCN modes include Night Scene, Surf and Snow, Food, Sunset, Kids, Pet, Candlelight, and Museum. (Chapter 4.) If you want to view a Help screen that explains the use of SCN or Capture modes, press the down key.
- **Metering mode.** Indicates whether Multi-Segment, Center-Weighted, or Spot metering is used. (Chapter 4.)

- **Exposure bracketing.** Shows that exposures are being bracketed. (Chapter 5.)
- **Flash mode.** Displays current electronic flash mode. Choices are Flash On, Flash On+Red-Eye, and Wireless mode when using any Capture/Scene/SCN setting. In addition, Auto Discharge (automatic pop-up) and Auto Discharge+Red-eye are available when using Scene/SCN modes, but not when using one of the Exposure modes (P, Sv, Tv, Av, M, or B). (Chapter 7.)
- **Focus mode.** Indicates whether Single Autofocus or Continuous Autofocus is used. (Chapter 5.)
- **Autofocus point.** Shows the position of the active AF point. (Chapter 5.)
- **Lens focal length.** Displays the focal length or zoom position of the lens at the time the Info button was pressed (it does not change if you zoom while the display is on the screen). (Chapter 6.)
- **Shutter speed.** The current shutter speed is shown here. (Chapter 4.)
- **F/stop.** Displays the current lens aperture. (Chapter 4.)
- **EV compensation.** Shows the amount of exposure compensation applied to the metered or set exposure, from +2.0 to –2.0 stops. (Chapter 4.)
- **Flash compensation.** If flash compensation has been dialed in, the amount is shown here. (Chapter 7.)
- **ISO sensitivity.** Shows current sensitivity setting, either ISO Auto or one of the fixed sensitivity settings from ISO 100 to 1600. (Chapters 3 and 4.)
- **ISO correction range.** If ISO Auto is set, this area of the LCD displays the ISO range that will be used to make corrections. For example, with 100-200 shown, only sensitivity settings from ISO 100 or 200 will be applied. (Chapter 4.)

The lower half of the Capture mode LCD display, pictured in Figure 2.19, has additional information. You'll find more in-depth descriptions of these settings in the chapters indicated.

- **White Balance.** This display shows the White Balance setting you've selected, from AWB (Automatic White Balance), through Daylight, Shade, Cloudy, Fluorescent light (three varieties),Tungsten Light, Flash, and Manual (custom). (Chapter 4.)
- **White Balance bias.** Shows the amount of fine-tuning of White Balance that you've set, using Blue/Amber and Green/Magenta axes. (Chapter 3.)
- **File format.** Displays the current file format, either JPEG, RAW, or RAW+ (RAW plus JPEG). (Chapter 3.)

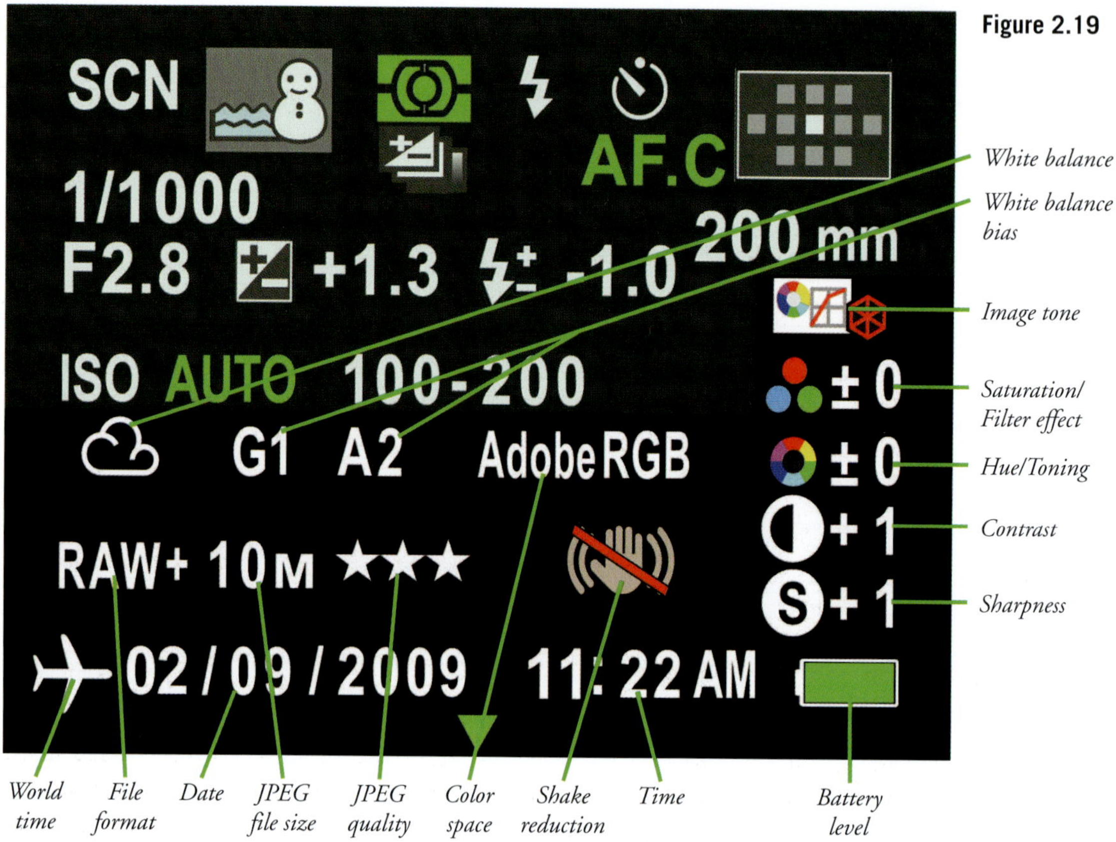

Figure 2.19

- **JPEG file size.** This shows the "recorded pixels" setting, or resolution of the image. Your choices include 10 megapixels (3872 × 2592), 6 megapixels (3008 × 2000), or 2 megapixels (1824 × 1216). (Chapter 3.)
- **JPEG quality.** The number of stars, from one star (Good), two stars (Better), to three stars (Best), indicates the amount of compression, and therefore the image quality, of a JPEG file. As the quality increases, the amount of space used on your memory card by the image increases; three stars takes the most space, and one star consumes the least amount. (Chapter 3.)
- **World time.** The K200D allows you to enter the time for both your "hometown" as well as one "destination" time zone, using the Set-Up menu, and then switch back and forth between them, as I'll explain in Chapter 3. When the airplane icon is shown, the time displayed indicates the time in your "destination" time zone. (Chapter 3.)

- **Date.** This shows the current date. (Chapter 3.)
- **Time.** This indicator displays the current time in either your "hometown" or "destination" time zone, depending on which you have activated in the World Time menu option within the Set-Up menu. (Chapter 3.)
- **Help screen.** Press the down key to display a help screen with more details about your current Exposure mode. When finished with the help screen, press the up key to return to the Capture information display.
- **Battery level.** Shows the amount of battery power remaining.
- **Color Space.** The Pentax K200D can save JPEG files using either of two different color spaces, or *gamuts*: sRGB (the default—best for display of images on your monitor and for output locally on an inkjet printer), and Adobe RGB (which has a different set of colors suitable for images that will be heavily edited, or output by a commercial printer). (Chapter 3.)
- **Shake reduction.** Indicates whether the K200D's anti-shake feature is turned on. The "hand" icon appears in green if the feature is activated; the "hand" has a diagonal red line drawn through it if shake reduction is turned off. Shake reduction is disabled when Bulb exposure is used, when you're using the 2-second self-timer, using the remote control, or wireless mode with an external flash. (Chapter 6.)
- **Image tone.** When the camera is set to one of the Exposure modes, P (Program), Sv (Sensitivity Priority), Tv (Shutter Priority), Av (Aperture Priority), M (Manual), or B (Bulb), you can press the Fn button and then the four-way controller center button to access the Custom Image feature and change Image Tone settings. The six Image Tone settings include Bright (the default), Natural, Portrait, Landscape, Vibrant, and Monochrome. You can further customize the attributes of any of these Image Tone settings using the four options described next. (Chapter 3.)
- **Saturation/Filter effect.** Use this option to modify the richness of the color, or, in Monochrome mode, to apply a filter effect. (Chapter 3.)
- **Hue/Toning.** Changes the overall hue bias of an image in any Image Tone mode except Monochrome; changes color tone (from bluish Cyanotype to brownish Sepia). (Chapter 3.)
- **Contrast.** Adjusts the relationship between the bright and dark areas of an image, from low contrast to high contrast. (Chapter 3.)
- **Sharpness.** Changes the contrast between edge boundaries of image elements, producing more or less sharpness. (Chapter 3.)

Through the Viewfinder

When you look through the viewfinder of the K200D, you'll see a row of green numbers and indicators, which represent the settings and modes that have been specified for your shot. Only some of the information about the settings of your shot will be shown at one time. Figure 2.20 shows what you'll see. The panel of data inside the viewfinder includes:

- **AF Frame.** The area bounded by these lines delineates the metered area when Multi-Segment metering is activated.
- **Spot Metering Frame.** Shows the circle that marks the metered area when Spot metering is activated.

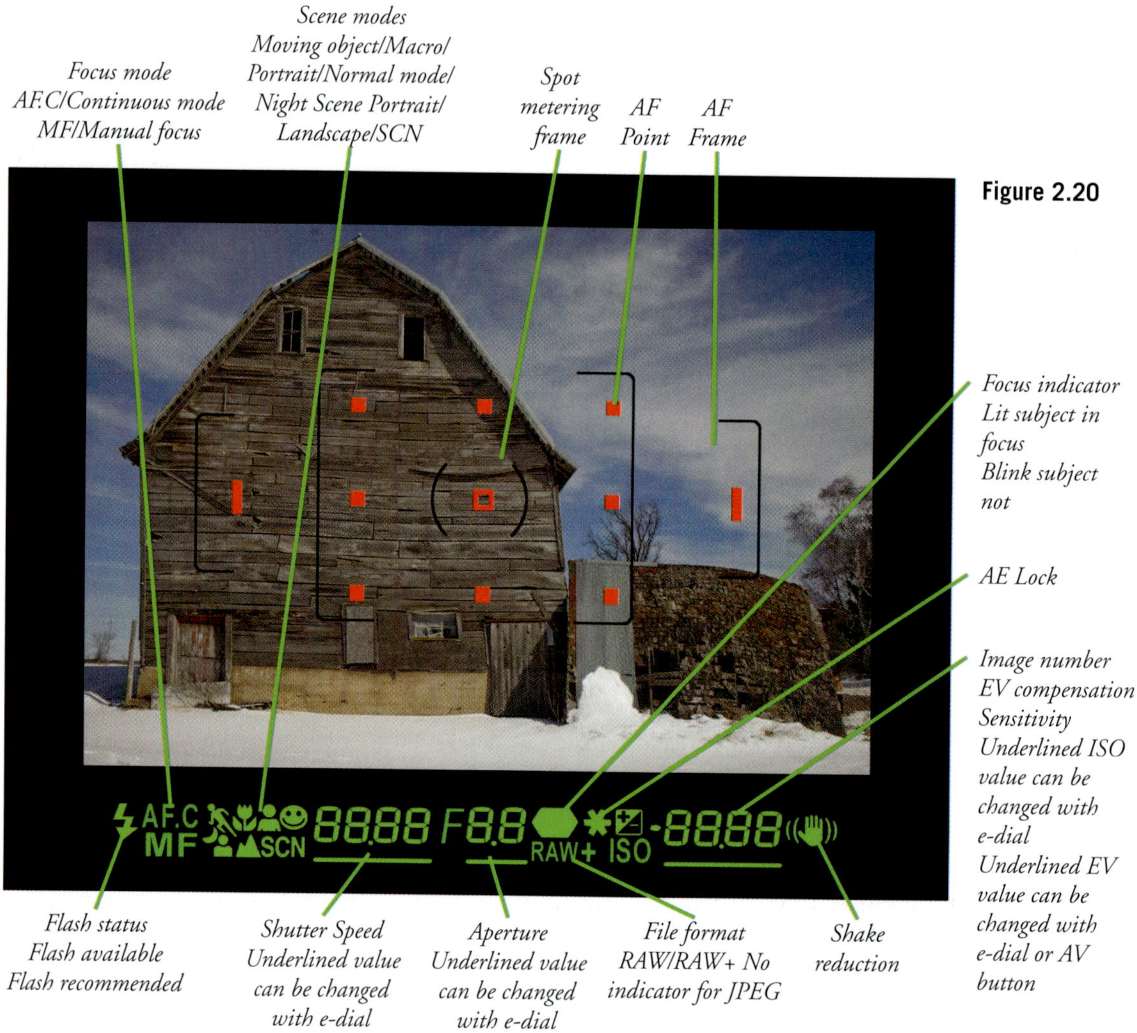

Figure 2.20

- **AE Lock.** Indicates that the K200D has locked exposure.
- **Shake Reduction.** When the hand icon appears in the viewfinder, the shake reduction switch is set to On and the feature is activated. Shake reduction is disabled when Bulb exposure is used, when you're using the 2-second self-timer, using the remote control, or wireless mode with an external flash.
- **Image Number/EV Compensation/Sensitivity.** This readout shows four things.
  - *The number of recordable images.* If no EV adjustments are set, this area shows the number of images that remain to be shot on your memory card, using the current quality and resolution settings. (The maximum number of recordable images that can be displayed is 999. If your memory card has a larger capacity, then 999 will be displayed instead of the correct number.) If EV compensation has been set, the recordable images display appears only after a picture is taken, and is replaced by the EV display when you partially depress the shutter release button.
  - *Current EV compensation.* If you've dialed in an EV adjustment, the "recordable images" display is shown immediately after a picture is taken, but otherwise, when the exposure meter is active, the amount of EV compensation is shown instead. Values between –2.0 to +2.0 are displayed. If the EV compensation display is underlined, you can change the EV value by holding down the EV/AV button and rotating the e-dial. The EV display will be underlined when you press the EV/AV button while using any Scene, SCN, or Exposure mode except for M (Manual) and B (Bulb).
  - *ISO sensitivity.* When Sv (Sensitivity Priority) mode is active, this area shows the current ISO setting. (You can press the EV/AV button to see any Exposure compensation instead.) The current ISO is also displayed when you press the controller center button when using modes other than Sv, but you can't change the value without using the Function menu, as described earlier in this chapter.
  - *Exposure difference in Manual mode.* When using M (Manual) mode, this area displays the difference between the actual exposure you have set, and the "correct" exposure, as determined by the K200D's light meter. The range shown will be +3.0 to –3.0 stops. For example, +2.0 indicates two stops' worth of overexposure and –1.0 indicates one stop of underexposure. A flashing +3.0 or –3.0 indicates that your current exposure varies by more than three stops from the recommended exposure. You'll find a *lot* more information on manual exposure, "stops," and other factors in Chapter 4.
- **Focus indicator.** When the focus indicator blinks, your subject is not in focus. When this icon is lit, the image is focused.

- **File format.** The viewfinder displays the file format you have set for taking pictures. RAW and RAW+ (RAW and JPEG) will be displayed, while JPEG won't.
- **Aperture and shutter speed.** These readouts show the current shutter speed and aperture. When either is underlined, you can change that setting on the e-dial. For example, if you're in Av mode, the aperture is underlined so that you can change it on the e-dial. The shutter speed, however, won't be underlined. In Tv mode, the shutter speed is underlined, but the aperture value is not, indicating that you can change the shutter speed with the e-dial.
- **Scene Modes.** When you've selected one of the Scene modes on the Mode dial, that image (or letters) appears in the view finder. The Scene modes that you select via the menus will not be listed individually; instead, just the letters SCN appear.
- **Focus mode/Manual focus.** The viewfinder shows what focus mode you've selected if it was AF.C or Continuous mode. No display occurs when you're in Single mode (AF.S). The display shows MF if you've switched out of Autofocus mode using the switch on the right front of the camera.
- **Flash status.** The flash icon appears in the viewfinder to tell you whether or not you need to use a flash. When it's lit, the flash is available. When it blinks, the flash is recommended, but not set.

Underneath Your K200D

The bottom of your camera (see Figure 2.21) houses the four lithium batteries and is the place where you attach a tripod. There's also a flexible rubber sealing connector for a battery grip, which is optional with the K200D. A battery grip contains a shutter release button and an AE-L button to accommodate shooting vertically.

Lens Components

The Pentax kit lens that comes with the K200D has several components, typical of those found in all Pentax lenses, shown in Figures 2.22 and 2.23.

- **Filter thread.** The thread on the front of a lens is for attaching a screw-in lens hood used for some lenses. You screw on the filter first, and then attach the hood to the screw thread on the front of the filter.
- **Lens hood bayonet.** This is used to mount the more common (and more popular) bayonet-mount style of lens hood. Attach the hood with the petals facing inward when not in use.

Figure 2.21

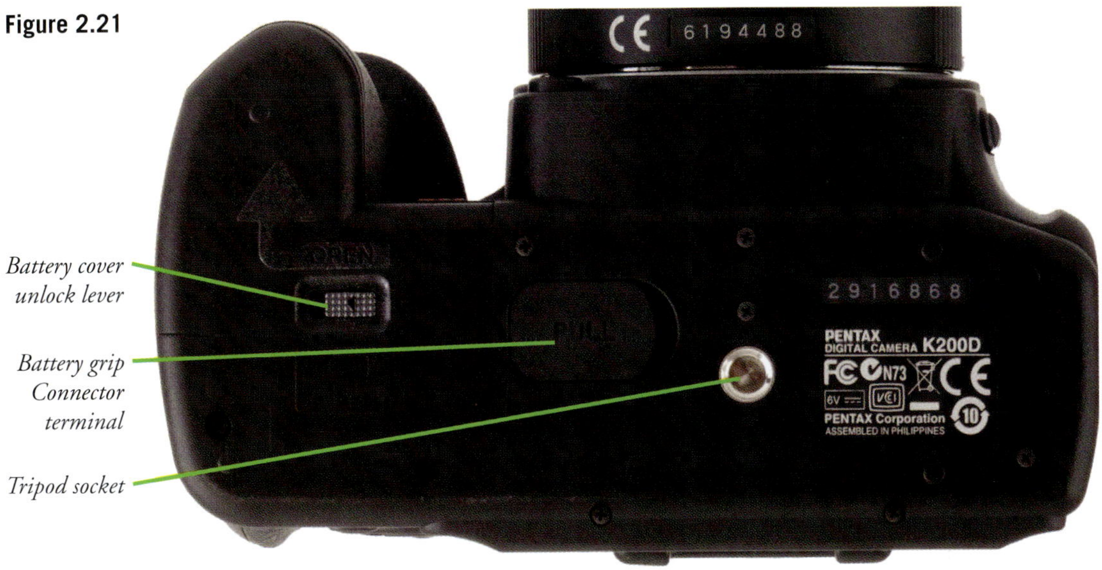

Figure 2.22

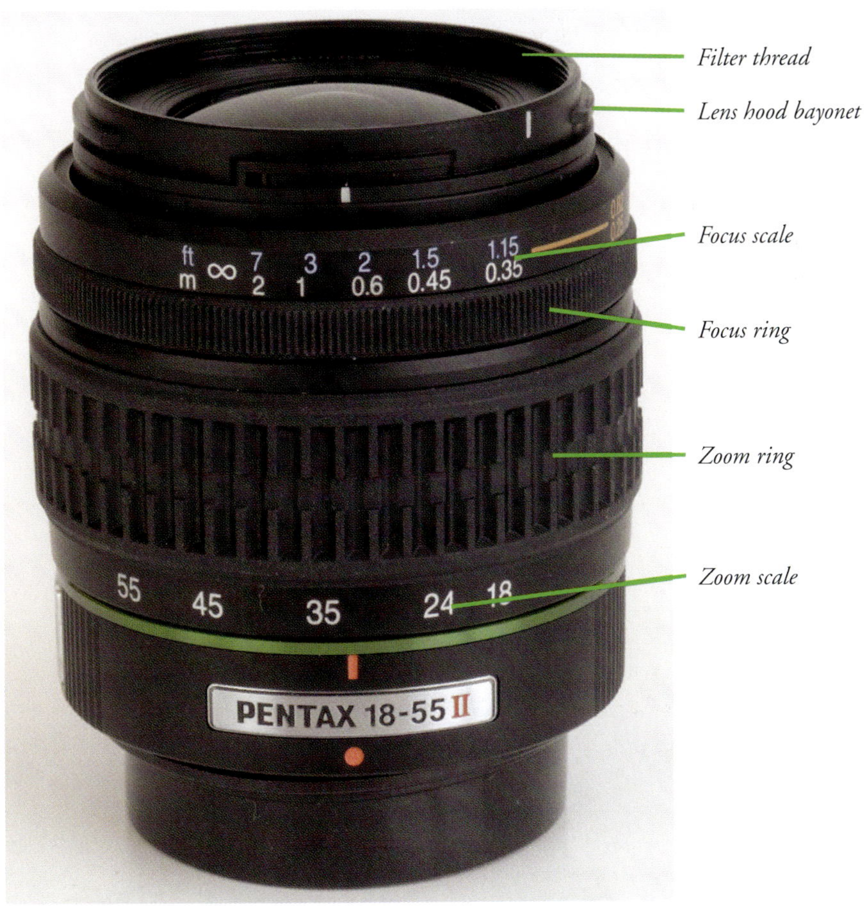

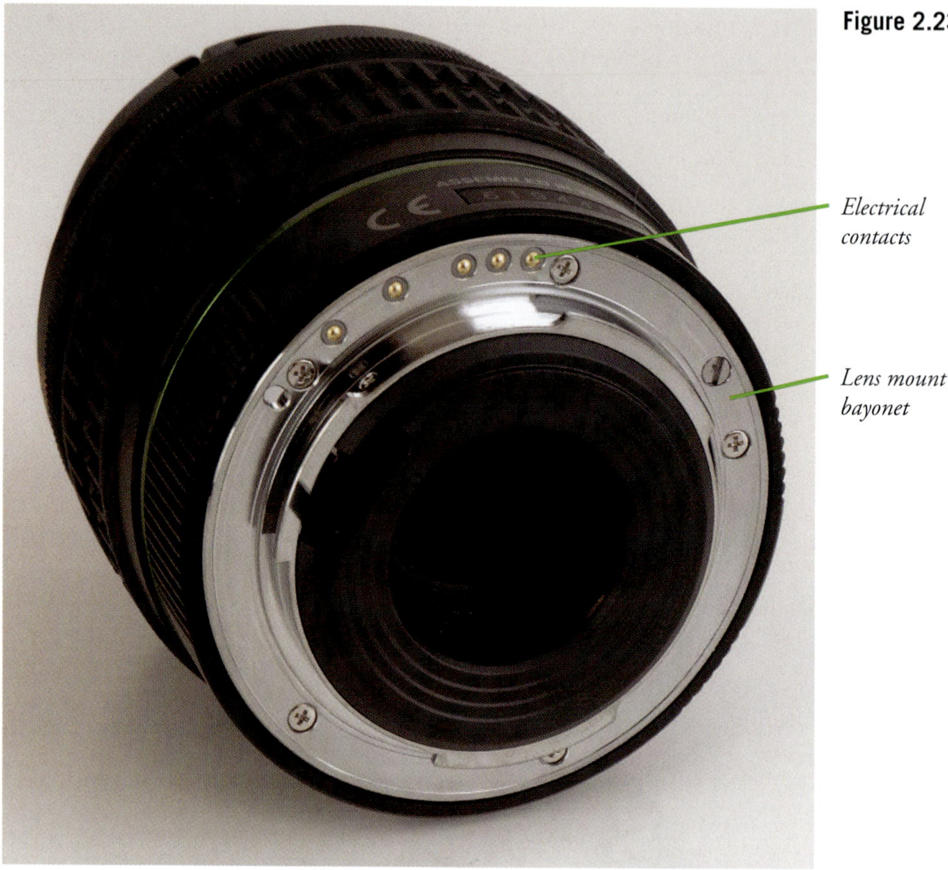

Figure 2.23

- **Focus scale.** The numbers that are printed on the focus ring move with the focus ring to measure the distance at which the lens has been focused. It's a useful indicator for double-checking autofocus, roughly evaluating depth-of-field, and for setting manual focus guesses.
- **Focus ring.** You turn this ring manually to focus when you're not using autofocus, or to fine-tune autofocus.
- **Zoom ring.** Turn this to zoom in and out.
- **Zoom scale.** The red marker is opposite the current focal length of a zoom lens.
- **Electrical contacts.** Allows the lens and camera body to communicate focus and exposure settings.
- **Lens mount bayonet.** Used to attach the lens to a matching mount on the camera body.

Playing Back Images

Reviewing images is a joy on the Pentax K200D's big 2.7-inch LCD. I introduced the basic functions in Chapter 1. To summarize, you can browse through the images you've taken by using these controls:

- **View most recent image.** Press the Playback button to display the last picture you took.
- **Change amount and type of information about the shot.** After pressing the Playback button, press the Info button to change the information display. The information display changes each time you press the Info button in the following repeating cycle: Standard (basic information about shot), either of two histogram displays, detailed information display, and no information display. I'll cover all these in this section.
- **Browse through images.** Push the right arrow to view the next image on the SD memory card, cycling around to the first image when you reach the last one taken. Push the left arrow to review previous images.
- **Rotate an image.** After pressing the Playback button, you can press the down arrow on the four-way controller to rotate an image. The image is rotated 90-degrees counterclockwise each time the button is pressed.
- **Zoom in and out.** After pressing the Playback button, you can magnify your image by turning the e-dial (located at the top-right backside of your camera). Turn it towards the right to zoom in (up to 16X), and towards the left to zoom out, and to change from full screen to thumbnail view. To move around within a magnified image, use the four-way controller buttons. Press the Playback button twice to exit a magnified display.

Changing the Info Display

Each time you press the Info button, the information display changes to the next option of four different data screens. Once you have set one of these four options, the K200D will use that type of display the next time you review an image, until you switch to one of the other types of information display:

- **Standard information.** In this mode, you can review your image, relatively unobstructed, with just three key pieces of information shown, plus three reminder icons. At upper left (as shown in Figure 2.24), you can see the file format information (JPEG, RAW, or RAW+); to the right is the folder and file number of the current image. In the lower-left corner you can see the shutter speed and aperture used to make the exposure. At lower right is a reminder icon representing the four-way controller pad; press left/right to see the previous/next image, and the down button to rotate the image 90 degrees. The two yellow icons at right appear only when the image has been given Protected status (the key icon), or is marked for printing (the printer icon).

- **Histogram displays.** Press the Info button when Standard information is shown, and one of two histogram displays appear. Figure 2.25 represents the Brightness/RGB display, which shows a thumbnail of the image with a separate histogram (tonal distribution) chart for brightness and for each of the red, green, and blue color channels. Figure 2.26 shows the image with only the brightness histogram chart overlaid. The pair of green up/down arrows indicate that you can switch from the current histogram to the other histogram mode by pressing the up/down keys. I'll explain more of what histograms are and how to use them in Chapter 4.

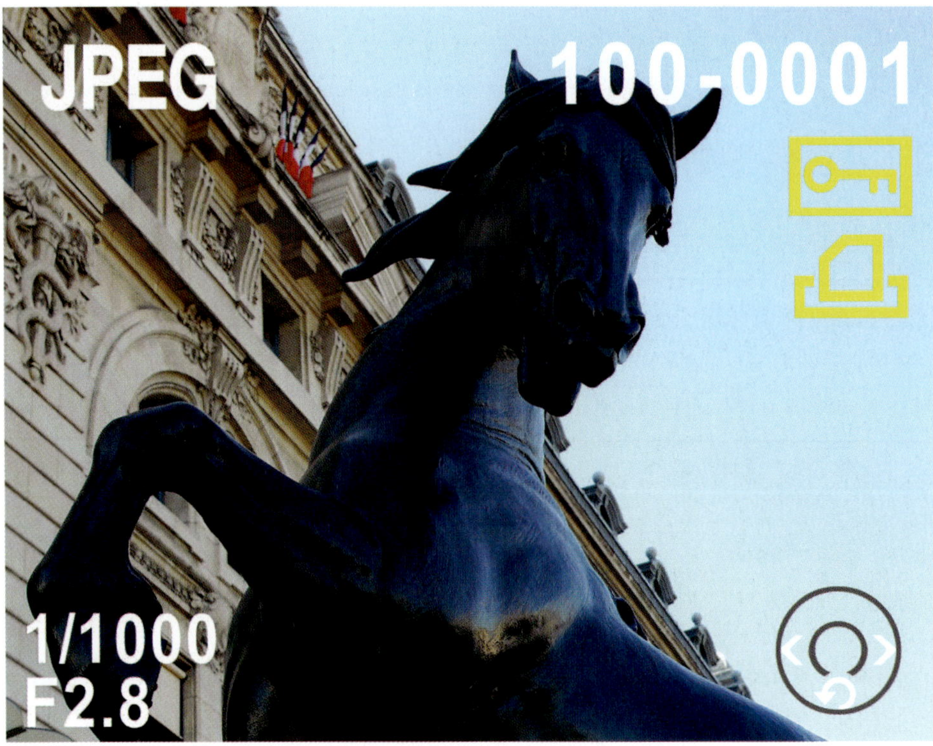

Figure 2.24 Standard information playback screen.

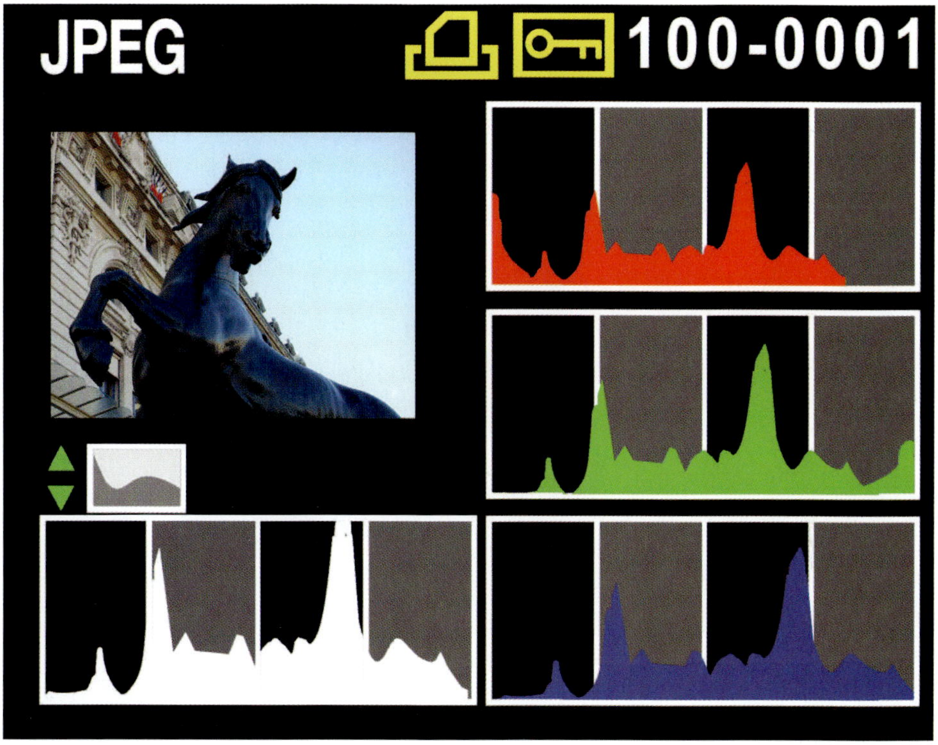

Figure 2.25
Brightness histogram information screen.

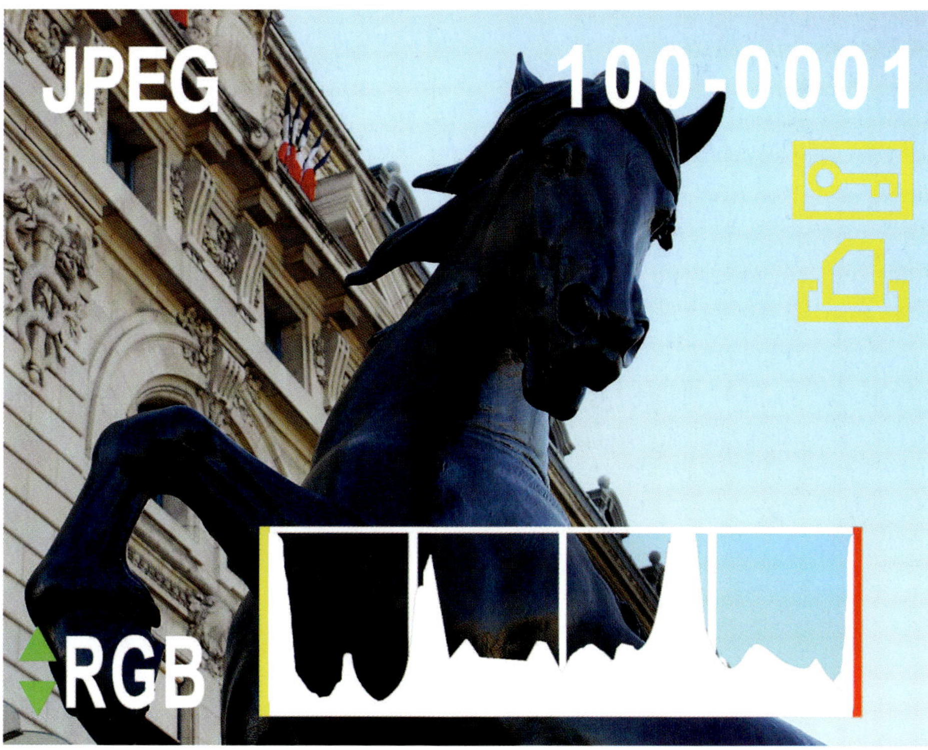

Figure 2.26
Brightness/RGB histogram information screen.

- **Detailed information.** This view is best for analyzing the shooting information for your image rather than for evaluating the photo itself, as only a small thumbnail is shown in the upper-left corner of the screen, as you can see in Figure 2.27. Everything from the focus point used to the lens' focal length, metering mode, flash mode, and any special effects you might have applied are shown. The labels for the figure show what each nugget of data on this screen represents. I'll discuss them in more detail in Chapters 3 and 4.
- **No information.** This version shows your image with no information overlay at all, as you can see in Figure 2.28.

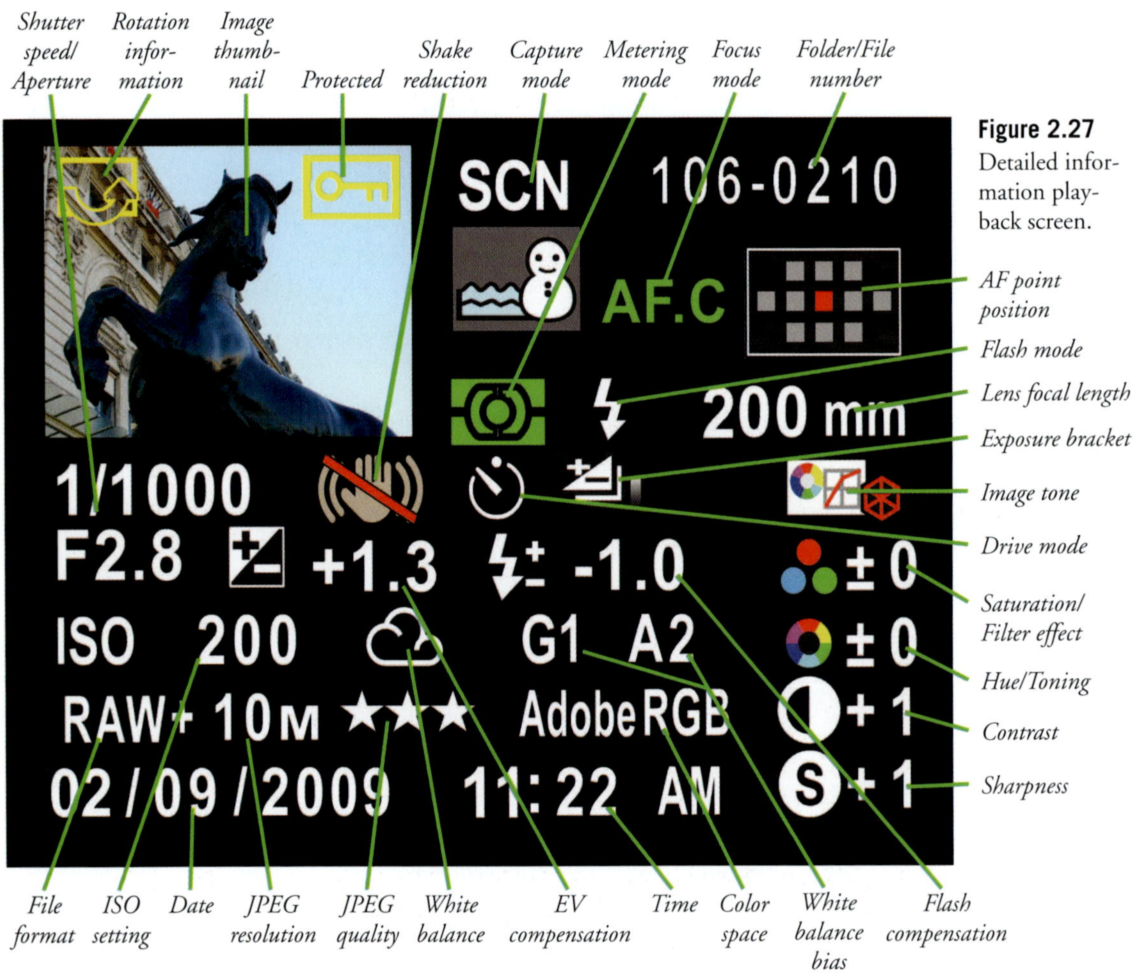

Figure 2.27 Detailed information playback screen.

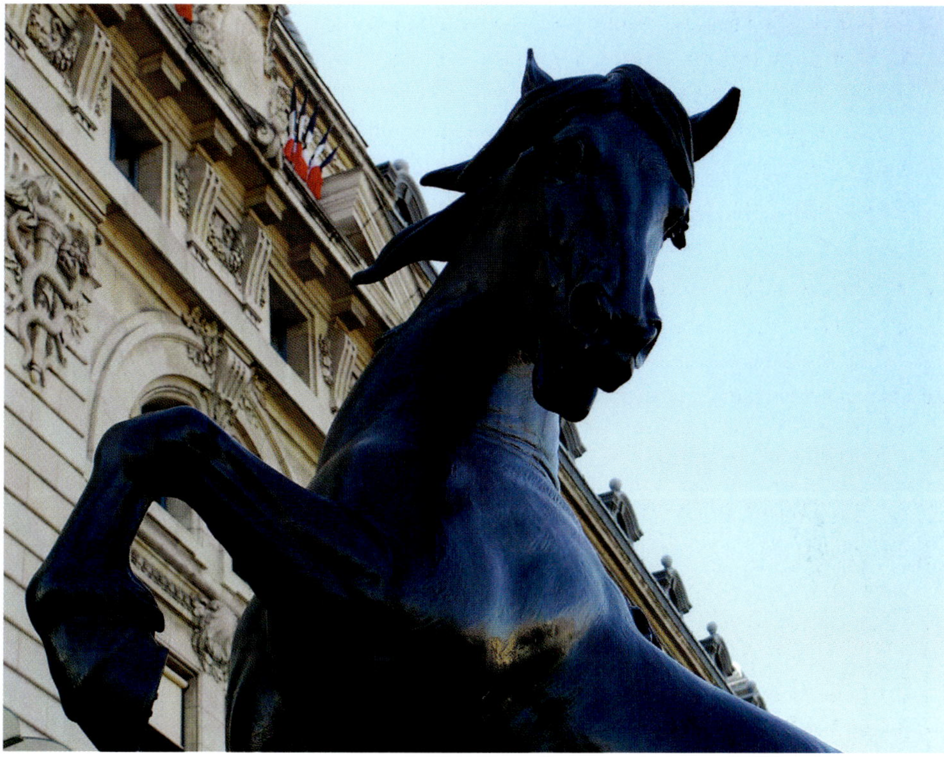

Figure 2.28 No information playback screen.

Basic Image Review

Here are the basics involved in reviewing images on the LCD screen (or on a television screen you have connected with a video cable). This section has the must-know information.

- **Start review.** To begin review, press the Playback button at the lower-left corner of the back of the K200D. The most recently viewed image will appear on the LCD.
- **Move back and forth.** To browse among images, use the left/right four-way controller keys as described earlier. When you reach the beginning/end of the photos in your folder, the display "wraps around" to the end/beginning of the available shots.
- **See different types of data.** To change the type of information about the displayed image that is shown, press the Info button as described in the previous section to cycle among your choices.

- **Zoom in and out.** When viewing an image, turn the e-dial to the right to enlarge the image in 16 steps from 1.2X to 16x. (The individual magnifications are 1.2X, 1.4X, 1.7X, 2X, 2.4X, 2.8X, 3.4X, 4X, 4.8X, 5.7X, 6.7X, 8X, 9.5X, 11X,14X, and 16X.) Press the four-way controller's OK center button to return to the original 1X view. You'll find more in the "Zooming" section that follows.
- **Move zoomed area within image.** In any zoomed view, a small navigation window will appear in the lower-left corner of the screen with a green navigation box that indicates the current zoomed portion of the photo within that, as shown in Figure 2.29. Note that the navigation window does *not* show a thumbnail version of the full image; it only represents the frame itself, with the green navigation window showing the relative size and position of the zoomed area. Use the left/right/up/down keys to move the green box around within the full frame. The larger image view on the screen will change to match. If you prefer to work without the navigation box as a guide, press the Info button and it will vanish.
- **Playback folder.** Image review generally shows you the images in the currently selected folder on your SD card. A given card can contain several folders (a new one is created anytime you exceed 500 images in the current folder, unless you're using auto bracketing).

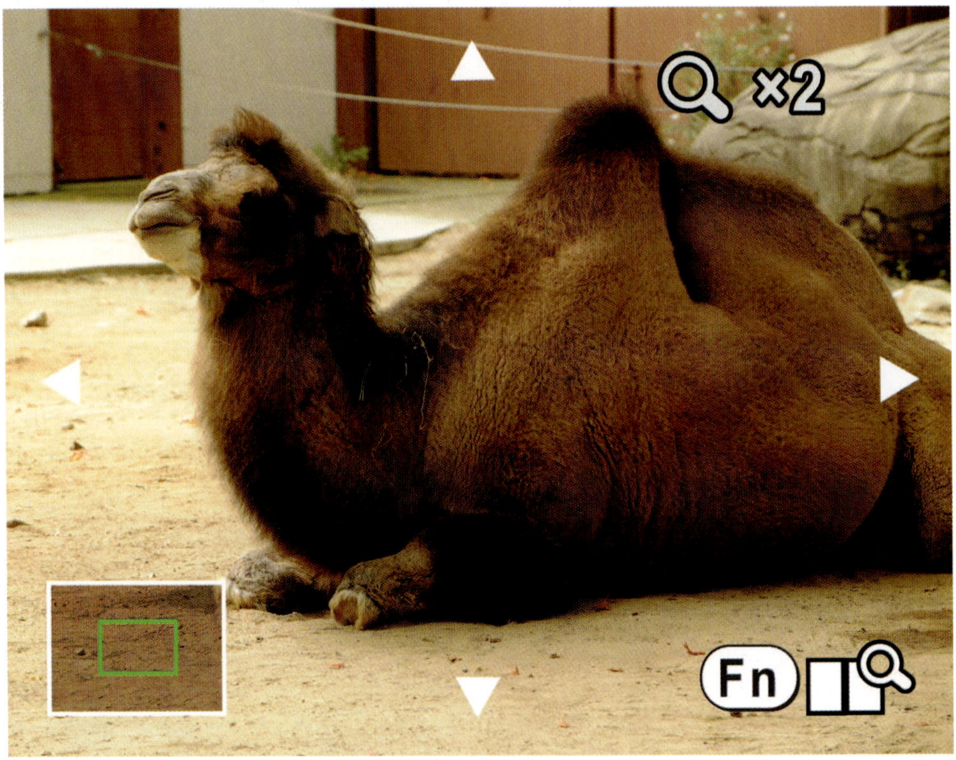

Figure 2.29
You can change the zoomed area within a frame using the four-way controller keys.

- **View thumbnail images.** To change the view from a single image to 4 or 9 thumbnails, follow the instructions in the "Viewing Thumbnails" section that follows later in this chapter.
- **Protect and delete images.** When viewing thumbnails or a single page image, press the Protect button to preserve the image against accidental deletion (a key icon is overlaid over the full page image), or the Trash button (twice) to erase it. You can Unprotect an image by viewing it and pressing the Protect button again. (To Protect or Unprotect all images on a card, view a single image, press the Protect button twice, and choose Protect All/Unprotect All from the screen that pops up.)
- **Cancel playback.** To cancel image review, press the Playback button again, or simply tap the shutter release button.

Zooming the Pentax K200D Playback Display

As I mentioned earlier, you can zoom in and out with the e-dial, and move the zoomed area around within the frame with the four-way controller keys. But the K200D's zooming functions have a couple of quirks you should know about.

- **Zoom guide/no guide.** The inset frame with green zoom area guide I described earlier is optional. Press Info to turn it off and on. You can still move the zoomed area around within the frame whether the zoom guide is visible or not.
- **Alternate zoom controls.** Once you've begun to zoom, the AV button (near the shutter release) and the AE-L button (to the right of the e-dial) have the same zoom in/zoom out functions. If you are viewing a full-screen image, rather than a zoomed version, these buttons have no effect; nor will the AE-L button zoom out further than 1.2X. You must still use the e-dial to zoom out further. For that reason, I recommend using the e-dial instead for zooming.
- **Quick zoom.** You can reprogram the camera so that the initial zoom display is a Quick Zoom value of 2X, 4X, 8X, or 16X rather than the default 1.2X. You'd want to use this option if you find that you frequently zoom in more tightly on an image during review, and want to skip the smaller increments. I'll show you how to make this change in the section on the Playback menu in Chapter 3.
- **Compare images.** When viewing a zoomed image, you can press the Fn button to compare that image with another image side by side. If you're viewing a full-frame, 1X image instead, you can press OK and then the Fn button to activate image comparison. I'll describe that feature next.
- **End zoom/picture review.** If you're viewing a full-frame or zoomed image, you can dismiss the image by tapping the shutter release button. You'll never have to worry about missing a shot because the camera was "busy" in picture review. When you partially depress the shutter release, the K200D's autofocus system and exposure meter springs to life, and you're ready to shoot.

Comparing Images

Sometimes it is useful to view multiple images at one time in order to compare them, or to look at a single image at two different magnifications. The Pentax K200D has a feature that shows a pair of vertical image slices on the screen side by side, so you can compare them easily. Just follow these steps to put this useful facility to work:

1. **Display dual images.** In Playback mode (with a full-size or zoomed-in review image on the LCD screen), press the Fn button, followed by the four-way controller's OK button. The image you are viewing will be shown on the screen as a pair of vertical slices from the image, within two different windows, as you can see in Figure 2.30.

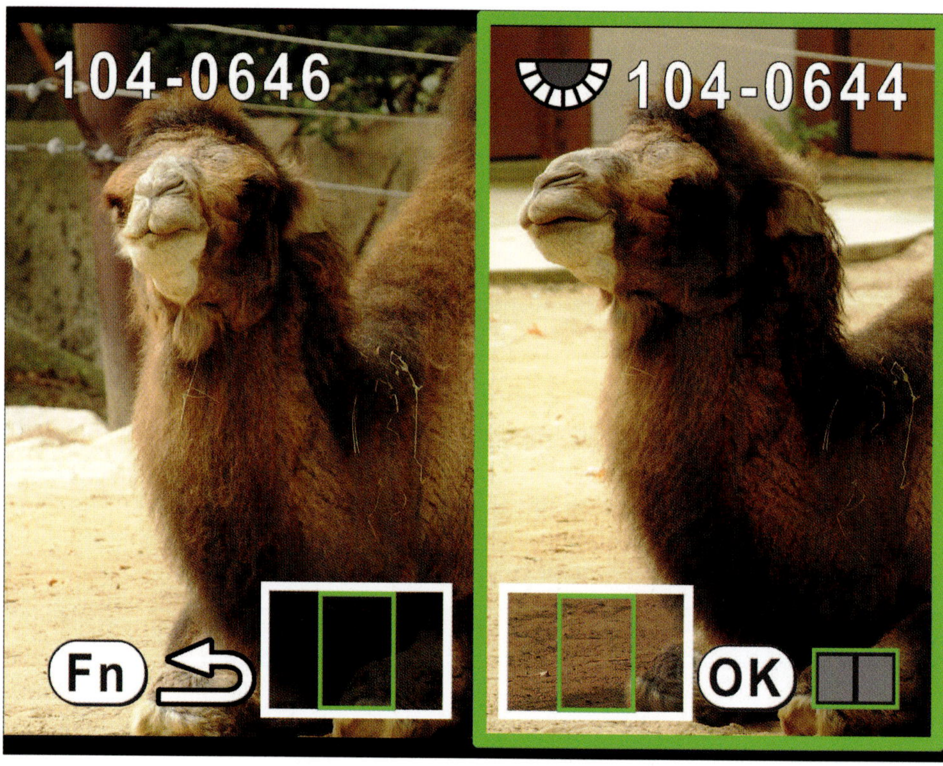

Figure 2.30 Compare images side by side.

2. **Show picture information.** Press the Info button to show the folder and picture number information for each of the two images, if that information is not already displayed. If it is shown, pressing the Info button hides it.
3. **Select left, right, or both images.** Once the dual display is shown, pressing the OK button cycles through highlighting (with a green outline) the left, right, or both images.
4. **Choose an image pair.** When the left or right images are surrounded by the green box, rotating the e-dial changes that image to the previous one on your memory

card (rotate the e-dial left) or the next one (rotate the e-dial right). This allows you to choose which two images to compare.

5. **Change viewed area.** While either image is highlighted with the green box, you can use the left/right/up/down controller keys to change the viewed portion of that image to some other position in the frame. Use this control when you don't want to look at the exact same area of both images.
6. **Zoom in and out.** After you've selected the image pair to compare, and have adjusted the viewed area, press the OK button to highlight both images simultaneously, surrounding them with a single green box. Then, rotate the e-dial to zoom in and out of both simultaneously, using the same magnification for both. If the Info display is activated, the zoom magnification will be shown. In this combined view, you can also use the four way controller keys to move the viewed area around within the frames of the original images. The Green button returns an enlarged view to the center of the display.
7. **Delete an image.** When one of the two images is highlighted with the green box, press the Trash button to delete that image.
8. **Return to normal view.** Press the Fn button to restore normal Playback.

Playback Images as a Slide Show

You can view a slide show of the images on your memory card. I'll show you how to set the display time for each image in Chapter 3, where you'll also learn how to use the Playback menu to initiate a slide show for display on the camera LCD, or a television/monitor that might be connected. However, you can easily activate a show using the Function menu. Just follow these steps.

1. **Activate review.** Press the Playback button to display the most recently shot image.
2. **Select the start image for the show.** Use the left/right keys to scroll to the image you want to be first in your slide show.
3. **Begin the slide show.** Press the Fn button to access the Function menu, then press the right key to commence the slide show.
4. **Jump ahead/back/pause/restart.** During the slide show, you can skip to the next image in the series by pressing the right controller key; back up to a previous image by pressing the left controller key; or pause the slide show by pressing the OK button. Press OK again to restart.
5. **Ending the show.** You can end the slide show and return the camera to Playback mode by pressing the controller down key, Playback button, or Menu button. End the show and return to Capture mode by pressing the shutter release; by rotating the power switch all the way clockwise; or by changing the Mode dial.

Viewing Thumbnails and Folders

The Pentax K200D provides other options for reviewing images in addition to zooming in and out. You can switch between single image view and either four or nine reduced-size thumbnail images on a single LCD screen. Figure 2.31 shows the nine-image view.

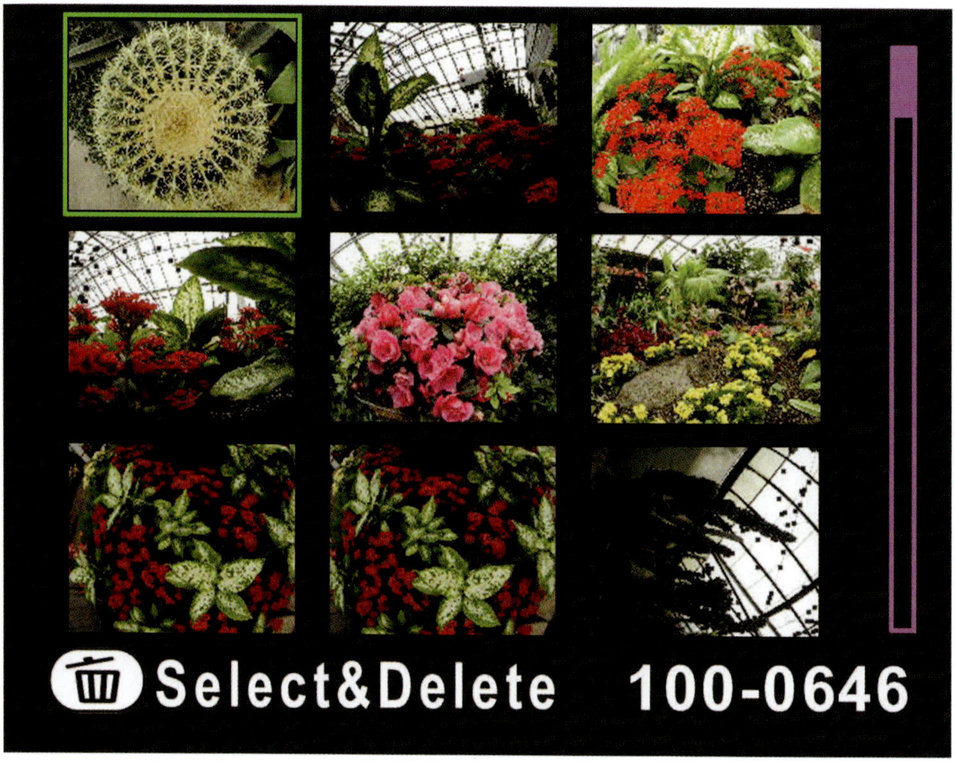

Figure 2.31
View thumbnails of images to rapidly find the photo you want.

Pages of thumbnail images offer a quick way to scroll through a large number of pictures quickly to find the one you want to examine in more detail. The K200D lets you switch quickly from single- to four- to nine-image views, with a scroll bar displayed at the right side of the screen to show you the relative position of the displayed thumbnails within the full collection of images in the folder on your memory card. To view thumbnails and folders, just follow these steps:

1. **Display thumbnails.** Press the Playback button to produce a single image display. Rotate the e-dial one click to the left to show thumbnails.
2. **Change number of thumbnails.** You can display four, nine, or 16 images at once. While viewing thumbnails, press the Fn button, and then press the left controller button to show four images; the up controller button to show nine images; and the right controller button to display 16 images.

3. **Navigate among thumbnails.** Use the four-way controller buttons to scroll among the available thumbnail images. If you have multiple folders on your memory card, each individual folder's images will be shown on separate screens.
4. **View a selected image.** Press the OK button to view a full screen version of a thumbnail that is highlighted by the green box.
5. **Return to full screen display.** When you are done browsing thumbnails, return to full screen view by rotating the e-dial one click to the right.
6. **Display contents of a folder.** If you want to jump directly to the contents of a folder on your memory card, rotate the e-dial to the left one additional click if you're viewing thumbnails, or two clicks to the left if you're using single-image view. Use the controller keys to select the folder you want to examine, and press the OK button to view that folder's images. They will be displayed using the thumbnail view that is currently active (4, 9, or 16 images). To return to thumbnail or single-image view, rotate the e-dial to the right one (thumbnail view) or two clicks (single-image view).

Removing Images

You can remove images from your memory card individually or as a group. Here are your options:

- **Format the card.** To remove all images from a memory card, even those that have been marked with Protect status, you should reformat the card. Press the Menu button, use the right controller key to choose the Set-up menu, press the down key to scroll to the Format command, and, finally, the right key to produce the Format screen. You can then select Format or Cancel.
- **Erase a single image.** To remove the currently displayed image, press the Trash button. You'll be shown a menu offering to delete the image, or to cancel the step. Highlight the choice you want, and press OK to either delete the image or cancel. If your image was taken using RAW+JPEG, the deletion menu will include Delete JPEG, Delete RAW, and Delete RAW+JPEG. You can choose to remove either format, or both.
- **Erase all images.** To remove all the images on the card, press the Trash button twice. A message asking Delete All Images On Memory Card appears. You can choose Delete All or Cancel. Make your choice and press the OK button to confirm. (Cancel is the default; you can also back out of the Delete All screen by pressing the Menu button.) Erasing all images doesn't return your card's file structure to its pristine state, so it's a good idea to format the card *in the camera* regularly, rather than simply erasing in the camera, and *especially* instead of erasing images from cards inserted in card readers connected to your computer.

- **Delete from thumbnail view.** When viewing thumbnails (turn the e-dial to the left one click during single-image playback), you can select individual thumbnails and mark each highlighted image. First, press the Trash button to produce a checkbox next to each thumbnail. Then, use the four-way controller to browse among the rest of your images. Press the OK button when each image you want to delete is highlighted. It will be marked with a checkmark, as shown in Figure 2.32. (You cannot mark Protected images; you must Unprotect them first.) When all the images you want to remove have been marked, press the Trash button again, and choose Select & Delete from the menu that appears. Press OK to remove the marked images.
- **Delete a folder.** When viewing folders as described earlier (turn the e-dial to the left two clicks during single-image play), use the four-way controller keys to highlight the folder you want to remove, and press the Trash button. A confirmation screen pops up. Choose Delete or Cancel, and press OK to confirm your choice. If there are Protected images in the folder you are deleting, an additional confirmation screen appears asking whether you want to Delete All or Leave All. Make your choice and press OK.

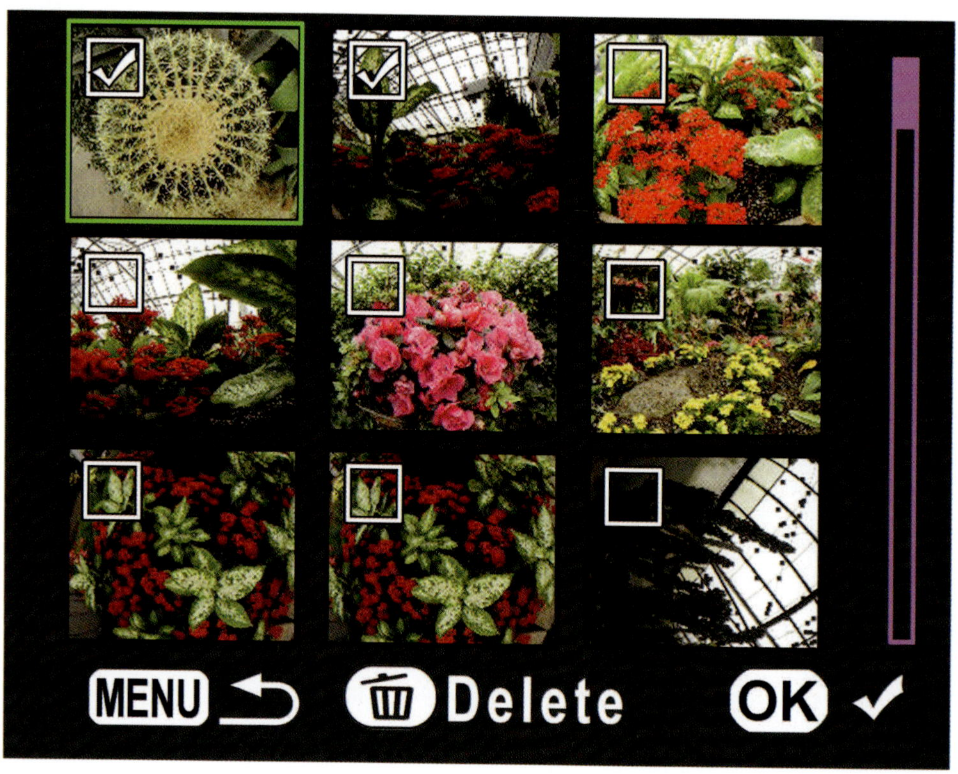

Figure 2.32 You can mark or unmark individual images for deletion in thumbnail view.

3

Setting Up Your Pentax K200D

When I first began using my Pentax K200D, I immediately noticed that, for an entry-level camera, this dSLR had an amazing number of options and settings that can be used to customize the way it operates. In terms of features, the K200D compares very favorably with its more advanced sibling, the Pentax K20D. Not only are you able to change shooting settings applied at the time the picture is taken, but you can adjust the way your camera behaves. Indeed, if your K200D doesn't operate in exactly the way you'd like, chances are you can make a small change in the Recording mode, Playback, Set-Up, and Custom Setting menus that will tailor the K200D to fit your needs. You'll find an array of choices ranging from the mundane—what White Balance setting to use—to unusual—the ability to choose Adobe's Digital Negative (DNG) format instead of RAW or JPEG. You'll find all these options in your Pentax's menu systems.

As I've mentioned before, this book isn't intended to replace the manual you received with your K200D, nor have I any interest in rehashing its contents. You'll still find the original manual useful as a standby reference that lists every possible option in exhaustive (if mind-numbing) detail—without really telling you how to use those options to take better pictures. There is, however, some unavoidable duplication between the Pentax manual and this chapter because I'm going to explain all the key menu choices and the options you may have in using them. You should find, though, that I will give you the information you need in a much more helpful format, with plenty of detail on why you should make some settings that are particularly difficult to understand.

Introducing the Pentax K200D's Menus

The Pentax K200D has four different menu systems, the SCN (or Scene) menu, the Playback Mode Function menu, Capture Mode Function menu, and the main menu system:

- **SCN menu.** This menu, shown in Figure 3.1, pops up when the Mode dial is set to the SCN position. It has eight additional Scene modes. You can learn more about using this menu in Chapter 1 in the section "Selecting a Scene Mode."
- **Playback Functions.** This menu, shown in Figure 3.2, appears when you press the Fn button while reviewing images in Playback mode. You can use it to select images for printing, play back your photos in a slide show, convert RAW files to JPEG format, apply filter effects, or compare two images side by side. Read more about this menu in "Using the Function Menus" in Chapter 2.
- **Capture Functions.** This menu appears when you press the Fn button while in Capture mode. (See Figure 3.3.) It includes options for changing the camera's Drive mode (Single Shot, Continuous Shot, Self-Timer, Remote Control, and Bracketing), ISO setting, White Balance adjustments, and electronic flash settings. An introduction to this menu can be found in "Using the Function Menus" in

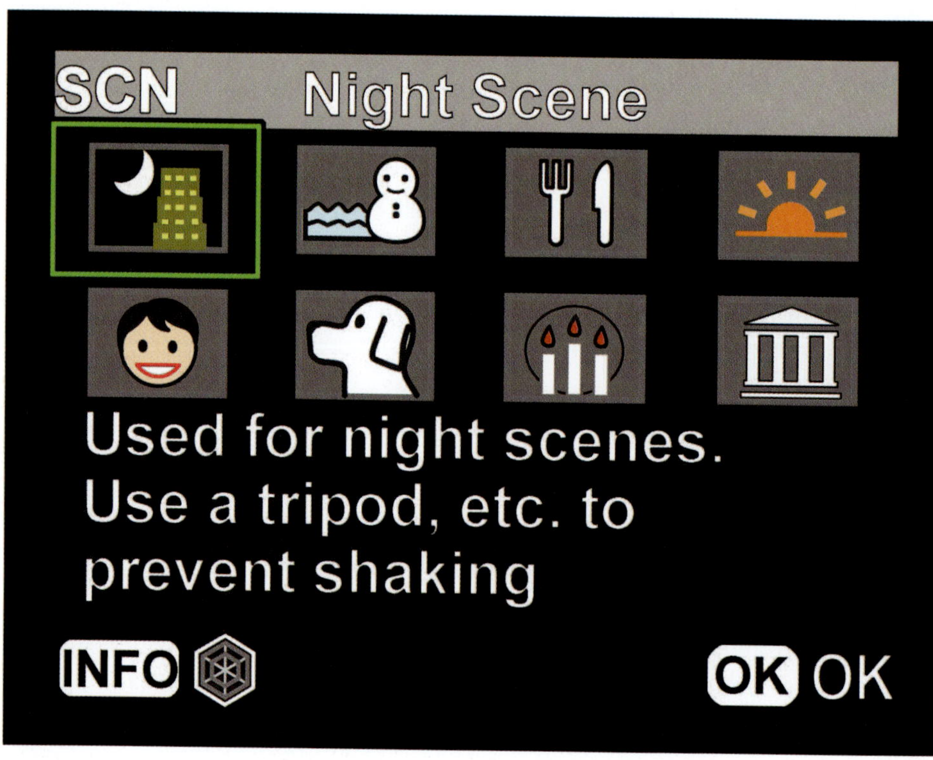

Figure 3.1 The SCN menu.

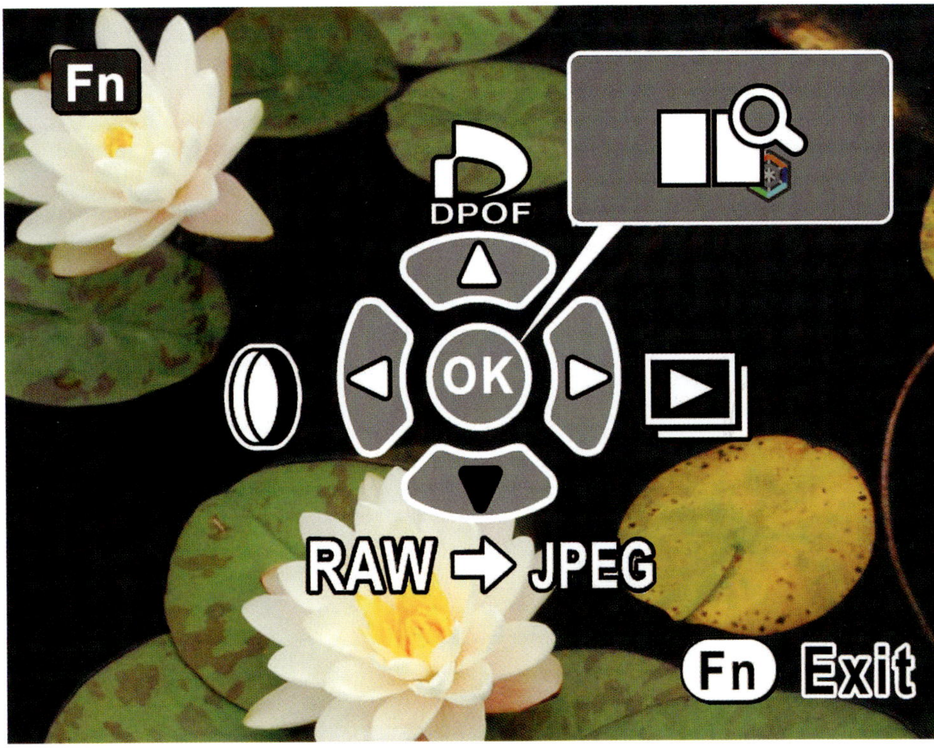

Figure 3.2 Playback Functions menu.

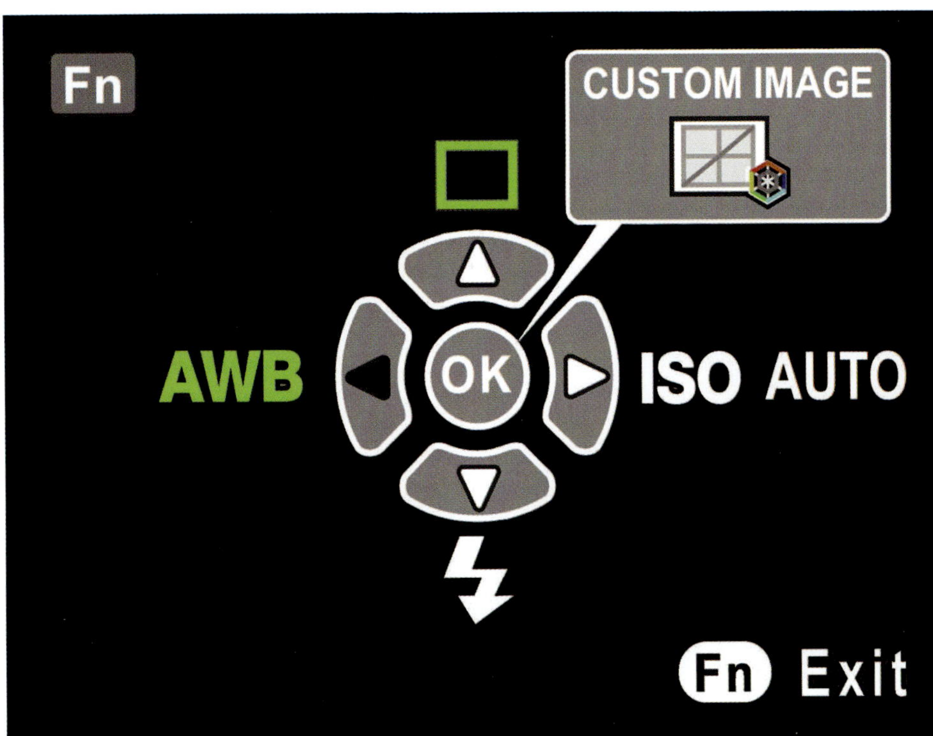

Figure 3.3 Capture Functions menu.

Chapter 2, but I'll also explain each of these functions in more detail later in this book. (ISO, White Balance, and Bracketing can be found in Chapter 4; Drive modes in Chapter 5; and flash options in Chapter 7.)

- **Main menus.** This menu system appears when you press the Menu button to the left of the LCD display. It includes four tabbed menus labeled Rec. Mode, Playback, Set-up, and Custom Setting. I'll describe each of these in the sections that follow.

Anatomy of the Pentax K200D's Main Menus

The K200D's main menu system includes four separate screens of entries, each located on a "tab" marked with an icon representing that menu's functions. Each tab includes from four to 24 entries, with a maximum of six shown on the screen at any one time. If a menu includes more than six entries, a scroll bar appears at the right side of the screen, and you can press the controller down button to scroll down to the additional entries that aren't visible. The four menu tabs, shown in Figure 3.4, are as follows:

- **Rec. Mode (Recording Mode).** A red camera icon lets you know you're working with the Recording Mode menu, which includes entries for autofocus and autoexposure settings, image size, quality, and file formats, as well as Color Space and functions of the RAW button.
- **Playback.** You'll find settings that control picture review display, slideshows, and other functions in this menu, marked with a blue right-pointing triangle when the menu is active.
- **Set-up.** A wrench icon marks the Set-up menu, which lets you format your memory card, turn the K200D's Beep sound on/off for functions of your choice, and set the time and date, brightness level of the LCD, power settings, and other frequently changed operation functions.
- **Custom Setting.** An orange C icon marks the Custom Setting menu when it's active, with 23 settings plus a Reset function, covering a large number of options that you won't be changing often. These include the order in which exposures should be bracketed; whether or not autofocus is used when triggering the camera with a remote control; or whether noise reduction should be applied during long exposures or when using high ISO settings.

The anatomy of the main menus generally follows the layout shown for the Recording Mode menu in Figure 3.4. The components are as follows:

- The top row includes tabs for the four menus, with the active menu's icon highlighted.
- The left column within each menu represents the name of the menu entry, such as AF Mode, or AE Metering. Note that some menu entries are abbreviated, but their

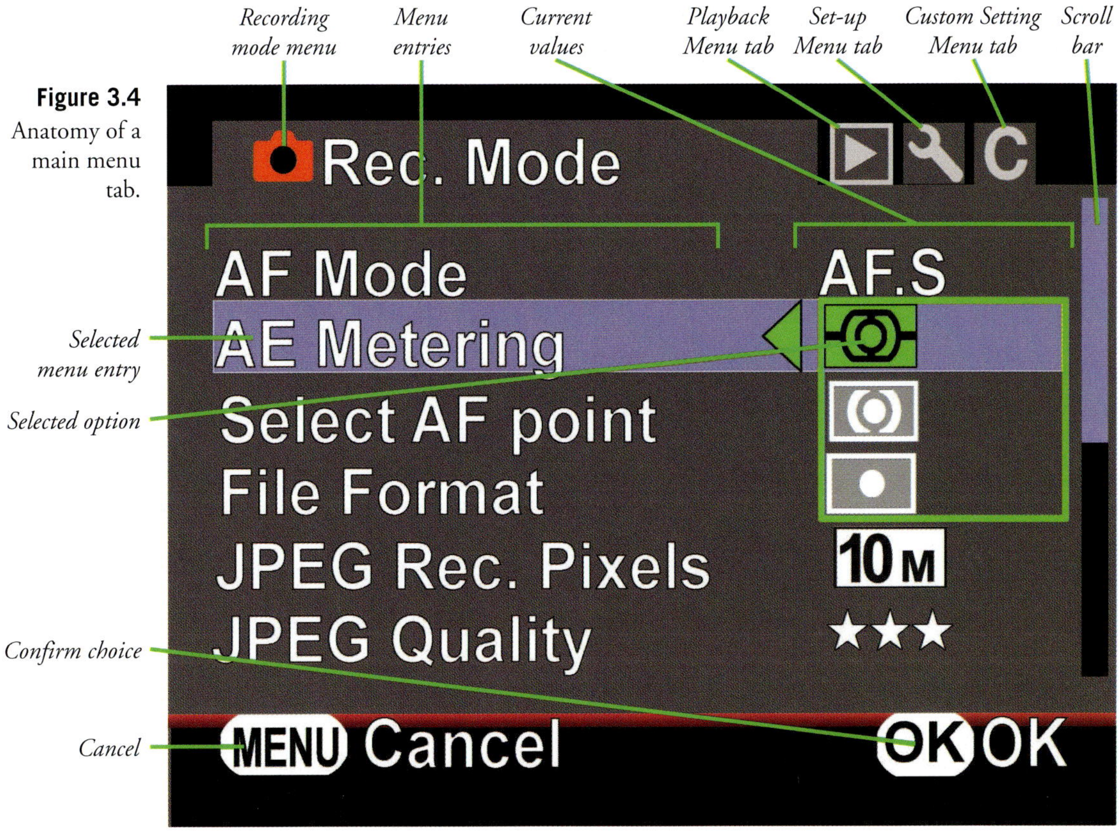

Figure 3.4 Anatomy of a main menu tab.

full name becomes visible when that entry is highlighted. For example, the JPEG Rec. Pixels entry becomes JPEG Recorded Pixels when it is selected.

- The right-hand column has an icon or text that shows either the current setting for that menu item, or which represents the function of that menu entry. When a particular menu item is highlighted and the right controller key is pressed, the available options pop up, as shown in the figure. Use the up/down keys to select the choice you want, and press OK to confirm it.
- A scroll bar appears at the right of the menu screen when additional menu entries are available. The position of the blue sliding "thumb" in the scroll bar (honest, that's what it's called) indicates the current position of the highlighted entry within the scrolling list. Use the up/down keys to scroll among the entries.
- The bottom row includes a Menu/Exit indicator when no entry has been activated, showing that you can exit the main menus by pressing the Menu button. This changes to Menu/Cancel when an entry is active, and an OK icon appears on the screen to indicate that you can press the four-way controller's OK button to confirm the highlighted option as your choice.

Navigating among the various main menus is easy and follows a consistent set of rules.

- **Press Menu to start.** Press the Menu button to display the main menu screens.
- **Choose menu tab.** Use the left/right four-way controller keys or the e-dial to choose the Rec. Mode, Playback, Set-up, or Custom Setting menu tab. Menu selection "wraps around"; if you continue scrolling left or right past the last menu tab, the first/last tab appears again.
- **Navigate among entries with the up/down keys.** The four-way controller has buttons at the up/down/left/right positions. Press the up/down keys to navigate among the menu entries.
- **Activate a menu entry.** Press the right button to activate a menu entry and the left button to de-activate it when you want to move to a different menu entry.
- **Choose options.** Once a menu entry has been activated, use the up/down buttons to select from the available options.
- **Confirm your selection.** Press the OK button to confirm your option. The menu entry is deactivated with the new setting indicated, and the menu entry remains highlighted in blue.
- **Leaving the menu system.** Press the Menu button to exit the main menus or tap the shutter release button. If you haven't confirmed your choice for a particular option, no changes will be made.

Recording Mode Menu

The buttons on the top of your camera, the e-dial and the Fn button on the back-right side are easily accessible and contain the settings you might change during a photo session. The green button and the Av buttons do things such as adjust EV compensation (exposure compensation) and reset exposure values in Program mode. The e-dial adjusts shutter speed, aperture, and ISO (in Sv Mode). The Fn button provides a similar setup to that of the point-and-shoot model cameras. It adjusts ISO mode, white balance, and flash modes. The Shooting menu options are accessed a bit less frequently when you're using your K200D. You might make these adjustments as you begin a shooting session, or when you move from one type of subject to another. The first screen of the Recording Mode menu was shown in Figure 3.4.

- AF Mode (autofocus)
- AE Metering
- Select AF point
- File Format
- JPEG Size

- JPEG Quality
- RAW File Format
- Color Space
- RAW Button Setting
- Memory
- Focal Length Input

AF Mode (autofocus)

This autofocus mode selection entry is available only when you are using one of the Exposure mode settings: Program, Sensitivity Priority (Sv), Shutter Priority (Tv), Aperture Priority (Av), Manual (M), or Bulb (B.) In any of the Mode dial Scene modes, or when using one of the SCN settings, the K200D chooses the autofocus method for you.

As I said in Chapter 1, you can manually focus the camera when the MF/AF switch on the left front side of the body is set to MF. You can also adjust focus manually after the camera has automatically focused when in AF mode. Press the shutter release down halfway and rotate the focusing ring on the camera. When the subject is in focus, the green focus indicator hexagon appears and you will hear a beep (unless you've disabled the beep for this function, as described later in this chapter). Even though you are focusing manually, the K200D is kind enough to help you by confirming sharp focus.

You might want to use Manual focus when shooting close-ups, because the range of sharpness (*depth-of-field*) is very shallow, and focusing the image yourself allows more precision in selecting the exact point of focus. Manual focus is also useful when you want to take advantage of the depth-of-field sharpness range to specify exactly what areas of your image are in focus for creative purposes. (This is called *selective focus.*) Manual focus also is useful if you are using an older lens that doesn't offer autofocus features. (I'll explain the use of these lenses in Chapter 7.)

Most of the time, however, you'll want to use the Pentax K200D's automatic focus features. This menu selection allows you to specify *when* the camera applies its focusing magic to your scene—either Single mode, or Continuous mode, as I originally described in Chapter 1:

- **AF.S: Single Mode.** This mode, sometimes called *Single Autofocus*, locks in a focus point when the shutter release button is pressed halfway down. You'll see a red square in the viewfinder that illuminates to indicate the focus point selected, a green octagonal focus confirmation indicator is shown at the bottom of the viewfinder, and the camera will emit a beep when the K200D has focused. The focus locks until you either release the button or press it all the way down to take the picture. If the subject begins moving, the camera switches to AF.C mode and tracks the movement by refocusing as necessary. This mode is best when your subject isn't moving, because you can set focus once on the subject of your choice, then change your composition and re-frame your image as you like. All the Scene/SCN Modes use this focus exclusively, except the Moving Object, Kids, and Pet modes. If the K200D isn't able to focus at all, the green octagon in the viewfinder will blink and the shutter release will be locked. This behavior is called *focus priority*; the shutter is disabled unless the image is sharply focused.

- **AF.C: Continuous Mode.** While the shutter release button is pressed halfway down, the focus locks on your subject, but the camera will refocus as required if the subject is moving. This mode can be selected when using P, Sv, Tv, Av, M, or B Exposure modes. The Moving Object Scene (Picture), Kids, and Pet SCN modes use this focus method exclusively. In order for the K200D to continually focus, you have to keep the shutter release button pressed halfway down. If the subject is slightly out of focus, as indicated by the flashing green octagon, the shutter button is *not* locked and the K200D can still take a picture when the shutter release is pressed all the way down. This behavior is called *release priority*; a photo will be taken when the shutter release is pressed, regardless of whether the image is in sharp focus. That can be helpful for action shots and other subject matter when you'd prefer to take a photo, even if slightly out of focus, rather than miss the picture entirely.

Tip

In dark scenes, there may not be enough light for the K200D to focus easily. When using AF.S mode, you can pop up the flash (if it isn't already elevated) by pressing the Flash Up button on the back-left corner of the camera. The flash will discharge several times when you partially depress the shutter release, providing enough illumination for automatic focus.

AE Metering

This menu entry allows you to select the area of the frame the Pentax K200D uses to calculate exposure: from multiple segments in 16 different metering zones; by emphasizing the center of the frame but taking into account the entire measurable area within the 16 zones; or by measuring exposure only from the center of the picture. I'll provide more details on obtaining the best exposure in Chapter 4. Here are the three choices you have available:

- **Multi-Segment metering.** Exposure is based on readings from 16 parts of the frame, which the K200D uses to make some intelligent guesses about what kind of photo you're taking based on the distribution of light and dark values (landscape, portrait, and so forth).

- **Center-Weighted metering.** Exposure is based on the entire frame, but with emphasis on subject matter in the center of the picture.
- **Spot metering.** Exposure is calculated based *only* on what's in the center of the frame within the round brackets shown in the viewfinder.

Select AF Point

Use this menu entry to specify how the primary autofocus point is selected from among the 11 different zones in the camera's viewfinder. The active AF point is displayed in the viewfinder screen, unless you've disabled that display using Custom Setting #8, as described later in this chapter. Your three AF point selection choices are as follows:

- **Auto.** The K200D chooses the best AF point from among 11 zones distributed throughout the center area of the frame. Your subject does not have to be centered for the camera to locate it. This is your best choice for fast-moving action and other scenes in which you don't know in advance where your main subject will be located at the moment of the exposure. The K200D will use its intelligence to choose the likely center of interest and lock focus on that AF point.
- **Select.** In this mode, you select one of those 11 focus points for more control of what you want in focus, using the controller's up/down/left/right keys. The center point is the default option unless you change it with the controller keys. The focus points don't "wrap around" left to right/right to left/ or up/down. When you reach the farthest focus point in any direction, the point movement stops. Use this method when you want to control the zone where focus is evaluated, particularly with subjects that are located away from the exact center of the frame. It's best for stationary subjects, or those that are moving very slowly, because it takes time to relocate the focus point manually.
- **Center.** The K200D uses the focus point in the center of your frame. Use this method when you know your main subject is going to be located in the middle of the frame. The camera automatically uses this method when you're using older lenses (which don't have DA, D FA, FA J, FA, or F in their names).

Tip

I'll explain how to use a technique called Catch-In Focus (also called *Trap Focus* outside the Pentax world) later in this chapter when I describe Custom Setting #22.

LOCKING FOCUS

Sometimes you'll want to use the autofocus system to focus on a subject that lies outside the 11 focus zones in the viewfinder. At other times, you'll want to lock focus on a particular point, even if the subject begins moving. (Perhaps you expect your subject to return to the original focus point, or another subject is moving towards that point—say, a baserunner heading for third while your original third-base runner dashes for home plate.)

To lock focus in such situations, switch from AF.C mode (which always refocuses as the subject moves) to AF.S mode, and press the AE-L button on the upper-right corner of the back of the camera. You must first enable the AE-L button for focus lock by using Custom Setting #4 (AE-L with AF Locked), and setting that option to ON. When CS#4 is set to OFF, the AE-L button locks *only* the exposure.

File Format

Your options within this menu entry are JPEG, RAW, or RAW+ (both JPEG and RAW file formats). So, you can elect to store only JPEG versions of the images you shoot, or you can save your photos as RAW images, which Pentax calls PEF, for Pentax Electronic Format files. Alternatively, you can choose the Adobe Digital Negative (DNG) RAW format, as described later in this chapter.

RAW images of either PEF or DNG type (with their .PEF or .DNG file extensions) consume more space on your memory card, but have the advantage of offering more flexibility during image editing (read on for more information on that). JPEG files (with their .JPG extensions) are more highly compressed and use less space on your memory card, but offer fewer options during image editing. Many photographers elect to save *both* JPEG and a RAW using the RAW+ choice, so they'll have a JPEG version that might be usable as-is, as well as the original "digital negative" RAW file in case they want to do some extensive processing of the image later. You'll end up with two different versions of the same file: one with a .jpg extension, and one with the .pef or .dng extension that signifies a RAW file. I'll offer some more detailed advice on choosing a file format later in this chapter.

JPEG Recorded Pixels

This setting allows you to choose the resolution of your image when shooting JPEG files. (RAW files are always saved at the highest resolution of 10 megapixels [3872 × 2592].) You can select:

- **10M.** Stores 10-megapixel JPEG images at 3872 × 2592-pixel resolution. This size allows making sharp prints as large as 10 × 12 –inches (according to Pentax; your results may differ).

- **6M.** Use this 3008 × 2000-pixel resolution to save some space on your memory card. Depending on your other settings (such as JPEG Quality), you can expect to make good prints from these 6-megapixel files that are as large as 8 × 10 inches.
- **2M.** This setting produces 1824 × 1216, two-megapixel files that are best for prints no larger than 5 × 7 inches.

JPEG Quality

This entry allows you to choose from Good (*), Better (**), or Best (***) JPEG quality levels, which are actually indicators of how much compression is used to make the image file smaller. The Good quality level produces the smallest image files, but with a loss of image detail that might be noticeable, as you can see in Figure 3.5. Best quality offers the clearest images, but the file sizes are as much as three times larger.

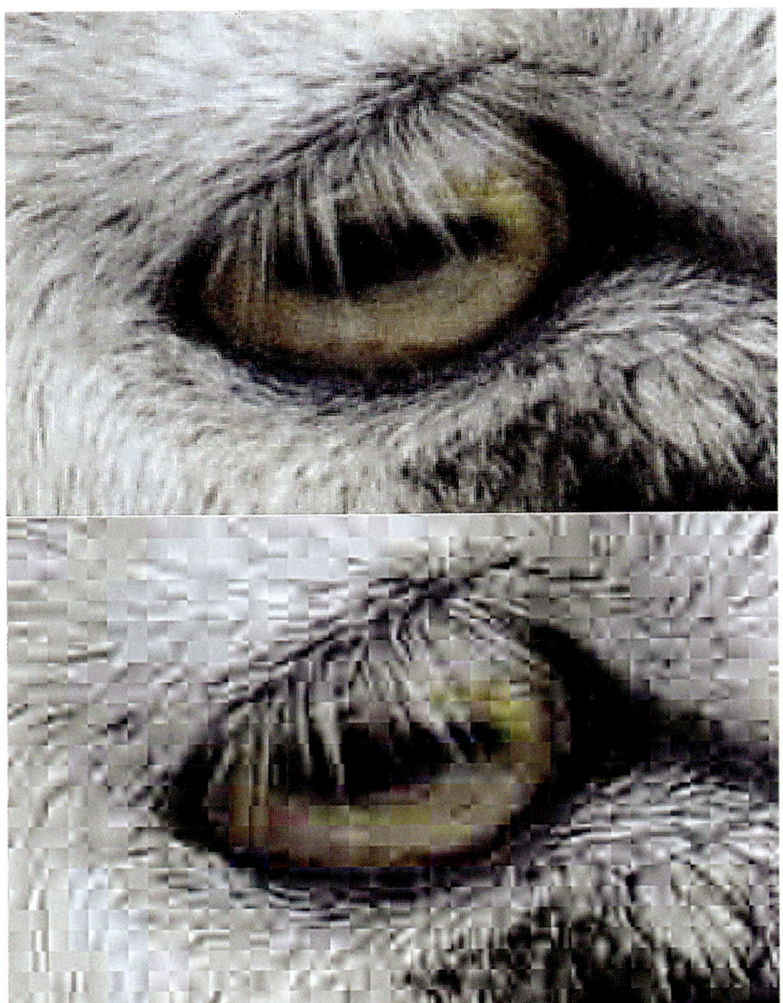

Figure 3.5
At low levels of JPEG compression, the image looks sharp even when you enlarge it enough to almost see the actual pixels (top); when using extreme JPEG compression (bottom) an image obviously loses quality.

In practice, you'll probably use the JPEG Best or RAW+ selections most often. Why so many choices, then? There are some advantages to using the JPEG Better and JPEG Good options. Settings that are less than max allow stretching the capacity of your memory card so you can shoehorn quite a few more pictures onto a single card. That can come in useful when on vacation and you're running out of storage, or when you're shooting non-critical work that doesn't require 10 megapixels of resolution (such as photos taken for real estate listings, web page display, photo ID cards, or similar applications). Some photographers like to record RAW+ so they'll have an excellent quality JPEG file review for minor manipulations, while retaining access to the original RAW file for serious editing.

For most work, using lower JPEG Recorded Pixels and JPEG Quality settings is false economy. You never know when you might actually need that extra bit of picture detail. Your best bet is to have enough memory cards to handle all the shooting you want to do until you have the chance to transfer your photos to your computer or a personal storage device.

However, reduced image quality can sometimes be beneficial if you're shooting sequences of photos rapidly, as the Pentax K200D is able to hold more of them in its internal memory buffer before transferring to the memory card. Still, for most sports and other applications, you'd probably rather have better, sharper pictures than longer periods of continuous shooting. Do you really need 10 shots of a pass reception in a football game, or six slightly different versions of your local basketball star driving in for a lay-up?

RAW File Format

This setting is the first in the second screen of the Recording Mode menu listings. You have two choices:

- **PEF.** This is Pentax's proprietary RAW format. To convert images saved in this format for your image-editing software, you'll need a utility that's compatible with PEF files, such as Adobe Camera Raw, Pentax Photo Browser, or Pentax Photo Laboratory. These allow you to tweak the settings normally made in the camera, and to save in another format, such as TIFF, JPEG, or DNG.
- **DNG.** Adobe's Digital Negative format is a non-proprietary file specification that functions as a kind of Rosetta Stone for RAW files among a broad range of digital camera types. All the captured information contained in Pentax PEF files can be included in the DNG version, which serves as a "universal" RAW format not only for Pentax, but for cameras produced by Nikon, Canon, Sony, Olympus, and other vendors. The advantage of DNG is that one type of file can be used and shared among anyone who has the Adobe DNG Converter software, or another utility that can translate the DNG format. The disadvantage is that few vendors, other than Pentax, have been enlightened enough to include a DNG option within their cameras, so Adobe's innovative format has not been used widely to date.

JPEG vs. RAW

You'll sometimes be told that Pentax's PEF or DNG RAW files are the "unprocessed" image information your camera produces, before it's been modified. That's nonsense. RAW files are no more unprocessed than camera film is after it's been through the chemicals to produce a negative or transparency. Your digital image undergoes a significant amount of processing before it is saved as a RAW file.

A RAW file is more similar to a film camera's processed negative. It contains all the information captured by the sensor, but with no sharpening, no application of any special filters or other settings you might have specified when you took the picture. Those settings are *stored* with the RAW file so they can be applied when the image is converted to a form compatible with your favorite image editor. However, using RAW conversion software such as Adobe Camera Raw, you can override those settings and apply settings of your own. You can select essentially the same changes there that you might have specified in your camera's picture-taking options.

RAW exists because sometimes we want to have access to all the information captured by the camera, before the camera's internal logic has processed it and converted the image to a standard file format. RAW doesn't save as much space as JPEG. What it does do is preserve all the information captured by your camera after it's been converted from analog to digital form.

So, why don't we always use RAW? Some photographers avoid using Pentax's RAW PEF or DNG files on the misguided conviction that they don't want to spend time in an image editor. But, if your basic settings are okay, such work is *optional*, and needs to be applied only when a particular image needs to be fine-tuned.

Although some photographers do save *only* in RAW format, it's common to use RAW+JPEG, or, if you're confident about your settings, just shoot JPEG and eschew RAW altogether. In some situations, working with a RAW file can slow you down a little. RAW images take longer to store on the memory card, and must be converted from RAW to a format your image editor can handle, whether you elect to go with the default settings in force when the picture was taken, or make minor adjustments to the settings you specified in the camera.

As a result, those who depend on speedy access to images or who shoot large numbers of photos at once may prefer JPEG over RAW. These photographers include wedding and sports shooters, who might take hundreds to more than a thousand pictures within a few hours.

JPEG was invented as a more compact file format that can store most of the information in a digital image, but in a much smaller size. JPEG predates most digital SLRs and was initially used to squeeze down files for transmission over slow dial-up connections. JPEG provides smaller files by compressing the information in a way that loses some image data. JPEG remains a viable alternative because it offers several different quality levels. At the highest quality Best level, you might not be able to tell the difference between the original RAW file and the JPEG version. If you don't mind losing some quality, you can use more aggressive Better compression with JPEG to cut the size again.

ANY FILE TYPE, ANY TIME

Say you're busy shooting and have your K200D set to a lower resolution or JPEG quality setting to capture images for a less-critical application (such as your Internet site) and suddenly, you see a photo-op that you dream of being printed in a wall-size poster. Your K200D can switch to RAW with the press of the RAW button, unlike most of the competition. I'll show you how to use this feature later in this section.

Color Space

Here you can choose between two different sets of colors—called *gamuts*—which is the range of colors that are available to represent an image. As you can see in Figure 3.6, you can select:

- **sRGB.** This setting, *standard RGB,* includes the range of colors that is recommended for images that are going to be output locally on your printer or viewed on your computer display, as this color space matches that of the typical inkjet printer and monitor fairly closely.
- **Adobe RGB.** This is an expanded color space useful for commercial and professional printing, and it can reproduce a wider range of colors, even though both color spaces reproduce the same absolute number of colors. There are 16.8 million when reduced to a 24-bit file from the original capture whether you're using sRGB or Adobe RGB, but Adobe RGB spreads these colors over a larger space.

You're probably surprised that the Pentax K200D doesn't automatically capture *all* the colors we see. Unfortunately, that's impossible because of the limitations of the sensor and the filters used to capture the fundamental red, green, and blue colors, as well as that of the phosphors used to display those colors on your camera and computer monitors. Nor is it possible to *print* every color our eyes detect, because the inks or pigments used don't absorb and reflect colors perfectly.

Instead, the colors that can be reproduced by a given device are represented as a color space that exists within the full range of colors we can see. That full range was defined by scientists at an international organization back in 1931.

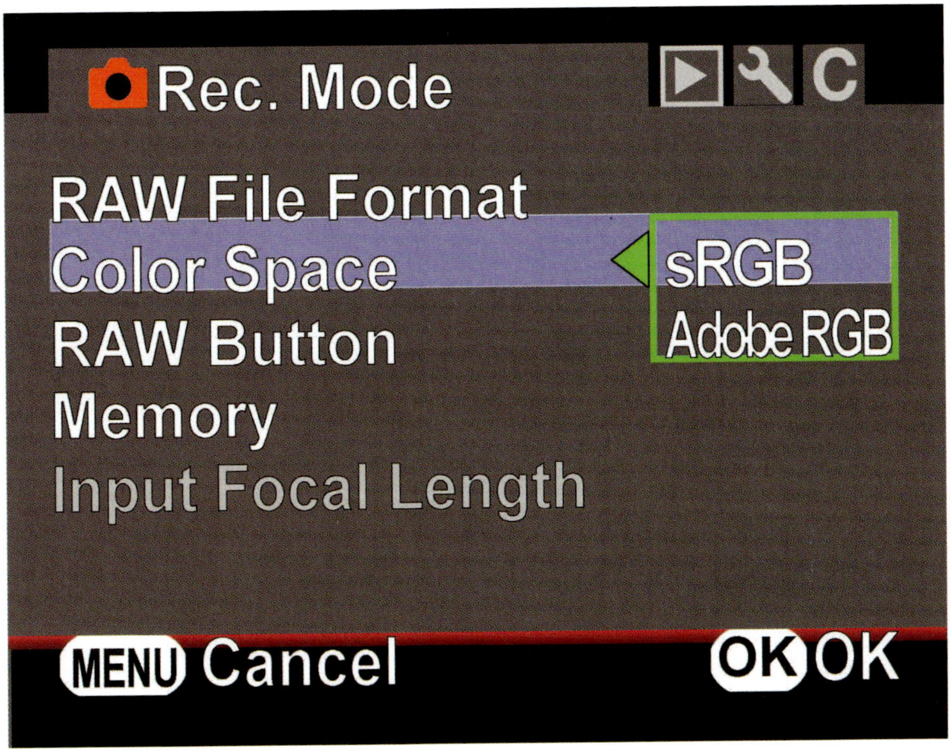

Figure 3.6 Choose a color space.

As I mentioned, regardless of which color space is used by the K200D, you end up with 16.8 million different colors that can be used in your photograph. (No one image will contain all 16.8 million!) But, the colors available will be *different.*

Adobe RGB is what is often called an *expanded* color space, because it can reproduce a range of colors that is spread over a wider range of the visual spectrum. Adobe RGB is useful for commercial and professional printing. You don't need this range of colors if your images will be displayed primarily on your computer screen or output by your personal printer.

The other color space, sRGB, is recommended for images that will be output locally on the user's own printer, as this color space matches that of the typical inkjet printer fairly closely, and it's the color gamut most photofinishers expect to receive from snapshooters. While both Adobe RGB and sRGB can reproduce the exact same 16.8 million absolute colors, Adobe RGB spreads those colors over a larger portion of the visible spectrum. Think of a box of crayons (the jumbo 16.8 million crayon variety). Some of the basic crayons from the original sRGB set have been removed and replaced with new hues not contained in the original box. Your "new" box contains colors that can't be reproduced by your computer monitor, but which work just fine with a commercial printing press.

SAVING BOTH COLOR SPACES

If you plan to use RAW+ (RAW+JPEG) for your photos, you can set sRGB as your color space. You'll have JPEGs suitable for output on your own printer, but you can still extract an Adobe RGB version from the RAW file at any time.

RAW Button Setting

Use this setting to specify the behavior of the RAW button, located on the front of the camera next to the K200 logo. What happens when the button is pressed depends on the format you are currently using, and the setting you make here:

- **JPEG --> [Choice].** If you're shooting JPEG, pressing the RAW button switches the K200D from JPEG shooting mode to JPEG (i.e., no change is made), RAW, or RAW+JPEG, depending on the *choice* you make here.
- **RAW-->[Choice].** If you're shooting RAW, pressing the RAW button switches the K200D from RAW shooting mode to JPEG, RAW (i.e., no change is made), or RAW+JPEG, depending on the *choice* you make here.
- **RAW+-->[Choice].** If you're shooting RAW+JPEG, pressing the RAW button switches the K200D from RAW+JPEG shooting mode to JPEG, RAW, or RAW+JPEG (no change is made), depending on the *choice* you make here.
- **Cancel Each Time.** When this option is highlighted, press the left/right controller keys to mark or unmark the check box. When the box is marked, each time you press the RAW button, the file format will be switched to the alternate format for one picture only. The K200D then reverts to the file format that had been in use before you pressed the RAW button. If the box is unmarked, the camera switches to the new file format setting "permanently"—or, at least, until the RAW button change is canceled doing one of the following: pressing the RAW button again, turning the camera off, rotating the Mode dial, accessing a different menu entry, or switching the camera from Capture mode to Playback mode to review an image.

Memory

Sometimes you make settings that you want to remain in force for the rest of your shooting session, but then revert to their default values when you turn the camera off. This clever option allows you to specify *which* settings the Pentax K200D should retain even when the camera is powered down and then switched on again. To mark or unmark settings to be memorized, scroll through the two pages of listings and press the left/right controller keys to add or remove a check from the box next to each option.

The settings you can save are as follows:

- Flash Mode
- Drive Mode
- White Balance
- Sensitivity (ISO Speed)
- EV Compensation value
- Flash Exposure Compensation value
- Playback Display
- Scene Display
- File No.

This menu can save you a lot of frustration if you realize what it can do for you. For example, it's very common for photographers to forget they have boosted the ISO setting of their camera to a high level, such as ISO 1600, while shooting indoors, only to end up overexposing the daylight exposures they make without first changing back to a lower setting. Or, you might add exposure compensation under particular lighting conditions, and then continue to shoot with that EV boost when you've moved on to a new scene. The Memory setting allows you to tell the K200D to return to the default value when you've switched the camera off.

File Number Setting

While most of the Memory Settings options simply store the current status for the setting listed, the File No. option is a special case, because it determines the file numbers used when writing your images to your SD card. Not understanding exactly how this works can result in some unintended consequences. I'll summarize what you need to know in this section.

Your Pentax K200D creates new file names using the templates shown in Table 3.1:

Table 3.1 Pentax File Name Conventions

Color Space	JPEG	Pentax RAW	Adobe Digital Negative
SRGB	IMGP*nnnn*.jpg	IMGP*nnnn*.pef	IMGP*nnnn*.dng
Adobe RGB	_IGP*nnnn*.jpg	_IGP*nnnn*.pef	_IGP*nnnn*.dng

So, an image named IMGP1002.jpg would be an sRGB picture; IMG1002.pef and IMGG1002.dng would be RAW files using the Pentax RAW and Adobe Digital Negative RAW formats, respectively. If the Adobe RGB color space was used instead, those three files would be named _IGP1002.jpg, _IGP1002.pef, and _IGP1002.dng, respectively. In the case of the RAW files, the color space you selected in the camera is used to build the file name, even though you can select the other color space when converting the file for manipulation in your image editor.

When the file numbers are reset, numbering of the *nnnn* portion of the file name begins again at 0001 and continues through 9999 before another reset occurs. Keep in mind that only 500 images are ordinarily stored in a given folder, so you might find images numbered IMGP0001*.xxx* (with *.xxx* being the file extension) through IMGP0500*.xxx* in a given folder, and images numbered IMGP501.aaa deposited in the next folder created. All you really need to know is that, until the file numbers are reset, image file names use the sequential numbers from 0001 through 9999, and the folders in which they reside depends on how many images are already in the folder.

The File No. entry determines when the reset back to 0001 takes place. You have two options:

- **On.** When the File No. box is checked in the Memory Status entry, the Pentax K200D remembers the last number assigned and applies a number that is one higher to the next image stored, going from 0001 to 9999. The number is assigned even if the picture is stored in a new folder. New folders are created any time the existing folder contains 500 images, unless Auto Bracketing is being used; in that case, all images in the bracketed set are stored in the same folder, even if the number exceeds 500. Use this option when you want to keep track of the total number of images you've taken with your camera, even if you've used several different memory cards. You'll have to carve a notch on the body of your K200D the first time you reach 9999 images, and every time thereafter, if you want to continue to keep count.
- **Off.** When the File No. box is unchecked in the Memory Status entry, the Pentax K200D resets and uses a value of 0001 for the first image in a new folder. Use this option when you want to organize your images by folders that contain 500 or fewer images, or you'll be using an image downloading utility that can apply new file names to images automatically as they are transferred from your camera or memory card to your computer. You'll find more information on this option in Chapter 8.

  Note that the file numbers appear in stored image files on the card; however, the number listed on the camera's LCD contains just the file folder number and the image number.

Focal Length Input

The current focal length of the lens mounted on the camera is used by the K200D when calculating the amount of shake reduction that is applied when the camera's anti-shake feature is switched on. Pentax lenses with DA, D FA, FA J, FA, or F in their names automatically provide this information to the camera. Other lenses do not, but you can input the focal length setting you'd like to use for such lenses using this menu option. It's available only when the Shake Reduction feature is turned on, and an applicable lens is mounted on the camera.

A listing of 34 different focal lengths, from 8mm to 800mm, appears with a default value of 35mm available in a horizontally scrolling list, as shown in Figure 3.7. You can use the controller left/right keys to select the value appropriate for your lens, or the closest value offered, such as 18mm (if you're using a 17mm lens). This setting is grayed out and not selectable when using lenses that communicate their focal length to the camera. Set Custom Setting #23, using the aperture ring set to Permitted when using older lenses.

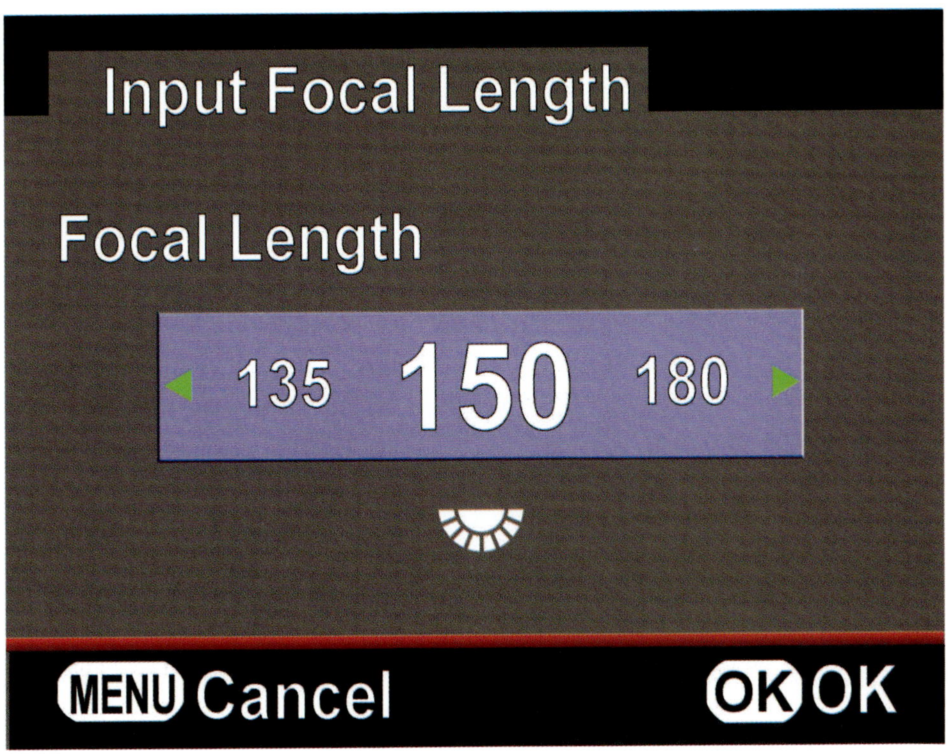

Figure 3.7 Help your camera's shake reduction operate more accurately by specifying a focal length for lenses that don't automatically supply this information.

Playback Menu

The Playback menu includes just five choices, shown in Figure 3.8, which allow you to specify some useful settings during picture review. You can make other Playback setting changes in the Custom Setting menu using CS #20 and CS#21, as described later in this chapter.

- Playback Display
- Instant Review
- Digital Preview
- Slide show

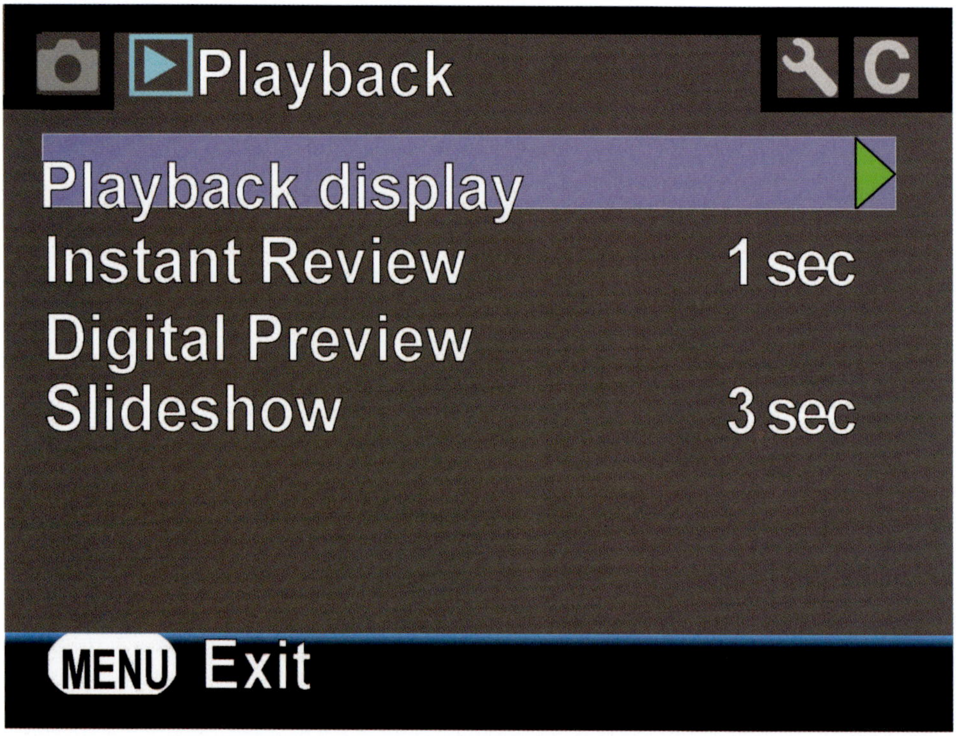

Figure 3.8
The Playback menu has four entries.

Playback Display

When reviewing images, the K200D can show flashing red pixels to indicate areas that are overexposed, and flashing yellow pixels to mark areas that are underexposed. These are commonly called "blinkies." This menu entry includes a Bright/Dark Area option with a check box, which can be marked and unmarked with the left/right controller keys. Mark the box to enable blinkies, and unmark the box to disable them (because you find the flashing pixels distracting or prefer to locate over- and under-exposed areas on your own).

The second option within this entry allows you to enable or disable the Quick Zoom feature, which automatically zooms in to a specified magnification when the Playback button is pressed to view an image. When you select Off, the default "zoom" level is 1X. You can also use the up/down controller keys to specify X2, X4, X8, and X16 default zoom levels that are used each time you review an image. This option is useful when you want to zoom in to a particular magnification each time you use picture review.

Instant Review

This menu entry lets you determine whether to display an instant review of the image you've just taken on the LCD and whether to show a histogram display and flashing yellow/red "blinkies." Your choices are:

- **Display time.** Highlight this entry, press the right controller button, and select from 1 second (really, too brief to be of much use other than as a confirmation a picture was actually taken), 3 seconds, 5 seconds, and Off, as shown in Figure 3.9. I usually select 5 seconds for most situations. You don't have to worry about this longer display interfering with your desire to take the next picture. Even while the Instant Review is shown, you can return to Capture mode and take another picture by tapping or pressing the shutter release. I set this option to Off when I am shooting concerts and other darkened areas where the lighted LCD might prove

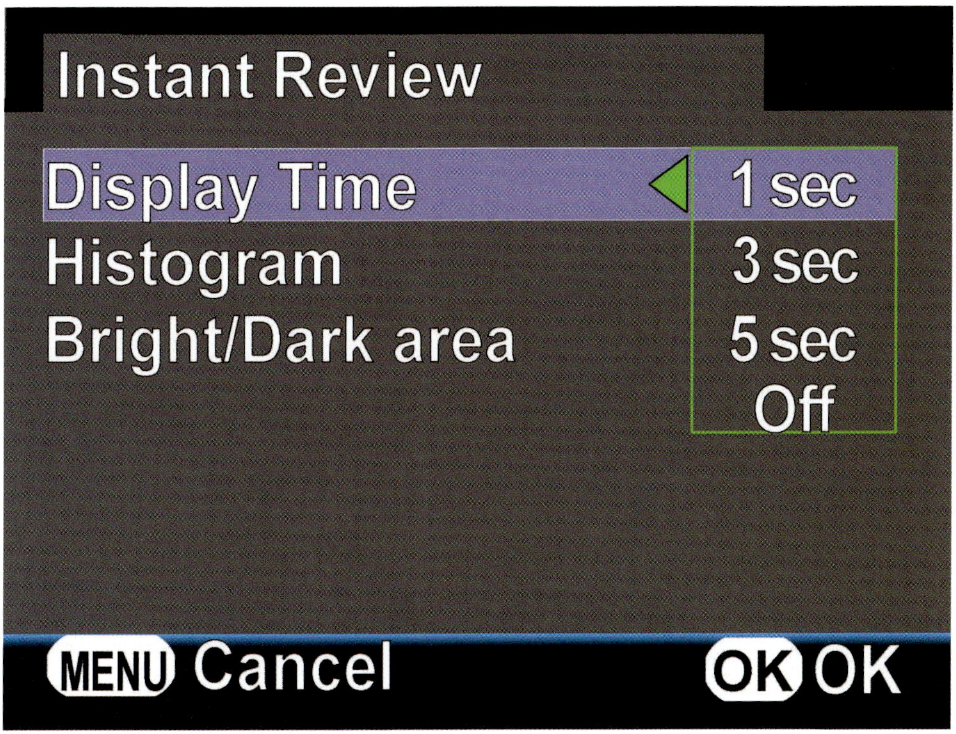

Figure 3.9
Specify the display time during instant review, as well as whether a histogram and bright/dark area "blinkies" are shown.

distracting or annoying to those behind me. I also use the Off setting when shooting sports in Continuous mode, because I rarely use Instant Review, preferring to take a peek at one of my action shots after a particular sequence is over. Remember that with or without Instant Review, you can look at the last picture taken at any time by pressing the Playback button.

- **Histogram display.** Highlight this option and press the left/right controller keys to enable or disable display of a histogram during Instant Review. (The check boxes for this option and the next one are obscured by the display time options in the figure.) You may find the histogram a help in determining whether your image is over- or under-exposed. While the Instant Review display is on the LCD, you can press the up/down controller keys to change the histogram from the standard brightness histogram to the detailed RGB histogram, which shows the image as a thumbnail, flanked by separate brightness, red, green, and blue histograms. I'll explain how to use histograms in Chapter 4.
- **Bright/Dark Area display.** Highlight this option and press the left/right controller keys to enable or disable display of flashing yellow (underexposed) and red (overexposed) pixels during Instant Review. The "blinkies" are a quick way to spot serious exposure problems.

Digital Preview

In Chapter 2, in the sidebar "Using Digital and Optical Preview," I described the difference between the Pentax K200D's conventional *optical* depth-of-field preview, and its innovative *digital* preview, which is an actual preview picture the camera takes prior to (or instead of) the actual picture. Digital and optical previews are activated by rotating the switch that rings the shutter release all the way clockwise.

This option lets you specify whether the histogram display and/or bright/dark area display are shown along with the Digital Preview image.

- **Histogram display.** Highlight this option and press the left/right controller keys to enable or disable display of a histogram during Digital Preview. While the Digital Preview is shown, press the up/down controller keys to change the histogram from the brightness histogram to the brightness/RGB histogram. I'll explain how to use histograms in Chapter 4.
- **Bright/Dark Area display.** Highlight this option and press the left/right controller keys to enable or disable display of flashing yellow (underexposed) and red (overexposed) pixels during Digital Preview.

Slide Show

I showed you how to activate a slide show of the images on your memory card in Chapter 2, using the Playback Functions menu. This menu entry lets you specify the interval between images, and whether the show should repeat when finished.

- **Interval.** Highlight this entry and choose 3, 5, 10, or 30 seconds. The 3 and 5-second intervals are best for traditional slide shows, in which the goal is to showcase a series of images one after another. The 10- and 30-second displays are suitable for "background" slide shows, such as those at a trade show or science fair exhibit, particularly if the K200D is connected to a television screen monitor. You can start the show, and it will cycle through the images at a leisurely pace.
- **Repeat Playback.** Highlight this entry and mark or unmark the check box to enable or disable repeating the slide show when it is finished. It's often desirable to display a slide show continuously at trade shows or exhibits, and your K200D makes a perfect slide projector when connected to a television set and—preferably—an AC power source.

Set-up Menu

The Set-up menu is used for adjustments on how your camera behaves in Capture mode during your shooting sessions, as opposed to the settings available in the Recording Mode menu, which adjusts how pictures are taken, and the Playback menu, which handles the settings controlling what the camera does during display of your picture after it's taken.

- Format
- Beep
- Date Adjust
- World Time
- Language
- Text Size
- Guide Display
- Brightness Level
- Video Out
- USB Connection
- Auto Power Off
- Folder Name
- Select Battery
- Pixel Mapping
- Dust Alert
- Dust Removal
- Sensor Cleaning
- Reset

Format

Use this setting, the initial entry on the first page of the Set-up menu (see Figure 3.10), to erase everything on your SD memory card and set up a fresh file system ready for use. When you navigate to Format, press the right arrow to get to a page with just two selections: Format and Cancel. If you choose Format and press the OK button, all your data will be deleted; Cancel and OK returns you to the Set-up menu. A progress screen appears while formatting is underway.

I recommend reformatting your memory card after each shooting session. While you can *move* files from the memory card to your computer, leaving behind a "blank" card, or *delete* files using the Trash can button during Playback, both options can leave behind stray files, including those that have been marked as Protected. Format removes those files completely (and beyond retrieval—unless you use a utility program like those described in Chapter 9) and establishes a fresh file system on the card, with all the file allocation table (FAT) pointers (which tell the camera and your computer's operating system where all the images reside) efficiently pointing where they are supposed to on a blank card.

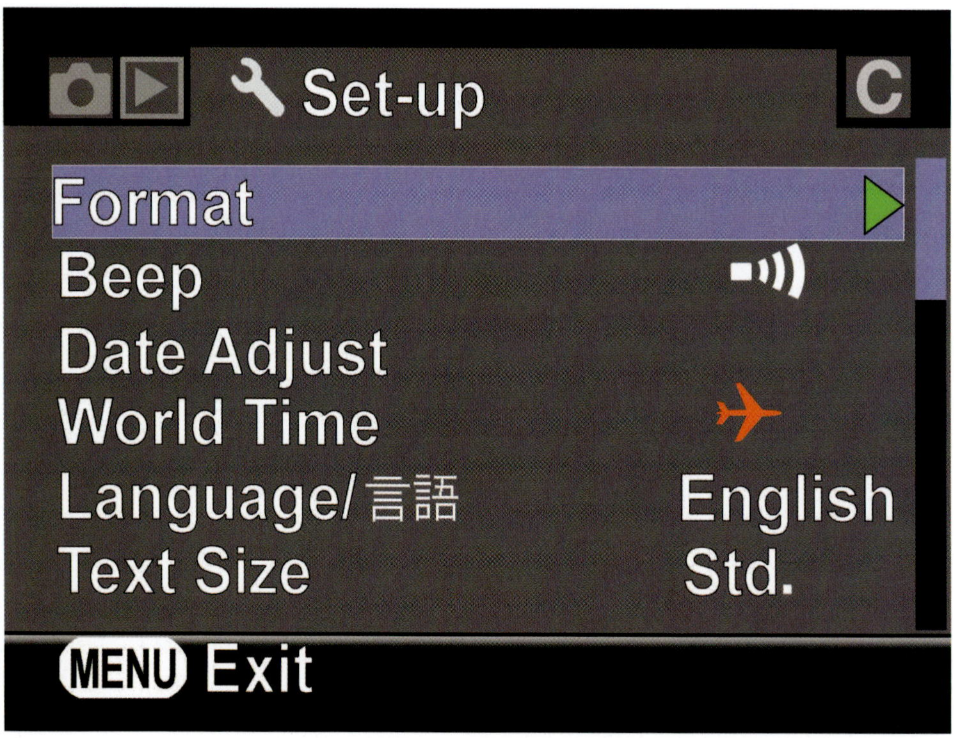

Figure 3.10 The first page of the Set-up menu has six entries.

Beep

You can turn the beep on or off individually for five different camera operations, or you can switch it off entirely. You may find the beeper noise for particular functions annoying, or you may be shooting in an environment (such as concerts, religious ceremonies, or museums) where such sounds are impolite. If you're one of those (bless you!) who turn your cell phones to vibrate when you're in the company of others (or even dining in a restaurant alone), you'll like this option.

Just navigate to the Beep menu entry using the four-way controller, highlight the beep item that you want to enable or disable, and use the left/right controller keys to mark or unmark the check box, as shown in Figure 3.11. The following features have beeps associated with them:

- **Setting.** The first entry listed among Beep options lets you turn the beeper on or off for all functions. Highlight the top entry and press the left/right controller keys to enable or disable all beeping functions. Individual functions can be silenced or enabled using the options listed next.
- **In-focus.** The camera beeps when correct focus has been achieved.
- **AE-L.** The beep sounds when autoexposure and/or focus is locked by a press of the AE-L button. I'll show you how to combine autoexposure lock and focus lock using the AE-L button in the discussion of Custom Setting #4 later in this chapter.

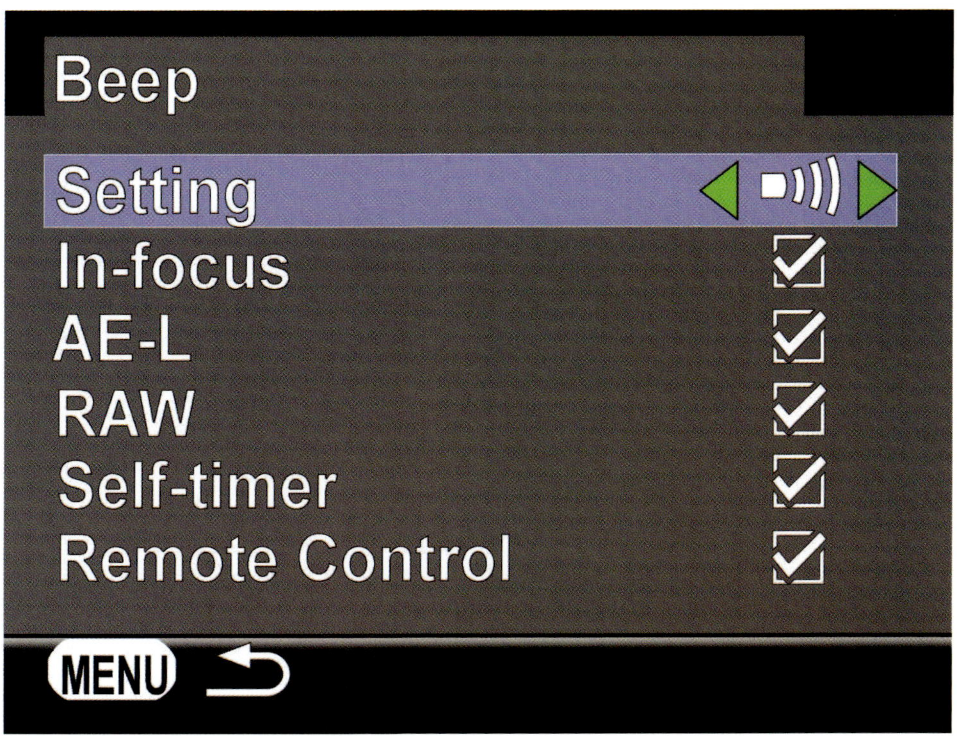

Figure 3.11
Mark the items you want to associate with beeps.

- **RAW.** You'll hear a beep each time you press the RAW button to change the file format, as discussed under the Recording Mode menu earlier in this chapter.
- **Self-timer.** During the self-timer countdown, the LED on the front of the handgrip blinks and the beeper can (optionally) provide an alert. Enable or disable that sound here.
- **Remote Control.** Beeps as the camera is triggered using the optional remote controller.

Date Adjust

Here's where you can adjust the date applied by your K200D to your "home" time zone. This information is embedded in the image file along with exposure information and other data. You can also specify an additional time zone as a "destination" time using the World Time adjustment, described next.

- **Date Style.** Choose among [mm/dd/yy], [dd/mm/yy], or [yy/mm/dd] styles, and specify either a 12-hour or a 24-hour clock. When Date Style is highlighted, use the left/right controller keys to select the option you want to change, and then the up/down keys to switch among the style and 12/24 hour options. Press the left controller key to return to the Date Adjust menu, or press OK if you're finished setting the date, time, and date style format. Press the Menu button to cancel and void any changes you've made.
- **Date.** Select the Date option with the left/right controller keys and move among the month, date, and year choices. Use the up/down keys to change the month, day, and year. Press the left controller key to return to the Date Adjust menu, or press OK if you're finished setting the date, time, and date style format. Press the Menu button to cancel and void any changes you've made.
- **Time.** Select the Time option with the left/right controller keys and move among the hour, minute, and AM/PM options, using the up/down keys to change them. Press the left controller key to return to the Date Adjust menu, or press OK if you're finished setting the date, time, and date style format. Press the Menu button to cancel and void any changes you've made.

World Time

Your Pentax K200D remembers two different time zones for you, a "home" time zone, which is set using the Date Adjust menu entry, described previously, and a "destination" time zone, which is an additional city that you want to track, usually because you are visiting there. You don't need to set the time for your Destination setting; once you've entered the correct date and time for your Home zone using Date Adjust, when you switch to the Destination time zone, the camera automatically adds or subtracts the correct number of hours to compensate.

This menu entry allows you to specify which world city is your default home time zone, and which is your default destination zone. You can also shift gears, so to speak, and tell your camera whether you are currently in your home zone or destination zone.

For example, if you live on the East Coast of the United States, you would set the time for Eastern Daylight or Eastern Standard time using the Date Adjust option described above. In addition, you might want to specify a second location, perhaps the West Coast, where you might have friends, relatives, colleagues, or another company office. You might find it particularly useful to have the World Time display available when you travel to that second time zone.

To use the World Time feature, follow these steps:

1. **Access World Time.** Highlight the World Time entry on the Set-up menu and press the right controller button to produce the World Time screen. (See Figure 3.12.)
2. **Choose Home or Destination Time modes.** The top line of the screen will show the icon of a house (your Home time zone) or an airplane (your Destination time zone). With the World Time line highlighted, press the left/right controller keys to switch to the zone you want as your current default, either Home or Destination. Once you've shifted to Home or Destination, the K200D will show those settings on the LCD and embed the local time in your images.

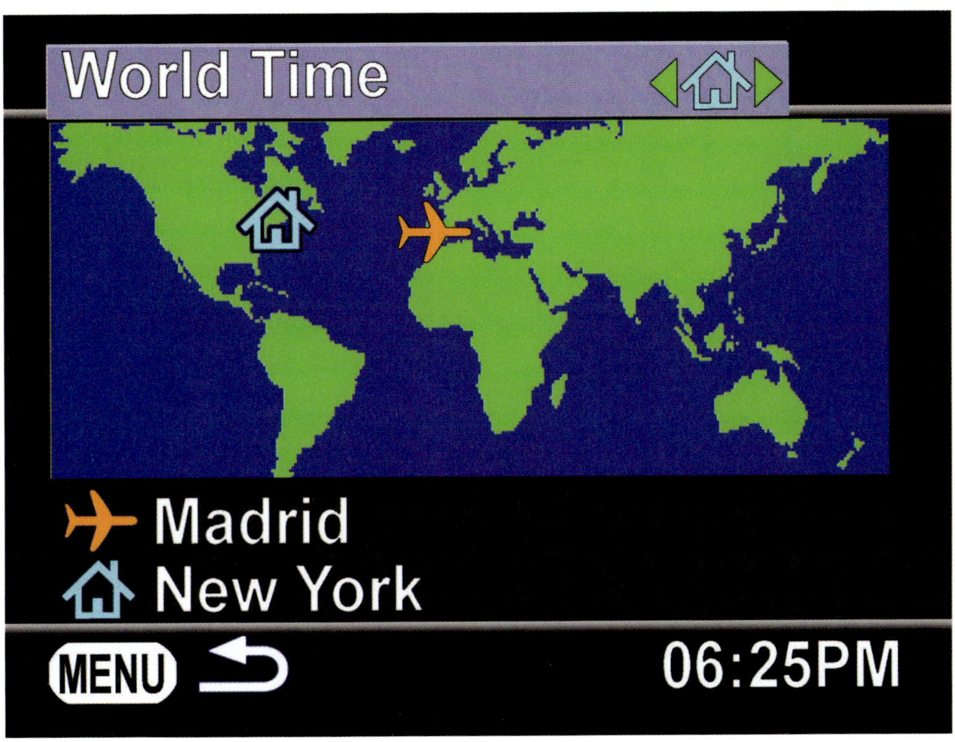

Figure 3.12
Change your display between your "home" and destination ("world") time.

3. **Specify city for Destination or Home zones.** Press the down key to highlight either the Destination or Home listings, then the right key to change to a world map dotted with possible cities. (See Figure 3.13.)

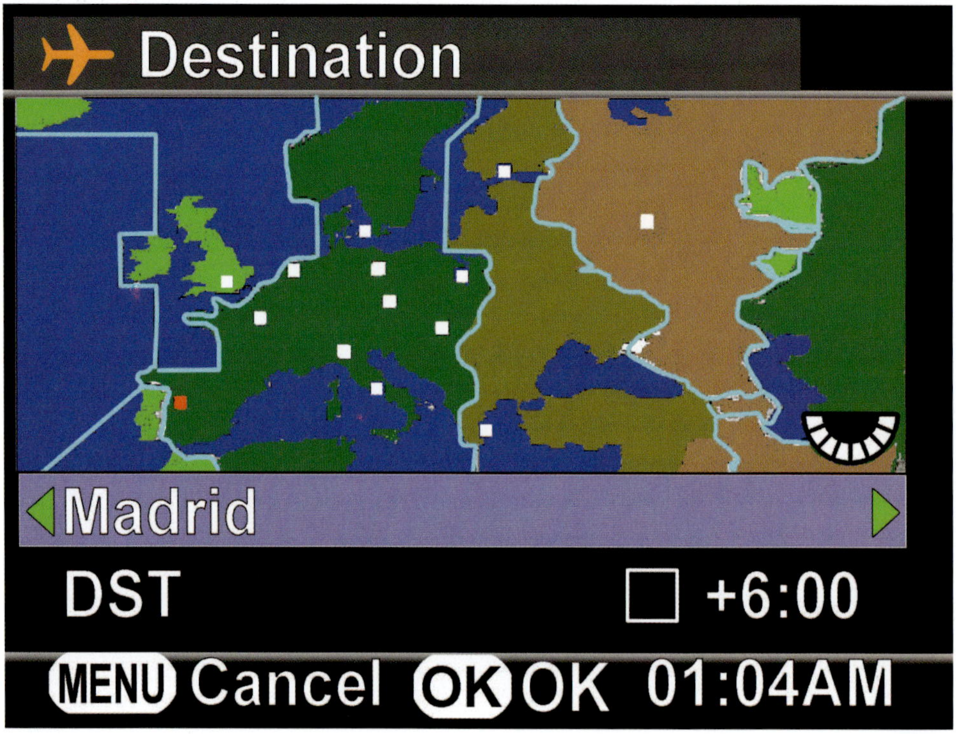

Figure 3.13
Select your destination city from this map.

4. **Choose the region.** Use the e-dial to select the region containing the city you want to specify.
5. **Select a specific city from those available.** With a city name highlighted, press the left/right keys to switch among available cities. Your selected city will be listed as the city name, and its location will blink on the world map.
6. **Enable/disable DST option.** When the city you want is listed, press the down key to highlight the DST (Daylight Savings Time) option, and then the left/right keys to mark or unmark the box that indicates that DST will be accounted for.
7. **Confirm your selection.** When you are satisfied with your setting, press the OK button to confirm your choice, or the Menu button to cancel World Time changes.

> **Tip**
>
> **Reminder:** Once you've set up Home and Destination cities for the World Time option, your K200D will display as its default whichever of the two zones you selected in Step 2. So, when you travel to your Destination time zone, you can set the camera to mark your files with your new local time, rather than the time at your original Home location. I use this feature a lot when traveling, so that the date stamps on my image files (not the pictures themselves, as is the case with some other digital cameras) reflect the time of day they were actually taken, rather than the time back home.

Language

Use this menu entry to select from 18 different languages that will be used to display your menus and other messages. Available languages include English French, German, Spanish, Portuguese, Italian, Dutch, Danish, Swedish, Finnish, Polish, Czech, Hungarian, Turkish, Russian, Korean, Japanese, and both Traditional and Simplified Chinese.

If you accidentally set the language to a tongue that is incomprehensible to you, don't panic. Press the Menu button and navigate to the menu marked with a wrench icon (in every language). That's the Set-up menu. Scroll down to the fifth entry, which is labeled "Language" in English, and press the right key. English will be offered as the choice in the upper-left corner of the screen that appears on the LCD.

Text Size

If you wear glasses and shoot without them, you may have difficulty reading the menu screens at times (even though you've set the viewfinder diopter correction for your vision). Use this menu option to set menu Text Size to Large (or back to Std—Standard) and when any menu item is selected, it will be shown in the text size you've specified.

Guide Display

This is the first entry on the second page of the Set-up menu (see Figure 3.14). It can be used to enable or disable a basic Guide Display, as shown in Figure 3.15 (or specify the amount of time the display is visible), each time you turn the camera on or change exposure modes with the Mode dial. Select Off, or choose from 3-second, 10-second, or 30-second display intervals. Most find that turning off the display or setting it for a brief display time works fine, because the same information can be called up by pressing the Info button. Note that when using any of the Scene modes, the Guide Display includes a typical sample thumbnail image of that type of shooting situation.

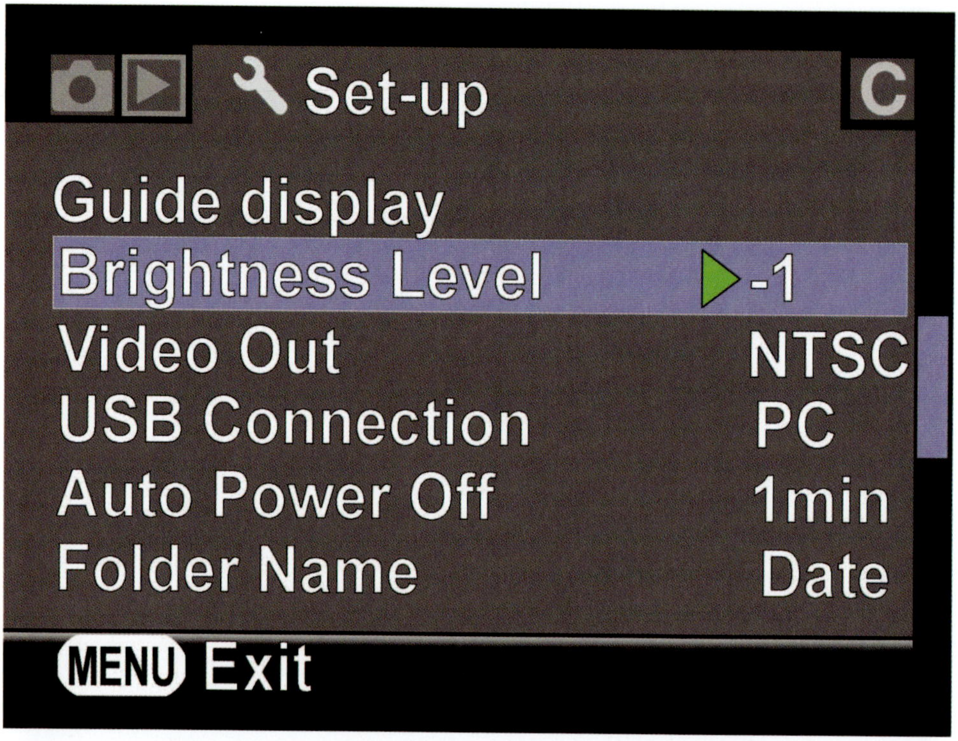

Figure 3.14
Guide Display is the first entry on the second page of the Set-up menu.

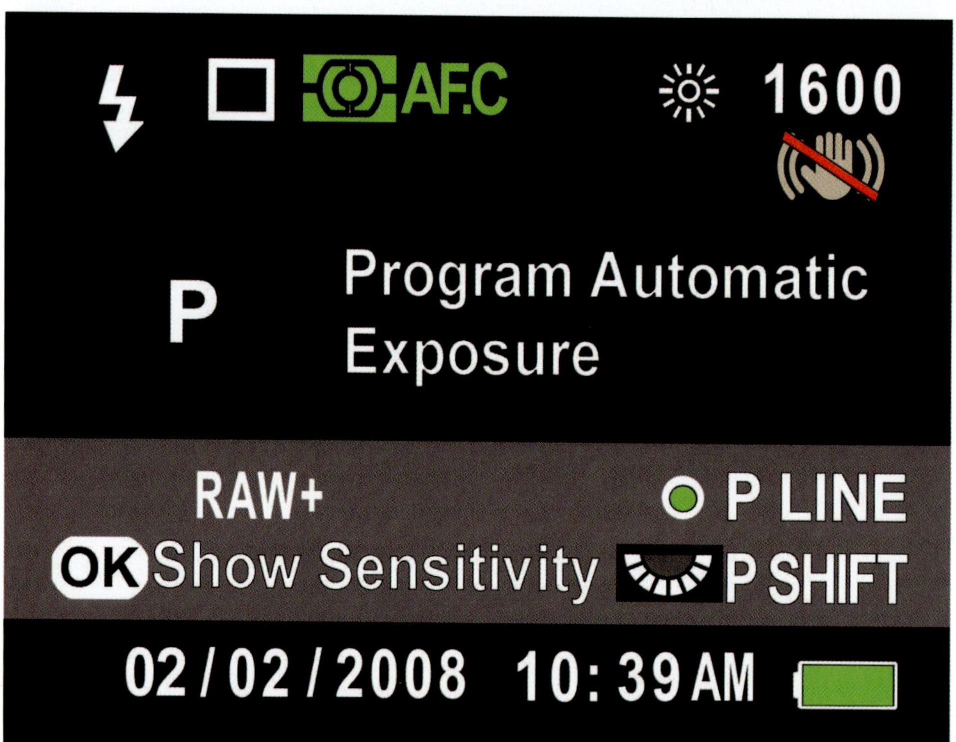

Figure 3.15
You can choose how long this informational display is shown each time you turn on the camera or change Exposure modes.

Brightness Level

Choose this menu option to adjust the intensity of the LCD display. A grayscale strip appears on the LCD, as shown in Figure 3.16. Use the left/right controller keys to adjust the brightness to a comfortable viewing level over a range of +7 to –7. Under the lighting conditions that exist when you make this adjustment, you should be able to see the full range of tones on the grayscale strip, from black to white. If the dark area at the left of the strip is the same tone for more than one increment, the brightness has been set too low. If the two whitest increments on the right end of the strip blend together, the brightness is too high. Brighter settings use more battery power, but can allow you to view an image on the LCD outdoors in bright sunlight. When you have the brightness you want, press OK to lock it in and return to the menu, or press the Menu button to cancel the adjustment.

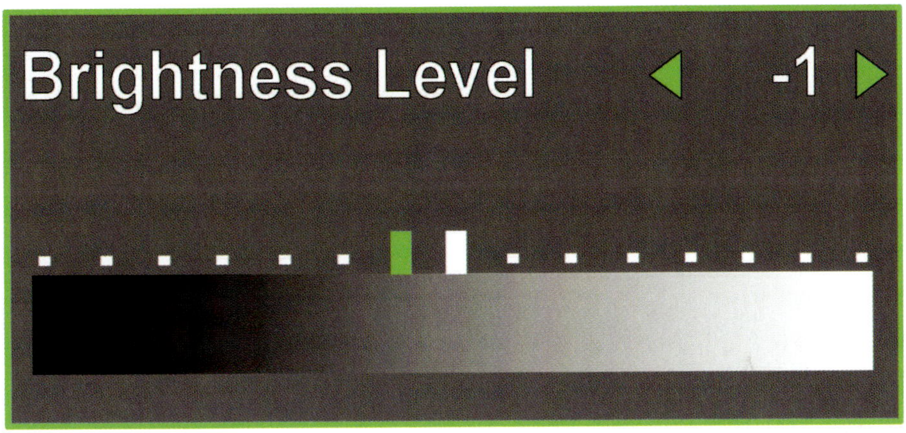

Figure 3.16 Adjust the LCD brightness so that all the grayscale tones are visible.

Video Out

This setting controls the output of the K200D when directed to a conventional video system though the video cable when you're displaying images. You can show these images on a monitor or connect to a VCR or other video device through the external device's yellow composite video input jack. You can select either NTSC, used in the United States, Canada, Mexico, many Central, South American, and Caribbean countries, much of Asia, and other countries; or PAL, which is used in the UK, much of Europe, Africa, India, China, and parts of the Middle East.

Your Pentax will select a default value for you, based on the region you select in the World Time settings, described earlier. If you change from Home to Destination, the Video Out setting uses the default for that city. You may need to adjust back to your Home setting in some cases. Perhaps you've toted a compact NTSC LCD monitor along with you to Europe, and want to view your images using the NTSC protocol, rather than PAL, even while your camera is using the appropriate European time stamp.

USB Connection

You can link your Pentax K200D to a computer (PC or Macintosh) or to a PictBridge-compatible printer using the USB cable bundled with your camera. This option allows you to specify which of the two types of connections you want to use.

You have just two choices: PC or PictBridge. When using the PC connection, your computer sees the K200D as just another hard disk peripheral device. You can drag and drop image files from the folders on the memory card to a folder on your computer. I'll provide more details on doing this in Chapter 8.

Printing Images in PictBridge Mode

In PictBridge mode, you can print your JPEG (but not RAW) pictures directly from the camera to a PictBridge-compatible printer (most newer printers are). When you connect the printer to the K200D, the camera in PictBridge mode automatically recognizes the printer. A menu like the one shown in Figure 3.17 appears on the monitor screen of the K200D.

You can then print single images or all images on the memory card, or choose to print images that have been marked using the DPOF Autoprint option (if no images are already marked for printing, this option will be grayed out and unavailable). The DPOF option, unlike the Single Image or All Image choices, doesn't allow you to change printer

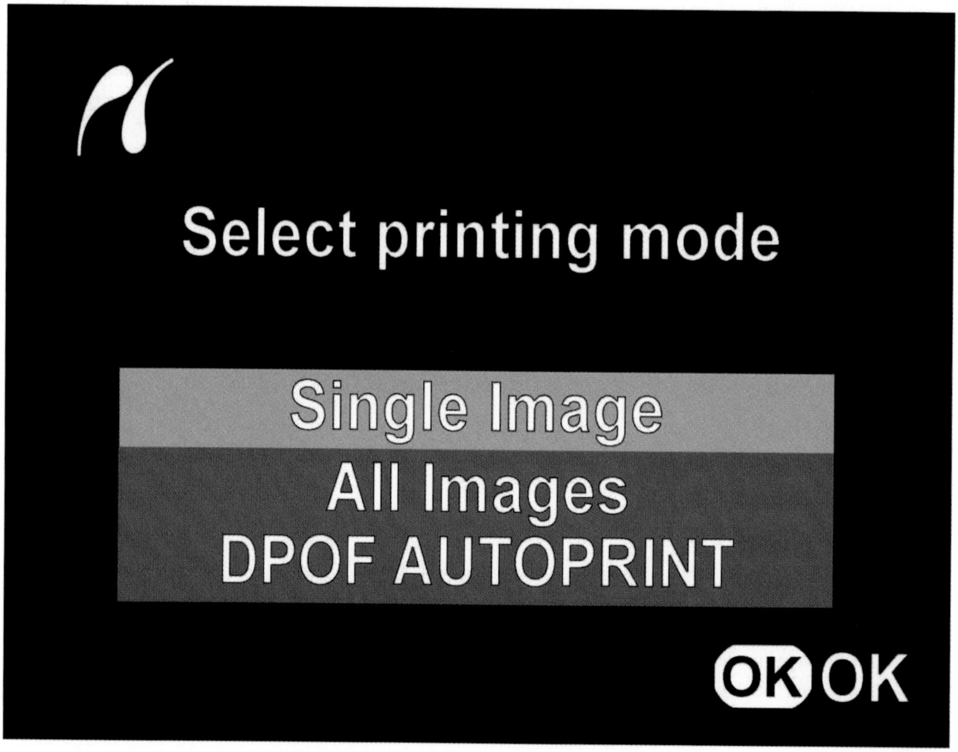

Figure 3.17 Print single images, all images, or use the DPOF Autoprint option.

settings for the images being printed. Use the Single Image or All Image modes when you want to choose paper size, paper type, image quality, or whether or not the prints will be borderless.

To print single images or all images, just follow these steps:

1. **Choose Single or All Images.** Use the up/down keys to select Single Image or All Images and press OK.
2. **Select individual images (Single Image only).** If printing just a single image, press the left/right keys to choose an image from those available on your memory card. If you are printing All Images, skip this step; the settings you apply in steps 3-8 apply to each image on the card, and cannot be specified individually.
3. **Choose number of copies.** Use the up/down keys to choose the number of copies, from 1 to 99.
4. **Add/remove Date.** Press the Fn button to mark or unmark the Date box, which determines whether the date is printed on the image.
5. **Confirm number of copies and date imprint.** Press the OK button to confirm your settings so far, and you'll be shown settings for:
   - **Paper Size.** Only the available paper sizes communicated by your PictBridge printer to the K200D may be selected.
   - **Paper Type.** Choose from *, **, or *** paper types, which is a somewhat unsatisfactory way of referring to the range between plain paper (*) and photo paper (***).
   - **Quality.** Again, you can choose from the amorphous * to *** indicators to choose Good, Better, or Best print quality.
   - **Border Status.** Indicates whether prints should be borderless or with borders.
6. **Access settings screen.** To change any of these settings, press the Fn button.
7. **Select any or all of Paper Size, Paper Type, Quality, and Border Status (with/without).** Use the up/down keys to highlight any of the settings you want to change.
8. **Change settings.** Press the right key to review and adjust any of the four settings. Press OK to confirm each option's settings.
9. **Return to Print According to Settings? Menu.** Press OK to return to the printing menu.
10. **Send your printing instructions to the printer.** Press OK one last time to print your image.

To print all images on the memory card that you have marked with the DPOF option (introduced in Chapter 2), just follow these steps:

1. In Playback mode while viewing an image you want to mark for printing, press the Fn button to view the screen shown in Figure 3.2. The screen shows an image of the four-way controller, with labels representing the functions you can activate by pressing the controller's keys.
2. Press the Up button to view the DPOF (Digital Print Order Format) screen.
3. Highlight Copies and use the left/right key to specify a number of copies, from 1 to 99.
4. Highlight Date and press the left/right keys to mark or unmark the Date box.
5. If you want to use the same Copies and Date parameters for all images on the memory card, press the Fn button. Each marked image will have a printer icon superimposed on it.
6. To mark or unmark additional images, rotate the e-dial to the right to view the next image, or to the left to see the previous image.
7. Repeat steps 3-5 to mark additional images.
8. When you're finished, press OK. You'll see a Data Being Recorded confirmation message before you're returned to the Playback screen.
9. Connect your K200D to a PictBridge-compatible printer, and when the PictBridge menu appears, select DPOF Autoprint and press OK to automatically print the images you've selected, using the number of copies and date imprint option you specified. The marked images can also be given to a photofinisher, which has equipment that can interpret your print order settings.

Auto Power Off

You might want your Pentax K200D to turn itself off after a brief interval of non-use, saving battery power. Or, you might prefer to keep the camera turned on and active for a longer period, ready for an instant grab shot. This setting allows you to choose automatic power-down intervals of 1, 3, 5, 10, or 30 minutes, or disable automatic shut-off completely with the Off setting. Note that even if the camera powers down, the status LCD on top of the K200D remains active, and you can return the camera to full operation by tapping the shutter release or pressing the Info or Playback buttons.

SAVING POWER WITH THE PENTAX K200D

There are several other techniques you can use to stretch the longevity of your K200D's battery. To get the most from each charge, consider these steps (some of which aren't described until later in this chapter):

- **Instant Review (Set-Up menu).** Turn off automatic image review after each shot. That 2.7-inch LCD uses a lot of juice, so reducing the amount of time it is used when you don't turn it off manually can boost the effectiveness of your battery. You can still review your images by pressing the Playback button. Or, leave image review on, but set the display for the minimum 1 second—and watch fast!
- **Use AF.S focus (Set-Up menu).** You'll find that single autofocus uses less power than continuous autofocus.
- **Turn off start-up Dust Removal.** If you turn your Pentax on and off a lot, you can disable the automatic application of the Dust Removal sensor shake each time the camera is powered up. The action is quite vigorous, and uses more than a little power. If you do this, you'll need to remember on your own to use the Dust Alert and Dust Removal options described later in this chapter and in Chapter 9.
- **Auto meter-off-delay (Custom Setting #3).** Set to 3 seconds if you can tolerate such a brief active time.
- **Disable AF point display (Custom Setting #8).** This one will save only a minuscule amount of power by disabling the display of the current AF point in red in the viewfinder.
- **Use Optical Preview (Custom Setting #18).** The K200D's Digital Preview actually takes a photo and displays it on your LCD, using more power than the Optical Preview, which simply shows an image in the viewfinder.
- **Turn off Guide Display (Set-Up menu).** You can always get the most important shooting information by pressing the Info button.
- **Reduce LCD brightness (Set-Up menu).** In the Set-up menu's Brightness Level option, select the lowest of the 14 brightness settings that work for you under most conditions. If you're willing to shade the LCD with your hand, you can often get away with lower brightness settings outdoors, which will further increase the useful life of your battery.
- **Reduce internal flash use.** No flash at all or fill flash use less power than a full blast.
- **Use a card reader.** When transferring pictures from your K200D to your computer, use a card reader instead of the USB cable. Linking your camera to your computer and transferring images using the cable takes longer and uses a lot more power.

Folder Name

As you take pictures, the Pentax K200D deposits the images into folders on your memory card containing up to 500 different pictures (unless you're using Auto Bracketing, in which case all the images in a sequence will be stored in the same folder, even if more than 500 images are created in that folder). You can choose the naming format for those folders here.

If you have viewed one of your memory cards' contents using a card reader, you noticed that the top-level folder on the card is always named DCIM. Inside that folder is another folder created by your camera. Cameras from different vendors use different folder naming conventions, and they can co-exist on the same card. For example, if your memory card is removed from your Pentax camera and used in, say, a camera from another vendor which also accepts SD, the other camera will create a new folder using a different folder name within the top-level DCIM directory.

By default, the Pentax K200D creates its folders using a three-number prefix (starting with 100 and going up to 999 if necessary), followed by two digits of the month and day, in the format MMDD or a different date format if specified in the Date Adjust menu entry. So, a folder containing images captured on February 8, 2009 might be deposited in a folder named 100_0208. If you happened to fill up that folder with 500 images, a new folder named 101_0208 would be created.

This menu option has just two options: Date, which uses the folder naming convention just described, or PENTX, which uses only a folder number and the string PENTX, as in 100PENTX, 101PENTX, and so forth. Use this option if you'd prefer not to have folders labeled with the current date.

Select Battery

This is the first option on the third screen of the Set-up menu (see Figure 3.18). If you own the optional D-BG3 battery grip, you can specify whether the K200D uses the camera's internal battery as the primary power source, whether the battery in the grip functions as the primary power source, or whether the camera should select its main battery automatically. Note that if batteries are installed in both, some power will be drawn from each, regardless of which setting you choose. Your options are as follows:

- **Auto Select.** In this mode, the K200D uses the battery that has the most power. It will then switch over to the other battery and use that until it's depleted. This setting is probably your best choice for any shooting session in which you feel you won't use up both batteries.
- **Body First.** With this setting, the Pentax uses the battery in the K200D first, and doesn't switch to the battery in the grip until the camera's power is depleted. I use this setting only when I am shooting both with and without grip and have several

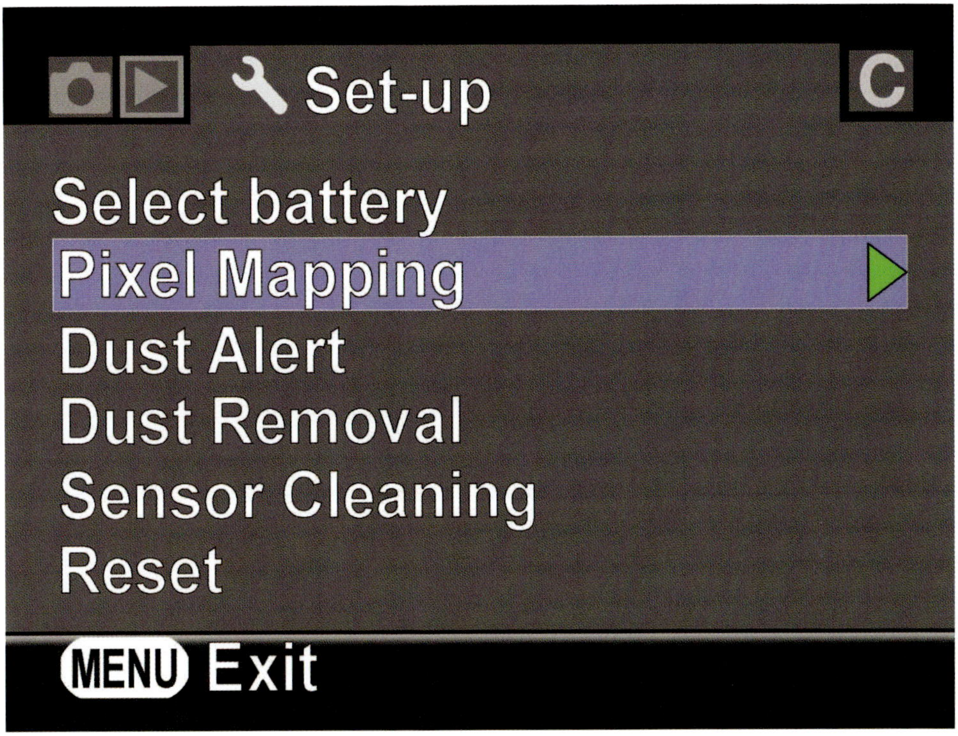

Figure 3.18
Select Battery is the first entry on the third screen of the Set-up menu.

additional replacement batteries. It allows me to keep the battery in the grip as fresh as possible in case I decide I need it on the spur of the moment. While shooting without the grip, I can remove and replace dead batteries in the body conveniently. If you are using the grip constantly, this option is not the best way to go.

- **Grip First.** When I have my grip attached to my camera for a full shooting session, I like to use this mode. The battery in the grip runs out first, and the camera shifts over to its internal battery until I have a chance to drop a new battery into the grip. If I think I may not have enough replacement batteries, I can often recharge the dead battery removed from the grip while I continue shooting.

Pixel Mapping

Use this option to tell your Pentax K200D to ignore "bad" pixels in the sensor. You can read more about the causes and fixes for such pixels in Chapter 9. Unlike the majority of digital SLRs, the Pentax has the facility built-in to "map out" these errant photosites.

Using this feature is simplicity itself. When you choose Pixel Mapping from the Set-up menu, a screen appears with the comment, "For checking the image sensor assembly to make adjustments," which doesn't really tell you very much (what *kind* of adjustments will be made?). Choose Pixel Mapping and press OK to start the process, or select

Cancel to back out of the screen. A "Data being processed" message appears, and then you're returned to the Set-up menu. Your defective pixels have been identified and the Pentax's pixel map updated so their information will be ignored in the future. Note that you cannot use this feature if battery power is low.

Dust Alert

This is not a setting, but, rather, it is a function that takes a "picture" of your sensor and provides an image that shows whether or not you have dust and other artifacts on your CCD. I'll explain how to use this option in Chapter 9.

Dust Removal

This is another function, rather than a setting, used to shake off dust on the sensor by shaking the CCD. You can perform the sensor-shaking from this menu, or mark a check box that will activate sensor cleaning each time the camera is turned on. I'll explain this feature in more detail in Chapter 9.

Sensor Cleaning

This function does not clean your sensor, but, instead, lifts up your mirror and opens the shutter so you can clean the sensor yourself using a blower, damp swab, or some other means. The "Troubleshooting" section in Chapter 9 shows you how to do this safely.

Reset

If you've been playing around with all of the camera's controls and you want to go back to all the default values for the settings in the menus, navigate to the Reset setting, the last in the Set-up menu. When you press the right arrow of the four-way controller, you'll be taken to a new page where it will say "Back to initial settings" at the top and give you two options at the bottom: Reset and Cancel. If you press Reset, all settings go to default and the screen goes blank.

Custom Setting

There are 23 options in the Custom Setting menu that modify how your camera behaves, plus a handy reset entry that returns all the settings to their defaults. Each of the custom settings from CS #1 to CS #23, are listed with a green numeral in the right-most column that shows the number representing their current value, from 1 to 4 (see Figure 3.19). Some custom settings have just two values (1 or 2) for On or Off, or some other pair of options. Others may have up to four different options, listed from 1-4 in their submenu. Although you don't need to learn what setting each number represents

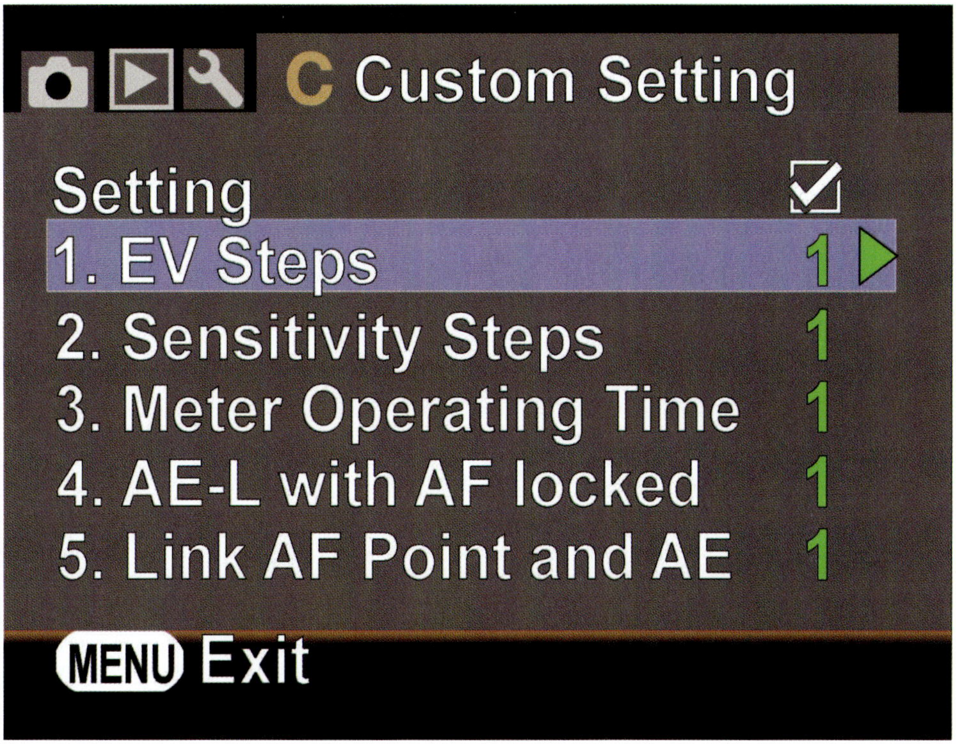

Figure 3.19 The green numeral in the right column represents the value of the current setting.

for each custom setting, it can be helpful to understand, at a glance, that, say, a 1 next to Preview Method means that Digital Preview is enabled, and a 2 means that Optical Preview is active.

To change a custom setting, highlight its menu entry and press the right key to produce a screen listing your options. Then, use the up/down keys to make your selection and the OK button to confirm it.

Custom Setting #0. Setting

The first entry in the Custom Setting menu is labeled Setting (it doesn't actually have a number), and can function as a sort of a temporary "reset" to restore each of the other custom settings to their default values until you activate your preferred options again.

Highlight the Setting entry and press the left/right keys to mark or unmark the check box. When the box is unmarked, each of the 23 custom settings revert to their default values (represented by the number 1). Mark the box to activate your custom settings instead. The customized options you've specified are not actually reset when the check box is unmarked; they are only temporarily ignored. If you want to actually reset the custom functions to their default values, use the Reset Custom Function entry, which follows CS #23 in the listing, and will be described later in this section.

Custom Setting #1. EV Steps

Options:

1. 1/2 EV steps

2. 1/3 EV steps

This setting tells the K200D the size of the "jumps" it should use when making exposure adjustments—either one-third, one-half, or one full stop. The increment you specify here applies to f/stops, shutter speeds, EV changes, and autoexposure bracketing. As with ISO sensitivity step value, you can select from 1/2 EV steps (the default) or 1/3 EV steps increments. Figure 3.20 shows the selection screen, which is typical of all the Custom Setting screens, with one to four options. (Because they are so similar, I won't provide sample screens for most of the other custom settings that follow.)

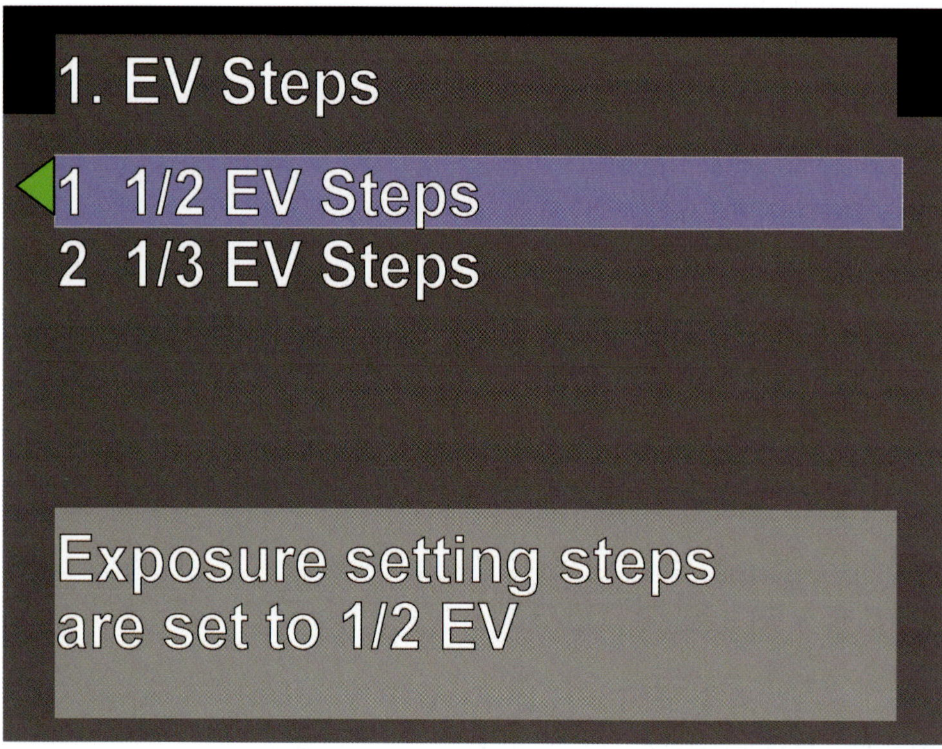

Figure 3.20
Choose 1/2 or 1/3 EV Steps.

With 1/2 stop increments, you will have larger and more noticeable changes between settings. The Pentax will use exposure compensation values of + or –0, .5, 1.0, 1.5, or 2.0 stops, and will use shutter speeds such as 1/60th, 1/125th, 1/250th, and 1/500th second, and f/stops including f/5.6, f/6.7, f/8, f/9.5, and f/11. These coarser adjustments are useful when you want more dramatic changes between different exposures.

Choose the 1/3 stop setting when you want the finest increments between shutter speeds and/or f/stops. For example, the Pentax will use exposure compensation values of + or

–0, .3, .7, 1.0, 1.3, 1.7, and 2.0 and shutter speeds such as 1/60, 1/80, 1/100, 1/125, 1/160 second, and 1/125th second, or f/stops such as f/5.6, f/6.3, f/7.1, and f/8, giving you (and the autoexposure system) maximum flexibility.

Custom Setting #2. Sensitivity Steps

Options:
1. 1 EV steps
2. As EV steps

This setting determines the size of the "jumps" it should use when making ISO adjustments (using the Capture Functions menu, as described in Chapter 2). The values (which don't appear in the menu themselves) would be:

- **I EV steps.** ISO 100, 200, 400, 800, 1600
- **1/2 EV steps.** ISO 100, 140, 200, 280, 400, 560, 800, 1100, 1600
- **1/3 EV steps.** ISO 100, 125, 160, 200, 250, 320, 400, 500, 640, 800, 1000, 1250, 1600

Custom Setting #3. Meter Operating Time

Options:
1. 10 sec.
2. 3 sec.
3. 30 sec.

This option determines how long the exposure meter remains active before shutting itself off. The default value of 10 seconds is usually enough under most circumstances, and allows a little idle time when you begin using the camera to frame an image. Use the 3-second setting to save power, especially when you expect to be shooting more or less constantly, so the quick time-out won't have much effect on the availability of the meter's readings. Use the 30-second option when you want to have the meter alive for longer periods while you contemplate and frame a shot. If your meter does time out, just tap the shutter release button to revive it.

Custom Setting #4. AE-L with AF Locked

Options:
1. Off
2. On

Use this setting to determine whether both exposure and focus are locked when the focus is locked. As you'll learn while becoming familiar with your Pentax K200D, the need to lock exposure, focus, or both doesn't always happen at the same time. At times, you'll want to freeze one or the other, or lock both simultaneously.

Exposure should be locked when you have framed your photo, are ready to shoot, and don't anticipate any events (such as a cloud passing in front of the sun) that will change the exposure settings as determined by the K200D's metering system. Focus should not be locked until the main subject you want as your center of interest is in sharp focus. Sometimes, this main subject is not located in one of the 11 focus zones in the viewfinder, and you may want to use AF.S (single autofocus) mode, adjust framing slightly to allow the camera to focus on your center of interest, lock focus, and then reframe to achieve the composition you want. In other situations, the desired point of focus can change if the subject is moving or begins moving. While AF.S will refocus a subject that begins moving after focus is locked, in such cases, you're better off using AF.C (continuous autofocus), which refocuses to follow active subjects. The K200D's Moving Object Scene mode also uses AF.C mode.

To determine how and when you should use this setting, you'll need to have a better understanding of how the AE-L button and shutter release interact than is provided in the confusing explanation offered in the Pentax manual. I'm going to clear up everything for you.

Locking Exposure and/or Autofocus.

When you are happy with the automatic exposure set by the Pentax K200D, there are two ways to lock in that exposure so that it does not change until either you have taken a picture (and the camera readies itself to calculate exposure for the next exposure) or you have unlocked exposure by *not* taking a picture. Lock exposure in either of these two ways:

- **Press the shutter release halfway with CS #4 set to On.** Focus is locked when you are using AF.A mode (or one of the Scene/SCN modes that operate in AF.A mode). If you're using AF.C mode, or AF.A mode and your subject begins moving, then *only* exposure is locked when the shutter release button is pressed halfway. In AF.C mode or AF.A mode with a moving subject, the camera will refocus as required to follow the subject.

  When CS #4 is set to Off, only focus is locked. Exposure will continue to adjust as the light changes or as you reframe the image. When CS #4 is set to On, *both* focus and exposure are locked, until you take a picture or you release the button.

- **Press the AE-L button.** When you press this button, the exposure is locked for as long as you continue holding down the AE-L button. A * indicator appears in the viewfinder and a beep (which you can disable in the Set-up menu) sounds. The exposure remains locked after you release the button, for a period of time ranging from one-half to twice the value set for the metering operating timer in CS #3 (usually about 5 to 20 seconds). Note that the AE-L button does not work in B (Bulb) exposure mode.

Custom Setting #5. Link AF Point and AE

Options:

1. Off

2. On

When using Multi-Segment metering, the Pentax K200D examines 16 different zones in the frame to calculate exposure. You'll find more on exposure metering in Chapter 4. This setting can be used to specify whether the camera takes into account the active autofocus point when determining focus settings, as follows:

- **1. Off.** In Multi-Segment mode, the camera calculates exposure based on the 16 exposure zones available. Use this option for most scenes, to take into account the entire frame rather than just the subject.
- **2. On.** The K200D calculates exposure based on the exposure zone in the focusing area that is linked to the active autofocus point. In other words, the camera assumes that the AF point of sharpest focus is the main subject, and bases exposure on that area of the frame. This choice may be best for subjects that are illuminated much differently from their surroundings, such as portraits of people with very light or very dark backgrounds.

Custom Setting #6. Auto Bracketing Order

Options:

1. 0 – +

2. – 0 +

3. + 0 –

4. 0 + –

This is the first entry on the second screen of Custom Setting options. When using automatic exposure bracketing (explained in Chapter 4 in more detail), you can choose the order in which adjustments are applied. Your choice is generally just a matter of personal preference in how you want your bracketed exposures to be presented.

- **1. 0 – +.** The first shot will have normal (as metered) exposure (0 compensation); the second has less exposure (– compensation); the third has additional exposure (+ compensation).
- **2. – 0 +.** The first shot will have less exposure than metered; the second will have normal exposure; the second has less exposure; the third has additional exposure.
- **3. + 0 –.** The first shot will have more exposure than metered; the second will have normal exposure; the third has less exposure.
- **4. 0 + –.** The first shot will have normal (as metered) exposure; the second will have additional exposure; the third has less exposure.

Custom Setting #7. Adjust White Balance

Options:

1. Off

2. On

When setting White Balance using the Capture Function menu, you can fine-tune the color by adjusting the bias in the blue/amber and magenta/green directions, as I'll describe in Chapter 4. This setting allows you to enable fine-tuning (giving you the most flexibility) or disable the option (reducing the chance that you'll accidentally change the color incorrectly). There are two options available with this setting:

- **1. Off.** You can only change the white balance using the preset choices that appear in Capture mode when you press the Fn button and the left arrow of the four-way controller to activate White Balance settings.
- **2. On.** You can fine-tune the White Balance settings. A small grid (which I'll explain in Chapter 4) appears, and the color bias can be adjusted by pressing the up key (more green); down key (more magenta); left key (more blue); or right key (more yellow/amber).

Custom Setting #8. Superimpose AF Area

Options:

1. On

2. Off

The selected AF point can be optionally highlighted in red in the viewfinder. This is largely a matter of personal preference, as the extra power consumption is minuscule.

- **1. On.** The selected AF point in the viewfinder is highlighted as a red light. This option can be especially useful for dim scenes to let you see exactly the point being used to calculate focus.
- **2. Off.** Disables the red AF point highlighting. Use when you find the red AF point distracting, or if your subject contains tones or illumination levels that make it difficult to see the highlighted point.

Custom Setting #9. AF in Remote Control

Options:

1. Off

2. On

Use this setting to specify whether autofocus should be used while using the optional Pentax Remote Control F. Remote shooting is sometimes used as an alternative to the self-timer to allow you to get into the picture, or simply to take a photo without touching the camera and thereby inducing vibration.

The K200D offers two remote control options in Drive mode (accessed from the Capture Functions screen by pressing the Fn button followed by the controller up key). In Standard remote mode, the shutter is triggered as soon as the release button on the remote is pressed. In Delayed remote mode, the shutter is triggered about three seconds after the button on the remote is pressed. In either case, if you plan to be in the photo yourself, you should already be in position. The Delay mode allows you to tuck the remote control away so it doesn't show in the picture.

This setting allows you to specify whether the autofocus system operates when the remote's release button is pressed:

- **1. Off.** The autofocus system does not operate when the remote's button is pressed. You must focus ahead of time, which means you'll need to focus by pressing the camera's shutter release button halfway before using the remote control. Then, release the shutter button and take your picture using the remote. This default setting is best when you are able to focus on your scene before taking the photo.
- **2. On.** When you press the release button on the remote, the camera's autofocus system will try to focus your image. If it is able to focus, a picture will be taken. If the camera is unable to focus, the photo will not be captured. This option is handy when subjects in the frame may be moving until just before the picture is taken, and there is plenty of light so that autofocus will be possible.

Custom Setting #10. Slow Shutter Speed Noise Reduction

Options:
1. On
2. Off

Visual noise is that awful graininess caused by long exposures and high ISO settings, and which shows up as multicolored specks in images. This setting helps reduce noise caused by long exposures/slow shutter speeds. This noise is rarely desirable in a digital photograph. There are easier and more controllable ways to add texture to your photos.

Slow shutter speeds allow more photons to reach the sensor, increasing your ability to capture a picture under low-light conditions. However, the longer exposures also increase the likelihood that some pixels will register random phantom photons, often because the longer an imager is "hot," the warmer it gets, and that heat can be mistaken for photons.

- **1. On:** For longer exposures, the K200D takes a second, blank exposure and compares that to the first image. Noise (pixels that are bright in a frame that *should* be completely black) in the "dark frame" image is subtracted from your original picture, and only the noise-corrected image is saved to your memory card. Because the noise-reduction process effectively doubles the time required to take and save a picture, you won't want to use this setting when you're rushed. Some noise can be removed later on, using tools like Bibble Pro or Photoshop.

- **2. Off:** This setting disables long exposure noise reduction. Use it when you want the maximum amount of detail present in your photograph, even though higher noise levels will result. This setting also eliminates the extra time needed to take a picture caused by the noise reduction process. If you plan to use only lower ISO settings (thereby reducing the noise caused by ISO amplification), the noise levels produced by longer exposures may be acceptable. For example, you might be shooting a waterfall at ISO 100 with the camera mounted on a tripod, using a neutral density filter and a long exposure to cause the water to blur. (Try exposures of 2 to 16 seconds, depending on the intensity of the light and how much blur you want.) To maximize detail in the non-moving portions of your photos, you can switch off Slow Shutter Speed noise reduction. You can compare images with and without noise reduction in Figure 3.21.

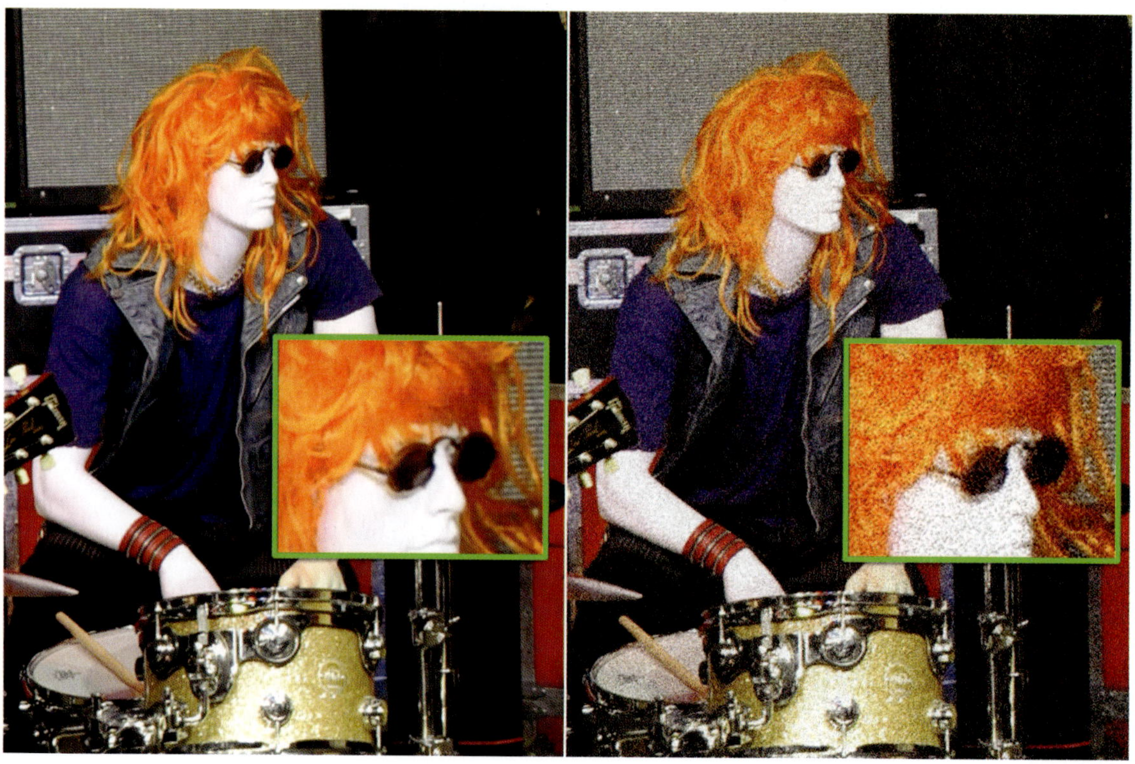

Figure 3.21 Noise reduction (left) reduces visual noise, but robs an image of some fine detail; photos without noise reduction may appear sharper, but grainier (right).

Custom Setting #11. High-ISO Noise Reduction

Options:

1. Off

2. Weakest

3. Weak

4. Strong

Depending on what kind of subject you are shooting, and how much noise reduction you want to apply, you can use this option to select Off, Weakest, Weak, or Strong High-ISO noise reduction.

Noise can also be caused by higher ISO sensitivity settings. The effects of high ISO noise are something like listening to a CD in your car, and then rolling down all the windows. You're adding sonic noise to the audio signal, and while increasing the CD player's volume may help a bit, you're still contending with an unfavorable signal to noise ratio that probably mutes tones (especially higher treble notes) that you really want to hear.

The same thing happens when the analog image signal is amplified: You're increasing the image information in the signal, but boosting the background fuzziness at the same time. Tune in a very faint or distant AM radio station on your car stereo. Then turn up the volume. After a certain point, turning up the volume further no longer helps you hear better. There's a similar point of diminishing returns for digital sensor ISO increases and signal amplification as well.

As the captured information is amplified to produce higher ISO sensitivities, some random noise in the signal is amplified along with the photon information. Increasing the ISO setting of your camera raises the threshold of sensitivity so that fewer and fewer photons are needed to register as an exposed pixel. Yet, that also increases the chances of one of those phantom photons being counted among the real-life light particles, too.

Some kinds of subjects may not require this kind of noise cancellation, particularly with images that have a texture of their own that tends to hide or mask the noise.

Custom Setting #12. OK Button when Shooting

Options:

1. Sensitivity/No. of Shots

2. Center of AF Point

3. Enable AF

4. Cancel AF

The four-way controller's center OK button can have several functions. You can choose which of these functions is active while you shoot.

Your options are as follows:

- **1. Sensitivity/No. of Shots.** This choice lets you specify whether the ISO speed setting or number of recordable shots remaining is displayed in the lower-right corner of the viewfinder. Ordinarily, the number of shots remaining is listed (up to a maximum displayable value of 999). When this option is selected, in all exposure modes except Sv, you'll see the ISO speed value at that location instead while the OK button is pressed. However, when you're using Sensitivity Priority (Sv) mode, the *ISO speed value* is displayed by default, and the number of recordable shots is shown *only* while the OK button is pressed.
- **2. Center of AF Point.** When this option is used, the active AF point jumps to the center AF point in the frame when the OK button is pressed. This can come in handy during action shooting and other situations when you want to make sure that the subject in the center of the frame is in sharp focus.
- **3. Enable AF.** This is a deceptively cool, if oddly named, option. It disables autofocus activation when the shutter release is pressed halfway, instead assigning this task to the OK button. When this option is active, you can lock exposure and autofocus separately. Press the shutter release button halfway to lock exposure (say, while framing an action shot), then press the OK button to lock autofocus when the subject you want to shoot is positioned in the frame. Press the shutter release the rest of the way to take your photo. This sounds more complicated than it is in real life.
- **4. Cancel AF.** Use this option if you sometimes want to de-activate autofocus quickly and use Manual focus instead. It's usually much faster than fumbling around for the AF/MF slide switch on the side of the camera lens mount. When active, press the OK button to manually focus. The MF indicator appears in the viewfinder window. Release the OK button to re-activate autofocus.

Custom Setting #13. e-dial in Program

Options:
1. Program shift
2. Tv
3. Av
4. Off

When using Program exposure mode, the e-dial can be used as a shortcut to several different functions. These include:

- **1. Program Shift.** When this option is selected, spinning the e-dial switches the K200D from Program mode to Program Shift mode. You can then rotate the e-dial to change from the metered exposure to other shutter speed/aperture combinations that provide the same exposure. To return to standard Program mode, press the Green button (located on top of the camera, southeast of the shutter release).

- **2. Tv.** When you've chosen this option, rotating the e-dial switches the K200D from Program mode to Tv (Shutter Priority) mode. You can then rotate the e-dial to change to a shutter speed of your choice, and the camera will select the correct aperture for the proper exposure. Press the Green button to return to Program mode.
- **3. Av.** When you've chosen this option, rotating the e-dial switches the K200D from Program mode to Av (Aperture Priority) mode. You can then rotate the e-dial to change to an aperture of your choice, and the camera will select the correct shutter speed for the proper exposure. Press the Green button to return to Program mode.
- **4. Off.** With this option active, rotating the e-dial while using Program mode has no effect.

Custom Setting #14. Green Button in Manual Mode

Options:
1. Program Line
2. Tv Shift
3. Av Shift
4. Off

When shooting in Manual Exposure mode you can get help in finding the right exposure. You can set the Green button to temporarily switch from Manual exposure to another exposure mode. This capability would come in handy when you're setting the exposure values yourself, and see a grab shot with illumination that might be different from the settings you've already made. Press the Green button, and the K200D will instantly switch from Manual exposure to one of the autoexposure methods you specified using this menu entry.

- **1. Program Line.** Sets the aperture and shutter speed to the exposure calculated using Program exposure when the Green button is pressed.
- **2. Tv Shift.** This option and the next are named confusingly. When you're using Manual exposure and press the Green button, the current aperture you've selected is locked in, and the K200D adjusts the shutter speed to set the correct exposure. The camera does *not* switch to Tv (Shutter Priority mode) and lock the shutter speed while adjusting the aperture, as you might think. This is a *Tv Shift* mode; the shutter speed (time value) shifts, or changes.
- **3. Av Shift.** Same deal. The Pentax *does not* switch to Av mode when the Green button is pressed. Instead, the shutter speed you'd set when using Manual mode is locked in, and the *aperture* is changed to achieve correct exposure.
- **4. Off.** Green button is disabled.

Custom Setting #15. Release when Charging

Options:

1. Off

2. On

Here's a simple one. Your Pentax K200D's built-in flash needs a second or two to recharge after you've taken a picture. When you've selected Off using this custom setting, the shutter release button is locked until the flash has recharged. Use that option when you want to make sure that you don't accidentally take a flash photo that might be underexposed.

- **1. Off.** Use this setting if you want to make sure you won't get any underexposed photos. In practice, the recycle time of your built-in flash will be fairly consistent at a given distance, so in any shooting session you'll quickly learn how to pace yourself so the flash can keep up with your snapshooting.
- **2. On.** At close distances, it's likely that the flash will have *almost* enough juice to take a usable picture, even if it's not fully charged. If getting any picture at all is more important than ensuring that you don't get an underexposed photo, use this option. You'll then be able to take a picture while the built-in flash is charging. This setting can be useful when your built-in flash is not the most important light source for the shot. If you're using the flash, say, as fill for the shadows, having a full charge might not be essential.

Custom Setting #16. Flash in Wireless Mode

Options:

1. On

2. Off

As you'll learn in Chapter 7, you can trigger an external electronic flash without a cord in *Wireless* mode, using the built-in flash as a controller for the external unit. To use this mode, you must set the power switch of the external flash unit to Wireless and then set it to the SLAVE mode. The camera must be set to Wireless mode, using the Capture Functions menu (press the Fn button) and by pressing the four-way controller's down key to access the flash options. You can choose from two options in this Custom Setting entry:

- **1. On.** The built-in flash fires, and will trigger the remote slave flash, which detects the burst. This mode is useful when the main exposure for a shot will come from one or more slave flash units, and you want some additional light from the built-in flash to serve as fill for the shadows.
- **2. Off.** The built-in flash functions as a controller for the remote slave flash, issuing a pre-flash burst that triggers the external unit, but not firing during the actual exposure. In this mode, all of the flash exposure will come from your remote unit(s).

Custom Setting #17. WB when Using Flash

Options:

1. Flash

2. Unchanged

Because the duration of electronic flash varies from very brief (about 1/1,000th second) to very, very brief (1/20,000th second or less with some units), the color temperature also changes. The K200D can automatically set the White Balance to flash when you're using a Pentax flash unit that is capable of reporting these changes to the camera. There are two options with this setting:

- **1. Flash.** White balance is set to flash when using flash. I recommend using this setting all the time.
- **2. Unchanged.** White balance setting doesn't change when using flash. You might want to use this setting if you're shooting RAW images and plan to set the white balance yourself when importing the images.

Custom Setting #18. Preview Method

Options:

1. Digital Preview

2. Optical Preview

Use this setting to specify the type of preview provided by the K200D when you rotate the Main switch all the way clockwise while the exposure meter is active. You can see either of two types of previews to gauge your camera's depth-of-field and composition at the actual f/stop that will be used to take the picture. (The normal view through the viewfinder shows an image at the lens's widest aperture, which won't reflect the true depth-of-field unless the picture happens to be exposed at that lens opening. Your options are as follows:

- **1. Digital Preview.** Use this mode for checking exposure, composition, and focus on the LCD before shooting. The camera takes an actual picture, which appears on the screen. You can then rotate the e-dial to zoom in and out of the preview image, with up to 16X magnification. Use the four-way controller keys to move the viewing window around in the zoomed image. Press the Fn button to save the preview as a new JPEG file. Or, press the shutter release halfway. The preview image vanishes from the LCD, and you can continue shooting in the normal way.
- **2. Optical Preview.** Use this mode when you simply want to check depth-of-field with the viewfinder. It's faster and uses less power.

Custom Setting #19. Display Sensitivity

Options:

1. Off

2. On

Use this option to specify whether the number of images remaining or the ISO sensitivity setting will be displayed on the top-panel LCD and in the viewfinder. You can set the OK button to display the attribute you don't specify here. Choose from:

- **1. Off.** If this option is chosen, the number of recordable images remaining will be displayed in the lower-right corner of the viewfinder and the LCD panel at the top of your camera.
- **2. On.** When this option is active, the ISO sensitivity value will be displayed in the lower-right corner of the viewfinder and the LCD panel at the top of your camera.

Custom Setting #20. Saving Rotation Info

Options:

1. On

2. Off

The K200D has a function that uses a sensor to rotate the image so that images shot in vertical orientation are rotated on the LCD screen and/or in your image editing application. This setting determines whether the orientation information is embedded in the image file; if you want to have vertical images rotated on your LCD screen, too, you'll need to use CS #21, described next.

- **1. On.** Turning this setting on tells the Pentax K200D to include camera orientation information in the image file. The orientation can be read by many software applications, including Adobe Photoshop and Photoshop Elements, as well as the camera's Playback feature.
- **2. Off.** Turn this feature off and none of the software applications will be able to determine the correct orientation for the image. I don't recommend using this option.

Custom Setting #21. Auto Image Rotation

Options:
1. On
2. Off

When you rotate the K200D to photograph vertical subjects in portrait, rather than landscape orientation, you probably don't want to view them tilted onto their sides later on. The K200D is way ahead of you. It has a directional sensor built in that can detect whether the camera was rotated when the photo was taken. You can apply this information in two different ways—to automatically rotate images when they are displayed on the camera monitor, or to automatically rotate images in your image-editing application.

This menu choice deals with whether the image should be rotated when displayed on the camera monitor. You might or might not want to do that. When Rotate Tall is activated, the Pentax K200D rotates pictures taken in vertical orientation on the LCD screen so you don't have to turn the camera to view them comfortably. However, this orientation also means that the longest dimension of the image is shown using the shortest dimension of the LCD, so the picture is reduced in size.

- **1. On.** Use this option if you'd rather not turn your camera to view vertical shots in their natural orientation, and don't mind the smaller image (see Figure 3.22).
- **2. Off.** Turn the feature off if, as I do, you'd rather see a larger image and are willing to rotate the camera to do so (see Figure 3.23).

Custom Setting #22. Catch-in Focus

Options:
1. Off
2. On

Catch-in, or *trap focus* is a popular technique for sports photography and other situations in which you know *where* the action is going to take place (such as at the finish line of a horse race), but you don't know exactly *when.* The solution is to prefocus on the point where the action will occur, and then tell your K200D not to actually take the photo until something moves into the prefocused spot. Sound magical? It's actually not as difficult to achieve as you think. The key is to decouple the focusing operation from the shutter release function.

To do that, you'll need to use a lens that is not focusing automatically, because you'll want to set the focus yourself manually on the position where the action will occur. So, use either a Manual focus lens, or a DA or FA lens with an AF/MF switch that has been set to MF. The technique will not work with a lens that does not have its own AF/MF switch (such as the 18-55mm kit lens often furnished with the K200D).

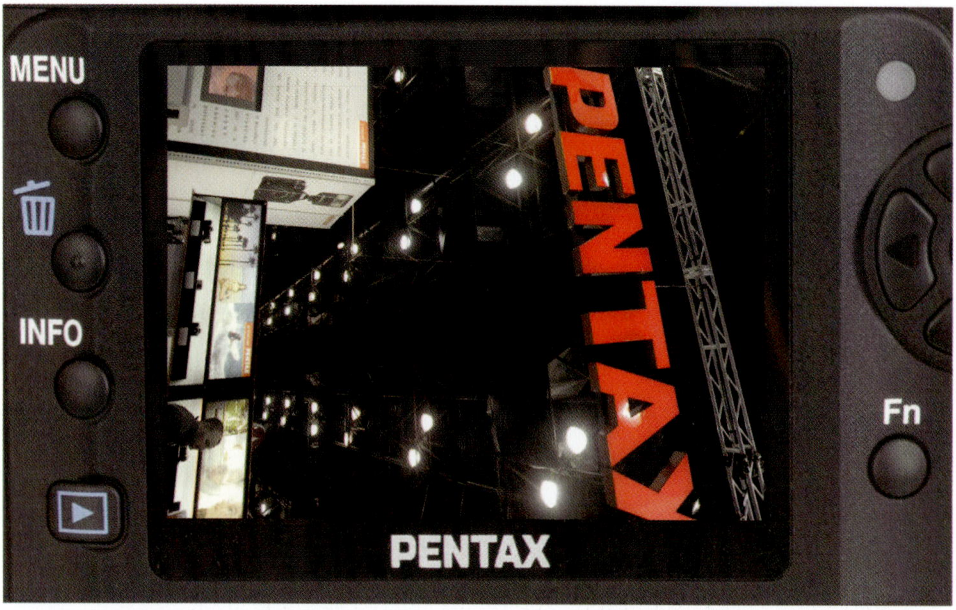

Figure 3.22
Without rotation, the image fills the LCD screen, but the camera must be rotated to view it.

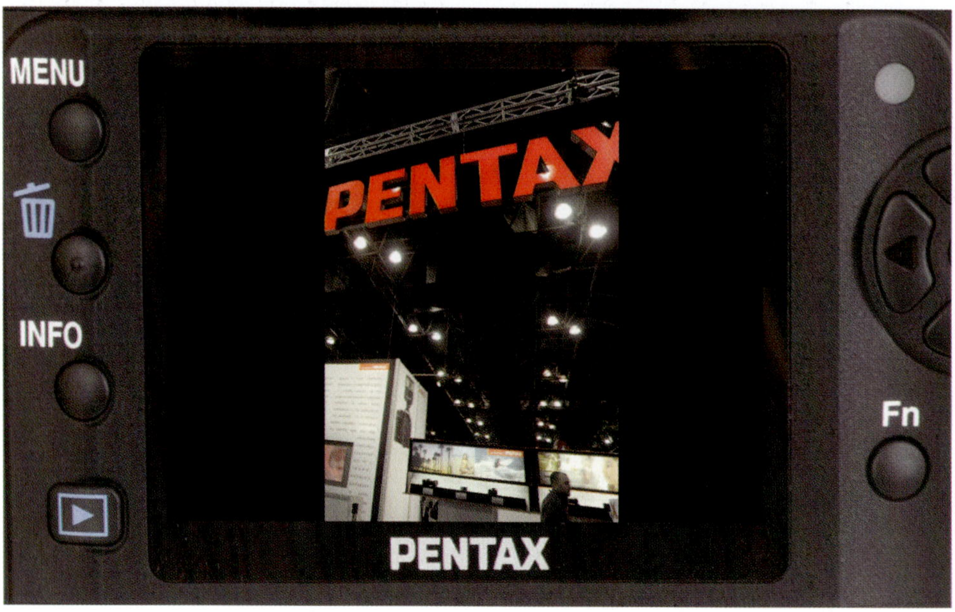

Figure 3.23
With rotation, the image is smaller, but can be viewed with the camera in a horizontal orientation.

Just follow these steps:

1. Make sure CS #22 is set to On, activating the feature.
2. Set the focus mode switch on the camera to AF. You want the K200D's autofocus mechanism to track the focus of subjects in your viewfinder; you simply don't want any focus changes to happen automatically. So, you'll have autofocus active, but not adjusting the focus of your lens because your lens has been set to Manual focus. (This will make more sense in a moment.)
3. In the Recording Mode menu, set the autofocus method to AF.S (single autofocus).
4. Manually focus on the position where the subject will appear when you want the photo to be taken, or at an equivalent distance.
5. Reframe your picture, if necessary, so that nothing is at the prefocused distance. (If an object occupies that spot, the K200D will take the photo immediately when you press the shutter release in the next step.)
6. Press and hold down the shutter release. The camera will not take a picture, because in AF.S mode, the shutter is locked until the subject is in focus.
7. The picture will be taken automatically when a subject moves into the prefocused area.

Custom Setting #23. Using Aperture Ring

Options:
1. Prohibited
2. Permitted

This setting determines whether or not you can set the f/stop using the aperture ring of a camera equipped with one. As you'll learn in Chapter 7, some lenses include a physical aperture ring for changing the lens opening on the lens itself, rather than having the f/stop set electronically by the camera. These lenses also may have an A (automatic) setting that enables the camera to set the aperture. Your choices:

- **1. Prohibited.** When this setting is used, the shutter will be locked if the lens is set to anything other than A (that is, to a particular f/stop), or if an f/stop is selected when using a lens that does not have an A. This prevents accidentally taking pictures with a manually adjusted aperture when your intent was to have the camera set the f/stop for you.
- **2. Permitted.** Use this setting if you want to take a photo even if the aperture has been set manually.

Custom Setting. Reset Custom Function

The last function follows the last item of the Custom Menu. It resets all 23 of the K200D's Custom Settings to their default value of 1, returning the CS entries to their factory settings. Unlike the setting I call CS #0, which only disables and restores your custom settings, this one truly resets them. If you want something other than the default value for any setting, you'll need to adjust each of them manually.

4

Fine-Tuning Exposure

When you bought your Pentax K200D, you probably considered your days of worrying about getting the correct exposure were over. To paraphrase an old Kodak tagline dating back to the 19th Century—the goal is, "you press the button, and the camera does the rest." For the most part, that's a realistic objective. The K200D is one of the smartest cameras available when it comes to calculating the right exposure for most situations. You can generally choose one of the Scene/SCN modes, or spin the Mode dial to Auto Pict, Program, Sensitivity Priority, Aperture Priority, or Shutter Priority and shoot away.

So, why am I including an entire chapter titled "Fine-Tuning Exposure?" As you learn to use your K200D creatively, you're going to find that the right settings—as determined by the camera's exposure meter and intelligence—need to be *adjusted* to account for your creative decisions or special situations.

For example, when you shoot with the main light source behind the subject, you end up with *backlighting*, which results in an overexposed background and/or an underexposed subject. The Pentax K200D recognizes backlit situations nicely, and can properly base exposure on the main subject, producing a decent photo. But what if you *want* to underexpose the subject, to produce a silhouette effect? Or, perhaps, you might want to flip up the K200D's built-in flash unit to fill in the shadows on your subject. The more you know about how to use your K200D, the more you'll run into situations where you want to creatively tweak the exposure to provide a different look than you'd get with a straight shot.

This chapter shows you the fundamentals of exposure, so you'll be better equipped to override the Pentax K200D's default settings when you want to, or need to. After all, correct exposure is one of the foundations of good photography, along with accurate focus and sharpness, appropriate color balance, freedom from unwanted noise and excessive contrast, as well as pleasing composition.

The Pentax K200D gives you a great deal of control over all of these, although composition is entirely up to you. You must still frame the photograph to create an interesting arrangement of subject matter, but all the other parameters are basic functions of the camera. You can let your K200D set them for you automatically, you can fine-tune how the camera applies its automatic settings, or you can make them yourself, manually. The amount of control you have over exposure, sensitivity (ISO settings), color balance, focus, and image parameters like sharpness and contrast make the K200D a versatile tool for creating images.

In the next few pages, I'm going to give you a grounding in one of those foundations, and explain the basics of exposure, either as an introduction or as a refresher course, depending on your current level of expertise. When you finish this chapter, you'll understand most of what you need to know to take well-exposed photographs creatively in a broad range of situations.

Getting a Handle on Exposure

In the most basic sense, exposure is all about light. Exposure can make or break your photo. Correct exposure brings out the detail in the areas you want to picture, providing the range of tones and colors you need to create the desired image. Poor exposure can cloak important details in shadow, or wash them out in glare-filled featureless expanses of white. However, getting the perfect exposure requires some intelligence—either that built into the camera, or the smarts in your head—because digital sensors can't capture all the tones we are able to see. If the range of tones in an image is extensive, embracing both inky black shadows and bright highlights, we often must settle for an exposure that renders most of those tones—but not all—in a way that best suits the photo we want to produce.

For example, look at the two typical tourist snapshots presented side by side in Figure 4.1. For the image on the left, the camera calculated exposure based—mostly—on the buildings in the background that are visible between the columns. The columns' shadows that wrap around the columns themselves are underexposed. Stepping back and pointing the camera upward produced the image at right. The ornate ceiling now receives the right amount of exposure, but the buildings in the background are badly overexposed. The camera's sensor simply can't capture detail in both dark areas and bright areas in a single shot.

The solution, such as it is, can be seen in Figure 4.2. The photo was reframed as a horizontal image, with no attempt to capture the detail in the ceiling. But by exposing for the intermediate areas of the column, it was possible to capture some detail in the bright highlights of the buildings in the background. The structures aren't perfectly exposed, but they aren't completely washed out, either. In some situations, this may be the best you can do without resorting to manipulation in an image-editing program like Photoshop or Photoshop Elements.

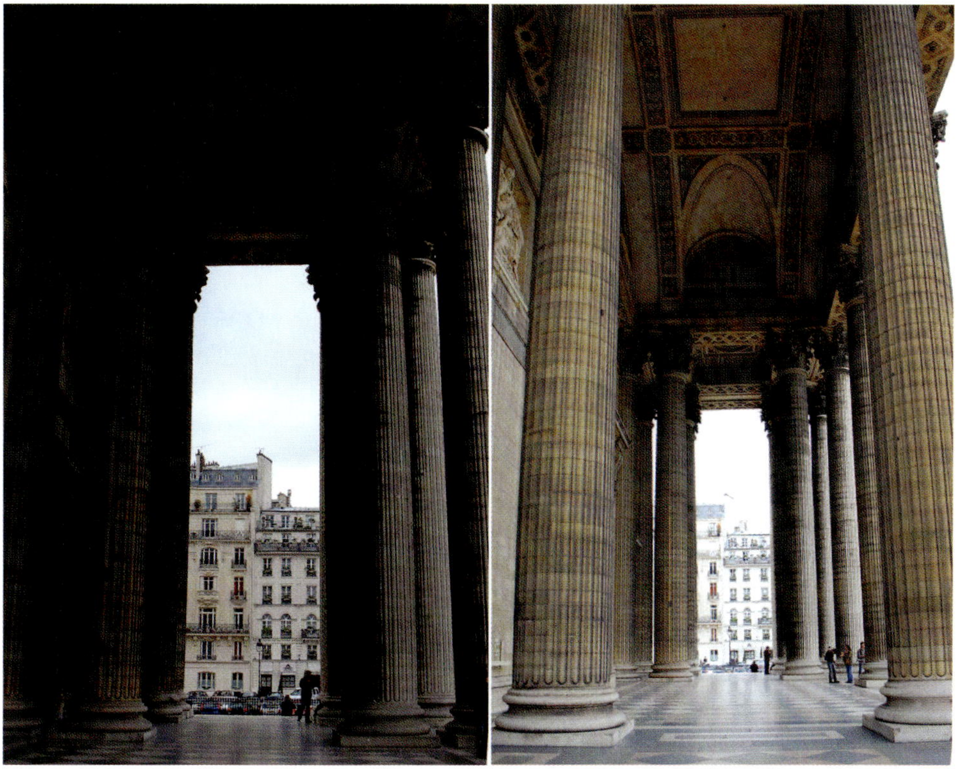

Figure 4.1 At left, the image is exposed for the background highlights, losing shadow detail. At right, the exposure captures detail in the shadows, but the background highlights are washed out.

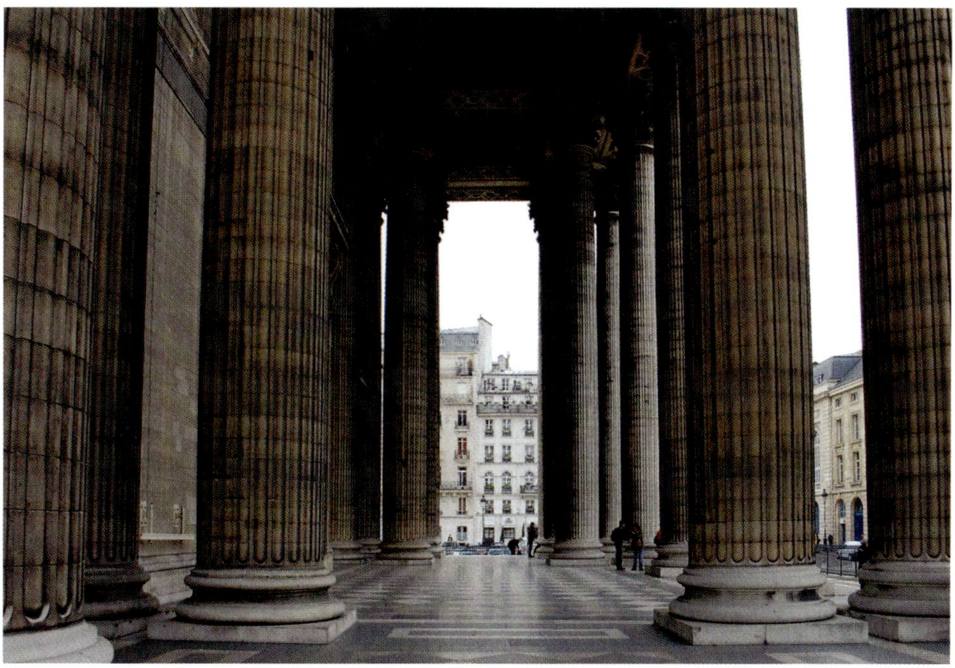

Figure 4.2 Reframing the shot and exposing for the middle shadows produces the best compromise exposure.

To understand exposure, you need to understand the six aspects of light that combine to produce an image. Start with a light source—the sun, an interior lamp, or the glow from a campfire—and trace its path to your camera, through the lens, and finally to the sensor that captures the illumination. Here's a brief review of the things within our control that affect exposure.

- **Light at its source.** Our eyes and our cameras—film or digital—are most sensitive to that portion of the electromagnetic spectrum we call *visible light.* That light has several important aspects that are relevant to photography, such as color, and harshness (which is determined primarily by the apparent size of the light source as it illuminates a subject). But, in terms of exposure, the important attribute of a light source is its *intensity.* We may have direct control over intensity, which might be the case with an interior light that can be brightened or dimmed. Or, we might have only indirect control over intensity, as with sunlight, which can be made to appear dimmer by introducing translucent light-absorbing or reflective materials in its path.
- **Light's duration.** We tend to think of most light sources as continuous. But, as you'll learn in Chapter 7, the duration of light can change quickly enough to modify the exposure, as when the main illumination in a photograph comes from an intermittent source, such as an electronic flash.
- **Light reflected, transmitted, or emitted.** Once light is produced by its source, either continuously or in a brief burst, we are able to see and photograph objects by the light that is reflected from our subjects towards the camera lens: transmitted (say, from translucent objects that are lit from behind): or emitted (by a candle or television screen). When more or less light reaches the lens from the subject, we need to adjust the exposure. This part of the equation is under our control to the extent we can increase the amount of light falling on or passing through the subject (by adding extra light sources or using reflectors) or by pumping up the light that's emitted (by increasing the brightness of the glowing object).
- **Light passed by the lens.** Not all the illumination that reaches the front of the lens makes it all the way through. Filters can remove some of the light before it enters the lens. Inside the lens barrel is a variable-sized aperture that is called a diaphragm that dilates and contracts to control the amount of light that enters the lens. You, or the Pentax's autoexposure system, can control exposure by varying the size of the aperture. The relative size of the aperture is called the *f/stop.* (See Figure 4.3.)
- **Light passing through the shutter.** Once light passes through the lens, the amount of time the sensor receives it is determined by the Pentax's shutter, which can remain open for as long as 30 seconds (or even longer if you use the Bulb setting) or as briefly as 1/4,000th second.

- **Light captured by the sensor.** Not all the light falling onto the sensor is captured. If the number of photons reaching a particular photosite doesn't pass a set threshold, no information is recorded. Similarly, if too much light illuminates a pixel in the sensor, then the excess isn't recorded or, worse, spills over to contaminate adjacent pixels. We can modify the minimum and maximum number of pixels that contribute to image detail by adjusting the ISO setting. At higher ISOs, the incoming light is amplified to boost the effective sensitivity of the sensor.

These factors—the quantity of light produced by the light source, the amount reflected or transmitted towards the camera, the light passed by the lens, the amount of time the shutter is open, and the sensitivity of the sensor—all work proportionately and reciprocally to produce an exposure. That is, if you double the amount of light that's available, increase the aperture by one stop, make the shutter speed twice as long, or boost the ISO setting 2X, you'll get twice as much exposure. Similarly, you can increase any of these factors while decreasing one of the others by a similar amount to keep the same exposure.

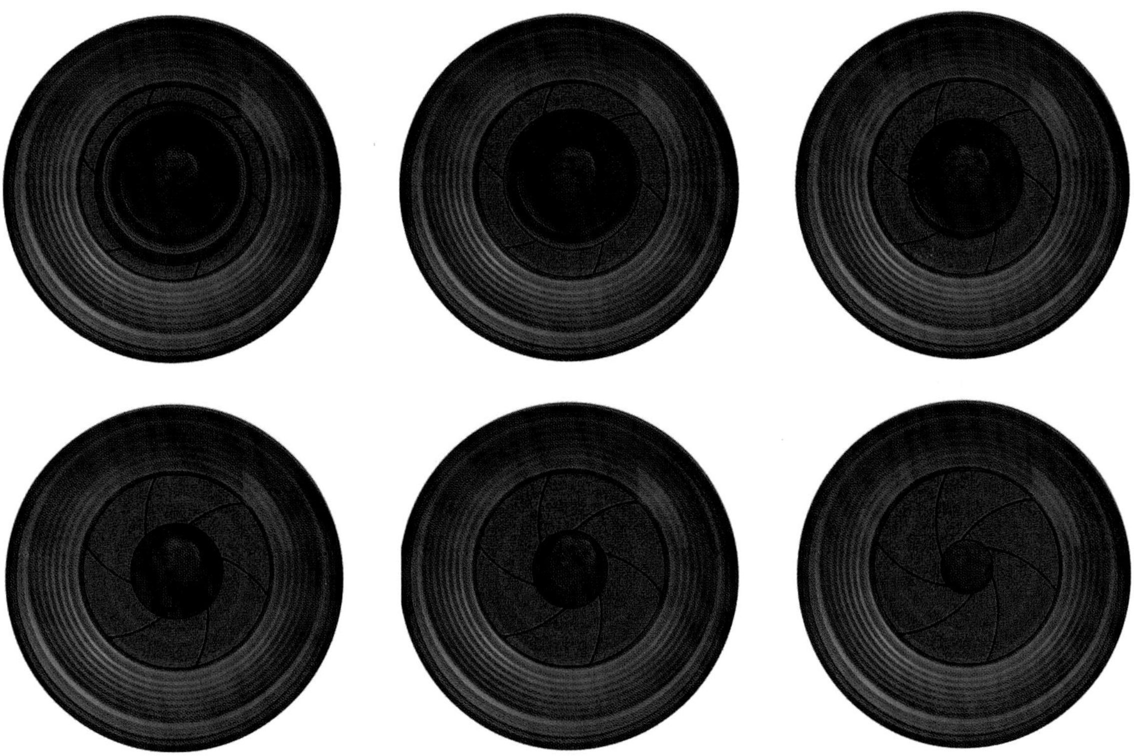

Figure 4.3 Top row (left to right): f/2, f/2.8, f/4; bottom row, f/5.6, f/8, f11.

F/STOPS AND SHUTTER SPEEDS

If you're *really* new to more advanced cameras (and I realize that many soon-to-be-ambitious photographers do purchase the K200D as their first digital SLR), you might need to know that the lens aperture, or f/stop, is a ratio, much like a fraction, which is why f/2 is larger than f/4, just as 1/2 is larger than 1/4. However, f/2 is actually *four times* as large as f/4. (If you remember your high school geometry, you'll know that to double the area of a circle, you multiply its diameter by the square root of two: 1.4.)

Lenses are usually marked with intermediate f/stops that represent a size that's twice as much/half as much as the previous aperture. So, a lens might be marked:

f/2, f/2.8, f/4, f/5.6, f/8, f/11, f/16, f/22, with each larger number representing an aperture that admits half as much light as the one before, as shown in Figure 4.3.

Shutter speeds are actual fractions (of a second), but the numerator is omitted, so that 60, 125, 250, 500, 1,000, and so forth represent 1/60th, 1/125th, 1/250th, 1/500th, and 1/1,000th second. To avoid confusion, Pentax uses quotation marks to signify longer exposures: 2", 2"5, 4", and so forth representing 2.0, 2.5, and 4.0-second exposures, respectively.

Most commonly, exposure settings are made using the aperture and shutter speed, followed by adjusting the ISO sensitivity if it's not possible to get the preferred exposure; that is, the one that uses the "best" f/stop or shutter speed for the depth-of-field (range of sharp focus) or action stopping we want (produced by short shutter speeds, as I'll explain later). Table 4.1 shows equivalent exposure settings using various shutter speeds and f/stops.

When the K200D is set for P mode, the metering system selects the correct exposure for you automatically, but you can change quickly to an equivalent exposure by holding down the shutter release button halfway ("locking" the current exposure), and then spinning the e-dial until the desired *equivalent* exposure combination is displayed. You

Table 4.1 Equivalent Exposures

Shutter speed	f/stop	Shutter speed	f/stop
1/30th second	f/22	1/500th second	f/5.6
1/60th second	f/16	1/1,000th second	f/4
1/125th second	f/11	1/2,000th second	f/2.8
1/250th second	f/8	1/4,000th second	f/2

can use this standard Program Shift feature more easily if you remember that you need to rotate the e-dial towards the *left* when you want to increase the amount of depth-of-field or use a slower shutter speed; rotate to the *right* when you want to reduce the depth-of-field or use a faster shutter speed. The need for more/less DOF and slower/faster shutter speed are the primary reasons you'd want to use Program Shift. I'll explain Program mode exposure shifting options in more detail later in this chapter.

In Aperture Priority (Av) and Shutter Priority (Tv) modes, you can change to an equivalent exposure using a different combination of shutter speed and aperture, but only by either adjusting the aperture in Aperture Priority mode (the camera then chooses the shutter speed) or shutter speed in Shutter Priority mode (the camera then selects the aperture). With Sensitivity Priority mode (Sv), you choose an ISO sensitivity setting, and the camera chooses *both* shutter speed and aperture. (This sounds a little like Program mode, which also chooses shutter speed and aperture.) But I'll cover all these exposure modes and their differences later in the chapter.

How the K200D Calculates Exposure

Your Pentax K200D calculates exposure by measuring the light that passes through the lens and is bounced up by the mirror to a 16-segment sensor located near the focusing surface, using patterns you can select (more on that later) and based on the assumption that each area being measured reflects roughly the same amount of light as a neutral gray card with 18-percent reflectance. That assumption is necessary, because different subjects reflect different amounts of light.

In a photo containing a white cat and a dark gray cat, the white cat might reflect five times as much light as the gray cat. An exposure based on the white cat will cause the gray cat to appear to be black, while an exposure based only on the gray cat will make the white cat washed out. Light-measuring devices handle this by assuming that the areas measured average a standard value of 18-percent gray, a figure that's been used as a rough standard (most vendors don't calibrate their metering for exactly 18-percent gray; the actual figure may be closer to 13 or 14 percent) for many years. Black, white, and gray cats have been a standard metaphor for many years, as well, so I'm going to explain this concept using a different, and more cooperative, life form: peppers.

Figure 4.4 shows three peppers. The yellow pepper at upper right represents a white cat, or any object that is very light but which contains detail that we want to see in the light areas. The red pepper in the lower center is a stand-in for a gray cat, because it has most of its details in the middle tones. The green pepper serves as our black cat, because it is a dark object with detail in its shadows.

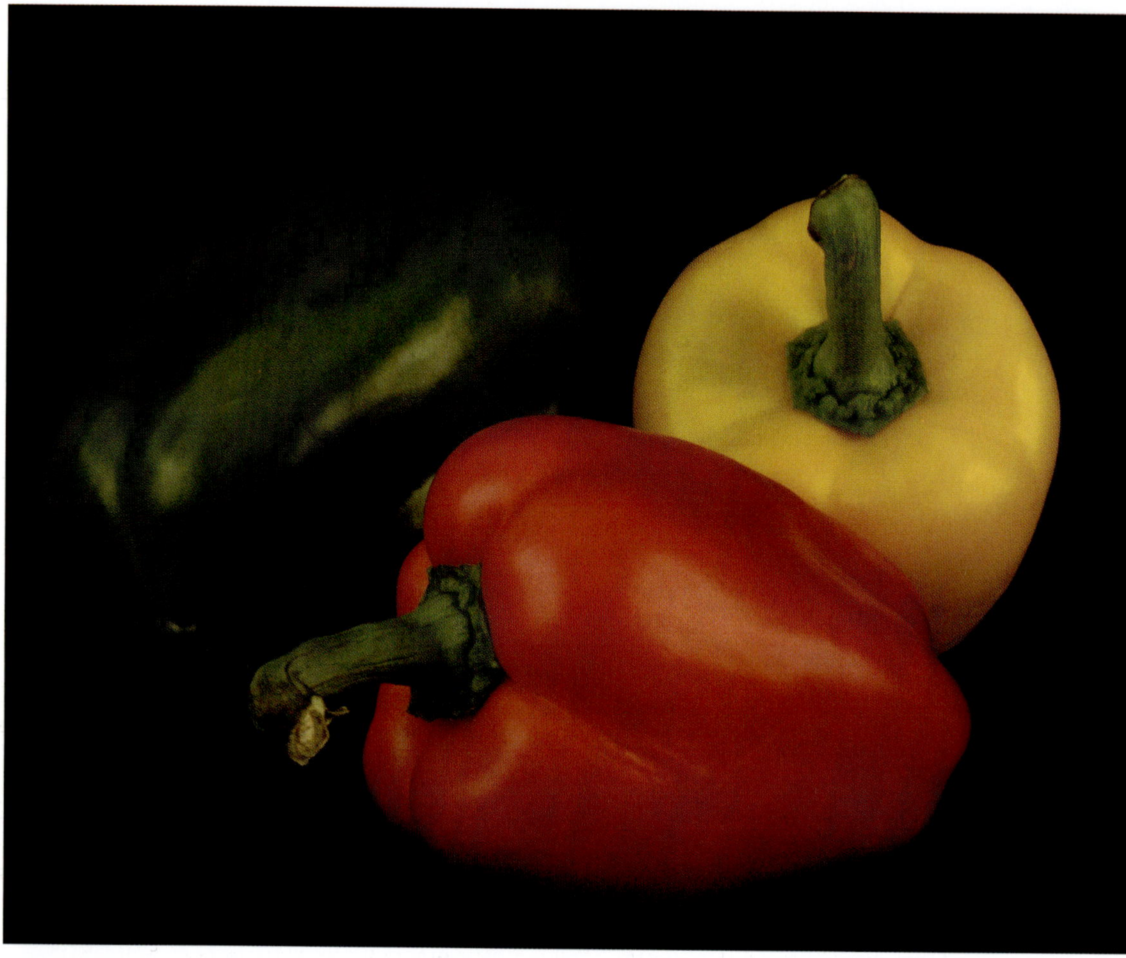

Figure 4.4 The yellow pepper, red pepper, and green pepper represent light, middle, and dark tones.

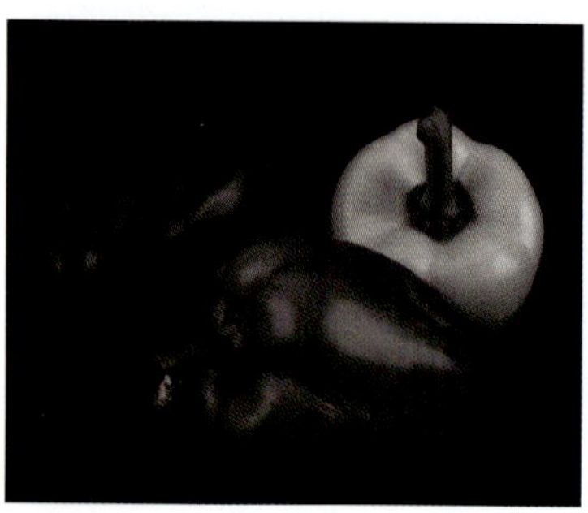

Figure 4.5 Exposing for the light-colored pepper in upper right renders the other two excessively dark.

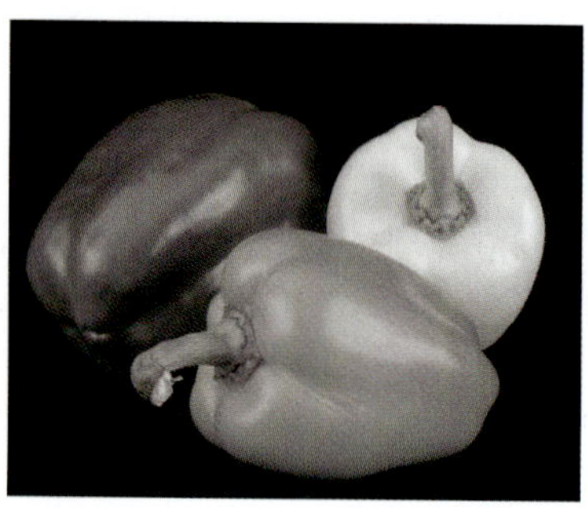

Figure 4.6 Exposing for the dark pepper (upper left) causes the two vegetables in the right half of the picture to become too light.

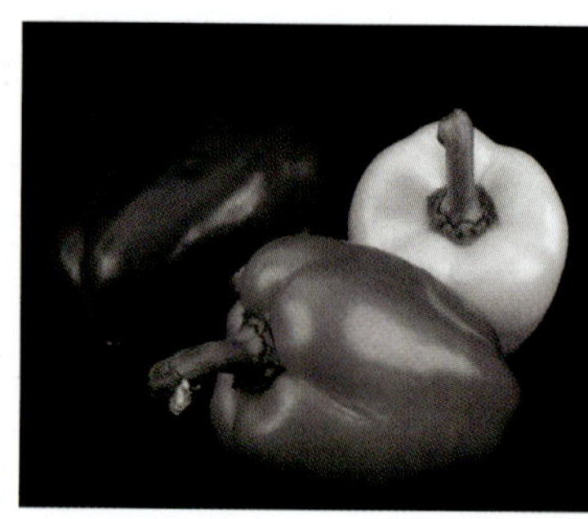

Figure 4.7 Exposing for the middle-toned red pepper produces an image in which the tones of all three subjects appear accurately.

The colors confuse the issue, so I'm going to convert our color peppers to black-and-white. For the version shown in Figure 4.5, the exposure was optimized for the white (yellow) paper, changing its tonal value to a medium, 18-percent gray. The dark (green) and medium-toned (red) peppers are now *too* dark. For Figure 4.6, the exposure was optimized for the dark (green) pepper, making most of its surface, now, fall into the middle-tone, 18-percent gray range. The yellow (light) and midtone (red) peppers are now too light.

The solution, of course, is to measure exposure from the object with the middle tones that most closely corresponds to the 18-percent gray "standard." Do that, and you wind up with a picture that more closely resembles the original tonality of the red, yellow, and green peppers, and which looks, in black-and-white, like Figure 4.7.

In the real world, you could calculate exposure the hard way, and arrive at accurate settings by pointing your K200D at an evenly lit object, such as an actual gray card or the palm of your hand (the backside of the hand is too variable). You'll need to increase the exposure by one stop in the latter case, because the human palm—of any ethnic group—reflects about twice as much light as a gray card. As you'll see, however, it's more practical though, to use your K200D's system to meter the actual scene.

F/STOPS VERSUS STOPS

In photography parlance, *f/stop* always means the aperture or lens opening. However, for lack of a current commonly used word for one exposure increment, the term *stop* is often used. (In the past, EV served this purpose, but Exposure Value and its abbreviation has been inextricably intertwined with its use in describing Exposure Compensation.) In this book, when I say "stop" by itself (no *f/*), I mean one whole unit of exposure, and I am not necessarily referring to an actual f/stop or lens aperture. So, adjusting the exposure by "one stop" can mean both changing to the next shutter speed increment (say, from 1/125th second to 1/250th second) or the next aperture (such as f/4 to f/5.6). Similarly, 1/3 stop or 1/2 stop increments can mean either shutter speed or aperture changes, depending on the context. Be forewarned.

In most cases, your camera's light meter will do a good job of calculating the right exposure, especially if you use the exposure tips in the next section. But if you want to double-check, or feel that exposure is especially critical, take the light reading off an object of known reflectance. Photographers sometimes carry around an 18-percent gray card (available from any camera store) and, for critical exposures, actually use that card, placed in the subject area, to measure exposure (or to set a custom white balance if needed).

Tip

Of course, if you use such a gray card, strictly speaking, you need to use about one-half stop *more* exposure than metered, because the K200D is calibrated for a lighter tone, rather than the 18-percent gray you just measured.

To meter properly, you'll want to choose both the *metering method* (how light is evaluated) and *exposure method* (how the appropriate shutter speeds and apertures are chosen based on the metered information). I'll describe both in the following sections.

MODES, MODES, AND MORE MODES

Call them modes or methods, the Pentax K200D seems to have a lot of different sets of options that are described using similar terms. Here's how to sort them out:

- **Metering mode.** These modes determine the *parts of the image* within the 16-zone array that are examined in order to calculate exposure. The K200D may look at many different points within the image, segregating them by zone (Multi-Segment metering), examine the same number of points, but give greater weight to those located in the middle of the frame (Center-Weighted metering), or evaluate only a limited number of points in a limited area (Spot metering).
- **Exposure mode.** These modes determine *which* settings are used to expose the image. The K200D may adjust the shutter speed, the aperture, or both, depending on the method you choose.
- **Scene/SCN modes.** These modes *combine* metering and exposure modes to determine exposure as well as other factors, such as focusing method, that are best suited for specific types of shooting situations.

Scene Modes Revisited

The K200D's Scene modes, both the ones that are on the Mode dial and those that are accessible from the LCD when the Mode dial is set to SCN, were introduced in Chapter 1. All these Scene modes are valuable when you don't have time to decide what the settings should be, and don't want a great deal of control over the exposure. To recap, the Pentax's Scene modes (see Figure 4.8) include:

- **Auto Pict.** The K200D figures out everything for you. This is the mode to use when you hand your camera to someone and ask them to take a picture of you. It will automatically select from any of the green-underlined Scene modes, as appropriate.

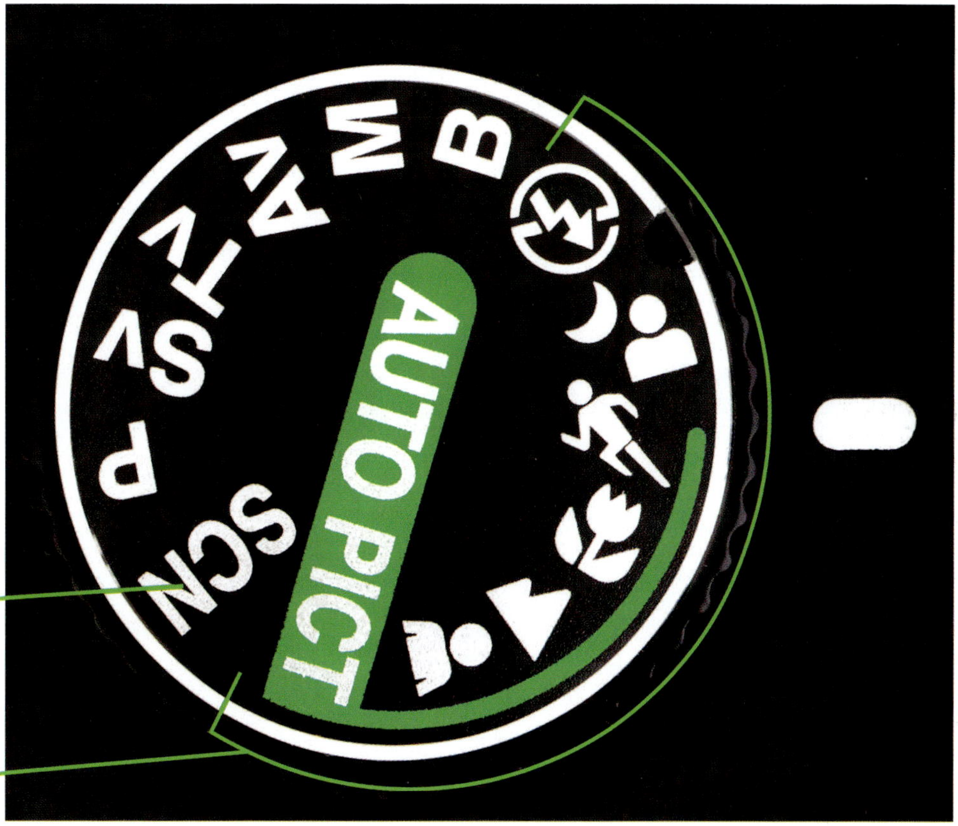

Figure 4.8
Scene modes available from the Mode dial.

- **Portrait.** The K200D will recognize your subject as being a person and adjust its aperture a bit wider for reduced depth-of-field, so the subject is clear and the background blurred.
- **Landscape.** The camera produces a bright, vivid image in which it attempts to put the entire frame in clear focus, both background and foreground. The Pentax uses smaller apertures to expand depth-of-field, and saturates the colors a bit.
- **Macro.** The K200D sets itself to properly focus in on extreme close-ups of objects like flowers and bugs.
- **Moving Object.** In this mode, the K200D uses fast shutter speeds to freeze action. It also uses continuous autofocus mode so that focus follows the subject as it moves throughout the frame.
- **Night Scene Portrait.** The camera attempts to detect human subjects at night, with shallower depth-of-field to emphasize the people in your photo. You might want to use a tripod with this mode, as the camera may leave the shutter open long enough to cause blur from camera shake.

Another eight modes are available when the Mode dial is set to the SCN position. The modes that appear on the LCD screen (see Figure 4.9) are:

- **Night Scene.** This mode isn't used for night portraits like the Night Scene Portrait mode available on the Mode dial. Instead, the camera is set for more general nighttime scenes, such as photos of a tall building at night, or nighttime city view, with a smaller f/stop used for greater depth-of-field. You might want to use a tripod here as the camera may leave the shutter open long enough to cause blur from camera shake.
- **Surf & Snow.** In this mode, the camera will compensate for bright backgrounds such as white sand beaches or snowy mountains by using faster shutter speeds. White balance will be adjusted so that the snow doesn't "white out" in your picture, thus keeping the texture of the snow's surface.
- **Food.** The K200D saturates the colors of the tasty objects that you put in the frame.
- **Sunset.** In this mode, the camera increases the contrast for more vivid dawn and dusk photos.
- **Kids.** In this mode, the K200D freezes the movement of active children, and uses continuous autofocus to follow their movement. The camera also makes adjustments to color, contrast, and sharpness to produce flattering skin tones.

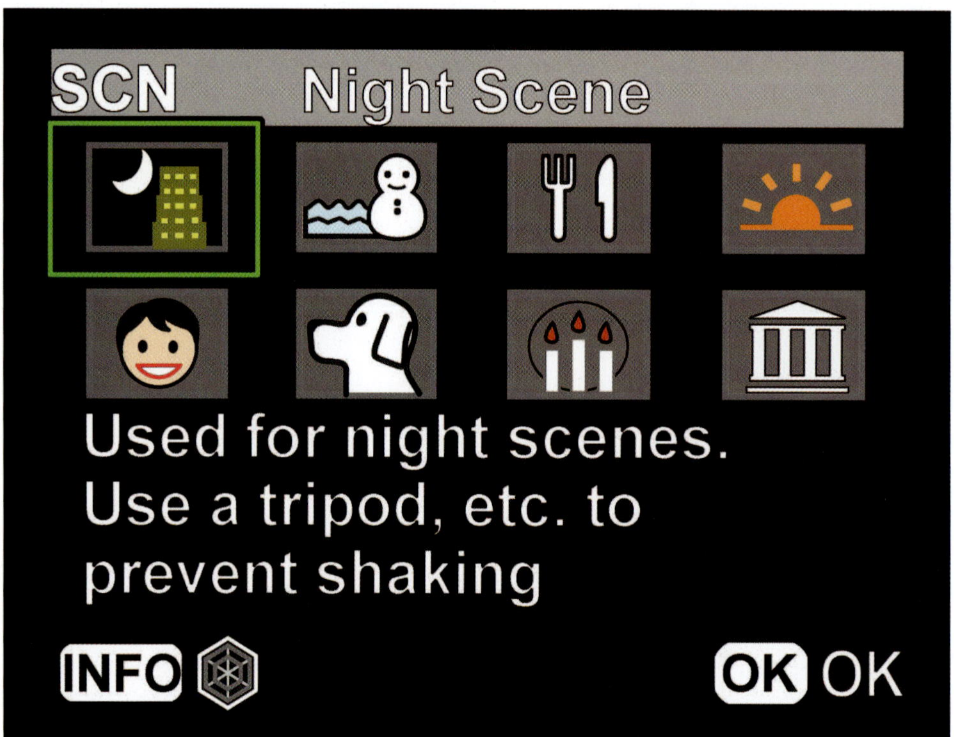

Figure 4.9 These eight Scene modes are available when the Mode dial is set to SCN.

- **Pet.** The K200D is ready for the movement of active pets.
- **Candlelight.** The K200D focuses properly and exposes for bright spots of light in a dark area.
- **Museum.** Flash is disabled, because flash is usually not permitted in a museum, and ISO speeds are increased to eliminate camera shake. You can also use this setting for religious ceremonies and other settings where flash is not desirable or allowed.

Choosing a Metering Method

The K200D has three different schemes for evaluating the light received by its exposure sensors, Multi-Segment, Center-Weighted, and Spot metering. Multi-Segment metering is always used when you select one of the Scene/SCN modes; you can't change to Center-Weighted or Spot metering when using Auto, Auto/No Flash, Portrait, Landscape, Child, Sports, Close-up, or Night Portrait modes. Exposure will generally be calculated well in one of these Scene modes, but the ability to choose an alternate metering method is one of the major reasons to select Program, Sensitivity Priority, Aperture Priority, Shutter Priority, or Manual exposure instead.

Multi-Segment Metering

For its Multi-Segment metering mode, the K200D slices up the frame into 16 different zones that cover most of the sensor area, shown in Figure 4.10. You can use Custom Setting #5 to specify that the zones are linked to the active autofocus points. When Multi-Segment metering is active, its icon appears in the center of the top line of the information display.

In all cases, the K200D evaluates the differences between the zones, and compares them with a built-in database of several hundred thousand images to make an educated guess about what kind of picture you're taking. For example, if the top sections of a picture are much lighter than the bottom portions, the algorithm can assume that the scene is a landscape photo with lots of sky. An image that includes most of the lighter portions in the center area may be a portrait.

Multi-Segment metering is best for most general subjects, because it is able to intelligently analyze a scene and make an excellent guess of what kind of subject you're shooting a great deal of the time. The camera can tell the difference between low-contrast and high-contrast subjects by looking at the range of differences in brightness across the scene. This mode is especially good for backlit scenes, where the illumination is coming from behind the subject.

Because the K200D has a fairly good idea about what kind of subject matter you are shooting, it can underexpose slightly when appropriate to preserve highlight detail when

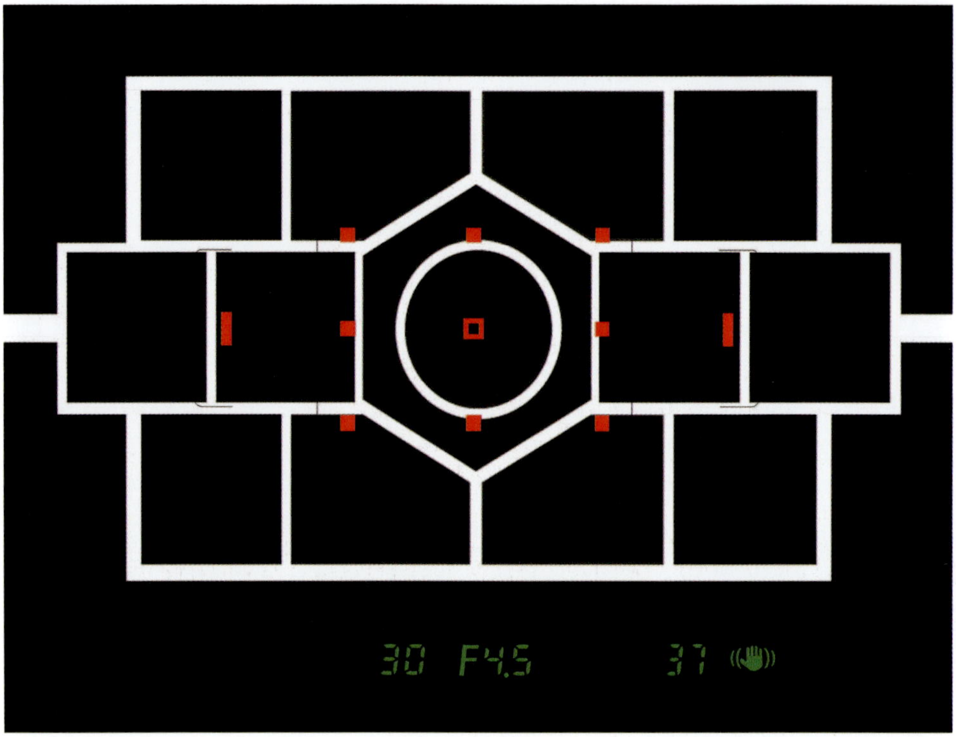

Figure 4.10 Multi-Segment metering uses 16 different zones, which can be linked to the autofocus points shown in red.

image contrast is high. (It's often possible to pull detail out of shadows that are too dark using an image editor, but once highlights are converted to white pixels, they are gone forever.)

As the manual notes, Multi-Segment metering is not possible when using a lens without a DA, D FA, FAJ, FA, F, or A designation, nor when the aperture is not set to A (Auto).

Center-Weighted Metering

In this mode, the exposure meter emphasizes a zone in the center of the frame, a little larger than the central hexagon shown in Figure 4.10, to calculate exposure. Most of the exposure is based on that central area, and the remaining exposure is based on the rest of the frame. The theory, here, is that, for most pictures, the main subject will be located in the center. So, if the K200D reads the center portion and determines that the exposure for that region should be f/8 at 1/250 second, while the outer area, which is a bit darker, calls for f/4 at 1/125 second, the camera will give the center portion the most weight and arrive at a final exposure of approximately f/5.6 at 1/250 second.

Center-Weighting works best for portraits, architectural photos, backlit subjects with extra-bright backgrounds (such as snow or sand), and other pictures in which the most important subject is located in the middle of the frame. As the name suggests, the light reading is *weighted* towards the central portion, but information is also used from the rest of the frame. If your main subject is surrounded by very bright or very dark areas, the exposure might not be exactly right. However, this scheme works well in many situations if you don't want to use one of the other modes. This mode can be useful for close-ups of subjects like flowers, or for portraits.

Spot Metering

Spot metering is favored by those of us who used to work with a hand-held light meter to measure exposure at various points (such as metering highlights and shadows separately). However, you can use Spot metering in any situation where you want to individually measure the light reflecting from light tones, midtones, or dark areas of your subject—or any combination of areas.

This mode confines the reading to a limited area in the center of the viewfinder, making up only the central portion of the image, roughly equivalent to the center circle in Figure 4.10. This is the only metering method you can use to tell the K200D exactly where to measure exposure. You'll find spot metering useful when you want to base exposure on a small area in the frame. If that area is in the center of the frame, so much the better. If not, you'll have to make your meter reading for an off-center subject and then lock exposure by pressing the shutter release halfway, or by pressing the AE-L button. This mode is best for subjects where the background is significantly brighter or darker. Figure 4.11 shows a picture of a lunar eclipse taken with the camera's metering system set to spot, yielding an exposure of 1/500th second at f/16 at a setting of ISO 400.

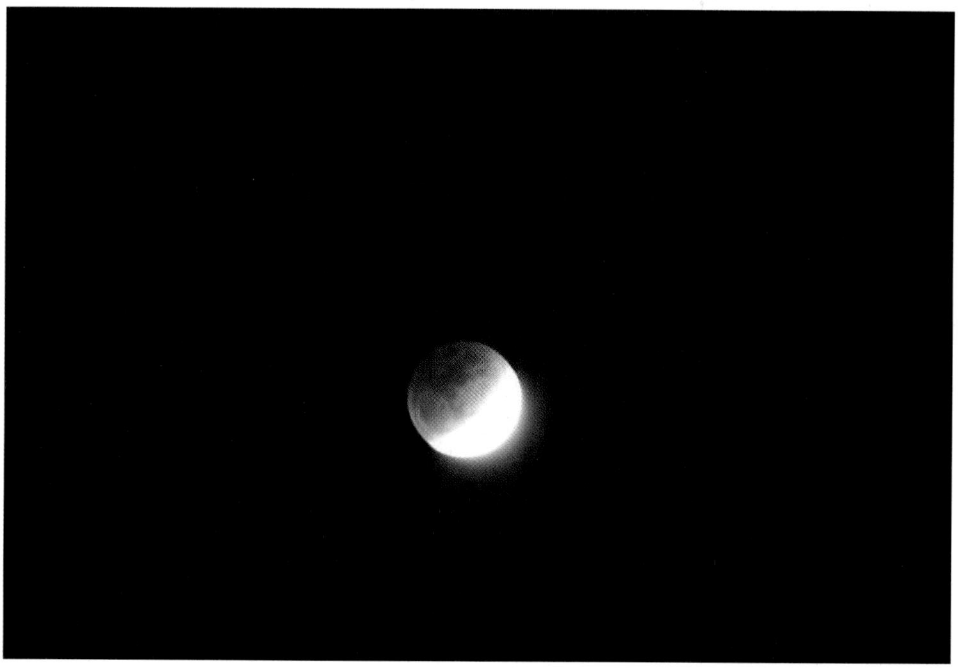

Figure 4.11
Lunar eclipse taken with exposure calculated using Spot metering.

Choosing an Exposure Method

The Pentax K200D's Scene/SCN modes choose an exposure method for you. But there are four semi-automated methods—Program, Sv, Av, Tv—and Manual, that you can use to choose how the appropriate shutter speed and aperture are selected. You can choose among them by rotating the Mode dial until the one you want is selected (see Figure 4.12). Your choice of which is best for a given shooting situation will depend on things like your need for lots of (or less) depth-of-field, a desire to freeze action or allow motion blur, or how much noise you find acceptable in an image. Each of the K200D's exposure methods emphasizes one aspect of image capture or another. This section introduces you to all of them.

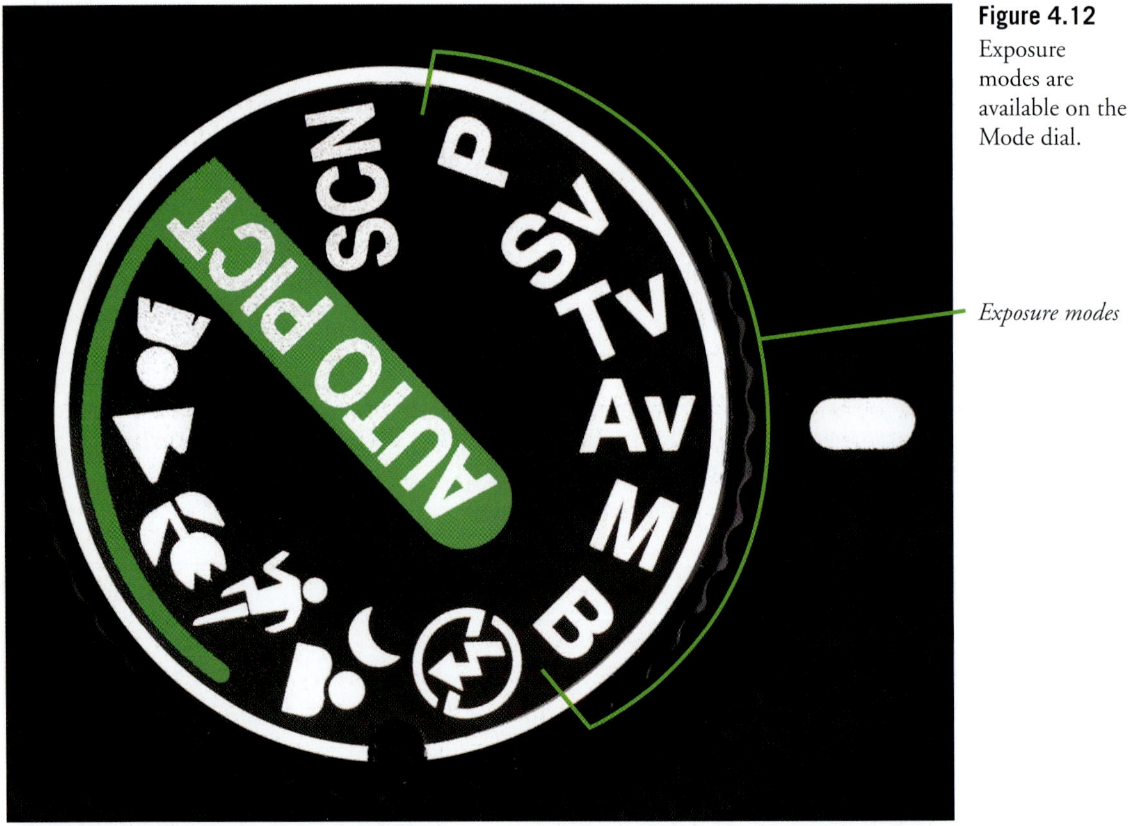

Figure 4.12 Exposure modes are available on the Mode dial.

In each Exposure mode, you can change some combination of shutter speed, f/stop, and ISO setting. The value that you can modify will be underlined in the viewfinder window.

Sensitivity Priority (Sv)

This mode allows you to specify a given fixed ISO value, with the K200D selecting both shutter speed and aperture. It's an unusual mode in the sense that most non-Pentax cameras don't have this option, although many have a kind of automatic ISO setting, or the ability to limit which ISO settings are used.

To use Sensitivity Priority, choose that mode with the Mode dial, and select an ISO setting using the e-dial. (Note that the ISO setting at bottom right in the viewfinder is underlined.) You can choose any value from ISO 100 to ISO 1600, using the increment you selected (either 1/3 or 1/2 stop) with CS #1, as described in Chapter 3. You can't select Auto ISO, nor can you use the Functions (Fn) menu to adjust ISO. If you want to add or subtract exposure using Exposure Compensation (described later in this chapter), you must hold down the Av button (located southwest of the shutter release on the top panel) and rotate the e-dial.

Sensitivity Priority is best used when you want to lock in a specific ISO setting, and the specific shutter speed and aperture aren't important. For example, you might want to use ISO 100 to provide the best overall contrast and tone, with the minimum amount of noise. In a brightly lit scene, it's unlikely that your shutter speed will venture into the low range and cause motion blur, and any aperture selected by the camera will provide adequate depth-of-field. So, you can use Sv and lock in that ISO 100 value. Or, you might want to fix the sensitivity at ISO 1600 in low-light situations. Unlike Auto ISO, the sensitivity setting won't vary at all as lighting conditions change.

To be honest, the reason that more cameras don't offer a Sensitivity Priority setting is that it doesn't provide much in the way of useful control. It's easy enough to lock in a specific ISO setting in any of the other Exposure modes, too, and they allow you to specify a shutter speed or aperture (or both).

Shutter Priority (Tv)

Shutter Priority (Tv) lets you choose the shutter speed you'd like to use, and the camera's metering system selects the appropriate f/stop. Perhaps you're shooting action photos and you want to use the absolute fastest shutter speed available with your camera (see Figure 4.13); in other cases, you might want to use a slow shutter speed to add some blur to a photo that would be mundane if the action were completely frozen (see Figure 4.14). Shutter Priority mode gives you some control over how much action-freezing capability your K200D brings to bear in a particular situation. The shutter speed indicator in the viewfinder will be underlined to show you can adjust the shutter speed.

You'll also encounter times when you select a shutter speed that's too long or too short for correct exposure under some conditions. I've shot outdoor soccer games on sunny Fall evenings and used Shutter Priority mode to lock in a 1/1,000th second shutter speed, only to find my K200D refused to shoot when the sun dipped behind some trees

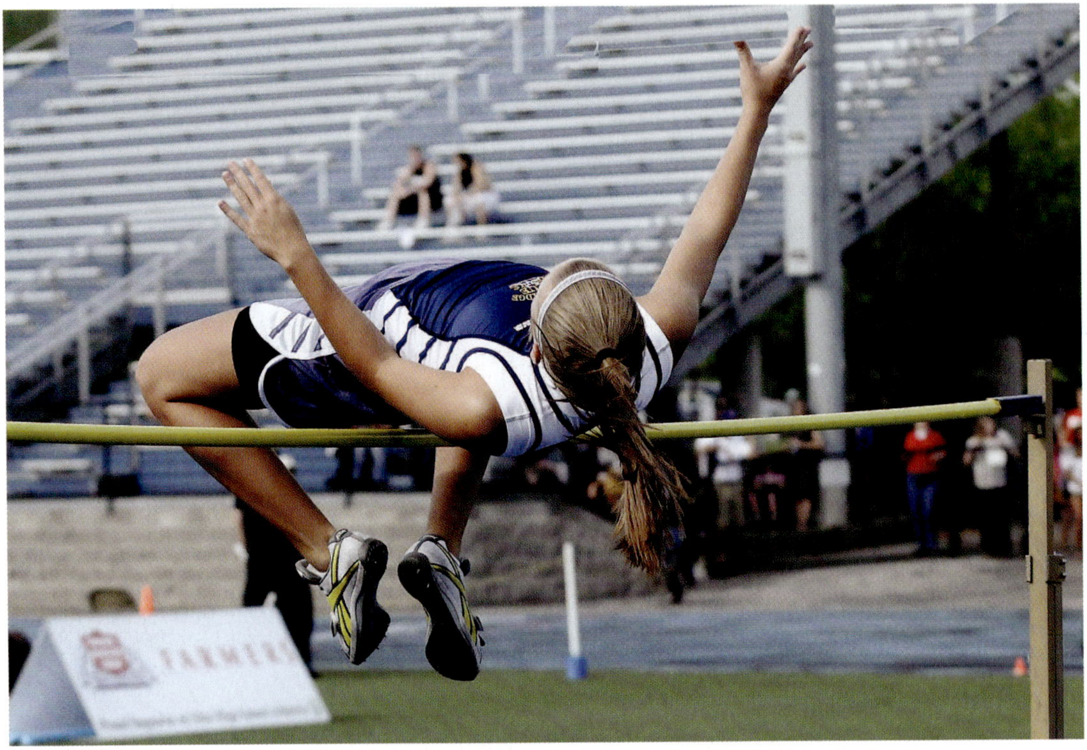

Figure 4.13 Lock the shutter at a high speed to freeze action.

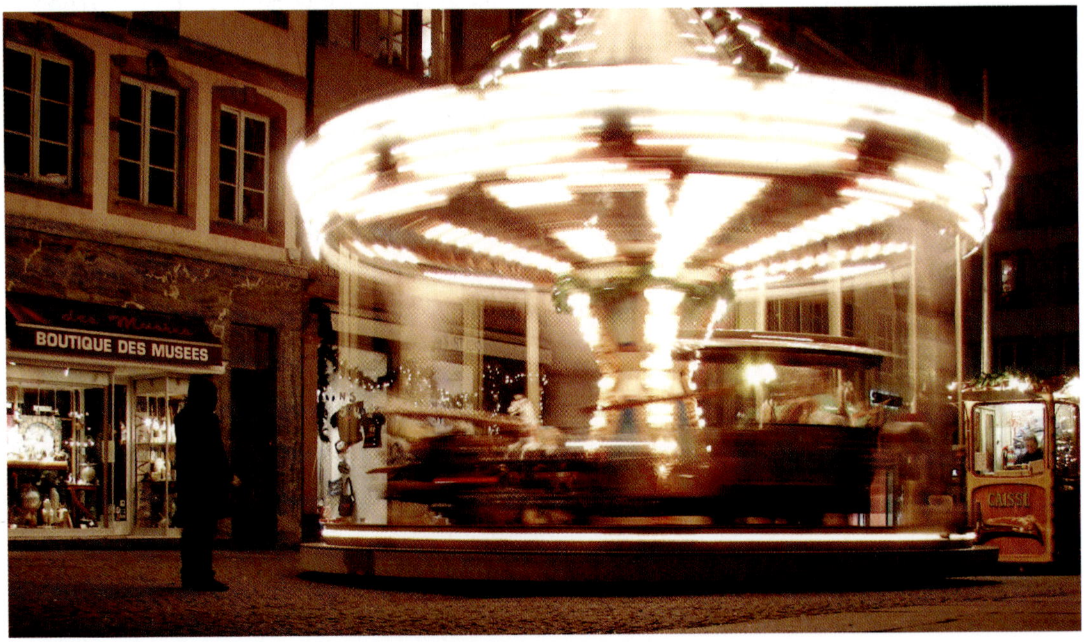

Figure 4.14 Use a slow shutter speed to introduce some interesting blur.

and there was no longer enough light to shoot at that speed, even with the lens wide open. It's possible to choose an inappropriate shutter speed. If that's the case, the lens aperture display in the viewfinder and on the top panel LCD will blink to indicate that a correct exposure is out of range.

Aperture Priority (Av)

In Av mode, you specify the lens opening used, and the K200D selects the shutter speed. Aperture Priority is especially good when you want to use a particular lens opening to achieve a desired effect. Perhaps you'd like to use the smallest f/stop possible to maximize depth-of-field in a close-up picture. Or, you might want to use a large f/stop to throw everything except your main subject out of focus, as in Figure 4.15. Maybe you'd just like to "lock in" a particular f/stop because it's the sharpest available aperture with that lens. Or, you might prefer to use, say, f/2.8 on a lens with a maximum aperture of f/1.4, because you want the best compromise between speed and sharpness.

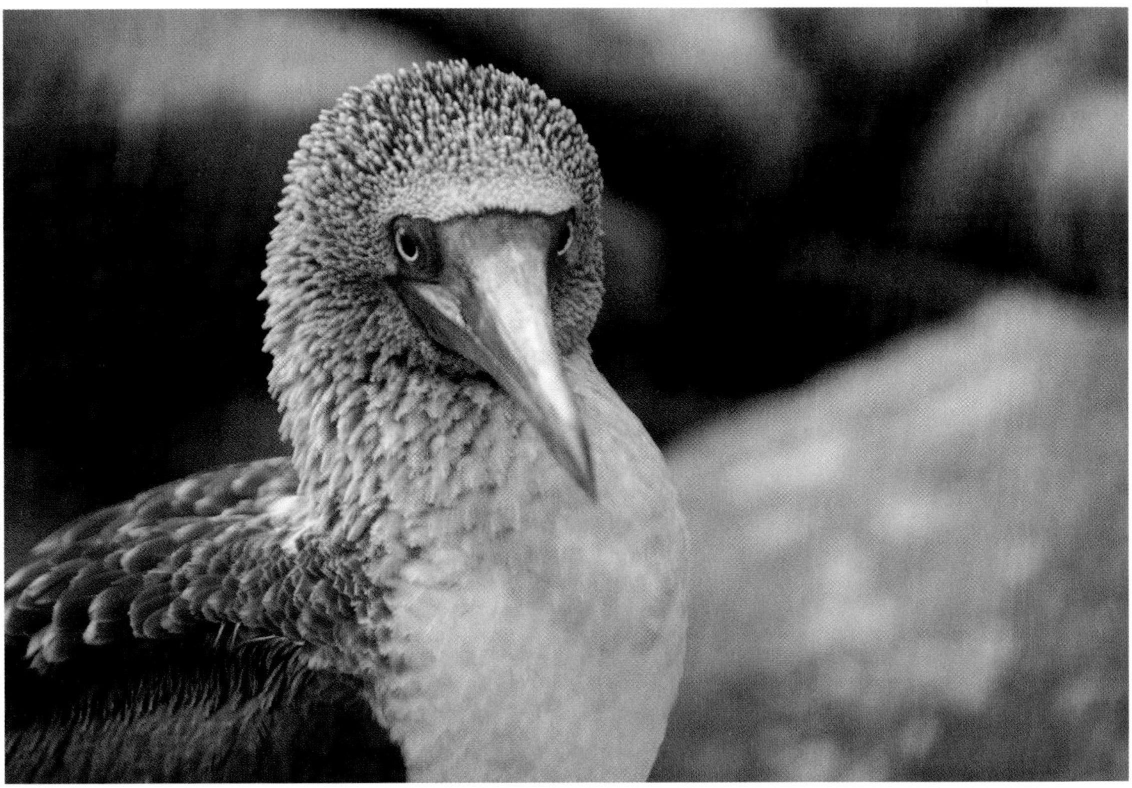

Figure 4.15 Use Aperture Priority to "lock in" a large f/stop when you want to blur the background.

Aperture Priority can even be used to specify a *range* of shutter speeds you want to use under varying lighting conditions, which seems almost contradictory. But think about it. You're shooting a soccer game outdoors with a telephoto lens and want a relatively high shutter speed, but you don't care if the speed changes a little should the sun duck behind a cloud. Set your K200D to Av, and adjust the aperture until a shutter speed of, say, 1/1,000th second is selected at your current ISO setting. (In bright sunlight at ISO 400, that aperture is likely to be around f/11.) Then, go ahead and shoot, knowing that your K200D will maintain that f/11 aperture (for sufficient DOF as the soccer players move about the field), but will drop down to 1/750th or 1/500th second if necessary should the lighting change a little.

If it's impossible to choose an appropriate shutter speed at the selected aperture, the shutter speed indicator in the viewfinder and the top-panel status LCD will blink. That's the major pitfall of using Av: you might select an f/stop that is too small or too large to allow an optimal exposure with the available shutter speeds. For example, if you choose f/2.8 as your aperture and the illumination is quite bright (say, at the beach or in snow), even your camera's fastest 1/4000th second shutter speed might not be able to cut down the amount of light reaching the sensor to provide the right exposure. Or, if you select f/8 in a dimly lit room, you might find yourself shooting with a very slow shutter speed that can cause blurring from subject movement or camera shake. Aperture Priority is best used by those with a bit of experience in choosing settings. Many seasoned photographers leave their K200D set on Av all the time.

When using Av mode, change the aperture by rotating the e-dial. If you want to add or subtract exposure using Exposure Compensation (described later), hold down the Av button on top of the camera and spin the e-dial.

Program Mode

Program mode (P) uses the K200D's built-in smarts to select the correct f/stop and shutter speed using a database of picture information that tells it which combination of shutter speed and aperture will work best for a particular photo. If the correct exposure cannot be achieved at the current ISO setting, the shutter speed and f/stop indicators will blink, and the electronic flash icon will appear, urging you to pop up the built-in flash. You can then elevate the flash, or boost or reduce the ISO to increase or decrease sensitivity, depending on the situation.

The K200D's recommended exposure can be overridden if you want. Use the EV setting feature (described later, because it also applies to Tv and Av modes) by pressing the Av button as you rotate the e-dial to add or subtract exposure from the metered value. And, as I mentioned earlier in this chapter, in Program mode you can rotate the e-dial to change from the recommended setting to an equivalent setting (as shown in Table 4.1) that produces the same exposure, but using a different combination of f/stop and shutter speed.

This is called "Program Shift" by Pentax. As I explained in Chapter 3, there are four variations on this mode, which Pentax dubs "hyper-program" modes. The mode used is determined by how you have set CS #13 to use the e-dial in the Custom Setting menu. Here's a recap of the four options you can select with that Custom Setting:

- **1. Program Shift.** When this option is selected, spinning the e-dial switches the K200D from ordinary Program mode to Program Shift mode. You can then rotate the e-dial to change from the metered exposure to other shutter speed/aperture combinations that provide the same exposure. The camera adjusts both values, as required. To return to standard Program mode, press the Green button (located on top of the camera, southeast of the shutter release).
- **2. Tv.** When you've chosen this option, rotating the e-dial switches the K200D from Program mode to Tv (Shutter Priority) mode. You can then rotate the e-dial to change to a shutter speed of your choice, and the camera will select the correct aperture for the proper exposure. The shutter speed will be underlined in the viewfinder, indicating that it can be adjusted. If an appropriate exposure can't be set, the aperture indicator in the viewfinder will blink. Press the Green button to return to Program mode.
  - **Left.** Spinning the e-dial to the left changes to an equivalent exposure with a longer shutter speed and smaller f/stop. Use this to add depth-of-field or when you want some motion blur that a longer shutter speed will produce.
  - **Right.** Spinning the e-dial to the right changes to an equivalent exposure with a shorter shutter speed (to better stop action) and a larger f/stop (to reduce depth-of-field). Use this to improve your ability to freeze movement, or to use selective focus with shallower DOF.
- **3. Av.** When you've chosen this option, rotating the e-dial switches the K200D from Program mode to Av (Aperture Priority) mode. You can then rotate the e-dial to change to an aperture of your choice, and the camera will select the correct shutter speed for the proper exposure. The aperture will be underlined, indicating it can be adjusted. If an appropriate exposure can't be set, the shutter speed indicator in the viewfinder will blink. Press the Green button to return to Program mode.
  - **Left.** Spinning the e-dial to the left changes to an equivalent exposure with a larger aperture (for less DOF) and a shorter shutter speed (to better stop action). Use this to improve your ability to freeze movement, or to use selective focus with shallower DOF.
  - **Right.** Spinning the e-dial to the right changes to an equivalent exposure with a smaller f/stop and longer shutter speed. Use this to add depth-of-field or when you want some motion blur that a longer shutter speed will produce.
- **4. Off.** With this option active, rotating the e-dial while using Program mode has no effect.

MAKING EXPOSURE COMPENSATION CHANGES

Sometimes you'll want more or less exposure than indicated by the K200D's metering system. Perhaps you want to underexpose to create a silhouette effect, or overexpose to produce a high-key look. It's easy to use the K200D's exposure compensation system to override the exposure recommendations. Press the Av button on the top of the camera (just southwest of the shutter release). Then rotate the e-dial right to add exposure, and left to subtract exposure. The EV change you've made remains for the exposures that follow, until you manually zero out the EV setting. The EV plus/minus icon appears in the viewfinder and monochrome status panel to warn you that an exposure compensation change has been entered. However, it's easy to miss—so, pay attention!

Manual Exposure

Part of being an experienced photographer comes from knowing when to rely on your K200D's automation (with Scene/SCN modes or P mode), when to go semiautomatic (with Tv or Av), and when to set exposure manually (using M). Some photographers actually prefer to set their exposure manually, as the K200D will be happy to provide an indication of when its metering system judges your manual settings provide the proper exposure, using the plus/minus indicator at the right of the viewfinder.

Manual exposure can come in handy in some situations. You might be taking a silhouette photo and find that none of the exposure modes or EV correction features give you exactly the effect you want. Set the exposure manually to use the exact shutter speed and f/stop you need. Or, you might be working in a studio environment using multiple flash units. The additional flash are triggered by slave devices (gadgets that set off the flash when they sense the light from another flash, or, perhaps from a radio or infrared remote control). Your camera's exposure meter doesn't compensate for the extra illumination, so you need to set the aperture manually.

Because, depending on your proclivities, you might not need to set exposure manually very often, you should still make sure you understand how it works. Fortunately, the K200D makes setting exposure manually very easy. Just set the Mode dial to Manual mode, and then turn the e-dial to set the shutter speed, and hold the Av button while rotating the e-dial to adjust the aperture. Press the shutter release halfway or press the AE-Lock button, and a plus/minus indicator at the right bottom edge of the viewfinder will show whether the current exposure you've selected is more or less than the recommended exposure.

Adjusting Exposure with ISO Settings

Another way of adjusting exposures is by changing the ISO sensitivity setting. Sometimes photographers forget about this option, because the common practice is to set the ISO once for a particular shooting session (say, at ISO 200 for bright sunlight outdoors, or ISO 800 when shooting indoors) and then forget about ISO. The reason for that is ISOs higher than ISO 200 or 400 are seen as "bad" or "necessary evils." However, changing the ISO is a valid way of adjusting exposure settings, particularly with the Pentax K200D, which produces good results at ISO settings that create grainy, unusable pictures with some other camera models.

Indeed, I find myself using ISO adjustment as a convenient alternate way of adding or subtracting exposure when shooting in Manual mode, and as a quick way of choosing equivalent exposures when in Program or Shutter Priority or Aperture Priority modes. For example, I've selected a Manual exposure with both f/stop and shutter speed suitable for my image using, say, ISO 200. I can adjust exposure using the Functions menu to change ISO to 400 (for one additional stop) or to 100 (for one less stop's worth of exposure). I keep my preferred f/stop and shutter speed in either case, but still adjust the exposure.

Or, perhaps, I am using Tv mode and the metered exposure at ISO 200 is 1/500th second at f/11. If I decide on the spur of the moment I'd rather use 1/500th second at f/8, I can change the ISO to 100. Of course, it's a good idea to monitor your ISO changes, so you don't end up at ISO 1600 accidentally.

ISO settings can, of course, also be used to boost or reduce sensitivity in particular shooting situations. The K200D can use ISO settings from ISO 100 up to ISO 1600. The camera can also adjust the ISO automatically as appropriate for various lighting conditions. When you choose the Auto ISO setting in the Shooting menu, as described in Chapter 3, the K200D adjusts the sensitivity dynamically to suit the subject matter, based on minimum shutter speed and ISO limits you have prescribed. You should use Auto ISO cautiously if you don't want the K200D to use an ISO higher than you might otherwise have selected.

Selecting an ISO Setting

To choose a fixed ISO setting or to choose Auto, follow these steps:

1. Tap the shutter release to activate Capture mode.
2. Press the Fn button to produce the Capture Functions screen.
3. Press the right controller button to access the Sensitivity screen (see Figure 4.16). The increments on the scale are either 1/2 or 1/3 stop, depending on your setting for CS #2 (Sensitivity Steps) in the Custom Setting menu, as described in Chapter 3.

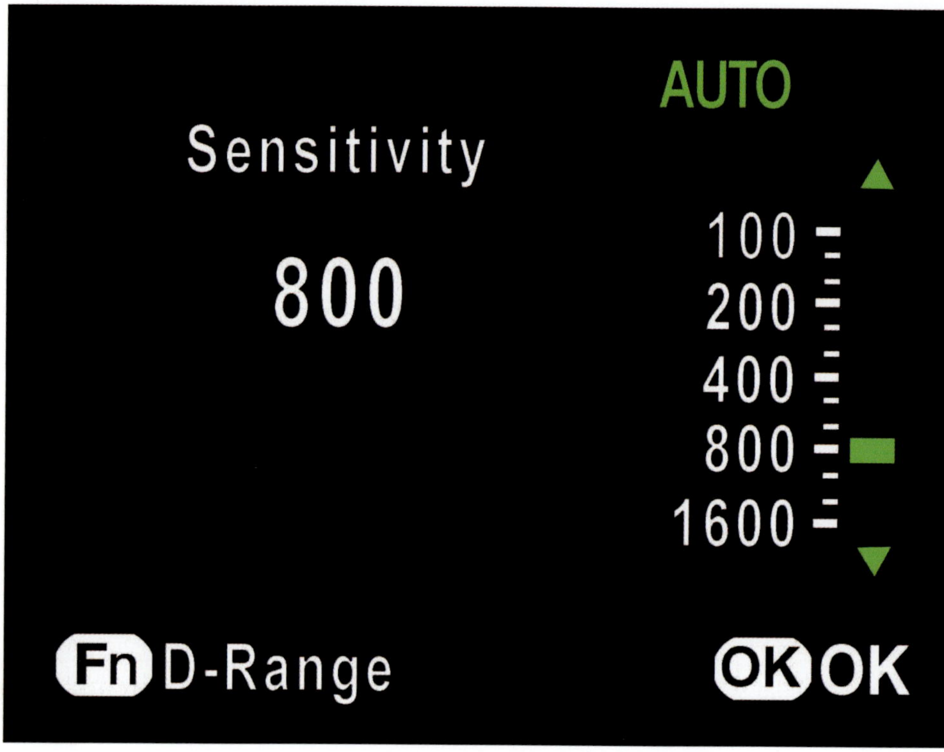

Figure 4.16
Sensitivity settings from ISO 100 to ISO 1600 can be selected.

4. Press the up/down controller keys to choose an ISO setting from ISO 100 to 1600 or Auto (located above the scale). (**Note:** If you're using Sv mode, the screen displays the current sensitivity, but you can't modify the setting.)
5. Press OK when finished to confirm your choice.

Selecting ISO Range in Auto

When you've selected Auto ISO, the K200D chooses an appropriate sensitivity for you, but you can select the range of ISO settings used. This prevents the camera from choosing an excessively enthusiastic (high) ISO setting when you want to rein in the amount of visual noise in your photos. To adjust the range of automatic correction, turn the e-dial. The permissible ISO range will be shown to the left of the scale, and indicated by a green bar to the right of the scale (see Figure 4.17). These changes are visible in the ISO menu summoned by the Fn button.

Expanding the Dynamic Range

When scenes have both extremely bright and extremely dark areas (high contrast), detail can be lost in the highlights, shadows, or both. The K200D can juggle pixel brightness values using mathematical formulas to effectively underexpose the image slightly, preserving highlight detail, and then boosting the underexposed shadows back to a normal

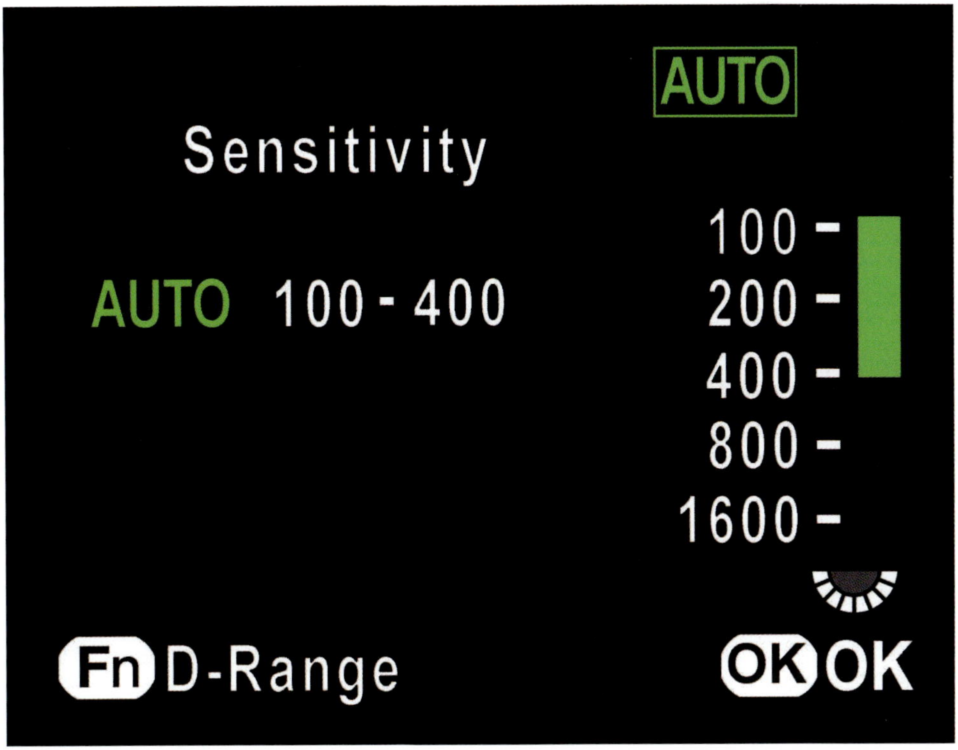

Figure 4.17 Specify the range of ISO settings used in Auto ISO mode.

rendition. This process produces an expanded dynamic range, at the cost of some picture detail.

To activate the Expand Dynamic Range feature, press the Fn button while the Sensitivity screen is displayed. A DR-Range 200% indicator appears under the current sensitivity display, showing that the feature is active. The ISO 100 setting is disabled, as the camera needs a certain amount of ISO "footroom" below the current ISO setting to operate.

Fixing Exposures with Histograms

While you can often recover poorly exposed photos in your image editor, your best bet is to arrive at the correct exposure in the camera, minimizing the tweaks that you have to make in post-processing. However, you can't always judge exposure just by viewing the image on your K200D's LCD after the shot is made. Your brightness setting for the LCD (specified in the Set-up menu as described in Chapter 3) and the amount of ambient (surrounding) light can affect the image on your screen. Instead, you are better off working with a histogram, which is a chart displayed on the K200D's LCD that shows the number of tones being captured at each brightness level. You can use the information to provide correction for the next shot you take.

You can view a histogram for an image displayed during playback by pressing the Info button until the brightness histogram appears, as shown in Figure 4.18. This screen provides a histogram at the bottom of the image that displays the distribution of luminance or brightness.

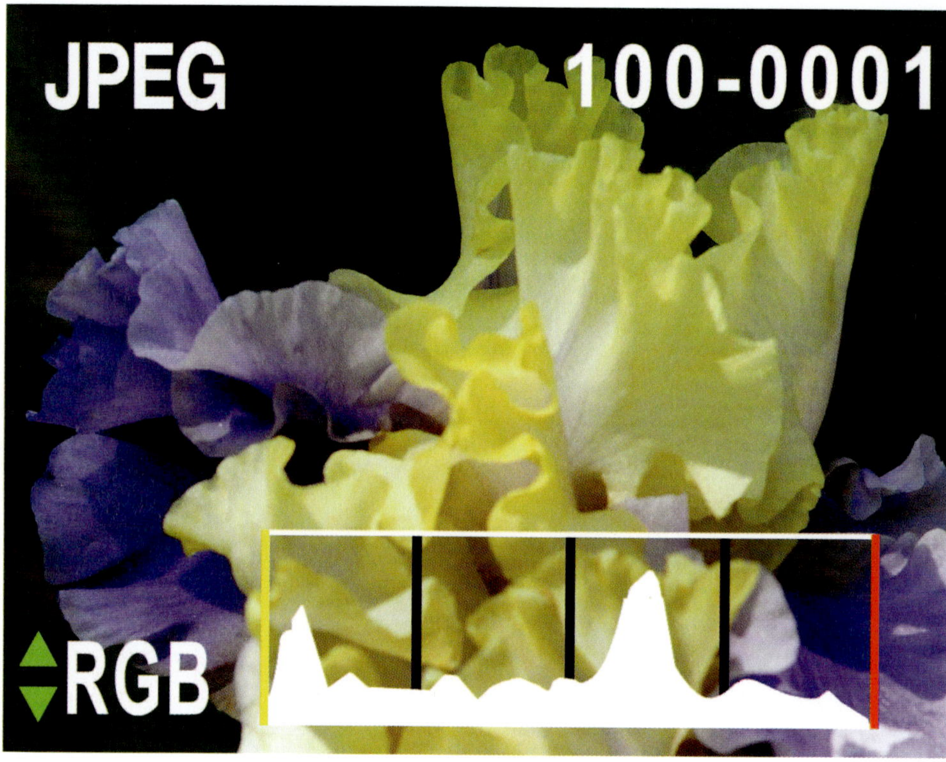

Figure 4.18
A histogram shows the relationship of tones in an image.

This histogram, called a brightness or *luminance* histogram, is a chart that includes a representation of up to 256 vertical lines on a horizontal axis that show the number of pixels in the image at each brightness level, from 0 (black) on the left side to 255 (white) on the right. (The LCD doesn't have enough pixels to show each and every one of the 256 lines, but, instead provides a representation of the shape of the curve formed.) The more pixels at a given level, the taller the bar at that position. If no bar appears at a particular position on the scale from left to right, there are no pixels at that particular brightness level.

As you can see, a typical histogram produces a mountain-like shape, with most of the pixels bunched in the middle tones, with fewer pixels at the dark and light ends of the scale. Ideally, though, there will be at least some pixels at either extreme, so that your image has both a true black and a true white representing some details. Learn to spot histograms that represent over- and underexposure, and add or subtract exposure using an EV modification to compensate.

For example, Figure 4.19 shows the histogram for an image that is badly underexposed. You can guess from the shape of the histogram that many of the dark tones to the left of the graph have been clipped off. There's plenty of room on the right side for additional pixels to reside without having them become overexposed. Or, a histogram might look like Figure 4.20, which is overexposed. In either case, you can increase or decrease the exposure (either by changing the f/stop or shutter speed in Manual mode or by adding or subtracting an EV value in A or S modes) to produce the corrected histogram shown in Figure 4.18, earlier, in which the tones "hug" the right side of the histogram to produce as many highlight details as possible. See "Making EV Changes" above for information on dialing in exposure compensation.

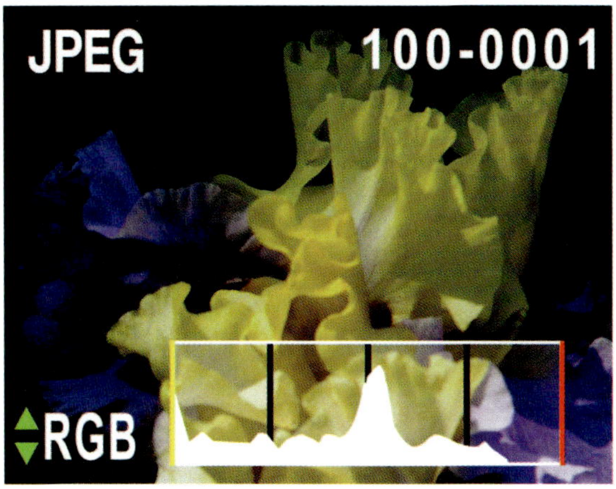

Figure 4.19 This histogram shows an underexposed image.

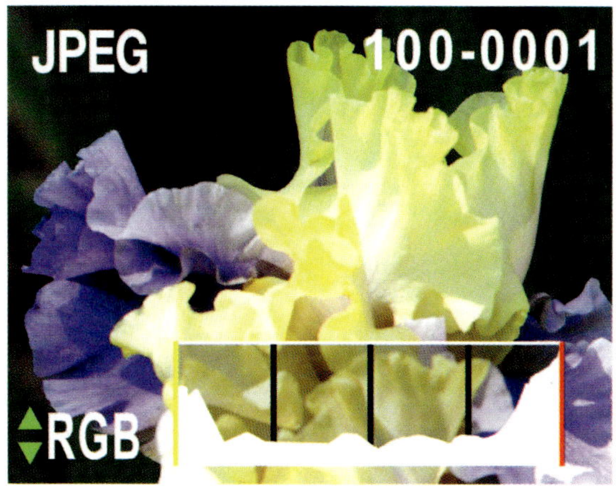

Figure 4.20 This histogram reveals that the image is overexposed.

The histogram can also be used to aid in fixing the contrast of an image, although gauging incorrect contrast is more difficult. For example, if the histogram shows all the tones bunched up in one place in the image, the photo will be low in contrast. If the tones are spread out more or less evenly, the image is probably high in contrast. In either case, your best bet may be to switch to RAW (if you're not already using that format) so you can adjust contrast in post processing.

When the brightness histogram is displayed, you can see even more information by pressing the up/down controller keys, to switch to a view that shows the image as a small thumbnail in the upper-left corner of the screen, with a brightness histogram below, and red, green, and blue (RGB) histograms arrayed at the right side (see Figure 4.21). The RGB histograms show the relative tones for each of the separate color channels. The channels can differ in rendition, and viewing their histograms makes it possible to see if one or more is "blown" (overexposed) or "blocked" (underexposed). There's not a lot you can do in the camera to modify the tones of individual colors, but advanced photographers can sometimes use the information to figure out fixes in their image editor.

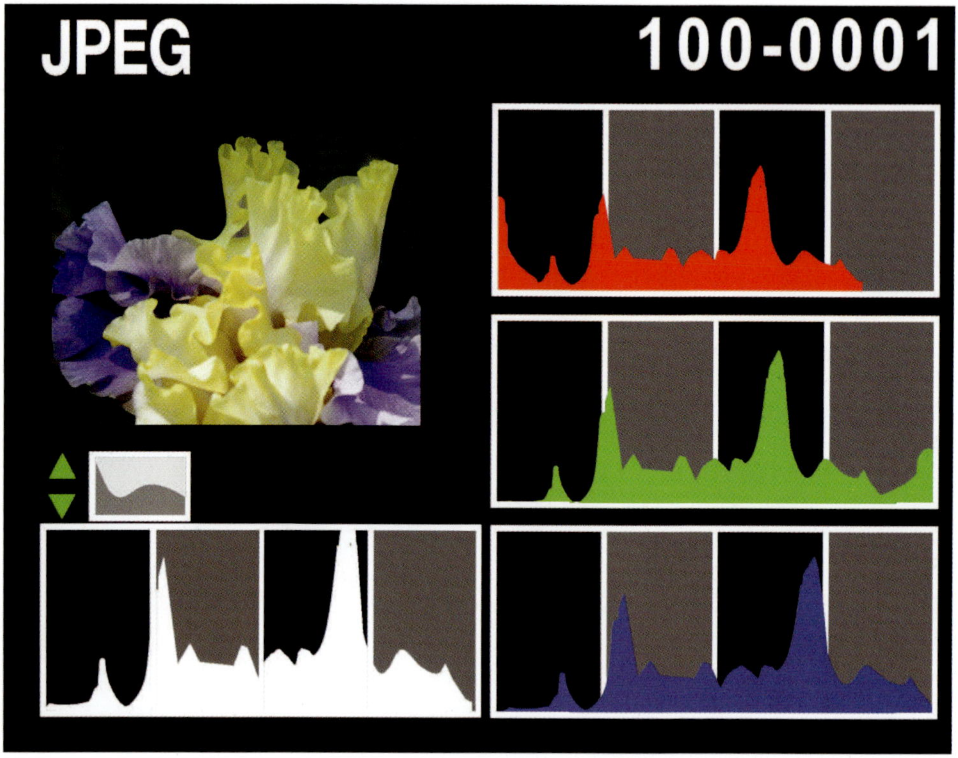

Figure 4.21 The combined brightness/RGB histogram provides the most information about tonal rendition of an image.

One useful, but often overlooked tool in evaluating histograms is the Bright/Dark area warning, which must be activated in the Playback Display menu entry described in Chapter 3. This feature causes the brightest/overexposed areas to blink red on the LCD screen during histogram review, while the underexposed areas blink yellow. (There are red and yellow vertical bars at the right and left edges of the histogram to help remind you.) These indicators can give you a better picture of what information is being lost to overexposure or underexposure.

In working with histograms, your goal should be to have all the tones in an image spread out between the edges, with none clipped off at the left and right sides. Underexposing (to preserve highlights) should be done only as a last resort, because retrieving the underexposed shadows in your image editor will frequently increase the noise, even if you're working with RAW files. A better course of action is to expose for the highlights, but, when the subject matter makes it practical, fill in the shadows with additional light, using reflectors, fill flash, or other techniques rather than allowing them to be seriously underexposed.

Bracketing

Bracketing is a method for shooting several consecutive exposures using different settings, as a way of improving the odds that one will be exactly right. Before digital cameras took over the universe, it was common to bracket exposures, shooting, say, a series of three photos at 1/125th second, but varying the f/stop from f/8 to f/11 to f/16. In practice, smaller than whole-stop increments were used for greater precision, and lenses with apertures that were set manually commonly had half-stop detents on their aperture rings, or could easily be set to a mid-way position between whole f/stops. It was just as common to keep the same aperture and vary the shutter speed, although in the days before electronic shutters, film cameras often had only whole increment shutter speeds available.

Today, cameras like the K200D can bracket exposures much more precisely, using an increment that you select. When this feature is activated, the K200D takes three consecutive photos: one at the metered "correct" exposure, one with less exposure ("underexposed"), and one with more exposure ("overexposed"), using an increment of your choice up to two stops. Just follow these steps:

1. Tap the shutter release to activate Capture mode.
2. Press the Fn button to produce the Capture Functions screen.
3. Press the up controller button to access the Drive Mode screen (see Figure 4.22). The increments on the scale are either 1/2 or 1/3 stop, depending on your setting for CS #1 (EV Steps) in the Custom Setting menu, as described in Chapter 3.

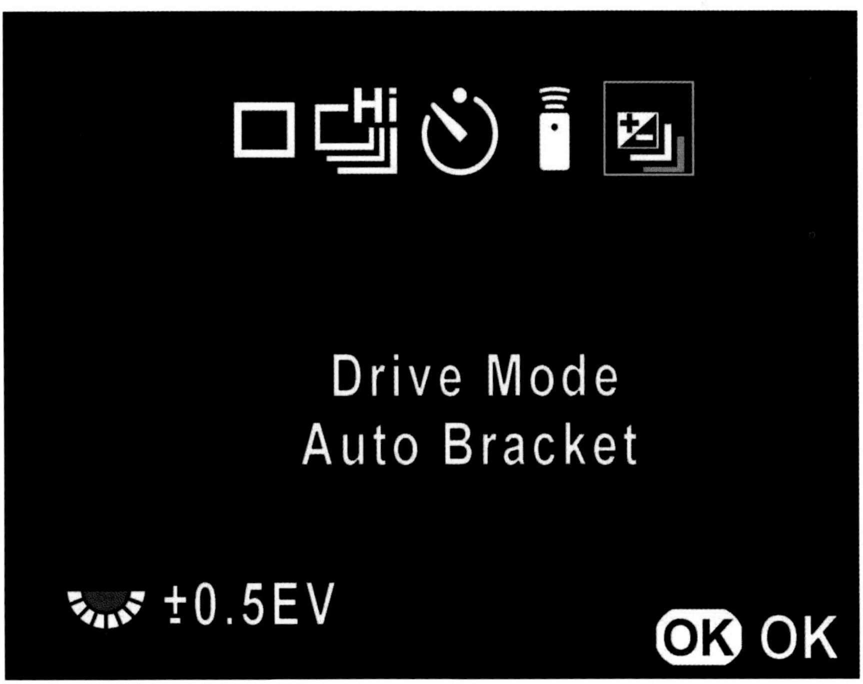

Figure 4.22 Select Auto Bracketing from the Drive mode menu.

4. Rotate the e-dial to choose a bracketing increment from 0.3 (or 0.5 with half-stop increments) to 2.0 stops.
5. Press OK to confirm your choice.
6. The bracketing indicator appears in the viewfinder and on the top-panel monochrome LCD (see Figure 4.23).
7. Press the shutter release and the K200D will take three consecutive photos bracketed using the increment you've chosen (Figure 4.24).

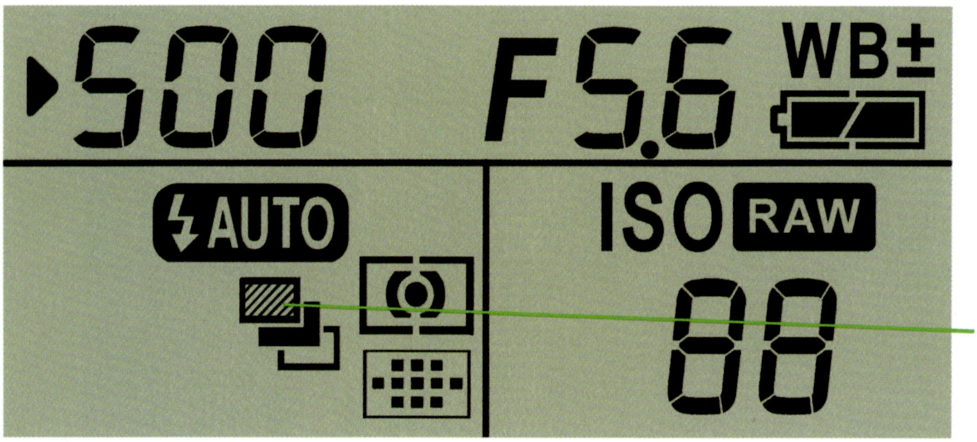

Figure 4.23
The bracketing indicator appears when the feature is activated.

More on Bracketing

There are a few additional things to keep in mind when using bracketing. Here's a quick summary:

- **Incremental improvements.** Use small increments, such as 1/3 f/stop to fine-tune exposure. Use larger increments, up to 2 full stops between photos, for dramatic differences that produce varied creative effects. Large increments are also useful when bracketing for images that you'll be merging to produce one high dynamic range (HDR) photo (discussed next).
- **Changing order.** By default the K200D exposes the first image at the metered exposure, the second with less exposure, and the third with extra exposure. A shorthand way of expressing this bracketing order is 0,–,+. You might prefer to use a different order, such as underexposure, metered exposure, overexposure (–,0,+), which makes it simpler to review, say, progressively lighter versions of the same image for comparison. Change the order using Custom Setting #6, as described in Chapter 3.
- **Cancel bracketing.** Like any Drive mode, once you've activated bracketing, it remains operational until you visit the Drive mode menu again and choose another mode, such as Single Shot. That's true, even if you shut the camera off: the next

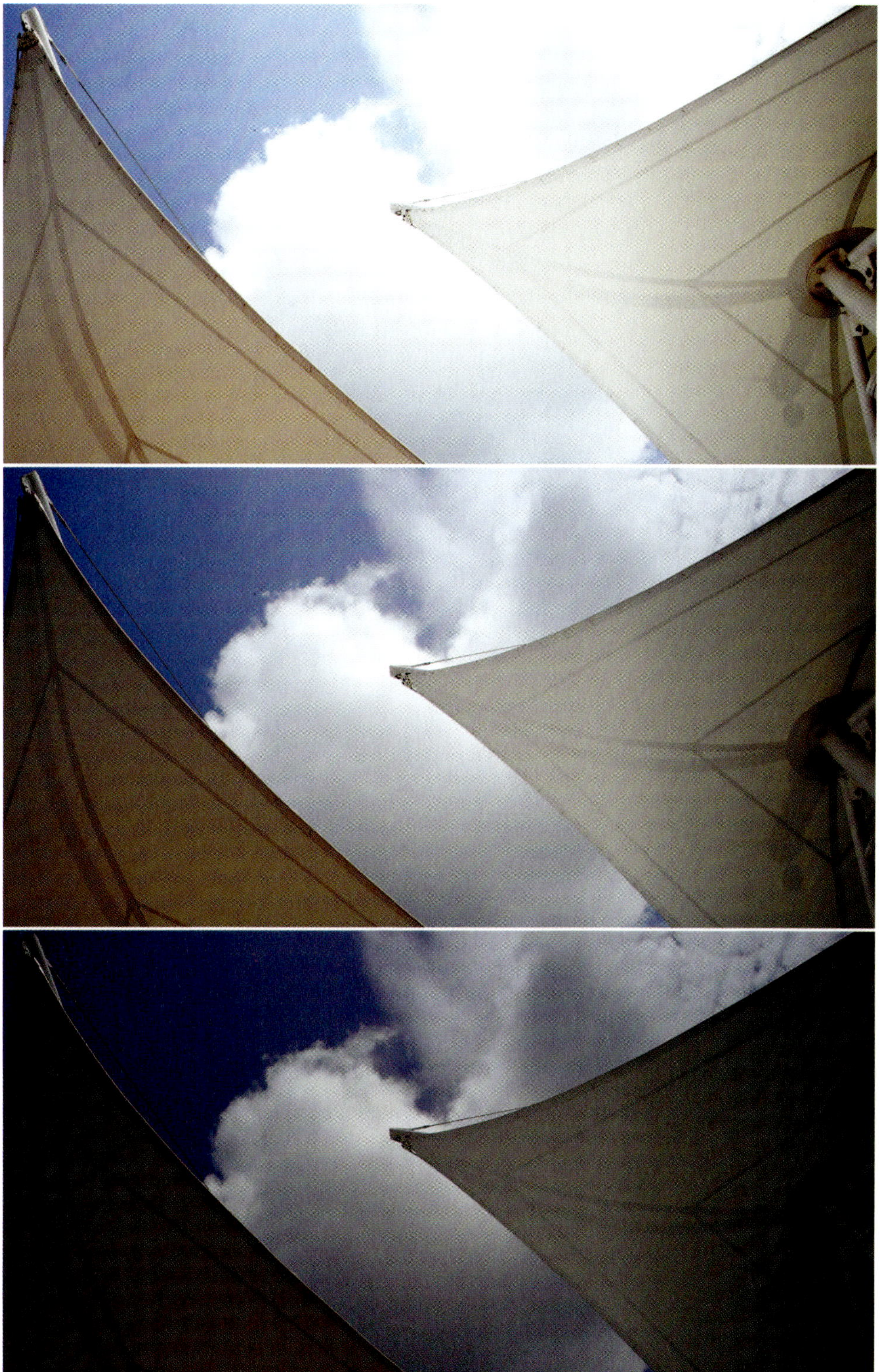

Figure 4.24
The flare caused by backlighting (center of each image) makes metering this scene tricky. Bracketing can give you three different versions; one with more exposure (top); the metered exposure (middle); and less exposure (bottom).

time you turn your K200D on, it will return to Bracketing mode. So, you must remember to turn this feature off when you no longer want to use it. Or, you can uncheck the "remember Drive Mode" box in the Menu entry in the Recording menu, and the K200D will then forget the current drive mode and return to Single Shot each time the camera is switched on.

- **Over, under.** Bracketing can't be set to cluster the exposures so that only overexposures or only underexposures are taken. Fortunately, however, you can trick the Pentax K200D into doing just that. Simply add or subtract exposure compensation using the Av button and e-dial, so that the "metered" exposure is more or less than it would be without an EV adjustment. For example, with the camera set for a +1EV and 1/3-step bracketing, you'll end up with one photo that's 1.3 stops more than the metered exposure, one that's 1.0 stops more than the metered exposure, and one that's 0.7 stops more than the metered exposure.

Bracketing and Merge to HDR

HDR (High Density Range) photography is, at the moment, an incredibly popular fad. There are even entire books that do nothing but tell you how to shoot HDR images. If you aren't familiar with the technique, HDR involves shooting two or three or more images at different bracketed exposures, giving you an "underexposed" version with lots of detail in highlights that would otherwise be washed out, an "overexposed" rendition that preserves detail in the shadows, and several intermediate shots. These are combined to produce a single image that has an amazing amount of detail throughout the scene's entire tonal range.

I call this technique a fad because the reason it exists in the first place is due to a (temporary, I hope) defect in current digital camera sensors. It's presently impossible to capture the full range of brightness that we perceive; digital cameras, including the Pentax K200D can't even grab the full range of brightness that *film* can see. But as the megapixel race slows down, sensor designers have already begun designing capture electronics that have larger density (dynamic) ranges, and I fully expect to see cameras within a few years that can produce images similar to what we're getting now with HDR manipulation in image editors.

HDR works like this: Suppose you wanted to photograph a dimly lit room that had a bright window showing an outdoors scene. Proper exposure for the room might be on the order of 1/60th second at f/2.8 at ISO 200, while the outdoors scene probably would require f/11 at 1/400th second. That's almost a 7 EV step difference (approximately 7 f/stops) and well beyond the dynamic range of any digital camera, including the Pentax K200D.

When you're using Merge to HDR, a feature found in Adobe Photoshop (similar functions are available in other programs, including Photomatix [www.hdrsoft.com; free to try, $99 to buy; also available with a Photoshop plug-in]), you'd take several pictures.

As I mentioned earlier, one would be exposed for the shadows, one for the highlights, and perhaps one for the midtones. Then, you'd use the Merge to HDR command (or the equivalent in other software) to combine all of the images into one HDR image that integrates the well-exposed sections of each version. You can use the Pentax K200D's bracketing feature to produce those images.

The images should be as identical as possible, except for exposure. So, it's a good idea to mount the K200D on a tripod, use a remote release, and take all the exposures in one burst. Just follow these steps:

1. Mount the K200D on a tripod and connect the remote release cable.
2. Set the camera to shoot RAW images, as described in Chapter 3.
3. Set bracketing to a 2-stop increment, as described above and in Chapter 3.
4. Change bracketing order to –, 0,+, if necessary. This will give you a continuous bracketed set of underexposed, metered exposure, and overexposed images.
5. Manually focus or autofocus the K200D.
6. Trigger the camera to expose your set of three images.
7. Copy your images to your computer and continue in Photoshop with the Merge to HDR steps listed next.

The next steps show you how to combine the separate exposures into one merged high dynamic range image. The sample images shown in Figures 4.25, 4.26, and 4.28 show the results you can get from a two-shot bracketed sequence. I merged only two pictures for simplicity, because the differences between three or more bracketed exposures, even when taken at exposures that are 2 stops apart, can be too subtle to show up well on the printed page.

1. If you use an application to transfer the files to your computer, make sure it does not make any adjustments to brightness, contrast, or exposure. You want the real raw information for Merge to HDR to work with. If you do everything correctly, you'll end up with at least two photos like the ones shown in Figures 4.25 and 4.26.
2. Load the images into Photoshop using your preferred RAW converter.
3. Save as .PSD files.
3. Activate Merge to HDR by choosing File > Automate > Merge to HDR.
4. Select the photos to be merged, as shown in Figure 4.27, where I have specified the two PSD files. You'll note a check box that can be used to automatically align the images if they were not taken with the K200D mounted on a rock-steady support.
5. Once HDR merge has done its thing, you must save in .PSD to retain the file's full color information, in case you want to work with the HDR image later. Otherwise, you can convert to a normal 24-bit file and save in any compatible format.

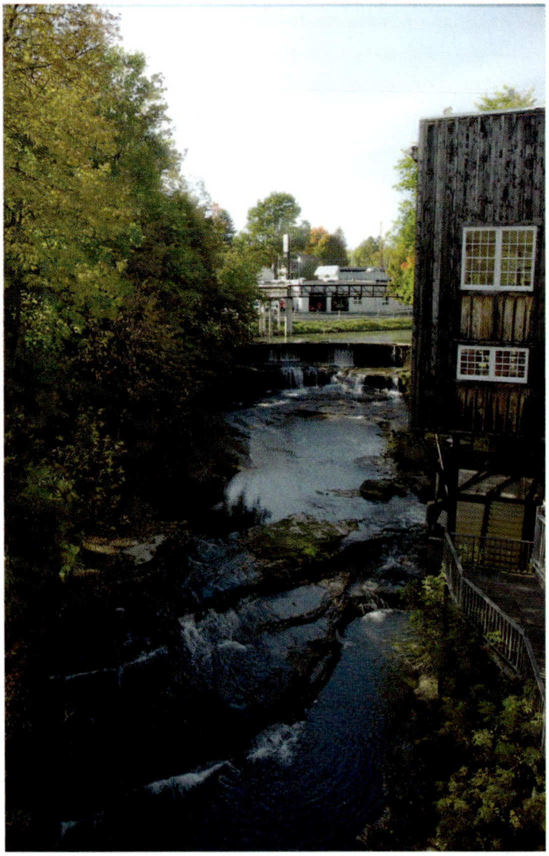

Figure 4.25 Make one exposure for the shadow areas.

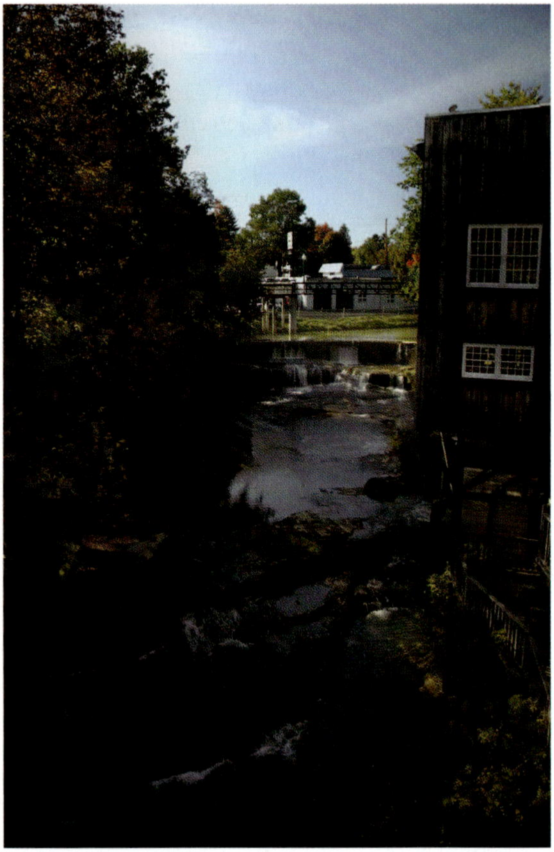

Figure 4.26 Make a second exposure for the highlights, such as the sky.

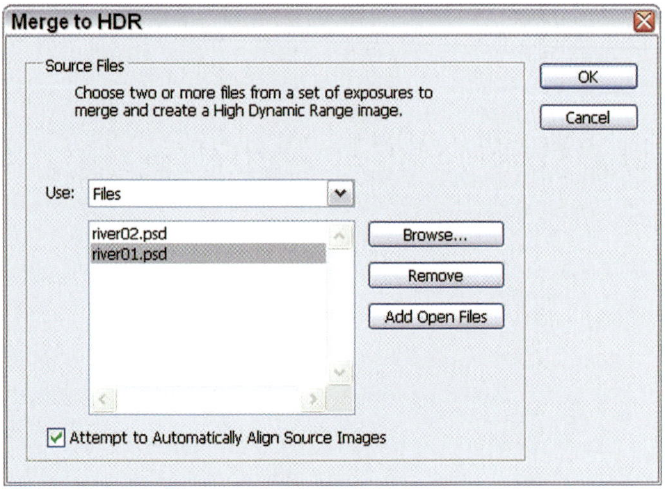

Figure 4.27 Use the Merge to HDR command to combine the two images.

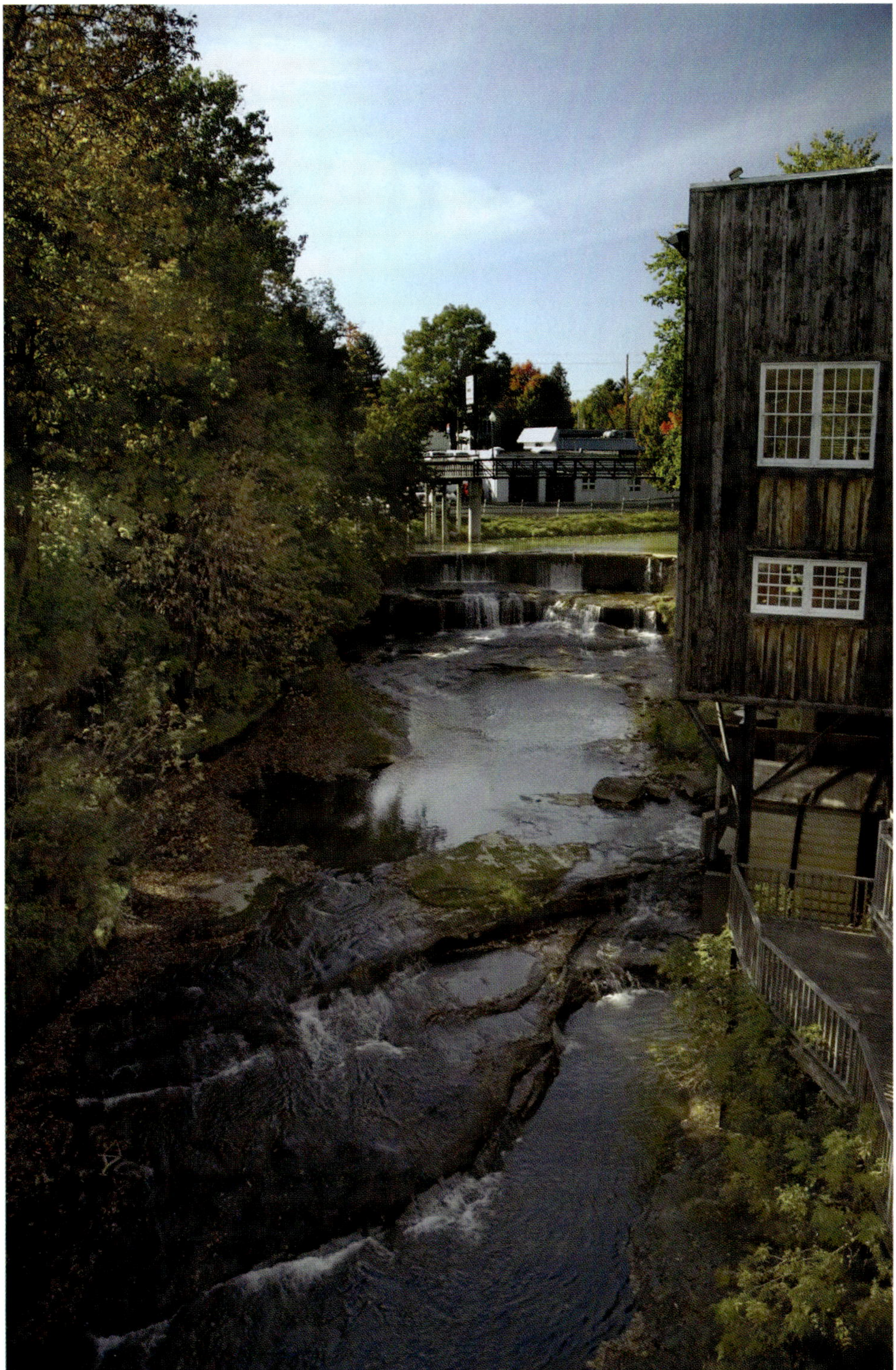

Figure 4.28 You'll end up with an extended dynamic range photo like this one.

If you do everything correctly, you'll end up with a photo like the one shown in Figure 4.28, which has the properly exposed foreground of the first shot, and the well-exposed sky of the second image. Note that, ideally, nothing should move between shots. In the example pictures, the river is moving, but the exposures were made so close together that, after the merger, you can't really tell.

What if you don't have the opportunity, inclination, or skills to create several images at different exposures, as described? If you shoot in RAW format, you can still use Merge to HDR, working with a *single* original image file. What you do is import the image into Photoshop several times, using Adobe Camera Raw to create multiple copies of the file at different exposure levels.

For example, you'd create one copy that's too dark, so the shadows lose detail, but the highlights are preserved. Create another copy with the shadows intact and allow the highlights to wash out. Then, you can use Merge to HDR to combine the two and end up with a finished image that has the extended dynamic range you're looking for.

5

Advanced Techniques for Your Pentax K200D

The typical new user of a sophisticated camera like the Pentax K200D passes through three stages on the road to proficiency. When the camera first came out of the box, you probably spent a lot of time learning its basic features, and setting it up to take decent pictures automatically, with little input from you. It probably felt great to gain the confidence to snap off picture after picture, knowing that a large percentage of them were going to be well-exposed, in sharp focus, and rich with color.

After you were comfortable with your camera, you began looking for ways to add your own creativity to your shots. You explored ways of tweaking the exposure, using selective focus, and, perhaps, experimenting with the different looks that various lens zoom settings (*focal lengths*) could offer.

The final, and most rewarding, stage comes when you begin exploring advanced techniques that enable you to get stunning shots that will have your family, friends, and colleagues asking you, "How did you *do* that?" These more advanced techniques deserve an entire book of their own (and I have one for you called *Digital SLR Pro Secrets*, also from Course Technology). But there is plenty of room in this chapter to introduce you to some clever things you can do with your K200D.

Beyond Good Exposure

In Chapter 4, you learned techniques for getting the *right* exposure, but I haven't explained all your exposure options just yet. You'll want to know about the *kind* of exposure settings that are available to you with the Pentax K200D. There are options that let you control when the exposure is made, or even how to make an exposure that's out of the ordinary in terms of length (time or bulb exposures). These capabilities all let you take pictures that are surprising and effective.

Short Exposures

Fast shutter speeds stop action because they capture only a tiny slice of time. Electronic flash also freezes motion by virtue of its extremely short duration—as brief as 1/20,000th second or less (with the top-of-the-line Pentax AF540FGZ electronic external flash). The K200D's 1/4,000 second shutter speed and its built-in flash unit both can give you these ultra-quick glimpses of moving subjects. An external flash offers even more versatility. You can read more about using electronic flash to stop action in Chapter 7.

In this chapter, I'm going to emphasize the use of short exposures to capture a moment in time. The K200D is fully capable of immobilizing all but the fastest movement using only its shutter speeds, which range all the way up to 1/4,000th second. While some cameras have speeds up to 1/8,000 second, those ultra-fast shutters are generally overkill when it comes to stopping action, and rarely needed for achieving the exposure you desire.

For example, if you wanted to use an aperture of f/1.8 at ISO 100 outdoors in bright sunlight, for some reason, the K200D's top shutter speed would more than do the job. You'd need a faster shutter speed only if you moved the ISO setting to a higher sensitivity, and you probably wouldn't do that if your goal was to use the widest f/stop possible. Under *less* than full sunlight, 1/4,000th second is more than fast enough for any conditions you're likely to encounter.

When it comes to stopping action, most sports can be frozen at 1/2,000th second or slower, and for many sports a slower shutter speed is actually preferable—for example, to allow the wheels of a racing automobile or motorcycle, or the propeller on a classic aircraft to blur realistically. Figure 5.1 is one example. The 1/500th second shutter speed more or less stopped the soccer players in mid-stride, but there is still enough blur in their legs and the ball to provide a feeling of motion. If the ball were perfectly sharp, it might look on first glance as if it were suspended in mid-air. The blur tells us that this shot wasn't faked.

But if you want to do some exotic action-freezing photography without resorting to electronic flash, the K200D's top shutter speed is at your disposal. Here are some things to think about when exploring this type of high-speed photography:

- **You'll need a lot of light.** High shutter speeds cut very fine slices of time and sharply reduce the amount of illumination that reaches your sensor. To use 1/4,000th second at an aperture of f/6.3, you'd need an ISO setting of 1,600—even in full daylight. To use an f/stop smaller than f/6.3 or an ISO setting lower than 1,600, you'd need *more* light than full daylight provides. (That's why electronic flash units work so well for high-speed photography when used as the sole illumination; they provide both the effect of a brief shutter speed and the high levels of illumination needed.)

- **Forget about reciprocity failure.** If you're an old-time film shooter, you might recall that very brief shutter speeds (as well as very high light levels and very *long* exposures) produced an effect called *reciprocity failure,* in which given exposures ended up providing less than the calculated value because of the way film responded to very short, very intense, or very long exposures of light. Solid-state sensors don't suffer from this defect, so you don't need to make an adjustment when using high shutter speeds (or brief flash bursts).
- **No elongation effect.** This is another old bugaboo that has largely been solved through modern technology, but I wanted to bring it to your attention anyway. In olden times, cameras used shutters that traveled horizontally. To achieve faster shutter speeds, focal plane shutters (located just in front of the plane of the sensor) open only a smaller-than-frame-sized slit so that, even though the shutter is already

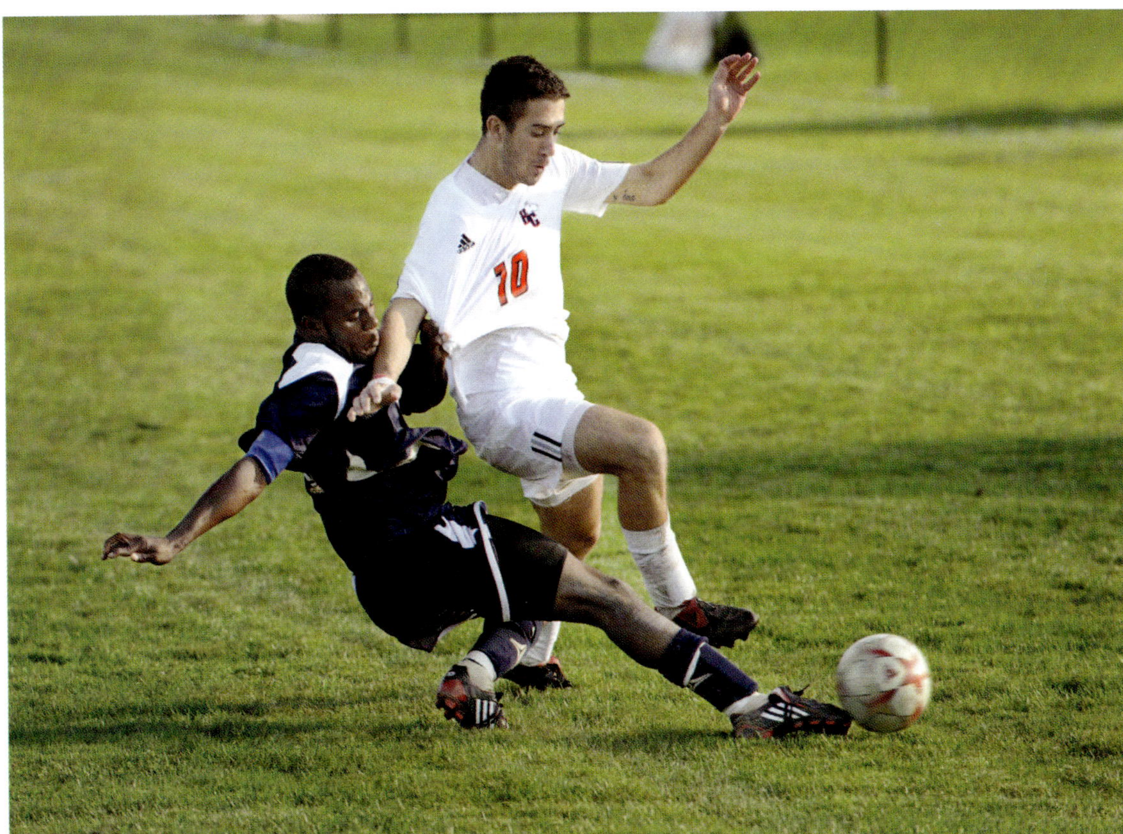

Figure 5.1 A little blur can be a good thing, as the soccer ball adds excitement to this action shot.

traveling at its highest rate of speed, the film/sensor is exposed for a briefer period of time as the slit moves across the surface. At very short shutter speeds, and with subjects moving horizontally at very fast velocities, it was possible for the subject to partially "keep up" with the shutter if it were traveling in the same direction as the slit, producing an elongated effect. Conversely, subjects moving in the opposite direction of shutter motion could be compressed. Today, shutters like those in the K200D move vertically and at a higher maximum rate of speed. So, unless you're photographing a rocket blasting into space, and holding the camera horizontally to boot (or shooting a racing car in vertical orientation), it's almost impossible to produce unwanted elongation/compression.

- **Don't combine high shutter speeds with electronic flash.** You might be tempted to use an electronic flash with a high shutter speed. Perhaps you want to stop some action in daylight with a brief shutter speed and use electronic flash only as supplemental illumination to fill in the shadows. Unfortunately, under most conditions you can't use flash in subdued illumination with your K200D at any shutter speed faster than 1/180th second, the top speed that syncs with electronic flash. That's the fastest speed at which the camera's focal plane shutter is fully open: at shorter speeds, the "slit" described above comes into play, so that the flash will expose only the small portion of the sensor exposed by the slit during its duration.

Working with Short Exposures

You can have a lot of fun exploring the kinds of pictures you can take using very brief exposure times, whether you decide to take advantage of the action-stopping capabilities of your built-in or external electronic flash or work with the Pentax K200D's faster shutter speeds. Here are a few ideas to get you started:

- **Take revealing images.** Fast shutter speeds can help you reveal the real subject behind the façade, by freezing constant motion to capture an enlightening moment in time. Legendary fashion/portrait photographer Philippe Halsman used leaping photos of famous people, such as the Duke and Duchess of Windsor, Richard Nixon, and Salvador Dali to illuminate their real selves. Halsman said, "*When you ask a person to jump, his attention is mostly directed toward the act of jumping and the mask falls so that the real person appears.*" Try some high-speed portraits of people you know in motion to see how they appear when concentrating on something other than the portrait.

- **Create unreal images.** High-speed photography can also produce photographs that show your subjects in ways that are quite unreal. A helicopter in mid-air with its rotors frozen or a motocross cyclist leaping over a ramp, but with all motion stopped so that the rider and machine look as if they were frozen in mid-air, make for an unusual picture. (See Figure 5.2.) When we're accustomed to seeing subjects in motion, seeing them stopped in time can verge on the surreal.

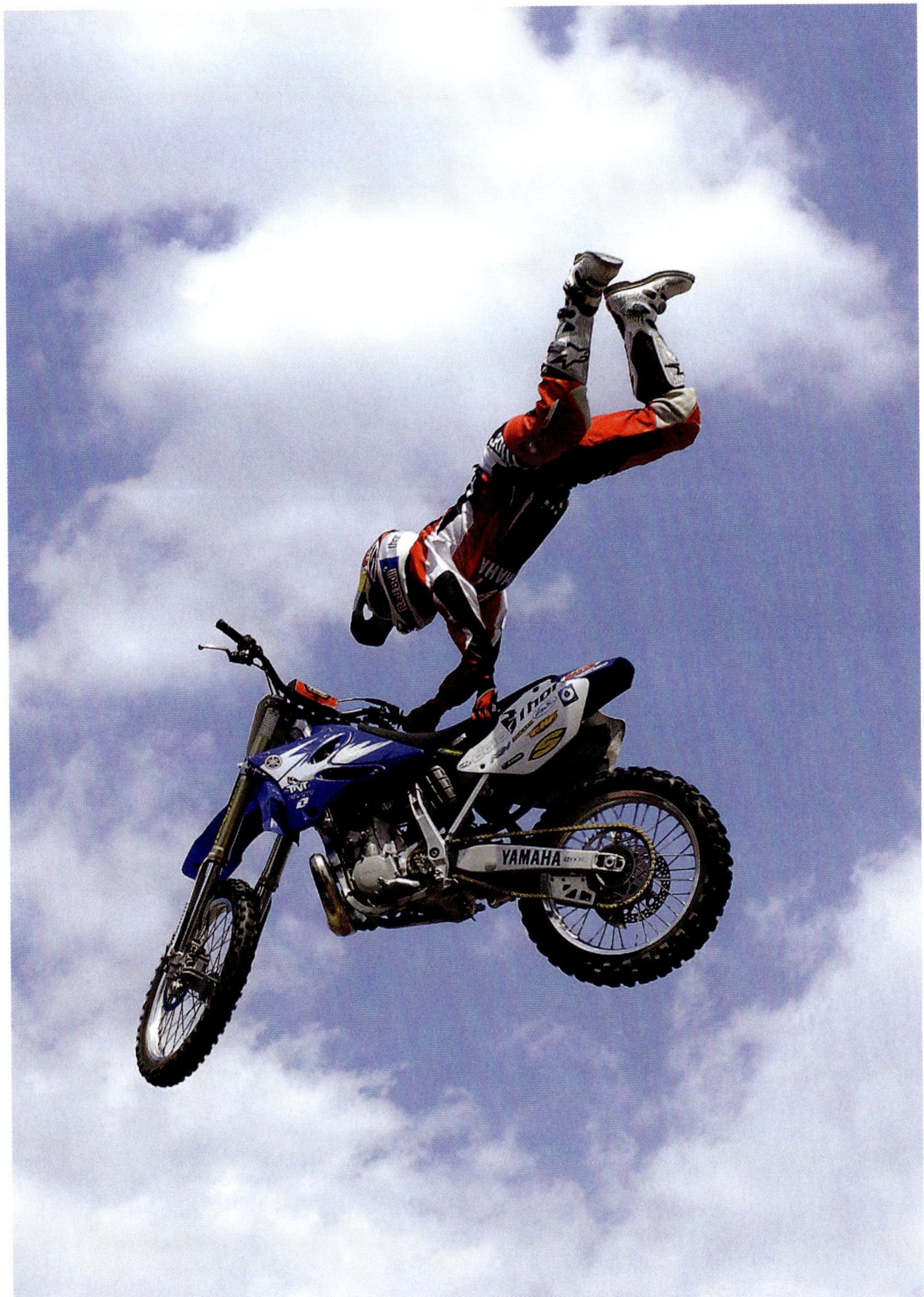

Figure 5.2
Freezing a leaping motocross rider in mid-air makes for an image that verges on the surreal.

- **Capture unseen perspectives.** Some things are *never* seen in real life, except when viewed in a stop-action photograph. Dr. Harold Edgerton's balloon bursts at MIT, starting in the 1930s, were only a starting point. Freeze a hummingbird in flight for a view of wings that never seem to stop. Or, capture the splashes as liquid falls into a bowl, as shown in Figure 5.3. No electronic flash was required for this image (and wouldn't have illuminated the water in the bowl as evenly). Instead, a clutch of high intensity lamps and an ISO setting of 1,600 allowed the K200D to capture this image at 1/2,000th second.

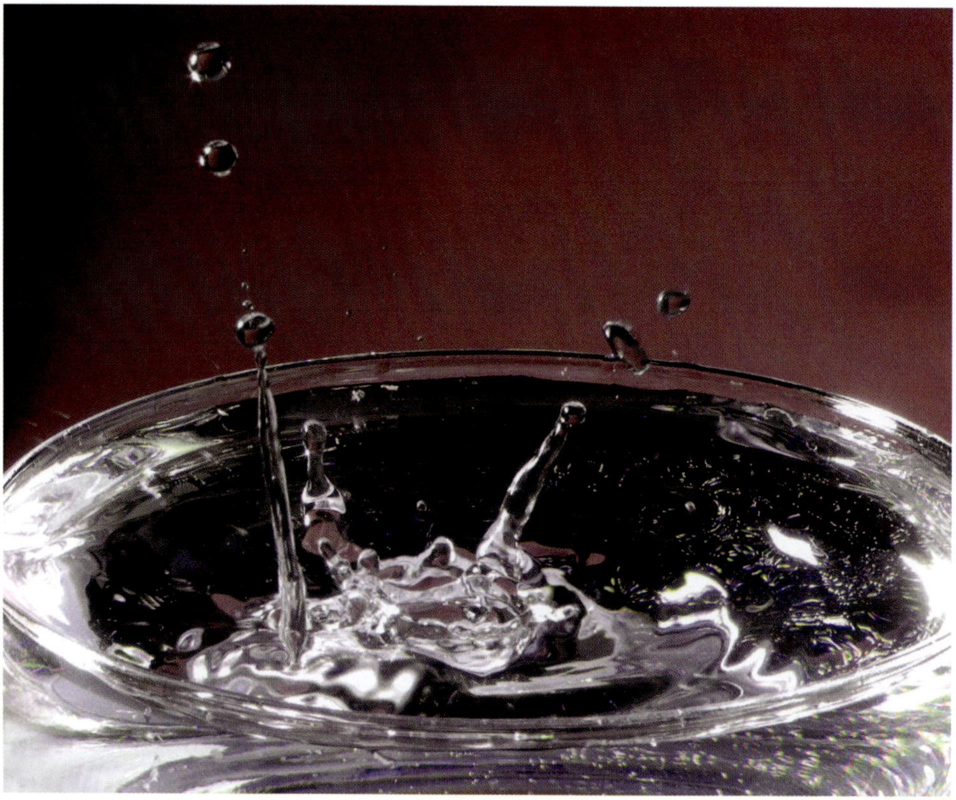

Figure 5.3
A large amount of artificial illumination and an ISO 1,600 sensitivity setting allowed capturing this shot at 1/2,000th second without use of an electronic flash.

- **Vanquish camera shake and gain new angles.** Here's an idea that's so obvious it isn't always explored to its fullest extent. A high enough shutter speed can free you from the tyranny of a tripod, making it easier to capture new angles, or to shoot quickly while moving around, especially with longer lenses. I tend to use a monopod or tripod for almost everything, and I end up missing some shots because of a reluctance to adjust my camera support to get a higher, lower, or different angle. If you have enough light and can use an f/stop wide enough to permit a high shutter speed, you'll find a new freedom to choose your shots. I have a favored

170mm-500mm lens that I use for sports and wildlife photography, almost invariably with a tripod, as I don't find the "reciprocal of the focal length" rule particularly helpful in most cases. (I would *not* handhold this hefty lens at its 500mm setting with a 1/500th second shutter speed under most circumstances, even given the forgiving nature of the K200D's Anti-Shake technology.) However, at 1/2,000th second or faster, it's entirely possible for a steady hand to use this lens without a tripod or monopod's extra support, and I've found that my whole approach to shooting animals and other elusive subjects changes in high-speed mode. Selective focus allows dramatically isolating my prey wide open at f/6.3, too.

Long Exposures

Longer exposures are a doorway into another world, showing us how even familiar scenes can look much different when photographed over periods measured in seconds. At night, long exposures produce streaks of light from moving, illuminated subjects like automobiles or amusement park rides. Extra-long exposures of seemingly pitch-dark subjects can reveal interesting views using light levels barely bright enough to see by. At any time of day, including daytime (in which case you'll often need the help of neutral density filters to make the long exposure practical), long exposures can cause moving objects to vanish entirely, because they don't remain stationary long enough to register in a photograph.

Three Ways to Take Long Exposures

There are actually three common types of lengthy exposures: *timed exposures, bulb exposures,* and *time exposures.* The K200D offers only the first two, but once you understand all three, you'll see why Pentax made the choices it did. Because of the length of the exposure, all of the following techniques should be used with a tripod to hold the camera steady.

- **Timed exposures.** These are long exposures from 1 second to 30 seconds, measured by the camera itself. To take a picture in this range, simply use Manual or Tv modes and use the e-dial to set the shutter speed to the length of time you want, choosing from preset speeds of 1.0, 1.5, 2.0, 3.0, 4.0, 6.0, 8.0, 10.0, 15.0, 20.0, or 30.0 seconds (if you've specified 1/2 stop increments for exposure adjustments), or 1.0, 1.3, 1.6, 2.0, 2.5, 3.2, 4.0, 5.0, 6.0, 8.0, 10.0, 13.0, 15.0, 20.0, 25.0, and 30.0 seconds (if you're using 1/3 stop increments). The advantage of timed exposures is that the camera does all the calculating for you. There's no need for a stop-watch. If you review your image on the LCD and decide to try again with the exposure doubled or halved, you can dial in the correct exposure with precision. The disadvantage of timed exposures is that you can't take a photo for longer than 30 seconds.

- **Bulb exposures.** This type of exposure is so-called because in the olden days the photographer squeezed and held an air bulb attached to a tube that provided the force necessary to keep the shutter open. Traditionally, a bulb exposure is one that lasts as long as the shutter release button is pressed; when you release the button, the exposure ends. To make a bulb exposure with the K200D, rotate the Mode dial to the Bulb position. (A bu indicator will appear in the viewfinder and on the top-panel monochrome LCD.) Then, press the shutter to start the exposure, and release it again to close the shutter. If you're using the Pentax Remote Control F infrared remote and have set the Drive mode to Remote, or are using the optional CS-205 cable switch, you can hold down the button on the unit to perform a bulb exposure.

Tip

Note that when using the bulb exposure mode, certain features are disabled or modified. Shake reduction is switched off, because it's unlikely to be of much help if you are hand-holding a bulb exposure, and you won't need it if the camera is mounted on a tripod for the bulb exposure. Exposure (EV) compensation, Continuous shooting, and Exposure Bracketing are also disabled. If you've set ISO sensitivity to Auto, sensitivity is fixed at ISO 200 if you've turned on the Dynamic Range Expansion option (as described in Chapter 4). If you've turned the feature off, it's fixed at ISO 100.

- **Time exposures.** This is a setting found on some cameras to produce longer exposures. With cameras that implement this option, the shutter opens when you press the shutter release button, and remains open until you press the button again. Usually, you'll be able to close the shutter using a mechanical cable release or, more commonly, an electronic release cable. The advantage of this approach is that you can take an exposure of virtually any duration without the need for special equipment (the tethered release is optional). You can press the shutter release button, go off for a few minutes, and come back to close the shutter (assuming your camera is still there). The disadvantages of this mode are exposures must be timed manually, and with shorter exposures it's possible for the vibration of manually opening and closing the shutter to register in the photo. For longer exposures, the period of vibration is relatively brief and not usually a problem—and there is always the release cable option to eliminate photographer-caused camera shake entirely. While the K200D does not have a built-in time exposure capability, you can simulate it with the bulb exposure technique, described previously.

Working with Long Exposures

Because the K200D produces such good images at longer exposures, and there are so many creative things you can do with long-exposure techniques, you'll want to do some experimenting. Get yourself a tripod or another firm support and take some test shots with long exposure noise reduction both enabled and disabled (to see whether you prefer low noise or high detail) and get started. Here are some things to try:

- **Make people invisible.** One very cool thing about long exposures is that objects that move rapidly enough won't register at all in a photograph, while the subjects that remain stationary are portrayed in the normal way. That makes it easy to produce people-free landscape photos and architectural photos at night or, even, in full daylight if you use a neutral density filter (or two or three) to allow an exposure of at least a few seconds. At ISO 100, f/22, and a pair of 8X (three-stop) neutral density filters you can use exposures of nearly two seconds; overcast days and/or even more neutral density filtration would work even better if daylight people-vanishing is your goal. They'll have to be walking *very* briskly and across the field of view (rather than directly toward the camera) for this to work. At night, it's much easier to achieve this effect with the 20- to 30-second exposures that are possible, as you can see in Figure 5.4.

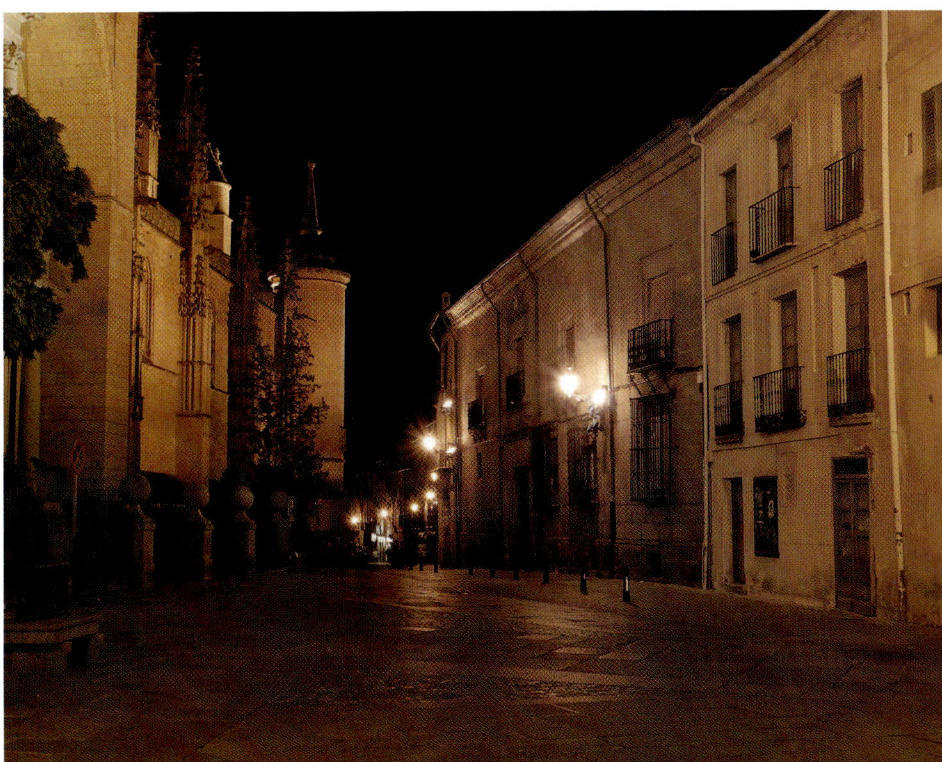

Figure 5.4 This alleyway is thronged with people, but you can't see them because of this 20 second exposure using only the available illumination.

- **Create streaks.** If you aren't shooting for total invisibility, long exposures with the camera on a tripod can produce some interesting streaky effects. Even a single 8X ND filter will let you shoot at f/22 and 1/6th second in daylight. Indoors, you can achieve interesting streaks with slow shutter speeds, as shown in Figure 5.5. For this shot, the camera lens was mounted on a monopod using the lens's tripod collar, and I loosened the collar and rotated the camera during a one second exposure.

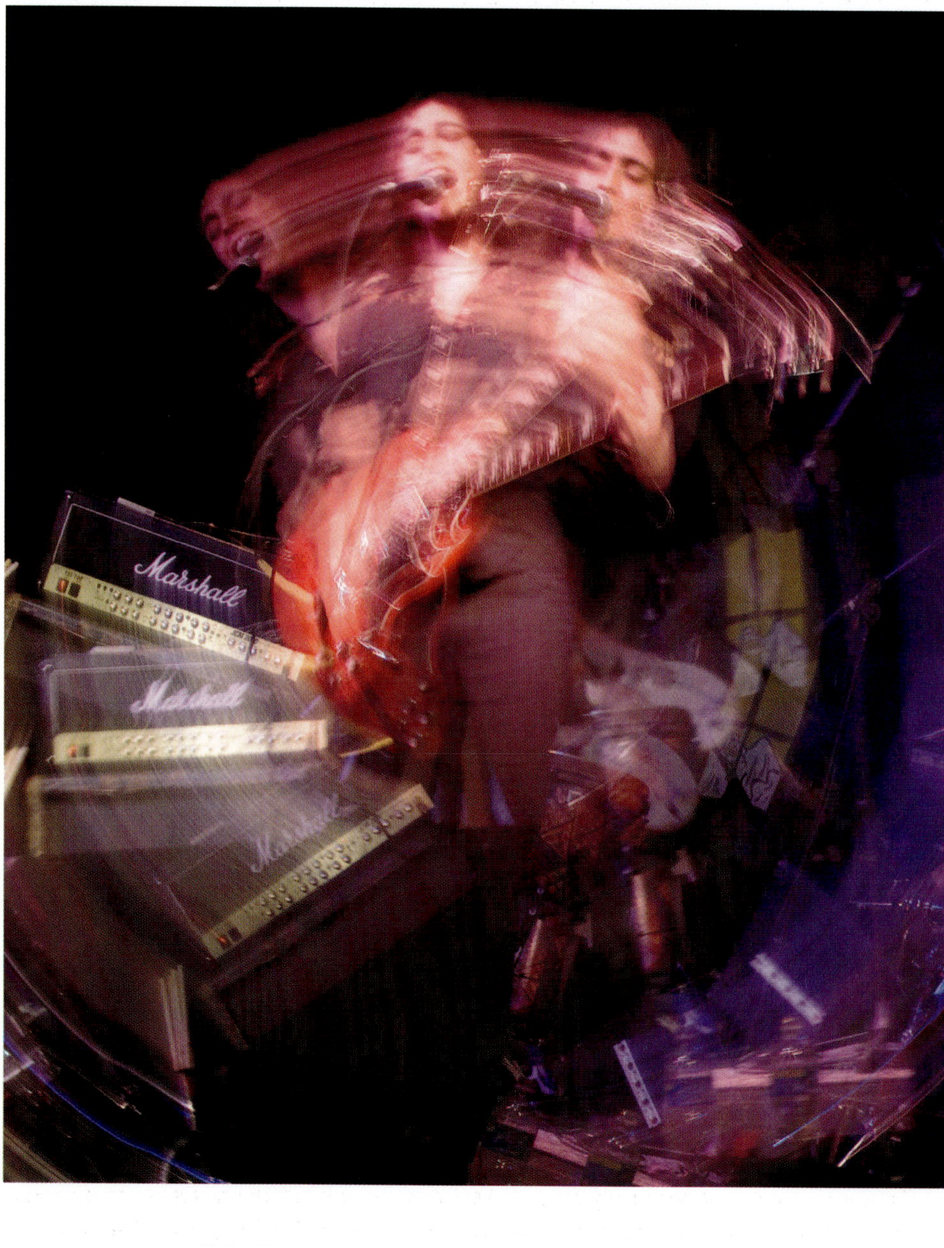

Figure 5.5
Rotating the camera during a long exposure produced this dynamic effect.

> **Tip**
>
> Neutral density filters are gray (non-colored) filters that reduce the amount of light passing through the lens, without adding any color or effect of their own.

- **Produce light trails.** At night, car headlights and taillights and other moving sources of illumination can generate interesting light trails. If you're shooting fireworks, a longer exposure may allow you to combine several bursts into one picture, as shown in Figure 5.6. Your camera doesn't even need to be mounted on a tripod; hand-holding the K200D for longer exposures adds movement and patterns to your trails.

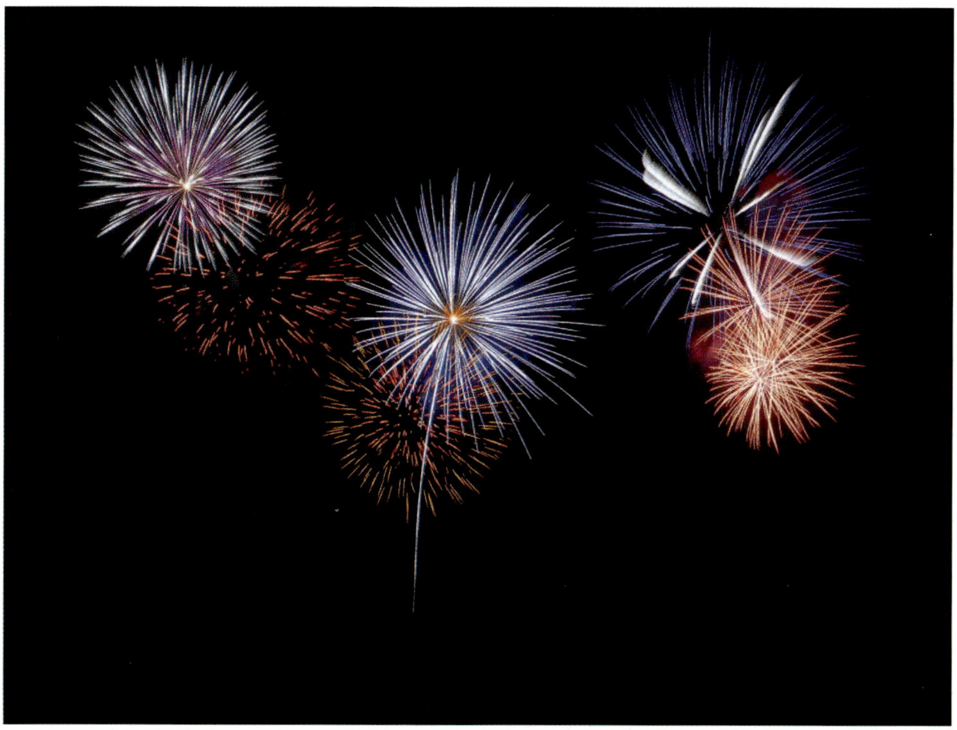

Figure 5.6 I caught the fireworks after a baseball game from a half-mile away, using a four-second exposure to capture several bursts in one shot.

- **Blur waterfalls, etc.** You'll find that waterfalls and other sources of moving liquid produce a special type of long-exposure blur, because the water merges into a fantasy-like veil that looks different at different exposure times, and with different waterfalls. Cascades with turbulent flow produce a rougher look at a given longer exposure than falls that flow smoothly. Although blurred waterfalls have become almost a cliché, there are still plenty of variations for a creative photographer to explore, as you can see in Figure 5.7. For this tripod shot, the water blurred nicely with a two-second exposure, but the cooperative water fowl remained immobile.

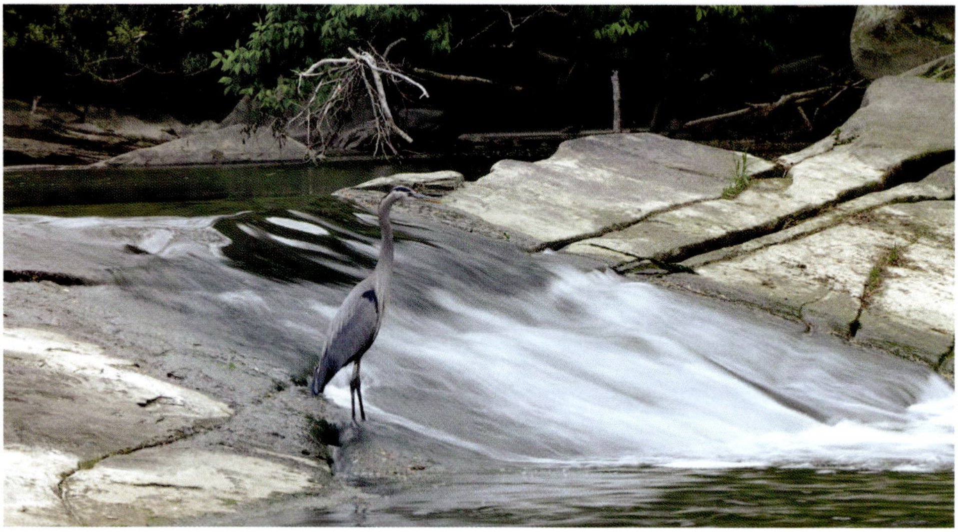

Figure 5.7
Long exposures can transform a waterfall into a display of flowing silk.

- **Show total darkness in new ways.** Even on the darkest, moonless nights, there is enough starlight or glow from distant illumination sources to see by, and, if you use a long exposure, there is enough light to take a picture, too. I was visiting a riverside park hours after sunset, but found that a 30-second exposure with the lens almost wide open revealed the scene shown in Figure 5.8, even though in real life, there was barely enough light to make out the closest tree. Although the photo appears as if it were taken at twilight or sunset, in fact the shot was made at 11 p.m.

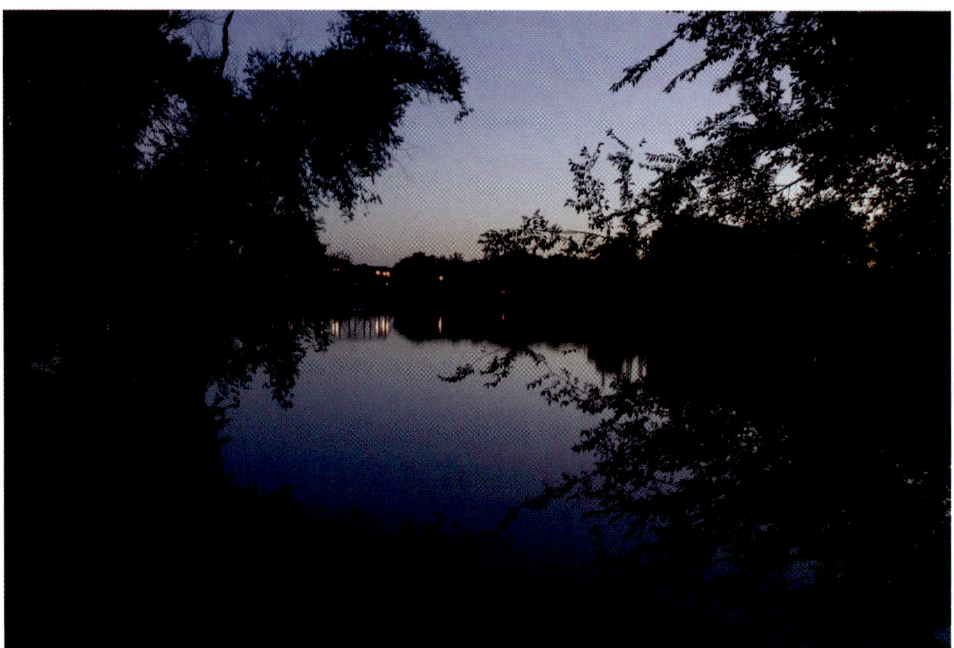

Figure 5.8
A 30-second exposure transformed this night scene into a picture apparently taken at dusk.

Delayed Exposures

Sometimes it's desirable to have a delay of some sort before a picture is actually taken. Perhaps you'd like to get in the picture yourself, and would appreciate it if the camera waited 12 seconds after you press the shutter release to actually take the picture. Maybe you want to give a tripod-mounted camera time to settle down and damp any residual vibration after the release is pressed to improve sharpness for an exposure with a relatively slow shutter speed. It's possible you want to explore the world of time-lapse photography. The next sections present your delayed exposure options.

Self-Timer

The K200D has a built-in self-timer with either the 12-second or 2-second timed delays.

Activate the timer by pressing the Fn button when in Capture mode, then pressing the controller up button to access the Drive Mode menu. Use the left/right keys to navigate to the self-timer icon. After selecting the self-timer icon (pressing the down cross key chooses the 12-second delay, and pressing the right cross key chooses the 2-second setting) press OK to lock in the choice. Press the OK button to confirm your choice. Then, press the shutter release button halfway to lock in focus on your subjects (if you're taking a self-portrait, focus on an object at a similar distance and use focus lock). When you're ready to take the photo, continue pressing the shutter release the rest of the way. The lamp on the front of the handgrip will blink slowly for ten seconds (when using the 12-second timer) and the beeper will chirp (if you haven't disabled it in the Set-up menu, as described in Chapter 3). During the final two seconds, the beeper sounds more rapidly and the lamp blinks at a furious pace until the picture is taken.

If you're using the 2-second delay, the mirror flips up as soon as the shutter release is pressed, which minimizes the tiny amount of camera shake that can occur when the mirror moves out of the way prior to exposure. This is something you might want to do if you're shooting close-ups, landscapes, or other types of pictures using the self-timer only to trip the shutter in the most vibration-free way possible. Forget to bring along your tripod, but still want to take a close-up picture with a precise focus setting? Set your digital camera to the self-timer function, then put the camera on any reasonably steady support, such as a fence post or a rock. When you're ready to take the picture, press the shutter release. The camera might totter back and forth for a second or two, but it will settle back to its original position before the self-timer activates the shutter. As with all Drive modes, the self-timer remains active until you turn it off—even if you power down the K200D. Remember to turn it off when you're finished. Although the self-timer icon appears on the top-panel LCD and rear LCD monitor in the information screen until the feature is turned off, it is easy to overlook.

Getting into Focus

Learning to use the Pentax K200D's autofocus system is easy, but you do need to fully understand how the system works to get the most benefit from it. Once you're comfortable with autofocus, you'll know when it's appropriate to use the manual focus option, too. The important thing to remember is that focus isn't absolute. For example, some things that look in sharp focus at a given viewing size and distance might not be in focus at a larger size and/or closer distance. In addition, the goal of optimum focus isn't always to make things look sharp. Not all of an image will be or should be sharp. Controlling exactly what is sharp and what is not is part of your creative palette. Use of depth-of-field characteristics to throw part of an image out of focus while other parts are sharply focused is one of the most valuable tools available to a photographer. But selective focus works only when the desired areas of an image are in focus properly. For the digital SLR photographer, correct focus can be one of the trickiest parts of the technical and creative process. A lot more is involved than simply remembering to set the slide switch on the left side of the camera to MF (manual focus) or AF (autofocus).

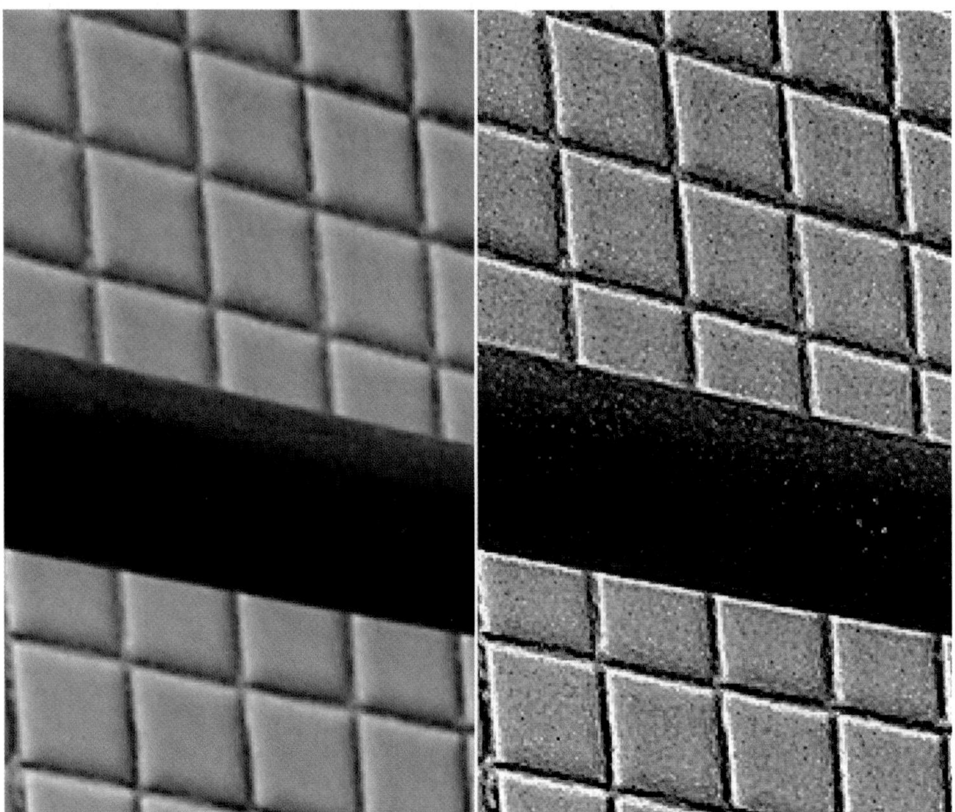

Figure 5.9
When there is little contrast between edges in an image (left), those edges appear to be blurry. When the contrast is increased (right), the edges appear to be sharper and better defined.

To make your job easier, the K200D has a precision eleven-point autofocus system that uses a separate sensor in the viewing system to measure the contrast of the image. When the contrast is highest at the active autofocus point(s), that part of the image is in sharp focus. In reality, blur is nothing more than the lack of contrast between edges in an image, as you can see in Figure 5.9.

The K200D's active focus points are represented by the eleven points visible in the viewfinder (see Figure 5.10), and can be selected automatically by the camera, or manually by you, the photographer.

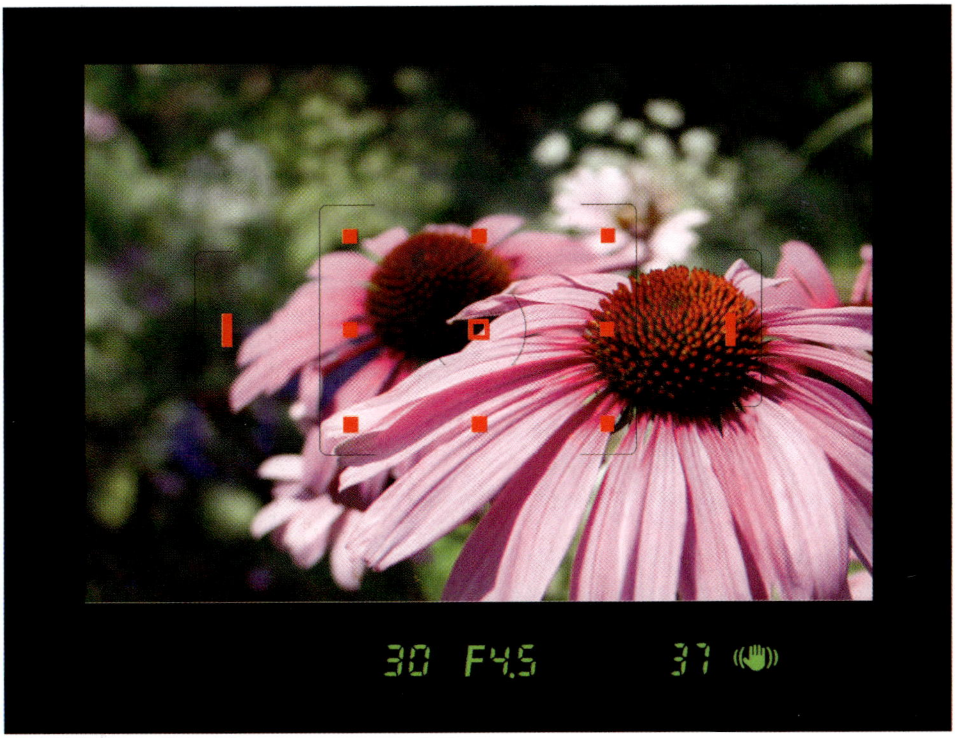

Figure 5.10 Any of the eleven autofocus points can be selected by the photographer manually or by the camera automatically.

Your camera's autofocus sensors require a minimum amount of light to operate, which is why autofocus capabilities are possible only with lenses having an f/5.6 or larger maximum aperture. If necessary, the AF assist beam built into the K200D and Pentax's dedicated flash units provide additional light that helps assure enough illumination for autofocus.

Focus Modes

The K200D has two AF modes: AF.S (also known as Single Autofocus) and AF.C (Continuous Autofocus). I'll explain all of these in more detail later in this section.

MANUAL FOCUS

With manual focus activated by sliding the switch on the left side of the camera body just below the RAW button, your K200D lets you set the focus yourself. There are some advantages and disadvantages to this approach. While your batteries will last slightly longer in manual focus mode, it will take you longer to focus the camera for each photo, a process that can be tricky. Modern digital cameras, even dSLRs, depend so much on autofocus that the viewfinders of models that have less than full-frame-sized sensors are no longer designed for optimum manual focus. Pick up any film camera and you'll see a bigger, brighter viewfinder with a focusing screen that's a joy to focus on manually. The K200D has a viewfinder that provides .85X magnification, and shows 96 percent of the image area captured by the sensor. (That means that with a 50mm focal length, the image appears to be 85 percent of life size.)

Focus Pocus

Although Pentax added autofocus capabilities in the 1980s, back in the day of film cameras, prior to that focusing was always done manually. Honest. Even though viewfinders were bigger and brighter than they are today, special focusing screens, magnifiers, and other gadgets were often used to help the photographer achieve correct focus. Imagine what it must have been like to focus manually under demanding, fast-moving conditions such as sports photography.

Focusing was problematic because our eyes and brains have poor memory for correct focus, which is why your eye doctor must shift back and forth between sets of lenses and ask "Does that look sharper—or was it sharper before?" in determining your correct prescription. Similarly, manual focusing involves jogging the focus ring back and forth as you go from almost in focus, to sharp focus, to almost focused again. The little clockwise and counterclockwise arcs decrease in size until you've zeroed in on the point of correct focus. As I mentioned earlier in this chapter, what you're looking for is the image with the most contrast between the edges of elements in the image.

The K200D's autofocus mechanism, like all such systems found in SLR cameras, also evaluates these increases and decreases in sharpness, but it is able to remember the progression perfectly, so that autofocus can lock in much more quickly and, with an image that has sufficient contrast, more precisely. Unfortunately, while the K200D's focus system finds it easy to measure degrees of apparent focus at each of the focus points in the viewfinder, it doesn't really know with any certainty *which* object should be in sharpest focus. Is it the closest object? The subject in the center? Something lurking *behind* the closest subject? A person standing over at the side of the picture? Many of the techniques for using autofocus effectively involve telling the K200D exactly what it should be focusing on.

Adding Circles of Confusion

But there are other factors in play, as well. You know that increased depth-of-field brings more of your subject into focus. But more depth-of-field also makes autofocusing (or manual focusing) more difficult because the contrast is lower between objects at different distances. So, autofocus with a 200mm lens (or zoom setting) may be easier than at a 28mm focal length (or zoom setting) because the longer lens has less apparent depth-of-field. By the same token, a lens with a maximum aperture of f/1.8 will be easier to autofocus (or manually focus) than one of the same focal length with an f/4 maximum aperture, because the f/4 lens has more depth-of-field *and* a dimmer view. That's why lenses with a maximum aperture smaller than f/5.6 can give your K200D's autofocus system fits.

To make things even more complicated, many subjects aren't polite enough to remain still. They move around in the frame, so that even if the K200D is sharply focused on your main subject, it may change position and require refocusing. An intervening subject may pop into the frame and pass between you and the subject you meant to photograph. You (or the K200D) have to decide whether to lock focus on this new subject, or remain focused on the original subject. Finally, there are some kinds of subjects that are difficult to bring into sharp focus because they lack enough contrast to allow the K200D's AF system (or our eyes) to lock in. Blank walls, a clear blue sky, or other subject matter may make focusing difficult.

If you find all these focus factors confusing, you're on the right track. Focus is, in fact, measured using something called a *circle of confusion.* An ideal image consists of zillions of tiny little points, which, like all points, theoretically have no height or width. There is perfect contrast between the point and its surroundings. You can think of each point as a pinpoint of light in a darkened room. When a given point is out of focus, its edges decrease in contrast and it changes from a perfect point to a tiny disc with blurry edges (remember, blur is the lack of contrast between boundaries in an image). (See Figure 5.11.)

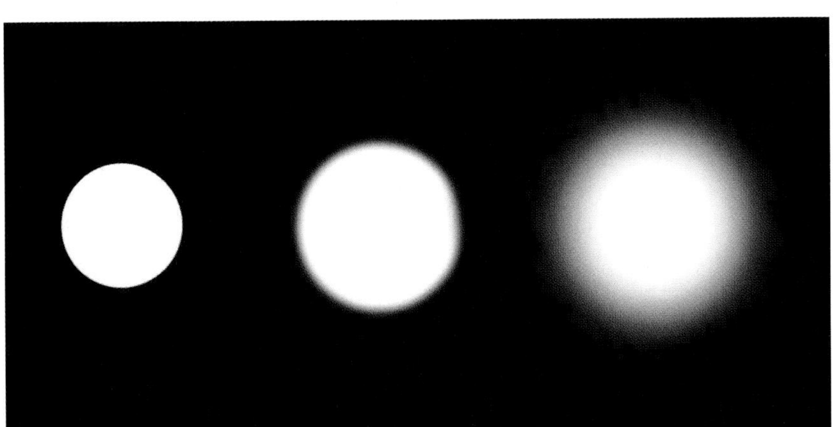

Figure 5.11
When a pinpoint of light (left) goes out of focus, its blurry edges form a circle of confusion (center and right).

If this blurry disc—the circle of confusion—is small enough, our eye still perceives it as a point. It's only when the disc grows large enough that we can see it as a blur rather than a sharp point that a given point is viewed as out of focus. You can see, then, that enlarging an image, either by displaying it larger on your computer monitor or by making a large print, also enlarges the size of each circle of confusion. Moving closer to the image does the same thing. So, parts of an image that may look perfectly sharp in a 5 × 7-inch print viewed at arm's length, might appear blurry when blown up to 11 × 14 and examined at the same distance. Take a few steps back, however, and it may look sharp again.

To a lesser extent, the viewer also affects the apparent size of these circles of confusion. Some people see details better at a given distance and may perceive smaller circles of confusion than someone standing next to them. For the most part, however, such differences are small. Truly blurry images will look blurry to just about everyone under the same conditions.

Technically, there is just one plane within your picture area, parallel to the back of the camera (or sensor, in the case of a digital camera), that is in sharp focus. That's the plane in which the points of the image are rendered as precise points. At every other plane in front of or behind the focus plane, the points show up as discs that range from slightly blurry to extremely blurry. In practice, the discs in many of these planes will still be so small that we see them as points, and that's where we get depth-of-field. Depth-of-field is just the range of planes that include discs that we perceive as points rather than blurred splotches. The size of this range increases as the aperture is reduced in size and is allocated roughly one-third in front of the plane of sharpest focus, and two-thirds behind it. The range of sharp focus is always greater behind your subject than in front of it (see Figure 5.12).

Making Sense of Sensors

The number and type of autofocus sensors can affect how well the system operates. As I mentioned, the Pentax K200D has eleven AF points. Cameras from other vendors may have as few as three autofocus sensors or as many as 51 (to date). The more AF points available, the more easily the camera can differentiate among areas of the frame, and the more precisely you can specify the area you want to be in focus if you're manually choosing a focus spot. The eleven found in the K200D is an excellent compromise: enough sensors to track moving objects, but not so many that prodigious (read: expensive) computing power is required in the camera to follow them all when calculating focus.

As the camera collects contrast information from the sensors, it then evaluates it to determine whether the desired sharp focus has been achieved. The calculations may include

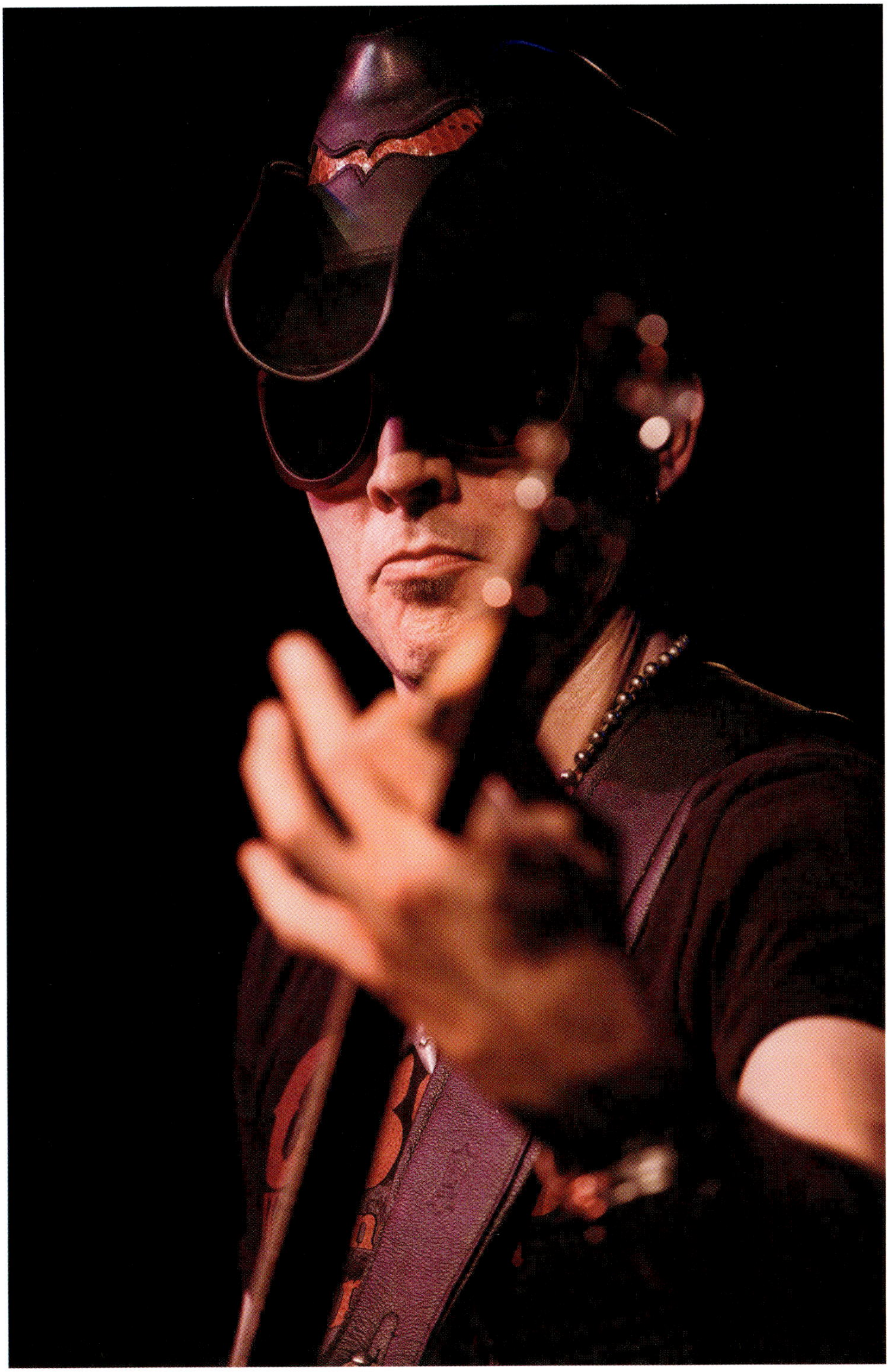

Figure 5.12
The musician is in sharp focus, but his hand and guitar are blurred, because the depth-of-field is limited.

whether the subject is moving, and whether the camera needs to "predict" where the subject will be when the shutter release button is fully depressed and the picture is taken. The speed with which the camera is able to evaluate focus and then move the lens elements into the proper position to achieve the sharpest focus determines how fast the autofocus mechanism is.

Although your K200D will almost always focus more quickly than a human, there are types of shooting situations where that's not fast enough. For example, if you're having problems shooting sports because the K200D's autofocus system manically follows each moving subject, a better choice might be to switch autofocus modes or shift into manual and prefocus on a spot where you anticipate the action will be, such as a goal line or soccer net. At night football games, for example, when I am shooting with a telephoto lens almost wide open, I often focus manually on one of the referees who happens to be standing where I expect the action to be taking place (say, a halfback run or a pass reception). When I am less sure about what is going to happen, I may switch to AF.C autofocus and let the camera decide.

Your Autofocus Mode Options

Choosing the right autofocus mode and the way in which focus points are selected is your key to success. Using the wrong mode for a particular type of photography can lead to a series of pictures that are all sharply focused—on the wrong subject. When I first started shooting sports with an autofocus SLR (back in the film camera days), I covered one game alternating between shots of base runners and outfielders with pictures of a promising young pitcher, all from a position next to the third base dugout. The base runner and outfielder photos were great, because their backgrounds didn't distract the autofocus mechanism. But all my photos of the pitcher had the focus tightly zeroed in on the fans in the stands behind him. Because I was shooting film instead of a digital camera, I didn't know about my gaffe until the film was developed. A simple change, such as locking in focus or focus zone manually, or even manually focusing, would have done the trick.

To save battery power, your K200D doesn't start to focus the lens until you partially depress the shutter release. But, autofocus isn't some mindless beast out there snapping your pictures in and out of focus with no feedback from you after you press that button. There are several settings you can modify that return at least a modicum of control to you. Your first decision should be whether you set the K200D to AF.S or AF.C. You can choose between these modes in the Recording Mode menu, as described in Chapter 3. When you've highlighted the mode of choice, press the OK button to confirm your selection. Although you can choose an autofocus mode even when the M/AF switch on the camera is set to MF (manual focus), your choice doesn't become active until you've moved the switch to the AF position.

AF.S

In this mode, also called *Single Autofocus*, focus is set once and remains at that setting until the button is fully depressed, taking the picture, or until you release the shutter button without taking a shot. For non-action photography, this setting is usually your best choice, as it minimizes out-of-focus pictures (at the expense of spontaneity). The drawback here is that you might not be able to take a picture at all while the camera is seeking focus; you're locked out until the autofocus mechanism is happy with the current setting. Because of the small delay while the camera zeroes in on correct focus, you might experience slightly more shutter lag. This mode uses less battery power.

When the focus point is locked in, you'll see a red square in the viewfinder that illuminates to indicate the focus point selected, a green octagonal focus confirmation indicator is shown at the bottom of the viewfinder, and the camera will emit a beep. The focus locks until you either release the button or press it all the way down to take the picture. If the subject begins moving, the camera switches to AF.C mode and tracks the movement by refocusing as necessary. This mode is best when your subject isn't moving, because you can set focus once on the subject of your choice, then change your composition and re-frame your image as you like. All the Scene/SCN modes use this focus exclusively, except the Moving Object, Kids, and Pet modes. If the K200D isn't able to focus at all, the green octagon in the viewfinder will blink and the shutter release will be locked. This behavior is called *focus priority*; the shutter is disabled unless the image is sharply focused.

AF.C

This mode, also known as *Continuous Autofocus*, is the mode to use for sports and other fast-moving subjects. In this mode, once the shutter release is partially depressed, the camera sets the focus but continues to monitor the subject, so that if it moves or you move, the lens will be refocused to suit. Focus and exposure aren't really locked until you press the shutter release down all the way to take the picture. This mode can be selected when using P, Sv, Tv, Av, M, or B Exposure modes. The Moving Object Scene (Picture) mode and Kids and Pet SCN modes use this focus method exclusively. In order for the K200D to continually focus, you have to keep the shutter release button pressed halfway down. If the subject is slightly out of focus, as indicated by the flashing green octagon, the shutter button is *not* locked and the K200D can still take a picture when the shutter release is pressed all the way down.

You'll often see Continuous Autofocus referred to as *release priority*. If you press the shutter release down all the way while the system is refining focus, the camera will go ahead and take a picture, even if the image is slightly out of focus. That can be helpful for action shots and other subject matter when you'd prefer to take a photo, even if slightly out of focus, rather than miss the picture entirely.

You'll find that AF.C produces the least amount of shutter lag of any autofocus mode: press the button and the camera fires. It also uses the most battery power, because the autofocus system operates as long as the shutter release button is partially depressed.

Selecting an Autofocus Point

One of the keys to achieving correct focus is having the camera calculate focus using the appropriate focus zone from among the eleven available areas. As I noted in Chapter 3, the active AF point is always displayed in the viewfinder screen with a red highlight, unless you've disabled that display using Custom Setting #8. There are three ways of choosing an AF zone, which can be selected in the Recording menu under the Select AF point entry:

- **Auto.** In this mode, the K200D selects the best focusing area for you, even if the subject is not centered in the frame. It chooses from among the 11 zones distributed throughout the center area, bounded by the brackets you can see in Figure 5.10 (shown earlier in this chapter). This mode is your best choice for fast-moving action and other scenes in which you don't know in advance where your main subject will be located at the moment of the exposure. The K200D will use its intelligence to choose the likely center of interest and lock focus on that AF point.
- **Select.** In this mode, you are able to choose one of those 11 focus points yourself, using the controller's up/down/left/right keys. The center point is used by default until you select a different focus area with the controller keys. The focus points don't "wrap around" left to right/right to left or up/down. When you reach the farthest focus point in any direction, the focus area shift stops. Use this method when you want to control the zone where focus is evaluated, particularly with subjects that are located away from the exact center of the frame. It's best for stationary subjects, or those which are moving very slowly, because it takes time to relocate the focus point manually.

  If you want to focus on a subject that is located outside the area covered by the 11 focus zones, follow the instructions in the next section.
- **Center.** The K200D uses the focus point in the center of your frame. Use this method when you know your main subject is going to be located in the middle of the frame. The camera automatically uses this method when you're using older lenses (which don't have DA, D FA, FA J, FA, or F in their names).

Locking Autofocus and/or Exposure

When you are happy with the focus and want to lock it, you can lock in focus or lock in focus *and* exposure, so that it does not change until either you have taken a picture (and the camera readies itself to calculate exposure for the next exposure), or you have unlocked exposure by *not* taking a picture. Lock focus and/or exposure in either of these two ways:

- **Press the shutter release halfway with CS #4 set to On.** Focus is locked when you are using AF.S mode (or one of the Scene/SCN modes that operate in AF.S mode). If you're using AF.C mode, or AF.S mode and your subject begins moving, then *only* exposure is locked when the shutter release button is pressed halfway. In AF.C mode or AF.S mode with a moving subject, the camera will refocus as required to follow the subject.

  When CS #4 is set to Off, only focus is locked. Exposure will continue to adjust as the light changes or as you reframe the image. When CS #4 is set to On, *both* focus and exposure are locked, until you take a picture or you release the button.

- **Press the AE-L button.** When you press this button, the exposure is locked for as long as you continue holding down the AE-L button. A * indicator appears in the viewfinder and a beep (which you can disable in the Set-up menu) sounds. The exposure remains locked after you release the button, for a period of time ranging from one-half to twice the value set for the metering operating timer in CS #3 (usually about 5 to 20 seconds). Note that the AE-L button does not work in B (Bulb) exposure mode.

Linking AF and AE Points

As I mentioned in Chapter 3, you can link the autofocus and autoexposure points (more or less), so that when you're choosing a focus point, you're also telling the Pentax K200D to give priority to that point when calculating exposure while using Multi-Segment metering. Remember that the camera looks at 16 different zones in the frame to calculate exposure, but there are only 11 autofocus zones, as shown in Figure 5.13.

Use CS #5 in the Custom Settings menu to link or unlink the AF and AE points, as described in Chapter 3. As a recap:

- **1. Off.** With this setting, AF and AE points are not linked when Multi-Segment metering is activated. The K200D calculates focus based on the active autofocus point selected by you or the camera, and figures exposure using the 16 exposure zones. Use this mode when you want to ensure that the entire scene is taken into account when figuring exposure, and not just the center of interest that is in sharp focus.

- **2. On.** Choose this option, and the K200D assigns exposure emphasis to the active autofocus point. The AF point of the main subject will be in sharpest focus, and exposure will be calculated based on that subject. Use this option for scenes in which the main subject is illuminated much differently from the surroundings. Backlit subjects, silhouettes, and many portraits fall into this category.

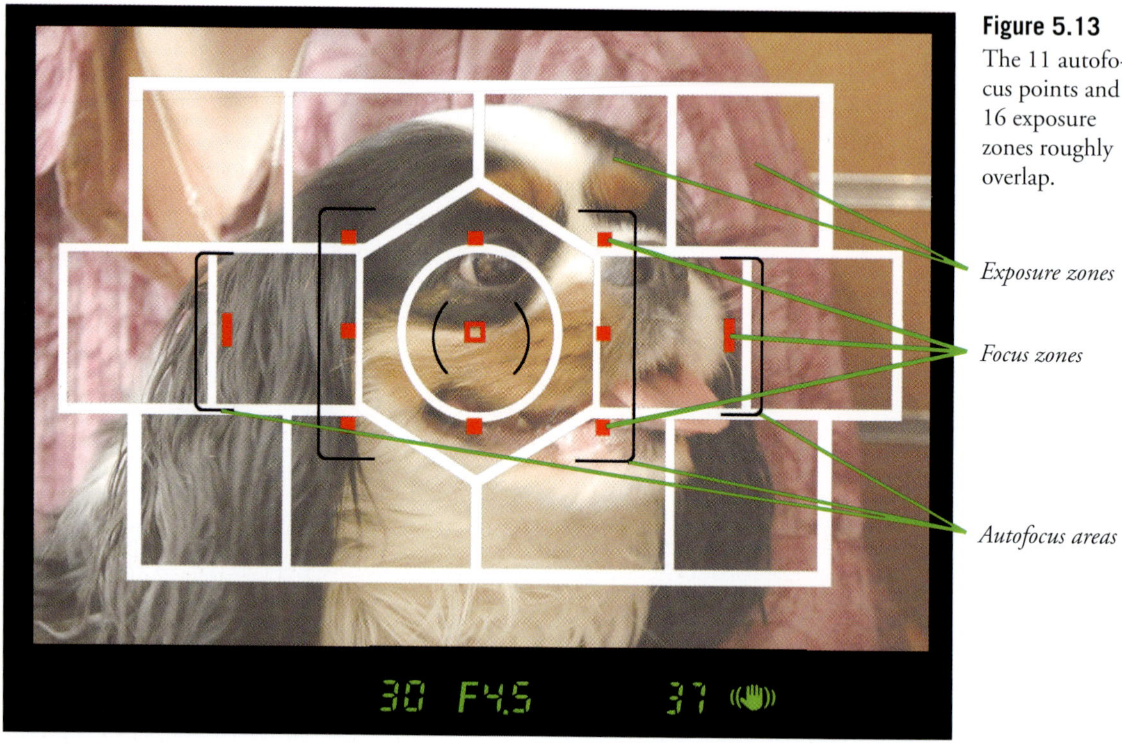

Figure 5.13
The 11 autofocus points and 16 exposure zones roughly overlap.

Continuous Shooting

The Pentax K200D's Hi and Lo Continuous Shooting modes remind me how far digital photography has brought us. The first accessory I purchased when I worked as a sports photographer some years ago was a motor drive for my film SLR. It enabled me to snap off a series of shots in rapid succession, which came in very handy when a fullback broke through the line and headed for the end zone. Pentax produced what it called "power winders" for its film cameras, including a gadget called the Motor Drive LX, which could fire off an entire 36 exposure roll of film in about eight seconds, at five frames per second. Later cameras from many vendors had motorized film transport built in.

Continuous shooting has long been a useful tool, because even a seasoned action photographer can miss the decisive instant when a crucial block is made, or a baseball superstar's bat shatters and pieces of cork fly out. Continuous shooting simplifies taking a series of pictures, either to ensure that one has more or less the exact moment you want to capture or to capture a sequence that is interesting as a collection of successive images.

The K200D's "motor drive" capabilities are, in many ways, much superior to what you get with a film camera. For one thing, a motor-driven film camera can eat up film at an incredible pace, which is why many of them are used with cassettes that hold hundreds of feet of film stock. At three to five frames per second (typical of film cameras), even a short burst of a few seconds can burn up as much as half of an ordinary 36 exposure roll of film. Digital cameras, in contrast, have reusable "film," so if you waste a few dozen shots on non-decisive moments, you can erase them and shoot more.

The increased capacity of digital film cards gives you a prodigious number of frames to work with. At a baseball game I covered earlier this year, I took more than 1,000 images in a couple hours. Yet, even shooting JPEG I could fit more than 450 different images without switching 2 GB memory cards. Even at the top speed of 2.8 frames per second that the K200D is capable of in Hi mode, that's a lot of shooting. Given an average burst of about four frames per sequence, I was able to capture hundreds of different sequences before I needed to swap cards. Figure 5.14 shows a typical short burst of three shots taken at a basketball game as a player drove in for a lay-up.

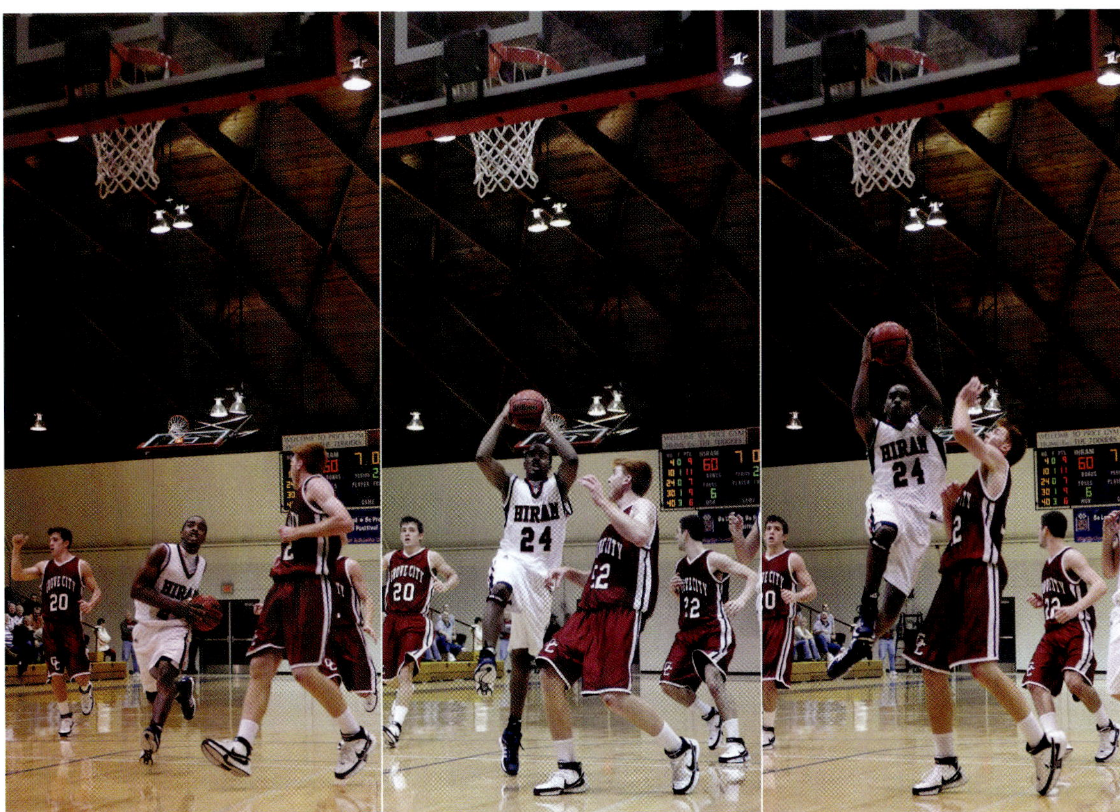

Figure 5.14 Continuous shooting allows you to capture an entire sequence of exciting moments as they unfold.

To use the K200D's Continuous Shooting modes, press the Fn button while in Capture mode to access the Capture Functions screen. Then, press the controller up button to view the Drive Mode menu, and use the left/right/up/down keys to navigate to the Continuous Shooting option. (See Figure 5.15.) Select either Hi (2.8 fps) or Lo (1.1 fps) and press OK to confirm your choice. You can shoot up to 4 frames continuously in Hi mode with the Quality Level set to the maximum (***), and if you use the Lo setting, you can shoot continuously at maximum JPEG quality at 1.1 frames per second until your memory card is full. Changing to RAW format limits the K200D to four frames, max, at both Hi and Lo settings.

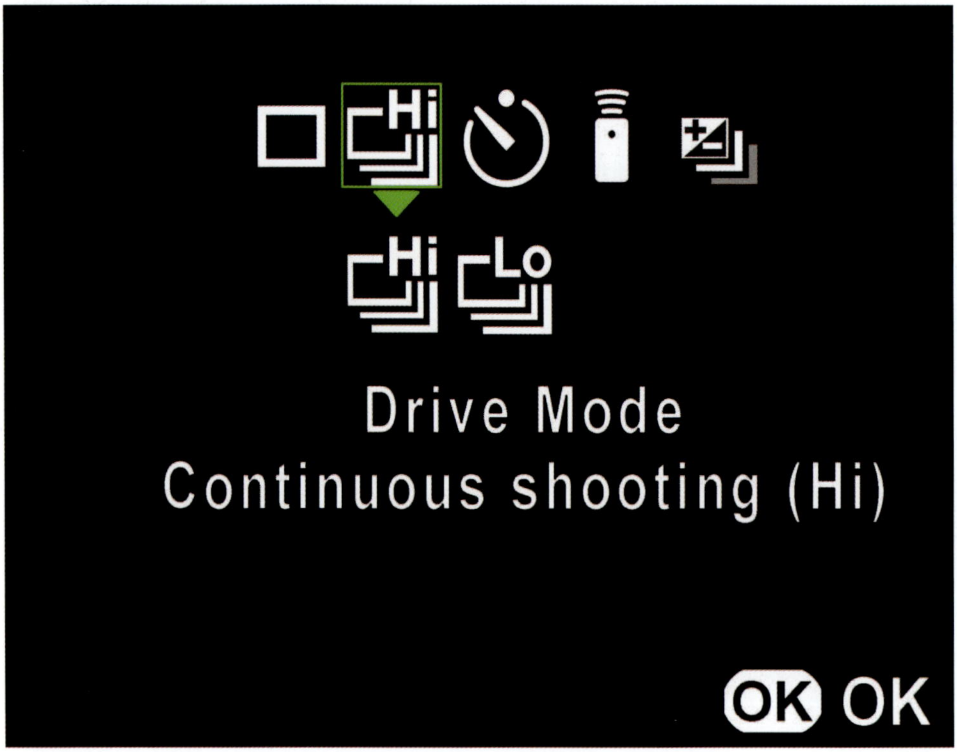

Figure 5.15
Press the Drive button and use the left/right cross keys to select Continuous Shooting.

The K200D will continually refocus during a sequence if the camera is set to AF.C mode or you are using the Moving Object, Kids, or Pet Scene/SCN mode modes. If AF.S is selected, focus will be set for the first picture in the sequence, and all subsequent shots will use the same focus. You'll want to select the appropriate focus mode before you begin shooting. You'll find that the highest frame rates are attained when using AF.S, because the K200D isn't taking time to refocus between shots. So, even with action photos, that may be your best choice if your subject is moving across the frame, or is standing in one place. If the subject is approaching the camera, you'll want to use AF.C, even if that means a slower frame rate.

If you use flash while in Continuous Shooting mode, your frame rate will slow down significantly as the K200D waits for the flash to recycle between shots. The shutter release locks while the flash is recharging. (You can tell the camera to go ahead and take a photo, anyway—without flash—by activating CS #15, Release when Charging, in the Custom Setting menu, as described in Chapter 3.)

As with all Drive modes, Continuous Shooting remains in force until you re-visit the Drive mode menu and change to another drive mode, or when you turn the camera off if you've unchecked the "remember Drive Mode" box in the Memory menu entry of the Recording menu. The Continuous Shooting icon appears on the top-panel LCD and on the back panel color LCD information screen until you turn it off, but again, it's easily overlooked.

Customizing White Balance

Back in the film days, color films were standardized, or balanced, for a particular "color" of light. Digital cameras like the K200D use a particular "white balance" matched to the color of light used to expose your photograph. The right white balance is measured using a scale called *color temperature.* Color temperatures were assigned by heating a mythical "black body radiator" and recording the spectrum of light it emitted at a given temperature in degrees Kelvin. So, daylight at noon has a color temperature in the 5,500 to 6,000 degree range. Indoor illumination is around 3,400 degrees. Hotter temperatures produce bluer images (think blue-white hot) while cooler temperatures produce redder images (think of a dull-red glowing ember). Because of human nature, though, bluer images are actually called "cool" (think wintry day) and redder images are called "warm" (think ruddy sunset), even though their color temperatures are reversed.

If a photograph is exposed indoors under warm illumination with a digital camera sensor balanced for cooler daylight, the image will appear much too reddish. (See Figure 5.16.) An image exposed outdoors with the white balance set for incandescent illumination will seem much too blue. (See Figure 5.17.) These color casts may be too strong to remove in an image editor from JPEG files, although if you shoot RAW, you can change the WB setting to the correct value when you import the image into your editor.

Mismatched White Balance settings are easier to achieve accidentally than you might think, even for experienced photographers. I'd just finished shooting some photos indoors with electronic flash and had manually set WB for flash. Then, I began taking more pictures using the incandescent interior lighting in this indoor fish market, and ended up with a few shots like Figure 5.16. Later that afternoon, outdoors, I had the White Balance set for indoor illumination, and the excessively blue image shown in

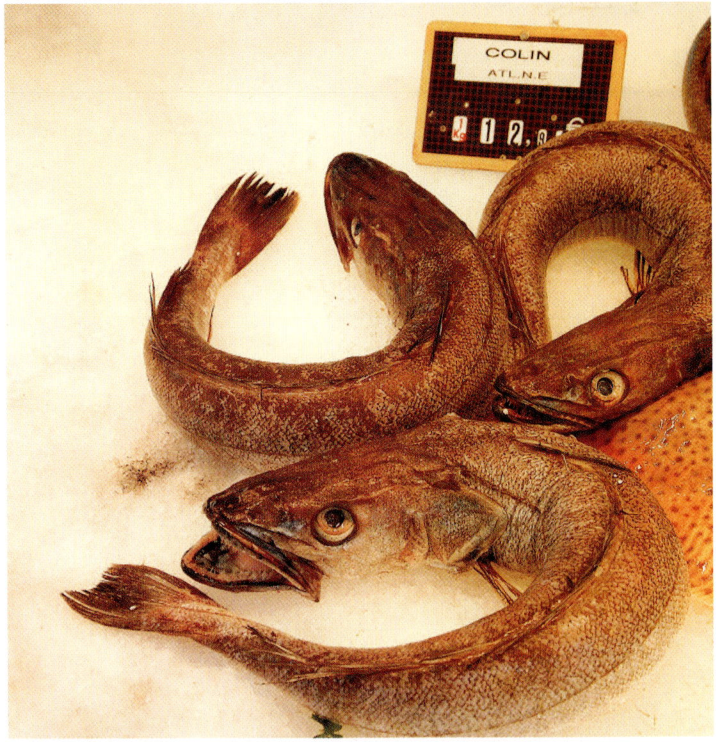

Figure 5.16
Indoor images taken under tungsten illumination with White Balance set to Daylight look too warm.

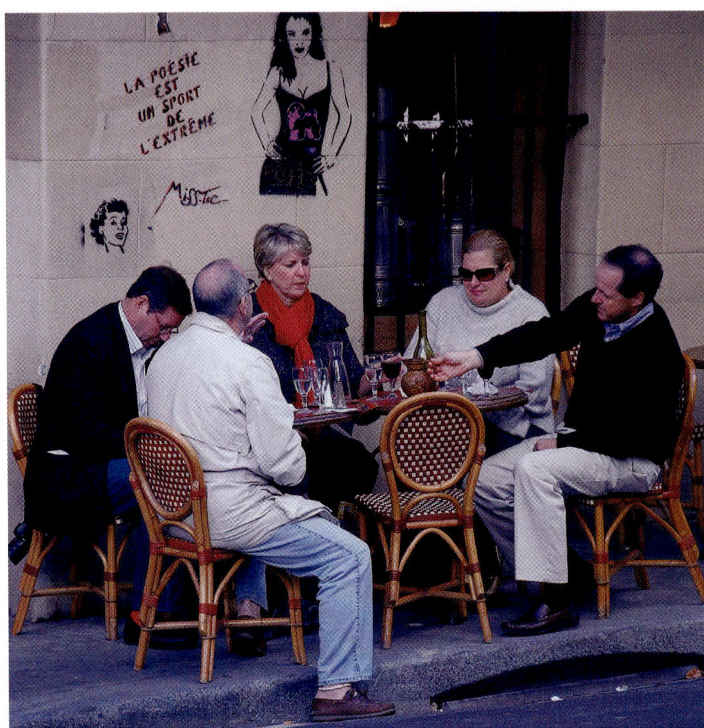

Figure 5.17
Images taken under daylight illumination with White Balance set to Tungsten look too blue or cold in tone.

Figure 5.17 resulted. I suppose I should salvage my reputation as a photo guru by admitting that both these images were taken "incorrectly" deliberately, as illustrations for this book; in real life, I'm excessively attentive to how my White Balance is set and never make mistakes like that. (Yeah, that's the ticket.)

Using a White Balance Preset

The K200D has six preset White Balance values you can select, corresponding to Daylight, Shade, Cloudy, Fluorescent, Tungsten, and Electronic flash illumination, plus an Automatic White Balance (AWB) setting that interprets a scene and sets a white balance for you. (Manual White Balance, the last entry in the column, will be discussed later in this chapter.) The preset values offer "close enough" settings that work in most typical situations:

- **Auto White Balance (AWB).** With this setting, the K200D looks at the color bias of neutral tones to see if they have the proper equal balance of red, green, and blue hues. If not, the camera calculates just how much the scene is biased, and adjusts the White Balance to a color temperature between 4000K and 8000K. Note that much interior illumination has a color temperature of less than 4000K, and so your camera may not sufficiently correct for indoor lighting when set to AWB.
- **Daylight.** In bright daylight or with a slight overcast, most of the illumination comes from the sun, so the 5200K setting applied by this preset provides accurate color and neutral tones in most situations.
- **Shade.** When your subject is in the shade, the illumination doesn't come directly from the sun. Instead, the light may come from the blue sky, or bounce off other objects to produce a diffuse illumination that has a higher (bluer) color temperature than daylight. So, the K200D uses a color temperature of 8000K at this setting.
- **Cloudy.** When clouds obscure the sun, the illumination is even more diffuse, but not quite as cold (blue) as shade in color temperature, so a setting of 6000K is used.
- **Fluorescent light.** This type of lighting doesn't have a true color temperature, and the actual color balance varies all over the map, depending on which type of tubes you're using. When you select this preset, you can choose from white fluorescents (W, about 4200K); neutral white (N, 5000K); and daylight fluorescent (D, 6500K).
- **Tungsten light.** Incandescent lamps produced especially for photographic purposes have a color temperature of either 3200K or 3400K. Common household variety lamps that you're more likely to encounter are somewhat warmer, so the K200D uses a color temperature of 2800K when this setting is selected.

- **Flash.** Electronic flash is supposed to be balanced for "daylight" (roughly 5000-5200K for much of the day), but it's not, strictly speaking. Indeed, the flash can vary in color temperature depending on its duration, as you'll learn in Chapter 7. When you're using the Pentax K200D's built-in flash unit, use this setting, which corresponds to the slightly bluer tone (5400K) that the flash generates—on average. As described in Chapter 3, the camera automatically changes the White Balance to this setting if you've set CS #17 (White Balance when using flash) to Flash in the Custom Setting menu. Use Unchanged instead if you want to leave the color balance as it was, perhaps for a special effect. I sometimes shoot wide-angle flash pictures with the White Balance set to Tungsten when I want to create a mixed-lighting clash between the part of the scene illuminated by flash, and the part illuminated by existing light. See Figure 5.18 for an example. It's a fisheye shot taken with the camera set for tungsten illumination, but with the flash fired to light up the foreground with an eerie blue cast.

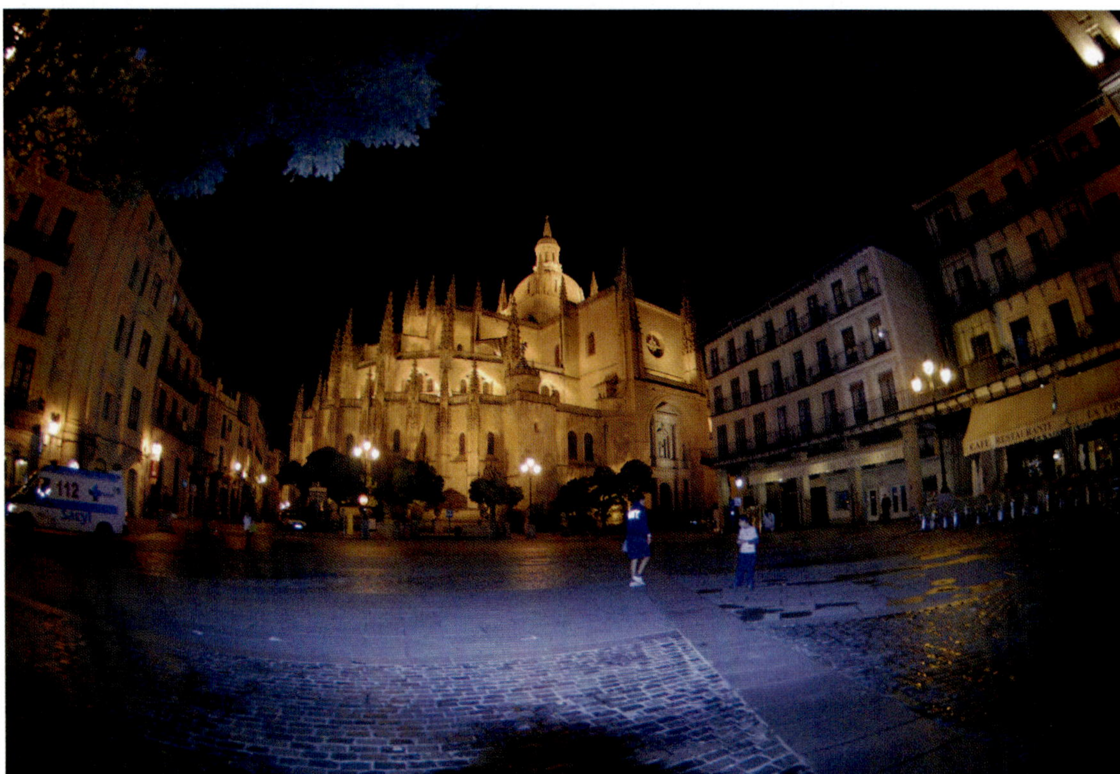

Figure 5.18 This fisheye shot mixes flash illumination and tungsten lighting.

Navigate to the White Balance settings by pressing the Fn button to produce the Custom Functions screen, and then press the left arrow of the four-way controller to activate the White Balance screen. There you will see icons for each of the White Balance settings arrayed along the left side of the LCD. You cannot change the White Balance in any of the Scene/SCN modes, but you can adjust the White Balance in all of the exposure modes (P, Sv, Tv, Av, M, or B). Navigate through them by pressing the up and down arrows of the four-way controller. If you don't know what the icons mean, that's no problem because the K200D spells them out on the LCD screen as you move though them.

The most efficient way to measure the white balance is to use the Digital Preview button to bring up a preview of your photo you have framed on the monitor screen. To do this, frame your photo, and instead of pressing the shutter release button, move the main switch to Digital Preview (to the icon just past the On button). A preview of your photo appears on the monitor screen along with the icons for changing the white balance as shown in Figure 5.19.

One of the settings for White Balance—Fluorescent Light—is divided into three choices, each choice a different type of fluorescent light. Each is marked with the Fluorescent Light icon next to a letter. The selections and letters are: Daylight (D), Neutral White (N), and White (W). (See Figure 5.20.)

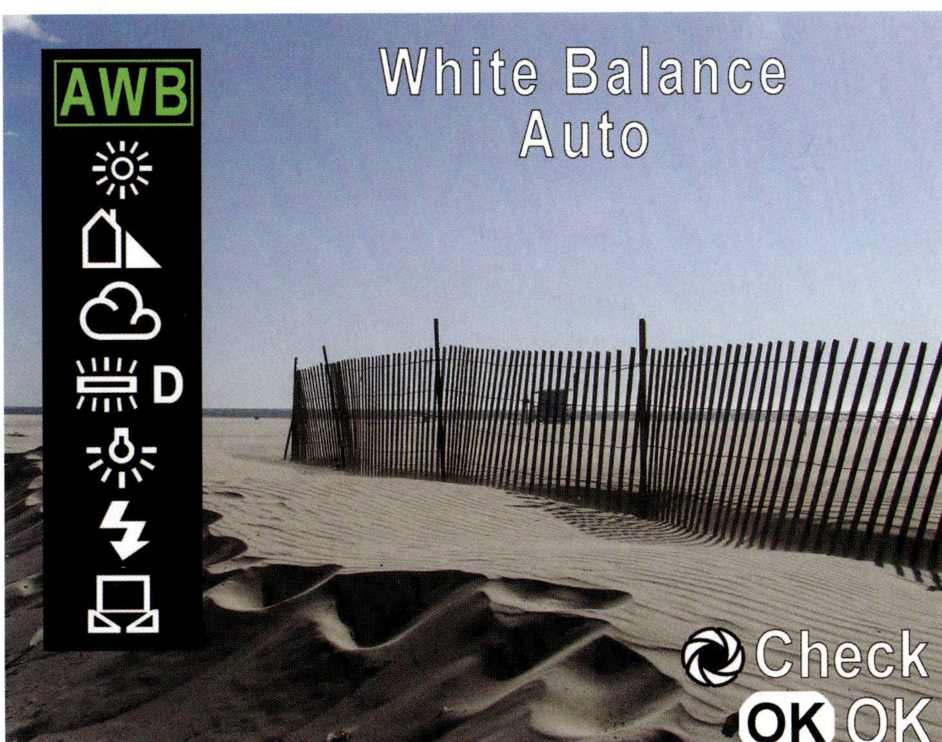

Figure 5.19
You can use a preview of your frame to try each of the White Balance settings on it before you shoot.

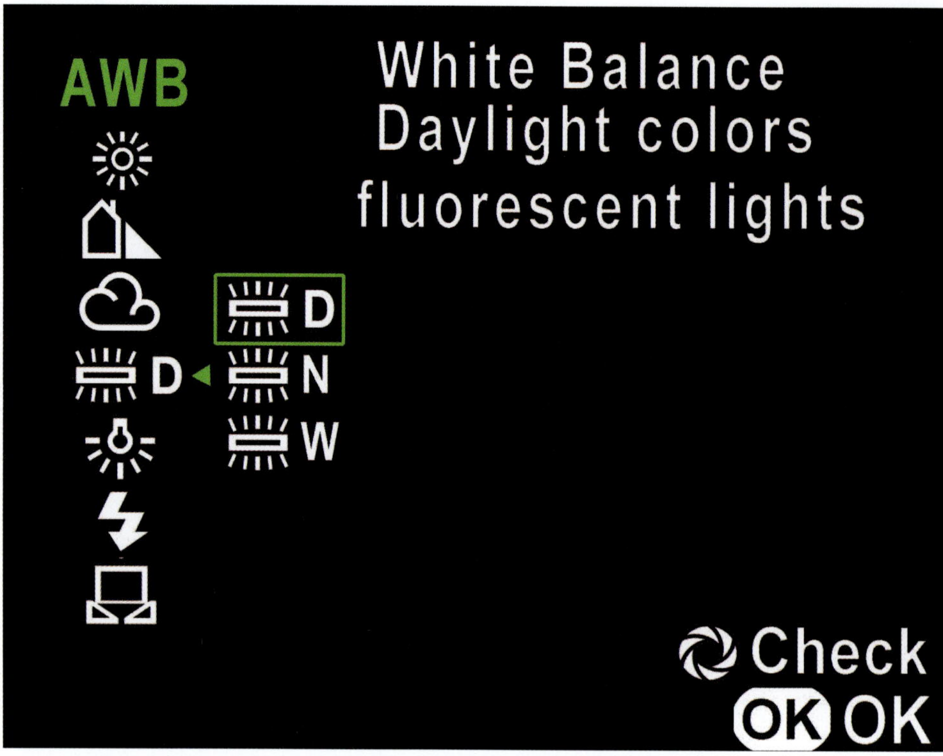

Figure 5.20
Choose from three varieties of fluorescent lights.

Fine-Tuning White Balance

You can further fine-tune any of the preset White Balance settings. To use White Balance adjustments, you must first activate this feature in the Custom Setting menu, using CS #7, first described in Chapter 3. Set the option to On, and when the White Balance screen appears, as described earlier, an additional control is shown on the LCD, just above the Check icon. It's a grid, with a green dot showing the current white balance "bias." Select a preset and press the right controller key. The adjustment screen appears. If you've used the Preview button to capture a preview image, the adjustment screen on the LCD will be overlaid on it, as in Figure 5.21.

When the yellow dot is in the center of the grid, the white balance has no bias at all. As the dot moves to the left or right, the bias is shifted towards blue (left) or amber/yellow (right.) Up and down movement on the grid changes the bias towards green (up) and magenta (down) hues. The color balance shift can be made both horizontally and vertically, so you could, for example, use the left/right/up/down controller keys to shift the bias three lines up and two lines to the left, producing a +3 green/+2 blue adjustment.

Use this feature to fine-tune the white balance of any of the presets to better suit your scene. You'll need to accumulate some experience before you can use this capability effectively. That's why the Custom Setting menu item is available to disable the adjustment until you're ready for it.

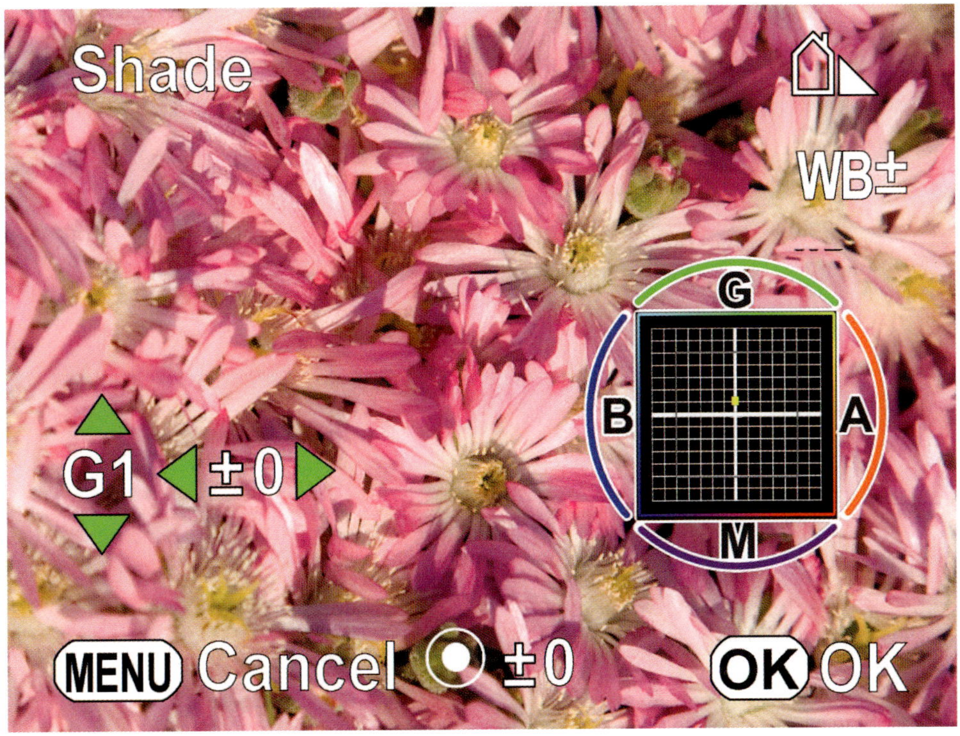

Figure 5.21
Shift white balance bias in the blue/amber or green/magenta directions.

Setting Manual White Balance

If the automatic white balance of one of the settings available (Daylight, Shade, Cloudy, Fluorescent Light, Tungsten Light, Flash) isn't suitable, you can set a White Balance value manually. You can set the White Balance manually in P, Sv, Tv, Av, or M modes.

To use Manual mode, navigate to the White Balance settings by pressing the Fn button and left arrow of the four-way controller. The Manual setting is the last one in the column. Navigate to it and press the right controller button. Then follow these steps:

1. Place a white sheet of paper under the illumination you want to evaluate.
2. Frame the paper in the viewfinder so it fills up the screen.
3. Press the shutter release button. An image of the white page appears on the LCD monitor. (See Figure 5.22.)
4. Rotate the e-dial if you'd like to use the entire frame as your white balance reference.
5. If you'd rather use part of the image as a reference, use the four-way controller keys to navigate to a spot on the screen that you'd like to use. A green box moves around the screen to show the currently selected area.

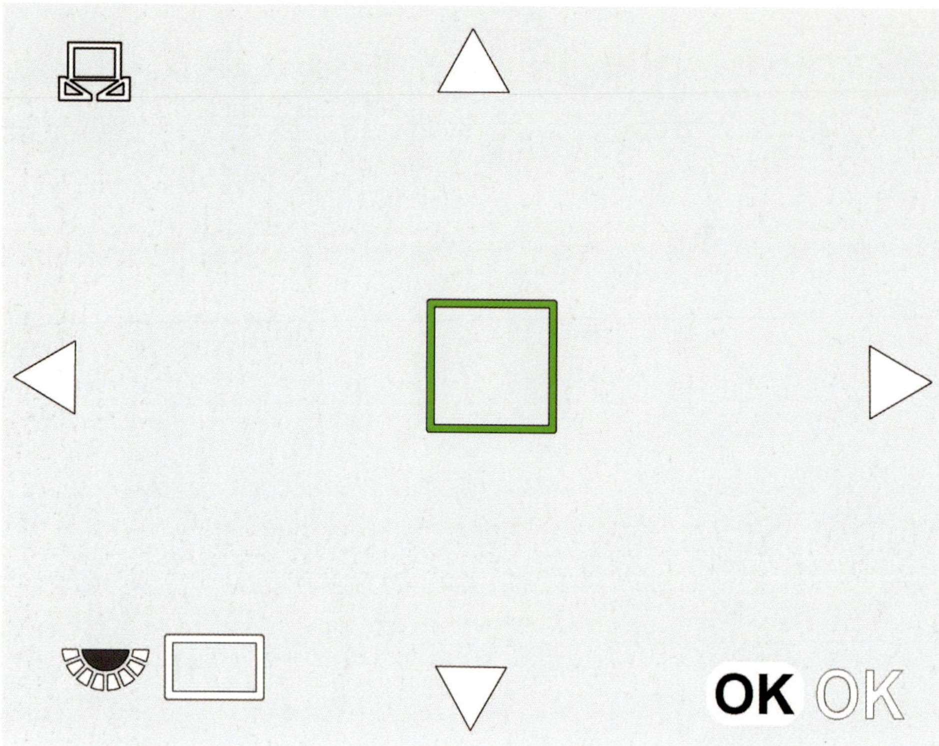

Figure 5.22
Choose an area of the captured image to be used as a white balance reference.

6. Press the OK button to lock in your manually measured white balance.
7. You can further fine-tune your manual white balance using the steps in the previous section.

Processing Options in Custom Image

The final advanced shooting option in this chapter is the use the Custom Image processing feature, which allows you to change a variety of image parameters and apply some special effects such as photographic filters and toning. This visual magic is available from the Custom Image screen of the Capture Functions menu (press the Fn button), and pops up when you press the center OK button.

When the screen appears, the last Image Tone selection you made is located in the upper-left corner of the screen. Press the left/right keys to highlight any of the six Image Tone options, labeled Bright, Natural, Portrait, Landscape, Vibrant, and Monochrome, as shown in Figure 5.23. Each of these represents a different basic image type, with preset parameters for things like color richness or contrast, but which you can modify to suit your own needs. When the Image Tone you want to work with is highlighted, press the down key to select one of four parameters that you can change. To modify the highlighted parameter, press the left/right controller keys.

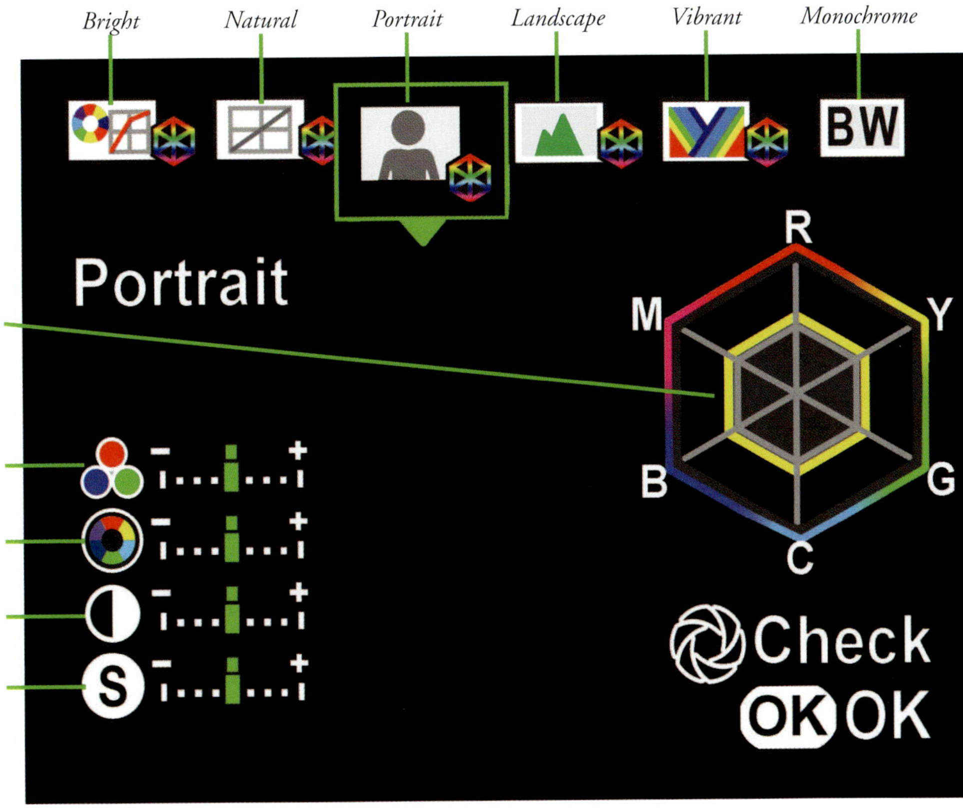

Figure 5.23
Select the Image Tone you want to modify.

To replace the blank background with a preview image, rotate the main switch around the shutter release button to the Digital Preview image position. The preview image will reflect any changes you make to an Image Tone setting as you make them.

For all the Image Tone choices other than Monochrome, you can choose Saturation, Hue, Contrast, and Sharpness. For the Monochrome Image Tone setting Filter Effect and Toning replace Saturation and Hue, but Contrast and Sharpness remain. Here's a quick description of each of these parameters:

- **Saturation (all but Monochrome).** You can adjust the richness of the color from low saturation (0 to –4) to high saturation (0 to +4). Lower saturation produces a muted look that can be more realistic for certain kinds of subjects, such as humans. Higher saturation produces a more vibrant appearance, but can be garish and unrealistic if carried too far. Boost your saturation if you want a vivid image, or to brighten up pictures taken on overcast days. As you adjust saturation, the hexagon in the center of the color wheel at the right side of the screen enlarges (as saturation increases) or contracts (as saturation decreases). A better indicator is an actual preview image, so I recommend that you activate one by rotating the main switch all the way clockwise, as I mentioned earlier. The preview will show the degree of saturation in effect much more visually.

- **Hue (all but Monochrome).** This parameter changes the bias of the image toward the red or yellow ends of the scale, with settings from 0 to –4 producing ruddier skin tones, and 0 to +4 creating more yellowish skin tones. The hexagon at right on the LCD monitor rotates to indicate the movement around the color wheel. Again, the preview image is a better indicator.
- **Contrast (all).** Compresses the range of tones in an image (increase contrast from 0 to +4) or expands the range of tones (from 0 to –4) to decrease contrast. Higher contrast images tend to lose detail in both shadows and highlights, while lower contrast images retain the detail but appear more flat and have less snap. The preview image is your only on-screen indicator of how your modification will affect your images.
- **Sharpness (all).** Increases or decreases the contrast of the edge outlines in your image, making the photo appear more or less sharp, depending on whether you've selected 0 (no sharpening) to up to +4 (extreme sharpening) or up to –4 (blurring). Remember that boosting sharpness also increases the overall contrast of an image, so you'll want to use this parameter in conjunction with the contrast parameter with caution. In addition to using the left/right buttons to adjust the amount of sharpening, you can spin the e-dial to switch between Sharpness and Fine Sharpness.
- **Filter Effect (Monochrome only).** This setting provides the look of black-and-white film when exposed through various color filters. The available filters include Green, Yellow, Orange, Red, Magenta, Blue, Cyan, Infrared Color, and None. Note that these filters change the *rendition* of a black-and-white image; they do not add any color to a monochrome photo. Old-time black-and-white film shooters will know what I am talking about. Everyone else should see the sidebar that follows for an explanation.
- **Toning (Monochrome only).** This option *does* add a color to a monochrome image. You can make the tone of your image colder (from 0 to –4) or warmer (from 0 to +4).

FILTERS VS. TONING

Although some of the color choices overlap, you'll get very different looks when choosing between Filter Effects and Toning. Filter Effects add no color to the monochrome image. Instead, they reproduce the look of black-and-white film that has been shot through a color filter. That is, Yellow will make the sky darker and the clouds will stand out more, while Orange makes the sky even darker and sunsets more full of detail. The Red filter produces the darkest sky of all and darkens green objects, such as leaves. Human skin may appear lighter than normal. The Green filter has the opposite effect on leaves, making them appear lighter in tone. Figure 5.24 shows the same scene shot with no filter, then Yellow, Green, and Red filters.

The Toning adjustment can be used to provide sepia (warm) or cyanotype (cold blue) images, simulating old-time photos. (See Figure 5.25.) Use either of these two settings when you want an antique look or a special effect, without bothering to recolor your shots in an image editor.

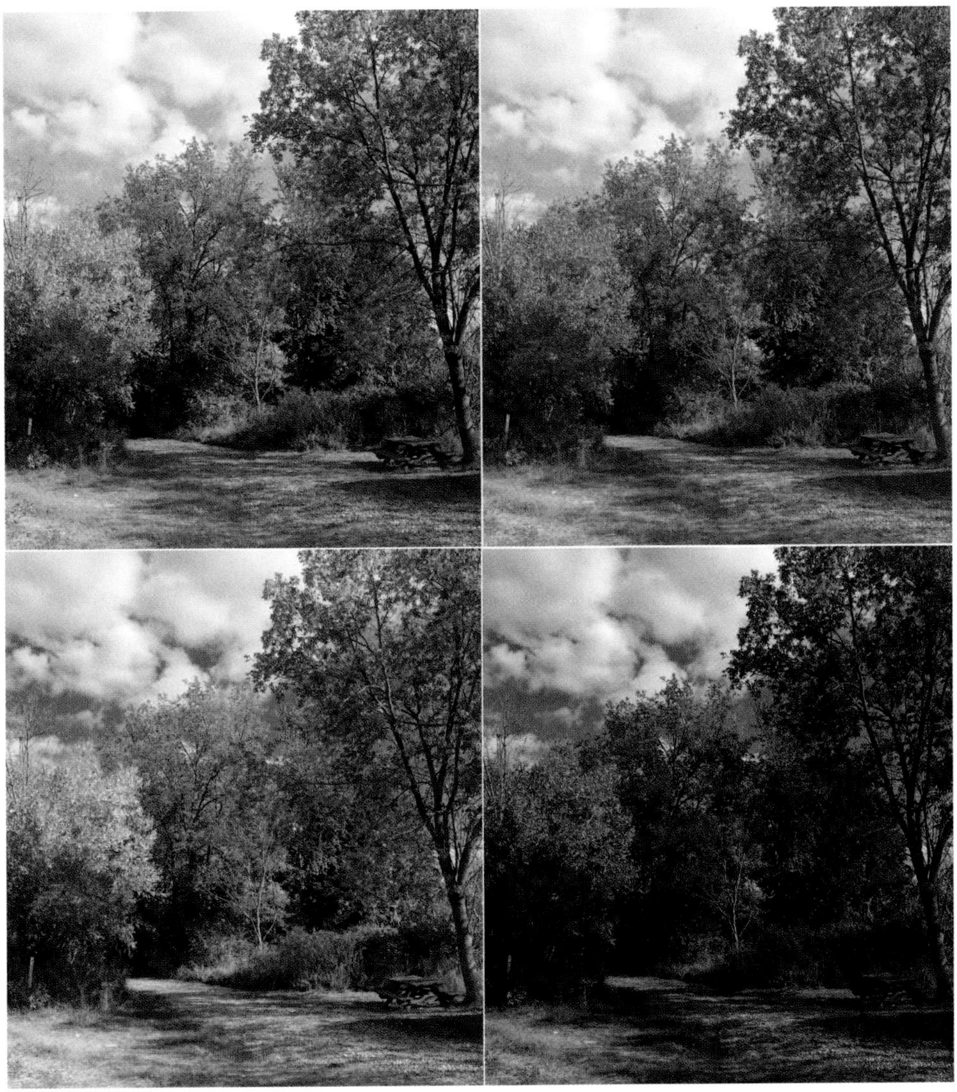

Figure 5.24 No filter (upper left); yellow filter (upper right); green filter (lower left), and red filter (lower right).

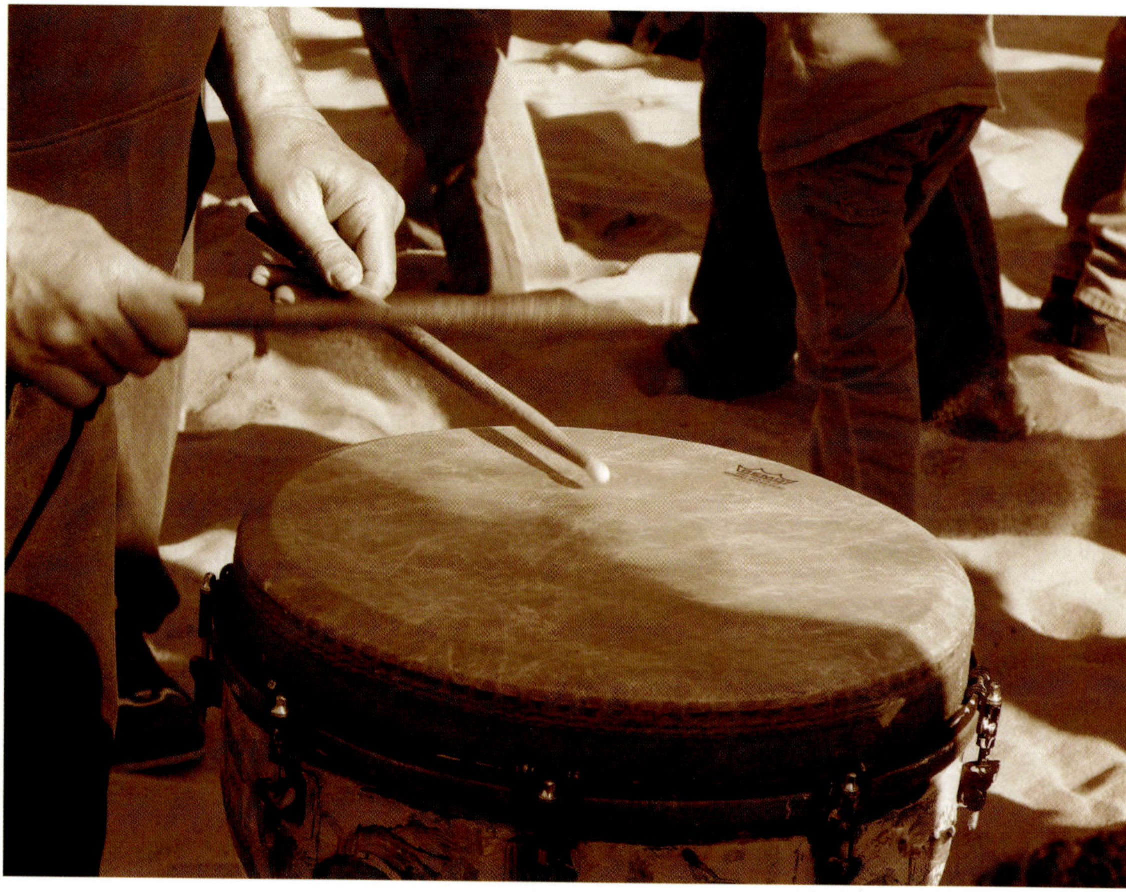

Figure 5.25 Sepia toning lends an old-time look to your photos.

Post-Processing with Digital Filters

The Image Tone features change the way your Pentax K200D exposes its images, introducing modifications to the photos as you snap them. Your camera also has a Digital Filter feature that can edit your photos after they've been exposed. Nothing is done to your original image. Instead, a copy of that photo is saved with the Digital Filters you've selected applied.

Digital Filters work only with JPEG images. To use them, press the Fn button while reviewing an image you want to modify in Playback mode. Press the Fn button to access the Playback Functions menu, and then click on the left key of the four-way controller. The screen that appears has a vertical row of six icons, each representing a digital filter with which you can manipulate your image. When an icon is selected using the down arrow of the four-way controller, your playback image adjusts according to the filter's characteristics. The name of the filter will also appear when you choose an icon.

I'm not a big fan of these digital filters, but they can be useful when you really, really need to make some changes in your camera, rather than in an honest-to-gosh image editor. (Say, you're rushed, lazy, don't have access to a computer, or need to send out an image in e-mail immediately.) Here are the tweaks that are available:

- **Black-and-White.** Changes a color image to black-and-white. There are no adjustments you can make here; it's a single-step filter. Press OK, and you'll be given the choice of saving the converted image under a new name, or canceling the operation.
- **Sepia Tone.** This filter changes an image to black-and-white and then adds a brown sepia tone. There are no modifications available, just Save or Cancel.
- **Color.** This option allows you to choose any of six different filters (Red, Magenta, Cyan, Blue, Green, and Yellow) using the left/right controller keys, and any of three different density levels, chosen with the e-dial. That gives you 18 different combinations. A color image is *not* converted to monochrome. This option actually applies a color cast of the selected hue and density to your color photo. If your image happens to be monochrome, you'll have a choice of 18 different sepia tones to apply instead.
- **Soft.** This Digital Filter fades your image subtly. You can select from three levels using the e-dial.
- **Illustration.** Photoshop-like filter that theoretically makes your image look as if it were drawn with a pen or pencil. In practice, though, what actually happens is that the camera applies a super-high degree of sharpening/contrast, in any of three levels selected with the e-dial. You're better off modifying the image in an image editor, unless you want to apply the effect now and then e-mail your shot off without ever passing it through editing software.
- **HDR (High Dynamic Range).** Gives more detail in the dark and light tones of the photo. (Again, theoretically.) Use the e-dial to adjust for three different levels. If you really want to expand the tonal range of an image, you're better off using an image editor or modifying the contrast using Image Tones and correct exposure.
- **Slim.** This Digital Filter lets you stretch your image horizontally or vertically. Rotate the e-dial to the left to make the image wider; to the right to slim it down.
- **Brightness.** This filter gives you 16 different levels of brightness from dark to light using the e-dial to make the adjustment.

6

Working with Lenses

If Pentax has one advantage over many of the other vendors of digital SLRs (other than making great, affordable cameras), it's the mind-bending assortment of high-quality lenses available to enhance the capabilities of cameras like the Pentax K200D. Pentax's official estimate (last updated in March 2006) is that there are 24 million compatible lenses that you can mount on your camera.

You can use most of the thousands of current and older lenses introduced by Pentax and third-party vendors in the last 50 years, although some older lenses require an adapter and won't have all the features found in the latest Pentax optics. (Don't expect autofocus from a 40-year-old manual focus lens, for example.) Accessory lenses can give you a wider view, bring distant subjects closer, let you focus closer, shoot under lower light conditions, or provide a more detailed, sharper image for critical work. Other than the sensor itself, the lens you choose for your dSLR is the most important component in determining image quality and perspective of your images.

This chapter explains how to select the best lenses for the kinds of photography you want to do.

But First, a Word from Our Sensor

One pervasive consideration that will trip us up in this chapter (and throughout this book) is the omnipresent *lens crop factor*. If the sensor is smaller than the standard 35mm film frame (24mm × 36mm), then any given lens will produce a field of view that's *cropped* from that full frame. To express the "real" field of view in 35mm terms, you must multiply a lens's focal length by the crop factor, which in the case of the Pentax

K200D is 1.5X. Other vendors, including Nikon, Canon, and Sony, sell dSLRs with a similar crop factor, but also offer several models with 1X (full-frame) sensors which provide the field of view shown for comparison in Figure 6.1.

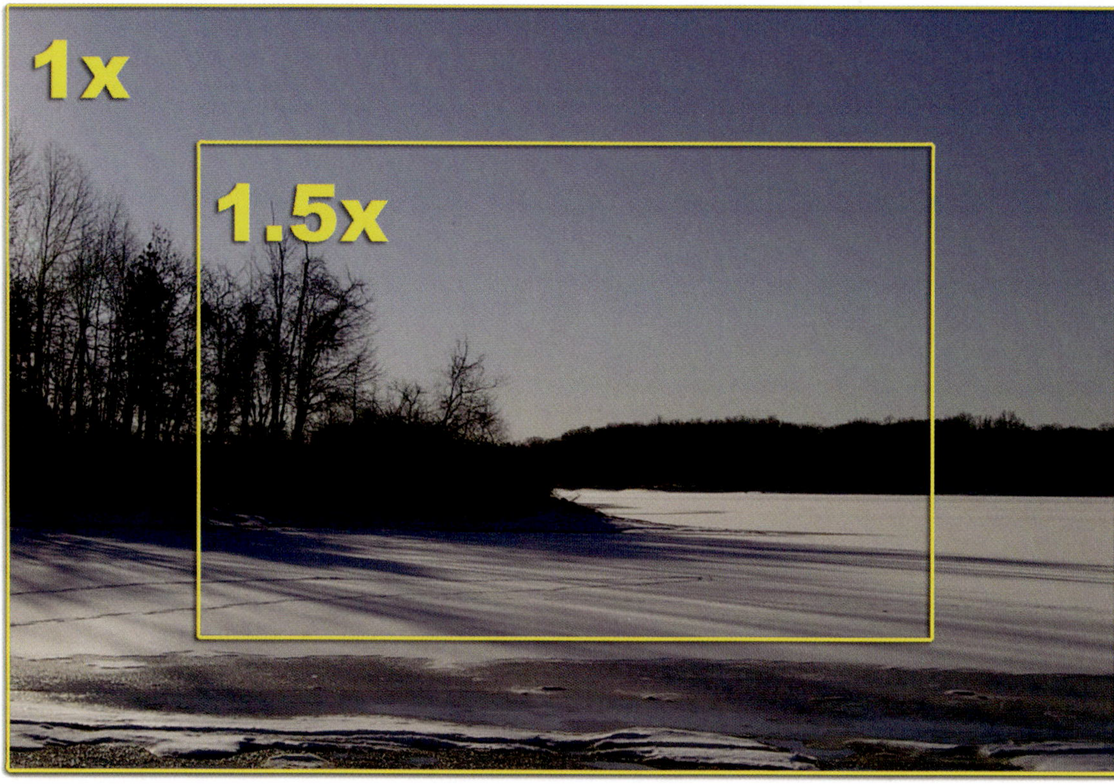

Figure 6.1 Pentax digital SLRs offer a 1.5X crop like the K200D, but other vendors market full-frame (1X crop) cameras.

The cropping effect is produced because the sensors of all Pentax digital SLRs to date are smaller than the sensors of the so-called "full-frame" cameras, which have a sensor that's the size of the standard 35mm film frame, 24mm × 36mm. Your K200D's sensor does *not* measure 24mm × 36mm; instead, it specs out at 23.5 × 15.7, which means that its diagonal measurement is about two-thirds that of a "full-frame" sensor, as shown by the yellow boxes in the figure. You can calculate the relative field of view by dividing the focal length of the lens by .667 (two-thirds). Thus, a 100mm lens mounted on a Pentax K200D has the same field of view as a 150mm lens on a 35mm film camera, like the Pentax Spotmatic that was the first SLR that I ever used. We humans tend to perform multiplication operations in our heads more easily than division, so such field of view comparisons are usually calculated using the reciprocal of .667—1.5—so we can multiply instead. (100 / .667=150; 100 × 1.5=150.)

This translation is generally useful only if you're accustomed to using full-frame cameras (usually of the film variety) and want to know how a familiar lens will perform on a digital camera. I strongly prefer *crop factor* over *lens multiplier*, because nothing is being multiplied; a 100mm lens doesn't "become" a 160mm lens—the depth-of-field and lens aperture remain the same. (I'll explain more about these later in this chapter.) Only the field of view is cropped. But *crop factor* isn't much better, as it implies that the 24 × 36mm frame is "full" and anything else is "less." I get e-mails all the time from photographers who point out that they own full-frame cameras with 36mm × 48mm sensors (like the Mamiya 645ZD or Hasselblad H3D-39 medium format digitals). By their reckoning, the "half-size" sensors found in "full-frame" cameras like the Canon EOS 1Ds Mark III or Nikon D700 are "cropped."

Of course, you may already be familiar with full-frame views from your use of Pentax (or other) 35mm film cameras. If so, you might find it helpful to use the crop factor "multiplier" to translate a lens's real focal length into the full-frame equivalent, even though nothing is actually being multiplied. Throughout most of this book, I've been using actual focal lengths and not equivalents, except when referring to specific wide-angle or telephoto focal length ranges and their fields of view.

Your First Lens

Some Pentax dSLRs are almost always purchased with a lens. The entry- and mid-level Pentax dSLRs, like the K200D or its stablemate the K2000D, are often bought by those new to digital photography, frequently by first-time SLR or dSLR owners who find the camera an irresistible bargain. Other Pentax models, including the more advanced Pentax K20D, are often purchased without a lens by veteran Pentax photographers who already have a complement of optics to use with their cameras.

I bought my K200D with the 18-55mm lens, even though I already had a suitable collection of lenses, because this lens is perfect to mount on the camera when I loan it to family members who have little photographic experience. Depending on which category of photographer you fall into, you'll need to make a decision about what kit lens to buy, or decide what other kind of lenses you need to fill out your complement of Pentax optics. This section will cover "first lens" concerns, while later in the chapter we'll look at "add-on lens" considerations.

When deciding on a first lens, there are several factors you'll want to consider:

- **Cost.** You might have stretched your budget a bit to purchase your Pentax K200D, so the 18-55mm f3.5-5.6 AL II kit lens helps you keep the cost of your first lens fairly low. In addition, there are other excellent moderately priced lenses available that will add from $100 to $300 to the price of your camera if purchased at the same time.

- **Zoom range.** If you have only one lens, you'll want a fairly long zoom range to provide as much flexibility as possible. Fortunately, there are several popular lenses for the K200D which have 3X to 5X zoom ranges, including an 18-250mm zoom, extending from moderate wide-angle/normal out to medium telephoto. Any of these are fine for everyday shooting, portraits, and some types of sports.
- **Adequate maximum aperture.** You'll want an f/stop of at least f/3.5 to f/4 for shooting under fairly low light conditions. The thing to watch for is the maximum aperture when the lens is zoomed to its telephoto end. You may end up with no better than an f/5.6 maximum aperture. That's not great, but you can often live with it, particularly when you are using your K200D's Shake Reduction capabilities, because you can often shoot at lower shutter speeds to compensate for the limited maximum aperture.
- **Image quality.** Your starter lens should have good image quality, because that's one of the primary factors that will be used to judge your photos. Even at a low price, several of the different lenses that can be used with the K200D include extra-low dispersion glass and aspherical elements that minimize distortion and chromatic aberration; they are sharp enough for most applications. If you read the user evaluations in the online photography forums, you know that owners of the kit lenses have been very pleased with its image quality.
- **Size matters.** A good walking-around lens is compact in size and light in weight.
- **Fast/close focusing.** Your first lens should have a speedy autofocus system (which is where the "supersonic" motor built into some of the latest Pentax lenses are an advantage). Close focusing (to 12 inches or closer) will let you use your basic lens for some types of macro photography.

Buy Now, Expand Later

The number of options available to you for the Pentax K200D is actually quite amazing, even if your budget is limited. Here's a list of Pentax's best-bet "first" lenses, including both inexpensive and pricier optics. Don't worry about sorting out the alphabet soup right now; I provide a list of Pentax lens "codes" later in the chapter.

- **smc P Pentax-DA 18-55mm f/3.5-5.6 AL II.** This new lens (see Figure 6.2) has improved image quality, and it provides the equivalent angle of view of a 27.5mm-84mm lens in the 35mm format. Its aspherical optical elements help make the lens smaller and lighter, and reduce aberrations.
- **smc P Pentax-DA 17-70mm f/4 AL [IF] SDM.** This $490 lens (see Figure 6.3) gives you a fixed f/4 aperture, and it uses the speedy Supersonic Drive Motor (SDM) autofocus system, which adjusts lens elements with a motor built into the lens, rather than the drive shaft in the body. It has both ED and aspherical elements to

compensate for chromatic and spherical aberration (described later) and, like the 18-55, has that rugged super protective coating on the front element.

- **smc P Pentax 16-50 f/2.8 ED AL [IF].** If you have $650 to spend, you might prefer this "star" lens, which has a constant f/2.8 aperture, and it goes a little wider than the kit lens at 16mm. It has the fast-focusing SDM autofocus technology, making it an all-around good choice for indoor sports. The ED and aspherical elements improve image quality.

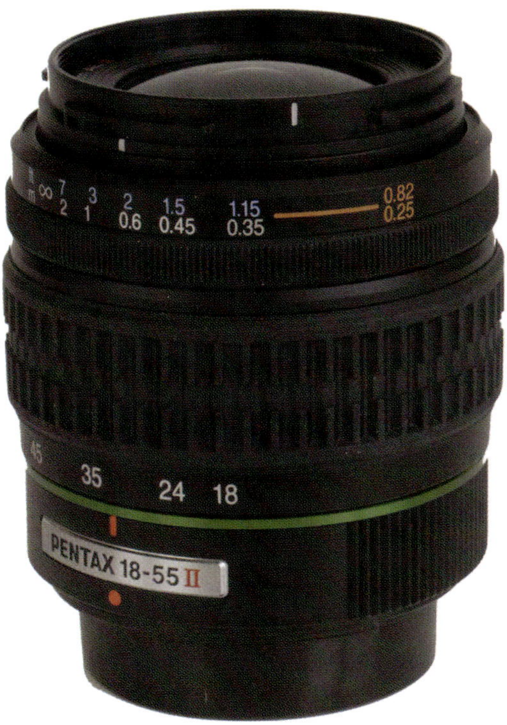

Figure 6.2 The Pentax K200D's 18-55mm kit lens is a bargain at less than $100.

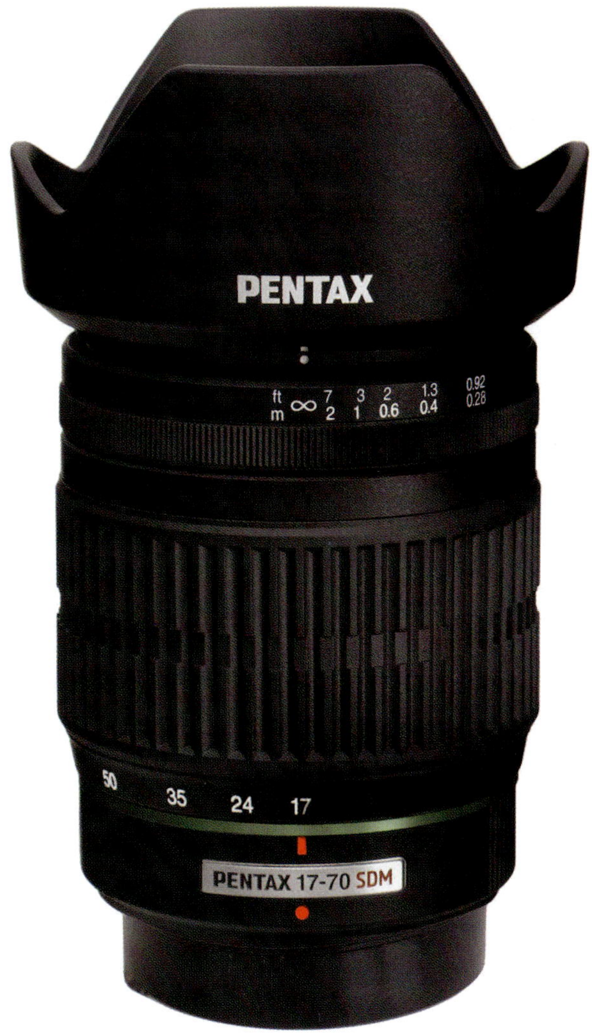

Figure 6.3 Slightly wider and longer, a lot faster, but costing five times as much, this 17-70mm f/4 lens is a good choice for the avid photographer.

What Lenses Can You Use?

The previous section helped you sort out what basic lens you need to buy with your Pentax K200D. Now, you're probably wondering what lenses can be added to your growing collection (trust me, it will grow). You need to know which lenses are suitable and, most importantly, which lenses are fully compatible with your Pentax K200D.

With the Pentax K200D, the compatibility issue is a simple one: It can use any Pentax lens that uses the K mount (introduced in 1975!), and earlier lenses, dating back to the 1960s, with an adapter. As far as third-party (non-Pentax) lenses go, your K200D will accept virtually all modern lenses produced by Tokina, Tamron, Sigma, and other vendors. If you come across a very old lens from third party vendors, you'll need to check with them to make sure it is compatible.

Using Really Old Lenses

Pentax has a long and glorious history of producing fine lenses. Pentax's original Asahiflex was a pioneer in the SLR arena back in the 1950s, but the company really came into its own in the '60s when the product line adopted the Pentax name and was imported into the US by a company called Honeywell. These cameras, including the incredibly popular TTL (through-the-lens) metering Pentax Spotmatic, used a 42mm diameter screw mount for its lenses. Other camera vendors "adopted" this mount, which came to be known as the Universal Pentax Screw Mount.

These lenses can be used today on your K200D in Manual focus mode, using what is called an M42-to-bayonet adapter. It sits flush with the Pentax's lens mount, and has a screw thread to accept M42 lenses. These optics are less convenient to use, because you lose autofocus (which was years in the future when these lenses were introduced), have to meter manually, and you must change the f/stop to the aperture you want to use.

Just set the AF/MF switch on the side of the K200D to MF (Manual focus), and choose Custom Setting Menu option Using Aperture Ring, and set to choice 2 (Permitted). Open the lens to its widest f/stop for easier viewing and focusing, and rotate the focusing ring until you see a sharp image. The green focus hexagon in the viewfinder will confirm sharp focus. Then, with the camera set for Program exposure, stop the lens down to the f/stop you want to use and press the shutter release halfway. The camera calculates the correct shutter speed for you.

Enter the K Mount

Pentax finally abandoned the screw mount in 1975, introducing the K mount, which, to make things short and sweet, is the mount used by every single Pentax film or digital SLR since then. So, any Pentax K mount lens can be used with your K200D, with a single exception—an early autofocus lens (actually, the *first* autofocus lens available anywhere) using something called the K_F mount, designed solely for the Pentax ME-F film camera. Of course, with older K mount lenses, some features, including autofocus, won't be available with lenses that didn't offer them originally.

Original K mount. The first K mount lenses communicated with the camera solely through a mechanical linkage that allowed stopping down the aperture at the time the picture was taken, and providing the camera with information about what f/stop has been selected on the aperture ring, so the correct shutter speed can be calculated. Obviously, the camera is unable to set the f/stop (only "read" what aperture you have selected), so these lenses operate only in Manual exposure mode, or the equivalent of what we call today *aperture priority.* Old lenses using the original 1975 K mount had no special designation; they'll be marked simply SMC (for Super Multi Coated) Pentax or SMC Pentax-M.

K_A mount. The mount was introduced in 1983, and it added six electrical contacts to the rear of the lens, which, in conjunction with an improved mechanical linkage, allows the camera to adjust the f/stop accurately. That improvement made shutter priority (where you choose the shutter and the camera selects an f/stop) and program exposure (where the camera sets both values) to be added to the Pentax film camera line's aperture priority autoexposure options.

K_{AF} and later versions. Later editions of the K mount starting with the K_{AF} in 1987, added a drive shaft built into the camera body, still present today in cameras like the K200D, which lets the camera change the focus of the lens efficiently. This made autofocus possible. A seventh electrical contact was added to send information from the lens to the camera including focal length, subject distance, and f/stop. Power contacts in the later editions of the K mount are used to provide juice for the latest SDM (Supersonic Drive Motor) lenses, which move diaphragm operation into the lens itself, rather than rely on the camera body driveshaft. The rear of the latest version of a K mount lens is shown in Figure 6.4.

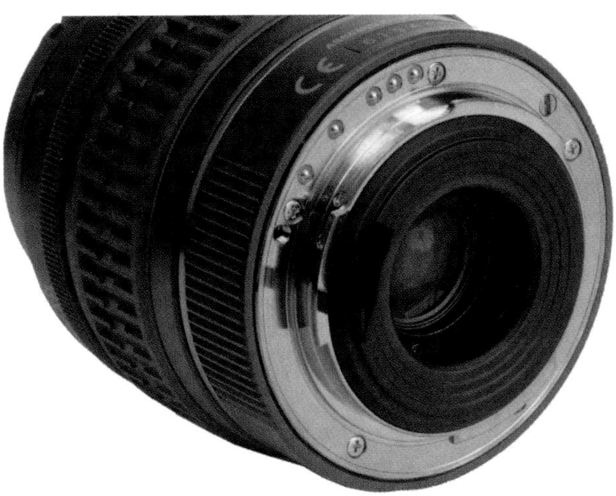

Figure 6.4
Electrical contacts on the back of the lens communicate with the camera body.

Pentax Lens Nomenclature

Unfortunately, Pentax has elected to apply a sometimes-bewildering alphabet soup of nomenclature to its lenses, and from time to time in the manual that came with your camera you'll see warnings about certain features that are only available if you use, say, a lens with a designation of FA, FA J, D FA, DA (ad nauseum). I haven't burdened you with these details because, for the most part, and for 99.9 percent of all Pentax K200D owners, they aren't relevant. Unless you're using a very old lens, it's compatible with every feature of the camera.

The only thing you really need to keep in mind is that, with any lens having an aperture ring (which allows you to set the f/stops on the lens), you need to leave it locked at the A or Automatic position so the camera can have full control over your lens. (It's likely that all or most of the lenses you own won't even have an aperture ring, so you can ignore that advice, too.)

In practice, Pentax lenses will have either an F or DA designation, which you'll know for sure, because the letters representing that lens series will be included in the name of the lens. Here's a quick summary:

- **F series.** Lenses with an F designation were the first practical autofocus Pentax lenses. They'll be marked with some variation of F or FA, and are compatible with both full frame (film) cameras, and digital cameras having a reduced sensor size. When an asterisk (star) is appended, that lens is a premium version, generally with superior optics and a large lens opening. You'll know that F* and FA* lenses are (almost) top of the line. The ultimate, ultrapremium lenses are labeled FA Limited. At the other end of the scale are FA-J lenses, an older "budget" line of optics, with a plastic lens mount and no aperture ring.
- **DA series.** Newer lenses belong to this series, and will be marked DA, DA* (Pentax calls this DA Star), or DA Limited. These lenses are designed specifically for digital cameras. The DA* lenses have one advantage over all other F and DA lenses: they have the Pentax Supersonic Drive Motor built in, and receive the SDM designation in their name. Note that not all DA lenses have the reduced image circle typical of optics designed for "cropped" sensors. Several of the DA Limited lenses (the 70mm f/2.4 and 40mm f/2.8), two DA* lenses (the 200mm f/2.8 and 300mm f/4), and the DA 35mm f/2.8 macro will all cover a full 24 × 36mm image frame. Of course, that's a moot point as I write this, as no Pentax digital full-frame camera is on the horizon.

You'll find other designations built into Pentax lens names. These include:

- **ED.** The ED (extra low dispersion) designation indicates that some lens elements are made of a special hard and scratch-resistant glass that minimizes the divergence of the different colors of light as they pass through, thus reducing chromatic aberration (color "fringing") and other image defects.

- **IF.** Pentax's *internal focusing* lenses change focus by shifting only small internal lens groups with no change required in the lens's physical length, unlike conventional double helicoid focusing systems that move all lens groups toward the front or rear during focusing. IF lenses are more compact and lighter in weight, provide better balance, focus more closely, and can be focused more quickly.
- **AL.** This designation indicates a lens that uses *aspheric elements*, which are lens components with a profile that is not a section of a sphere or cylinder. The more complex surfaces of these elements allow better correction of certain lens defects.
- **SMC/SMCP.** This abbreviation means *super multi-coated*, which is an attribute of lenses that are given several layers of chemical treatment to reduce partial reflection or flare from the lens surface. The SMCP variation denotes a lens with the rugged Super Protective coating which uses a special fluoride compound on the front surface of the lens that repels water and oil, while providing easier cleaning of fingerprints and other dirt. Virtually all Pentax lenses are super multi-coated, but it is included in the lens name because Pentax actually invented and patented the process in 1971. Other vendors use multi-coating on their lenses and filters, but only Pentax (and Hoya, now its parent company) can rightly use the super multi-coating designation.
- **II (etc.)** When Pentax introduces a new lens with the same specification as the old one, a Roman numeral is appended.

What Lenses Can Do for You

No one can afford to buy even a percentage of the lenses available. The sanest approach to expanding your lens collection is to consider what each of your options can do for you and then choose the type of lens and specific model that will really boost your creative opportunities. So, in the sections that follow, I'm going to provide a general guide to the sort of capabilities you can gain for your K200D by adding a lens to your repertoire.

- **Wider perspective.** Your 18-55mm kit lens has served you well for moderate wide-angle shots. Now you find your back is up against a wall and you *can't* take a step backward to take in more subject matter. Perhaps you're standing on the rim of the Grand Canyon, and you want to take in as much of the breathtaking view as you can. You might find yourself just behind the baseline at a high-school basketball game and want an interesting shot with a little perspective distortion tossed in the mix.
- **Bring objects closer.** A long lens brings distant subjects closer to you, offers better control over depth-of-field, and avoids the perspective distortion that wide-angle lenses provide. They compress the apparent distance between objects in your frame.

Don't forget that the Pentax K200D's crop factor narrows the field of view of all these lenses, so your SMC Pentax DA 50-200mm f/4-f5.6 ED lens looks more like a 75mm-300mm zoom through the viewfinder. The image shown in Figure 6.5 was taken using a wide 16mm lens, while the images in Figures 6.6 and 6.7 were taken from the same position as Figure 6.5, but with focal lengths of 40mm and 85mm, respectively.

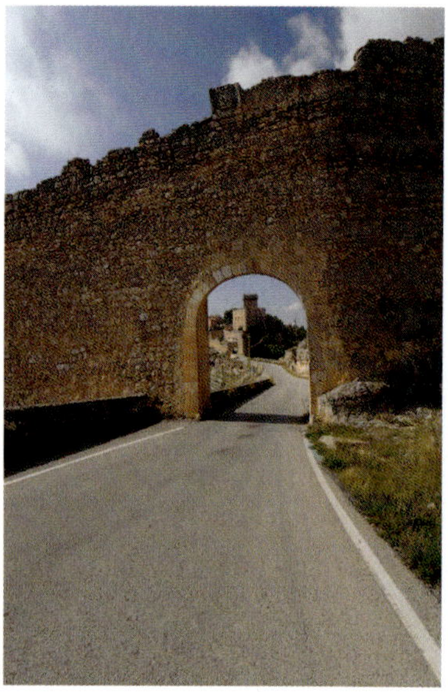

Figure 6.5 An ultra-wide-angle lens provided this view of an 8th Century castle.

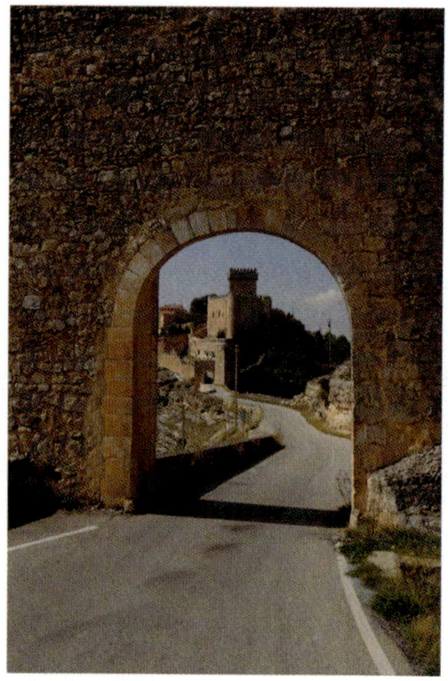

Figure 6.6 This photo, taken from roughly the same distance, shows the view using a "normal" lens.

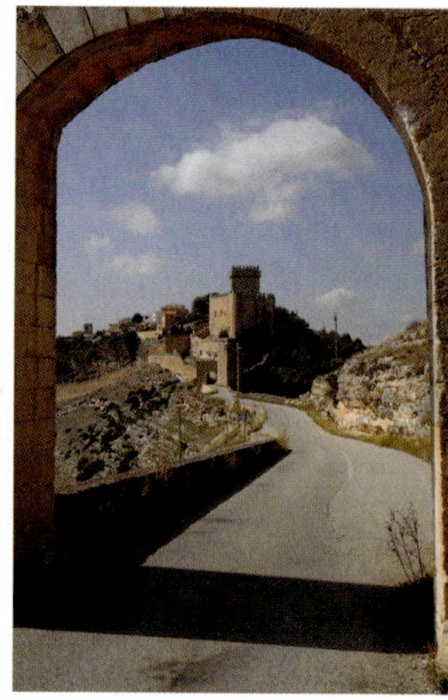

Figure 6.7 A medium telephoto lens captured this close-up view of the castle from approximately the same shooting position.

- **Bring your camera closer.** Macro lenses allow you to focus to within an inch or two of your subject. Pentax's best close-up lenses are all fixed focal length optics in the 50mm to 100mm range. But you'll find good macro zooms available from Sigma and others. They don't tend to focus quite as close, but they provide a bit of flexibility when you want to vary your subject distance (say, to avoid spooking a skittish creature).
- **Look sharp.** Many lenses are prized for their sharpness and overall image quality. While your run-of-the-mill lens is likely to be plenty sharp for most applications, the very best optics are even better over their entire field of view (which means no fuzzy corners), are sharper at a wider range of focal lengths (in the case of zooms), and have better correction for various types of distortion.
- **More speed.** Your nifty Pentax-DA 18-250mm f/3.5-6.3 ED lens might have the perfect focal length and sharpness for sports photography, but the maximum aperture for f/6.3 at 250mm won't cut it for night baseball or football games, or, even,

any sports shooting in daylight if the weather is cloudy or you need to use some ungodly fast shutter speed, such as 1/4,000th second. You might be happier to gain two and a half f/stops (while relieving your wallet of $800) with the Pentax SMCP-DA* 200mm f/2.8 ED (IF) SDM lens. Or, maybe you just need the speed and can benefit from an f/1.8 or f/1.4 prime lens. With any of these faster lenses you can continue photographing under the dimmest of lighting conditions without the need for a tripod or flash or an increase in your ISO sensitivity.

- **Special features.** Accessory lenses give you special features, close-up (macro) capabilities, or the fun factor of one of my personal favorites, the SMC Pentax-DA Fish-Eye 10-17mm f/3.54.5 ED [IF] lens.

Zoom or Prime?

Zoom lenses have changed the way serious photographers take pictures. One of the reasons that I own 12 SLR film bodies dating back to the pre-zoom days is that in ancient times it was common to mount a different fixed focal length prime lens on various cameras and take pictures with two or three cameras around your neck (or tucked in a camera case) so you'd be ready to take a long shot or an intimate close-up or wide-angle view on a moment's notice, without the need to switch lenses. It made sense (at the time) to have a half-dozen or so bodies (two to use, one in the shop, one in transit, and a couple backups). Zoom lenses of the time had a limited zoom range, were heavy, and not very sharp (especially when you tried to wield one of those monsters hand-held). That's all changed today. Smaller, longer, sharper zoom lenses are available.

When selecting between zoom and prime lenses, there are several considerations to ponder. Here's a checklist of the most important factors. I already mentioned image quality and maximum aperture earlier, but those aspects take on additional meaning when comparing zooms and primes.

- **Logistics.** As prime lenses offer just a single focal length, you'll need more of them to encompass the full range offered by a single zoom. More lenses mean additional slots in your camera bag, and extra weight to carry. Just within Pentax's line alone you can choose from a good selection of general purpose prime lenses in 14mm, 21mm, 31mm, 35mm, 40mm, 43mm, 50mm, 55mm, 70mm, 77mm, 200mm, 300mm, and 600mm focal lengths. Of course, nine of them are overlapped by the 18-250mm zoom I mentioned earlier. Even so, you might be willing to carry an extra prime lens or two in order to gain the speed or image quality that lens offers.
- **Image quality.** Prime lenses usually produce better image quality at their focal length than even the most sophisticated zoom lenses at the same magnification. Zoom lenses, with their shifting elements and f/stops that can vary from zoom position to zoom position, are in general more complex to design than fixed focal length lenses. That's not to say that the very best prime lenses can't be complicated as well.

However, the exotic designs, aspheric elements, and low-dispersion glass can be applied to improving the quality of the lens, rather than wasting a lot of it on compensating for problems caused by the zoom process itself.

- **Maximum aperture.** Because of the same design constraints, zoom lenses usually have smaller maximum apertures than prime lenses, and the most affordable zooms have a lens opening that grows effectively smaller as you zoom in. The difference in lens speed verges on the ridiculous at some focal lengths. For example, the 18mm-55mm basic zoom gives you a 55mm f/5.6 lens when zoomed all the way out, while prime lenses in that focal length commonly have f/1.8 or faster maximum apertures. Figure 6.8 shows an image of legendary bluegrass performer "Doctor" Ralph Stanley, taken with an f /1.8 lens.

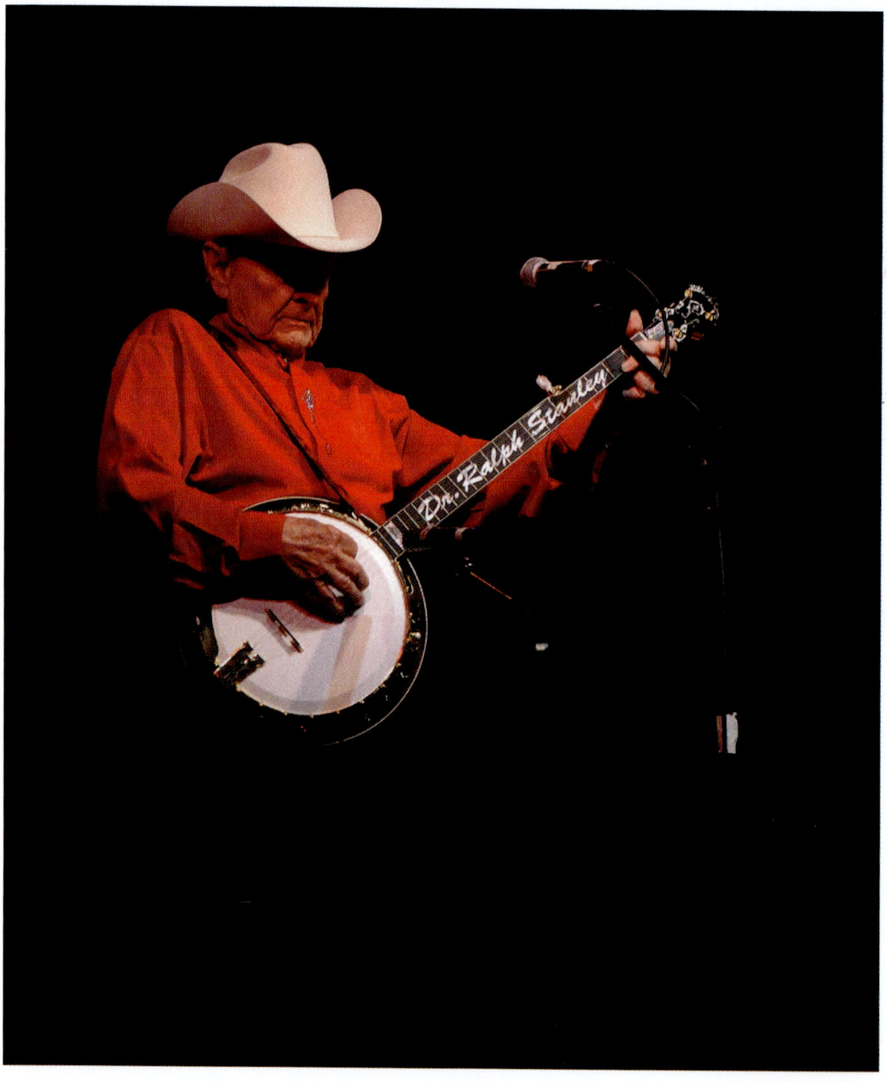

Figure 6.8
A lens with an f/1.8 maximum aperture was perfect for this hand-held photo at a concert.

- **Speed.** Using prime lenses takes time and slows you down. It takes a few seconds to remove your current lens and mount a new one, and the more often you need to do that, the more time is wasted. If you choose not to swap lenses, when using a fixed focal length lens you'll still have to move closer or farther away from your subject to get the field of view you want. A zoom lens allows you to change magnifications and focal lengths with the twist of a ring and generally saves a great deal of time.

Categories of Lenses

Lenses can be categorized by their intended purpose—general photography, macro photography, and so forth—or by their focal length. The range of available focal lengths is usually divided into three main groups: wide-angle, normal, and telephoto. Prime lenses fall neatly into one of these classifications. Zooms can overlap designations, with a significant number falling into the catch-all wide-to-telephoto zoom range. This section provides more information about focal length ranges, and how they are used.

When the 1.5X crop factor (mentioned at the beginning of this chapter) is figured in, any lens with an equivalent focal length of 10mm to 16mm is said to be an *ultra-wide-angle lens*; from about 16mm to 30mm is said to be a *wide-angle lens. Normal lenses* have a focal length roughly equivalent to the diagonal of the film or sensor, in millimeters, and so fall into the range of about 30mm to 40mm on a K200D. *Short telephoto lenses* start at about 40mm to 70mm, with anything from 70mm to 250mm qualifying as a conventional *telephoto.* For the Pentax K200D, anything from about 300mm-400mm or longer can be considered a *super-telephoto.*

Using Wide-Angle and Wide-Zoom Lenses

To use wide-angle prime lenses and wide zooms, you need to understand how they affect your photography. Here's a quick summary of the things you need to know.

- **More depth-of-field.** Practically speaking, wide-angle lenses offer more depth-of-field at a particular subject distance and aperture. (But see the sidebar below for an important note.) You'll find that helpful when you want to maximize sharpness of a large zone, but not very useful when you'd rather isolate your subject using selective focus (telephoto lenses are better for that).
- **Stepping back.** Wide-angle lenses have the effect of making it seem that you are standing farther from your subject than you really are. They're helpful when you don't want to back up, or can't because there are impediments in your way.
- **Wider field of view.** While making your subject seem farther away, as implied above, a wide-angle lens also provides a larger field of view, including more of the subject in your photos.

- **More foreground.** As background objects retreat, more of the foreground is brought into view by a wide-angle lens. That gives you extra emphasis on the area that's closest to the camera. Photograph your home with a normal lens/normal zoom setting, and the front yard probably looks fairly conventional in your photo (that's why they're called "normal" lenses). Switch to a wider lens and you'll discover that your lawn now makes up much more of the photo. So, wide-angle lenses are great when you want to emphasize that lake in the foreground, but problematic when your intended subject is located farther in the distance.
- **Super-sized subjects.** The tendency of a wide-angle lens to emphasize objects in the foreground, while de-emphasizing objects in the background can lead to a kind of size distortion that may be more objectionable for some types of subjects than others. Shoot a bed of flowers up close with a wide angle, and you might like the distorted effect of the larger blossoms nearer the lens. Take a photo of a family member with the same lens from the same distance, and you're likely to get some complaints about that gigantic nose in the foreground.
- **Perspective distortion.** When you tilt the camera so the plane of the sensor is no longer perpendicular to the vertical plane of your subject, some parts of the subject are now closer to the sensor than they were before, while other parts are farther away. So, buildings, flagpoles, or NBA players appear to be falling backwards, as you can see in Figure 6.9. While this kind of apparent distortion (it's not caused by a defect in the lens) can happen with any lens, it's most apparent when a wide angle is used.
- **Steady cam.** You'll find that you can hand-hold a wide-angle lens at slower shutter speeds, without need for vibration reduction, than you can with a telephoto lens. The reduced magnification of the wide-lens or wide-zoom setting doesn't emphasize camera shake like a telephoto lens does.
- **Interesting angles.** Many of the factors already listed combine to produce more interesting angles when shooting with wide-angle lenses. Raising or lowering a telephoto lens a few feet probably will have little effect on the appearance of the distant subjects you're shooting. The same change in elevation can produce a dramatic effect for the much-closer subjects typically captured with a wide-angle lens or wide-zoom setting.

DOF IN DEPTH

The depth-of-field (DOF) advantage of wide-angle lenses is diminished when you enlarge your picture; believe it or not, a wide-angle image enlarged and cropped to provide the same subject size as a telephoto shot would have the *same* depth-of-field. Try it: take a wide-angle photo of a friend from a fair distance, and then zoom in to duplicate the picture in a telephoto image. Then, enlarge the wide shot so your friend is the same size in both. The wide photo will have the same depth-of-field (and will have much less detail, too).

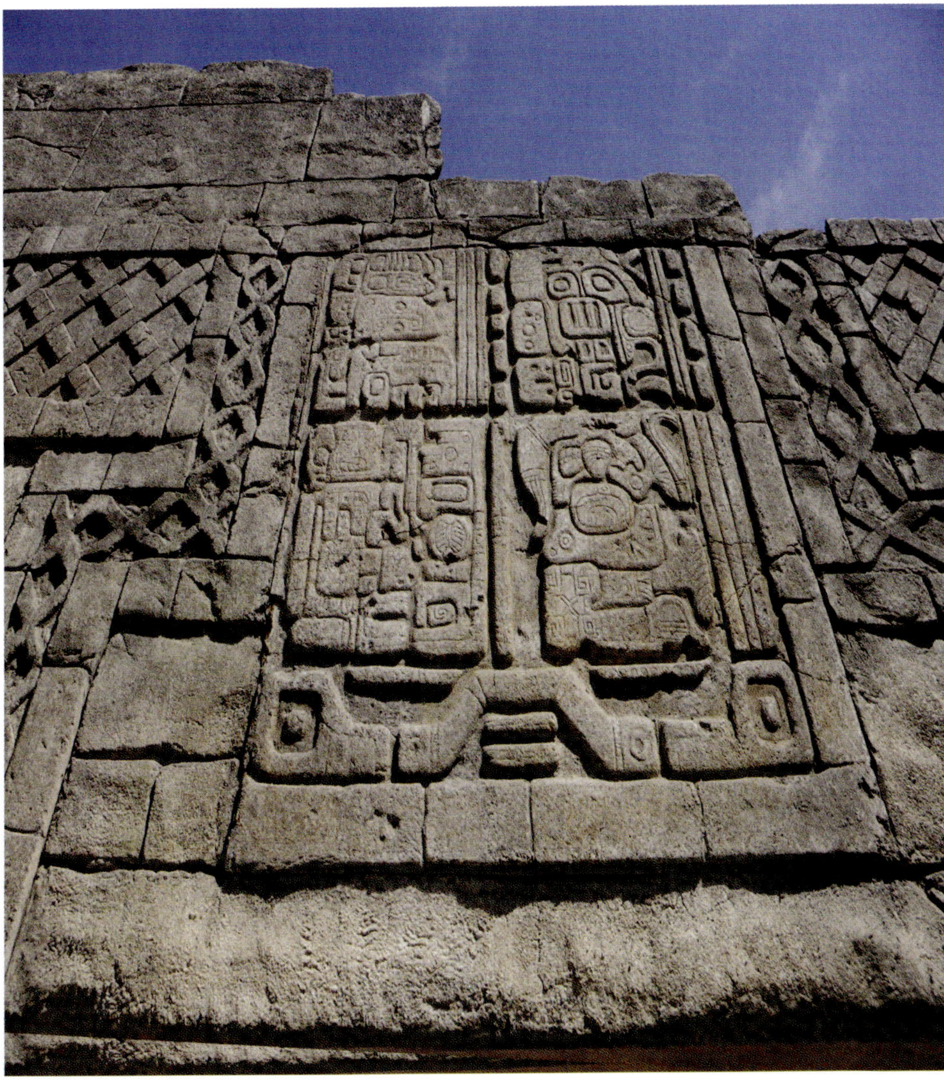

Figure 6.9
Tilting the camera back produces this "falling back" look in architectural photos.

Avoiding Potential Wide-Angle Problems

Wide-angle lenses have a few quirks that you'll want to keep in mind when shooting so you can avoid falling into some common traps. Here's a checklist of tips for avoiding common problems:

- **Symptom: converging lines.** Unless you want to use wildly diverging lines as a creative effect, it's a good idea to keep horizontal and vertical lines in landscapes, architecture, and other subjects carefully aligned with the sides, top, and bottom of the frame. That will help you avoid undesired perspective distortion. Sometimes it helps to shoot from a slightly elevated position so you don't have to tilt the camera up or down.

- **Symptom: color fringes around objects.** Lenses are often plagued with fringes of color around backlit objects, produced by *chromatic aberration*, which is produced when all the colors of light don't focus in the same plane or same lateral position (that is, the colors are offset to one side). Some kinds of chromatic aberration can be reduced by stopping down the lens, while all sorts can be reduced by using lenses with low diffraction index glass (or ED elements, in Pentax nomenclature) and by incorporating elements that cancel the chromatic aberration of other glass in the lens.
- **Symptom: lines that bow outward.** Some wide-angle lenses cause straight lines to bow outwards, with the strongest effect at the edges. In fisheye (or *curvilinear*) lenses, this defect is a feature, as you can see in Figure 6.10. When distortion is not desired, you'll need to use a lens that has corrected barrel distortion. Manufacturers

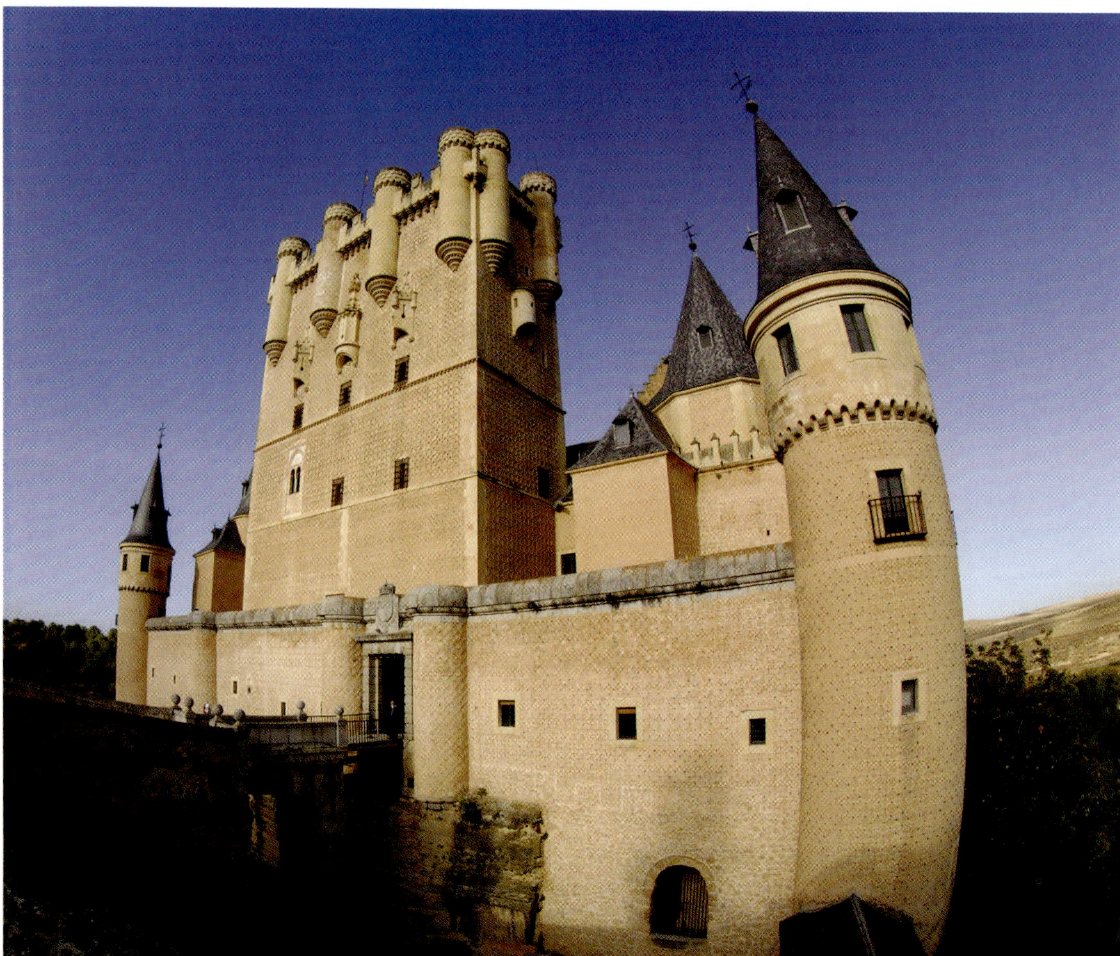

Figure 6.10 Many wide-angle lenses cause lines to bow outwards towards the edges of the image; with a fisheye lens, this tendency is considered an interesting feature.

like Pentax do their best to minimize or eliminate it (producing a *rectilinear* lens), often using *aspherical* lens elements (which are not cross-sections of a sphere). You can also minimize barrel distortion simply by framing your photo with some extra space all around, so the edges where the defect is most obvious can be cropped out of the picture. Some image editors, such as Photoshop and Photoshop Elements have a lens distortion correction feature.

- **Symptom: dark corners and shadows in flash photos.** The Pentax K200D's built-in electronic flash is designed to provide even coverage for lenses as wide as 17mm. If you use a wider lens, you can expect darkening, or *vignetting*, in the corners of the frame. At wider focal lengths, the lens hood of some lenses can cast a semi-circular shadow in the lower portion of the frame when using the built-in flash. Sometimes removing the lens hood or zooming in a bit can eliminate the shadow. Mounting an external flash unit can solve both problems.

Using Telephoto and Tele-Zoom Lenses

Telephoto lenses also can have a dramatic effect on your photography, and Pentax is especially strong in the long-lens arena, with lots of choices in many focal lengths and zoom ranges. You should be able to find an affordable telephoto or tele-zoom to enhance your photography in several different ways. Here are the most important things you need to know. In the next section, I'll concentrate on telephoto considerations that can be problematic—and how to avoid those problems.

- **Selective focus.** Long lenses have reduced depth-of-field within the frame, allowing you to use selective focus to isolate your subject. You can open the lens up wide to create shallow depth-of-field, or close it down a bit to allow more to be in focus. The flip side of the coin is that when you *want* to make a range of objects sharp, you'll need to use a smaller f/stop to get the depth-of-field you need. Like fire, the depth-of-field of a telephoto lens can be friend or foe. Figure 6.11 shows a photo of a holiday tree ornament photographed using a telephoto macro lens and wider f/stop to de-emphasize the other portions of the background.
- **Getting closer.** Telephoto lenses bring you closer to wildlife, sports action, and candid subjects. No one wants to get a reputation as a surreptitious or "sneaky" photographer (except for paparazzi), but when applied to candids in an open and honest way, a long lens can help you capture memorable moments while retaining enough distance to stay out of the way of events as they transpire.
- **Reduced foreground/increased compression.** Telephoto lenses have the opposite effect of wide angles: they reduce the importance of things in the foreground by squeezing everything together. This compression even makes distant objects appear to be closer to subjects in the foreground and middle ranges. You can use this effect as a creative tool to squeeze subjects together.

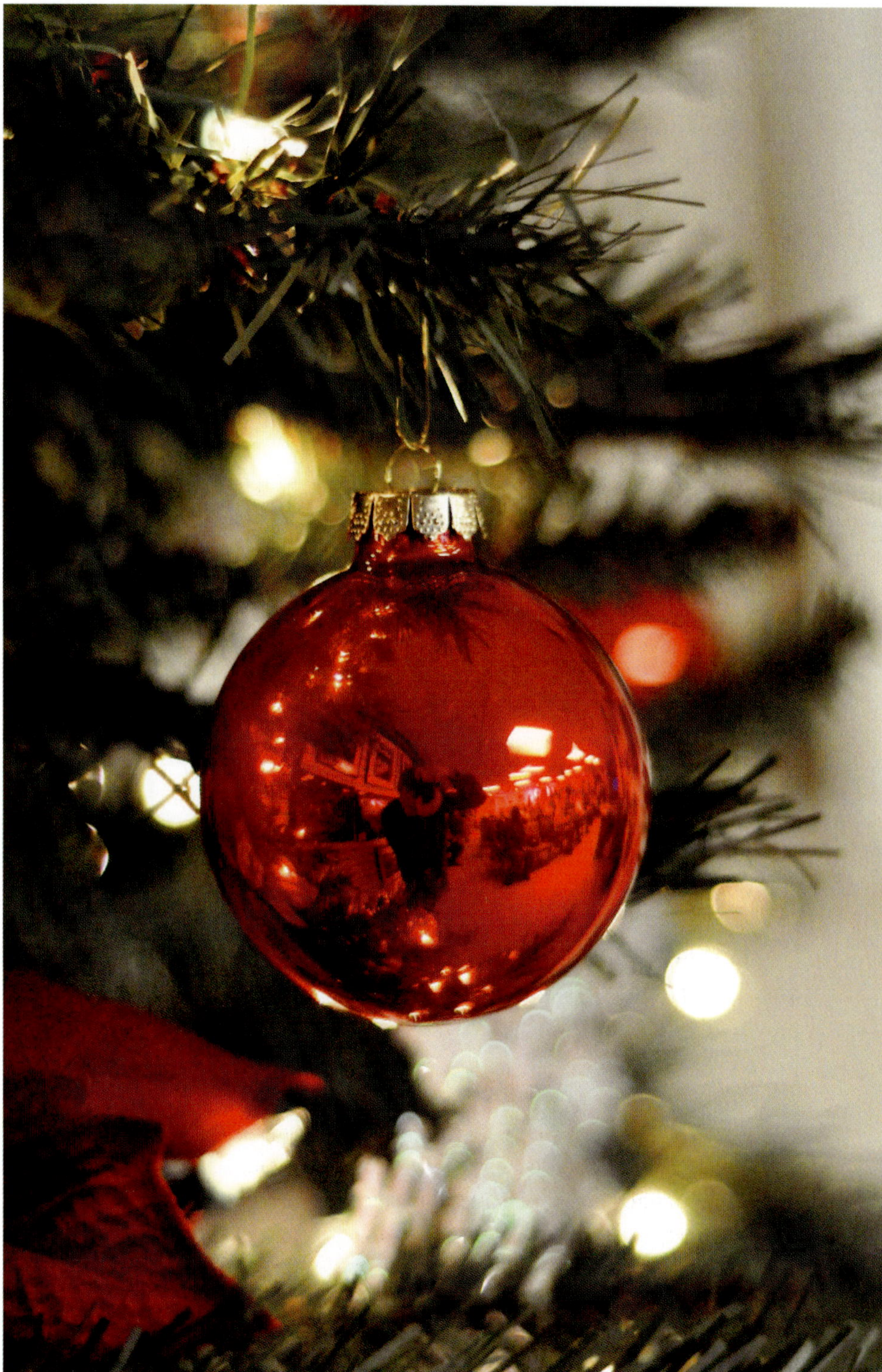

Figure 6.11
A wide f/stop helped isolate the tree ornament, while allowing the background to go out of focus.

- **Accentuates camera shakiness.** Telephoto focal lengths hit you with a double-whammy in terms of camera/photographer shake. The lenses themselves are bulkier, more difficult to hold steady, and may even produce a barely perceptible see-saw rocking effect when you support them with one hand halfway down the lens barrel. Telephotos also magnify any camera shake. It's no wonder that vibration reduction is popular in longer lenses.
- **Interesting angles require creativity.** Telephoto lenses require more imagination in selecting interesting angles, because the "angle" you do get on your subjects is so narrow. Moving from side to side or a bit higher or lower can make a dramatic difference in a wide-angle shot, but raising or lowering a telephoto lens a few feet probably will have little effect on the appearance of the distant subjects you're shooting.

Avoiding Telephoto Lens Problems

Many of the "problems" that telephoto lenses pose are really just challenges and not that difficult to overcome. Here is a list of the seven most common picture maladies and suggested solutions.

- **Symptom: flat faces in portraits.** Head-and-shoulders portraits of humans tend to be more flattering when a focal length of 50mm to 85mm is used. Longer focal lengths compress the distance between features like noses and ears, making the face look wider and flat. A wide-angle might make noses look huge and ears tiny when you fill the frame with a face. So stick with 50mm to 85mm focal lengths, going longer only when you're forced to shoot from a greater distance, and wider only when shooting three-quarters/full-length portraits, or group shots.
- **Symptom: blur due to camera shake.** Use a higher shutter speed (boosting ISO if necessary); consider using Shake Reduction; or mount your camera on a tripod, monopod, or brace it with some other support. Of those three solutions, only the first will reduce blur caused by *subject* motion; shake reduction or a tripod won't help you freeze a racecar in mid-lap.
- **Symptom: color fringes.** Chromatic aberration is the most pernicious optical problem found in telephoto lenses. There are others, including spherical aberration, astigmatism, coma, curvature of field, and similarly scary-sounding phenomena. The best solution for any of these is to use a better lens that offers the proper degree of correction, or stop down the lens to minimize the problem. But that's not always possible. Your second-best choice may be to correct the fringing in your favorite RAW conversion tool or image editor. Photoshop CS4's Lens Correction filter (found in the Filter > Distort menu) offers sliders that minimize both red/cyan and blue/yellow fringing.

- **Symptom: lines that curve inward.** Pincushion distortion is found in many telephoto lenses. You might find after a bit of testing that it is worse at certain focal lengths with your particular zoom lens. Like chromatic aberration, it can be partially corrected using tools like the correction tools built into Photoshop and Photoshop Elements.
- **Symptom: low contrast from haze or fog.** When you're photographing distant objects, a long lens shoots through a lot more atmosphere, which generally is muddied up with extra haze and fog. That dirt or moisture in the atmosphere can reduce contrast and mute colors. Some feel that a skylight or UV filter can help, but this practice is mostly a holdover from the film days. Digital sensors are not sensitive enough to UV light for a UV filter to have much effect. So you should be prepared to boost contrast and color saturation in your Picture Controls menu or image editor if necessary.
- **Symptom: low contrast from flare.** Lenses are furnished with lens hoods for a good reason: to reduce flare from bright light sources at the periphery of the picture area, or completely outside it. Because telephoto lenses often create images that are lower in contrast in the first place, you'll want to be especially careful to use a lens hood to prevent further effects on your image (or shade the front of the lens with your hand).
- **Symptom: dark flash photos.** Edge-to-edge flash coverage isn't a problem with telephoto lenses as it is with wide angles. The shooting distance is. A long lens might make a subject that's 50 feet away look as if it's right next to you, but your camera's flash isn't fooled. You'll need extra power for distant flash shots, and probably more power than your K200D's built-in flash provides. Use an external flash (see more on accessory units in the next chapter).

Telephotos and Bokeh

Bokeh describes the aesthetic qualities of the out-of-focus parts of an image and whether out-of-focus points of light—circles of confusion—are rendered as distracting fuzzy discs or smoothly fade into the background. *Boke* is a Japanese word for "blur," and the h was added to keep English speakers from rendering it monosyllabically to rhyme with *broke.* Although bokeh is visible in blurry portions of any image, it's of particular concern with telephoto lenses, which, thanks to the magic of reduced depth-of-field, produce more obviously out-of-focus areas.

Bokeh can vary from lens to lens, or even within a given lens depending on the f/stop in use. Bokeh becomes objectionable when the circles of confusion are evenly illuminated, making them stand out as distinct discs, or, worse, when these circles are darker in the center, producing an ugly "doughnut" effect. A lens defect called spherical aberration may produce out-of-focus discs that are brighter on the edges and darker in the center, because the lens doesn't focus light passing through the edges of the lens exactly as it does light going through the center. (Mirror or *catadioptric* lenses also produce this effect.)

Other kinds of spherical aberrations generate circles of confusion that are brightest in the center and fade out at the edges, producing a smooth blending effect, as you can see at right in Figure 6.12. Ironically, when no spherical aberration is present at all, the discs are a uniform shade, which, while better than the doughnut effect, is not as pleasing as the bright center/dark edge rendition. The shape of the disc also comes into play, with round smooth circles considered the best, and nonagonal or some other polygon (determined by the shape of the lens diaphragm) considered less desirable.

If you plan to use selective focus a lot, you should investigate the bokeh characteristics of a particular lens before you buy. Pentax user groups and forums will usually be full of comments and questions about bokeh, so the research is fairly easy.

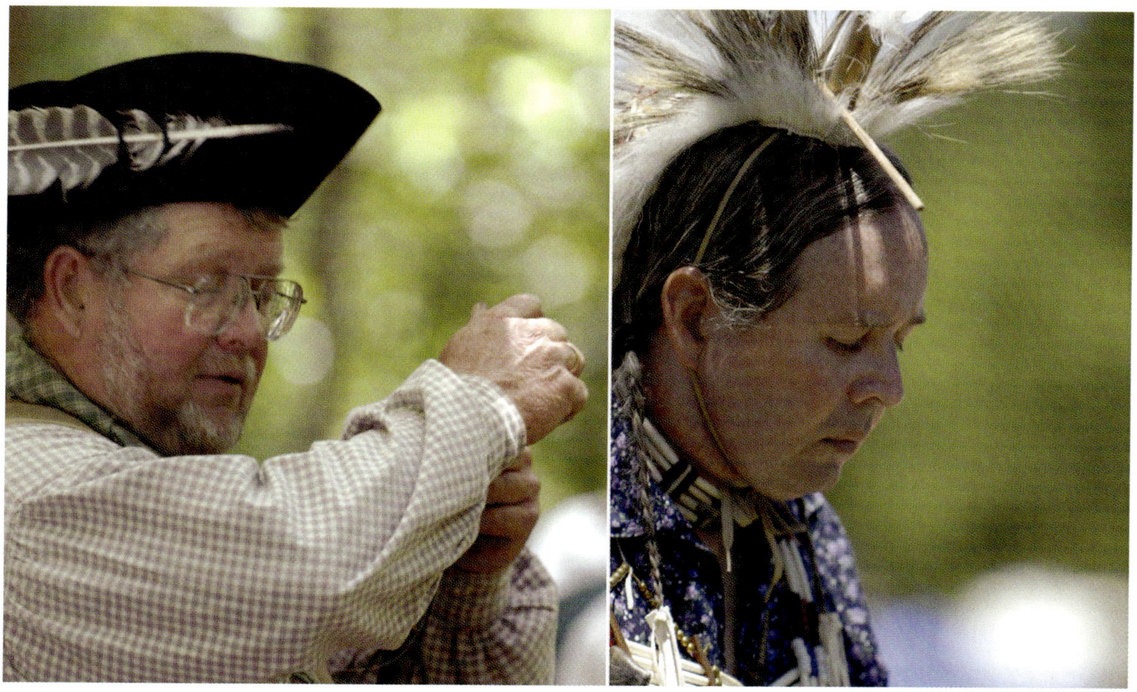

Figure 6.12 Bokeh is less pleasing when the discs are prominent (left), and less obtrusive when they blend into the background (right).

Add-ons and Special Features

Once you've purchased your telephoto lens, you'll want to think about some appropriate accessories for it. There are some handy add-ons available that can be valuable. Here are a couple of them to think about.

Lens Hoods

Lens hoods are an important accessory for all lenses, but they're especially valuable with telephotos. As I mentioned earlier, lens hoods do a good job of preserving image contrast by keeping bright light sources outside the field of view from striking the lens and, potentially, bouncing around inside that long tube to generate flare that, when coupled with atmospheric haze, can rob your image of detail and snap. In addition, lens hoods serve as valuable protection for that large, vulnerable, front lens element. It's easy to forget that you've got that long tube sticking out in front of your camera and accidentally whack the front of your lens into something. It's cheaper to replace a lens hood than it is to have a lens repaired, so you might find that a good hood is valuable protection for your prized optics.

When choosing a lens hood, it's important to have the right hood for the lens, usually the one offered for that lens by Pentax or the third-party manufacturer. You want a hood that blocks precisely the right amount of light: neither too much light nor too little. A hood with a front diameter that is too small can show up in your pictures as vignetting. A hood that has a front diameter that's too large isn't stopping all the light it should. Generic lens hoods may not do the job.

When your telephoto is a zoom lens, it's even more important to get the right hood, because you need one that does what it is supposed to at both the wide-angle and telephoto ends of the zoom range. Lens hoods may be cylindrical, rectangular (shaped like the image frame), or petal shaped (that is, cylindrical, but with cut-out areas at the corners which correspond to the actual image area). Lens hoods should be mounted in the correct orientation (a bayonet mount for the hood usually takes care of this).

Telephoto Converters

Teleconverters (often called telephoto extenders outside the Pentax world) multiply the actual focal length of your lens, giving you a longer telephoto for much less than the price of a lens with that actual focal length. These converters fit between the lens and your camera and contain optical elements that magnify the image produced by the lens. Pentax offers an especially good 2X S Teleconverter, but it's expensive at $385. Sigma and Kenko are among the vendors who offer these accessories at a more reasonable price, in magnifications of 1.4X and 2.0X. A teleconverter transforms, say, a 200mm lens into a 280mm or 400mm optic, respectively. Given the K200D's 1.5X crop factor, your 200mm lens now has the same field of view as a 420mm or 600mm lens on a full-frame camera. At around $300-$400 each, converters are quite a bargain, aren't they?

Actually, there are some downsides. While extenders retain the closest focusing distance of your original lens, autofocus may be maintained only if the lens's original maximum aperture is f/4 or larger (for the 1.4X extender) or f/2.8 or larger (for a 2X extender). The components reduce the effective aperture of any lens they are used with, by one f/stop with the 1.4X converter and two f/stops with the 2X extender. So, your 200mm f/2.8 lens becomes a 280mm f/4 or 400mm f/5.6 lens. Although converters are precision optical devices, they do cost you a little sharpness, but that improves when you reduce the aperture by a stop or two. If you're shooting under bright lighting conditions, these extenders make handy accessories. I recommend the 1.4X version because it robs you of very little sharpness and only one f/stop.

Macro Focusing

Some telephotos and telephoto zooms available for the Pentax K200D have particularly close focusing capabilities, making them *macro* lenses. Of course, the object is not necessarily to get close (get too close and you'll find it difficult to light your subject). What you're really looking for in a macro lens is to magnify the apparent size of the subject in the final image. Camera-to-subject distance is most important when you want to back up farther from your subject (say, to avoid spooking skittish insects or small animals). In that case, you'll want a macro lens with a longer focal length to allow that distance while retaining the desired magnification.

Pentax makes three lenses that are officially designated as macro lenses. The SMC Pentax D FA Macro 50mm f/2.8 is an excellent lens for shooting close-ups when it isn't desirable or necessary to put some distance between you and your subject. The other macro lenses include the SMC Pentax D FA Macro 100mm f/2.8, which puts you farther away from your subject, which can be useful when shooting skittish creatures, like the fellow shown in Figure 6.13. There is also a 35mm macro lens for those who want close-up capabilities in a "normal" walk-around lens.

You'll also find macro lenses, macro zooms, and other close-focusing lenses available from Sigma, Tamron, and Tokina. If you want to focus closer with a macro lens, or any other lens, you can add an accessory called an *extension tube*, which moves the lens farther from the focal plane, allowing it to focus more closely. Pentax also sells add-on close-up lenses, which look like filters, and allow lenses to focus more closely.

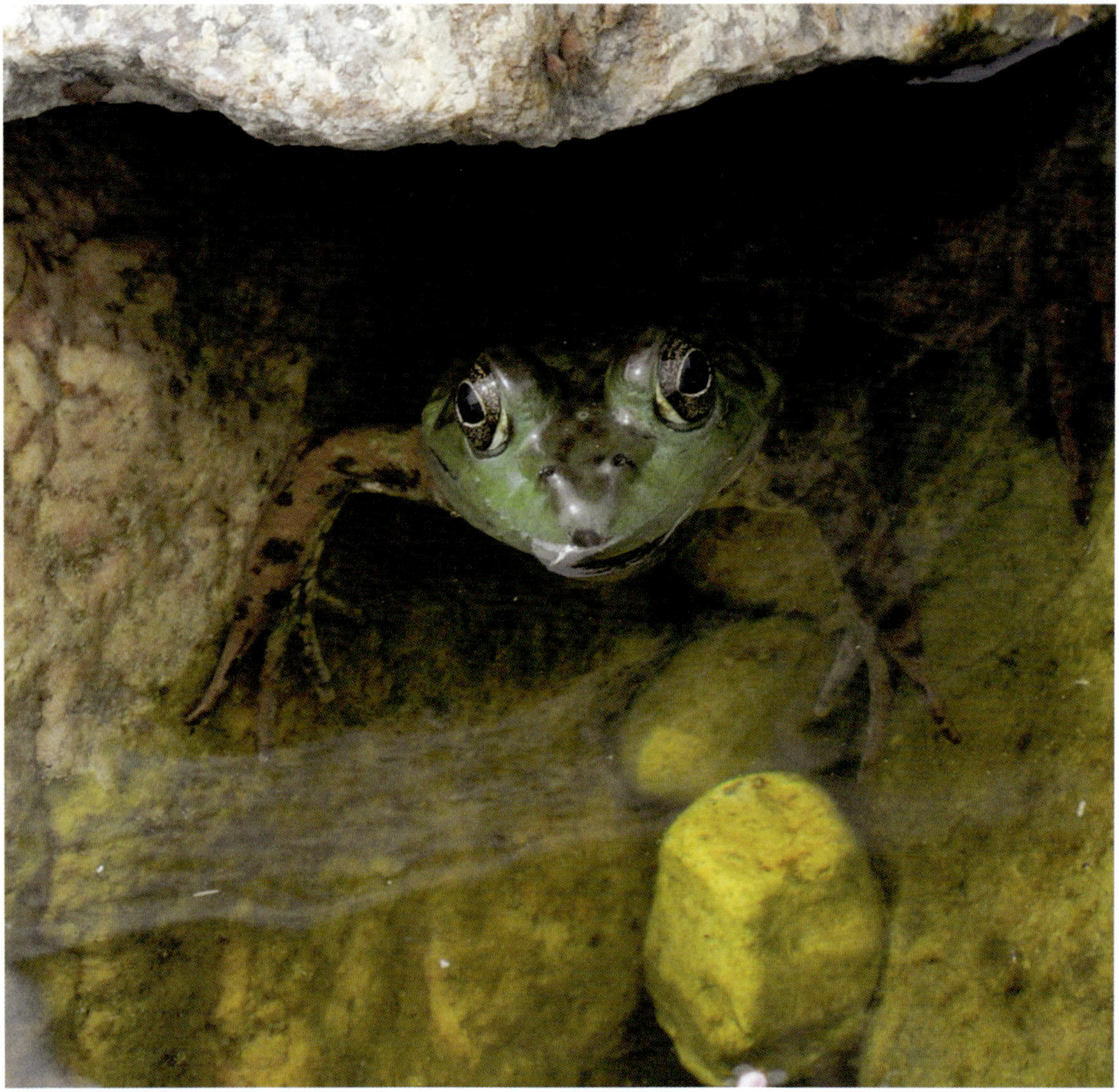

Figure 6.13 A telephoto macro lens allows you to shoot close-ups from a distance.

Anti-Shake and Your Lenses

Vendors like Nikon and Canon sell special lenses with Anti-Shake features built in. With your Pentax K200D, *every* lens you own has image stabilization. Anti-Shake provides you with camera steadiness that's the equivalent of at least two or three shutter speed increments. The camera incorporates a ball-bearing-mounted oscillator with a quartet of electromagnets that surround the "floating" image sensor. A set of angular velocity sensors detect camera movement and relay the amount of compensation needed to the electromagnets, which adjust the sensor to compensate for the movement.

The system activates only when the shutter release is pressed, so, unlike systems built into the lens, Pentax's Anti-Shake uses only negligible battery power. Pentax's system uses the focal length of the lens to calculate the amount of adjustment, so it works automatically only with F, FA, D-FA, DA*, and DA lenses that supply this data to the camera. As I described in Chapter 3, you can enter the focal length of other lenses manually.

This extra margin can be invaluable when you're shooting under dim lighting conditions or hand-holding a long lens for, say, wildlife photography. Perhaps that shot of a foraging deer calls for a shutter speed of 1/1,000 second at f/5.6 with your lens. Relax. You can shoot at 1/250 second at f/11 and get virtually the same results, as long as the deer doesn't decide to bound off.

Or, maybe you're shooting a high-school play without a tripod or monopod, and you'd really, really like to use 1/15 second at f/4. Assuming the actors aren't flitting around the stage at high speed, your wide-angle lens can grab the shot for you at its wide-angle position. However, keep these facts in mind:

- **Anti-Shake doesn't stop action.** Unfortunately, no stabilization is a panacea to replace the action-stopping capabilities of a higher shutter speed. Image stabilization applies only to camera shake. You still need a fast shutter speed to freeze action. Anti-Shake works great in low light, when you're using long lenses, and for macro photography. It's not always the best choice for action photography, unless there's enough light to allow a sufficiently high shutter speed. If so, stabilization can make your shot even sharper.
- **Stabilization doesn't slow you down.** The process of adjusting the sensor to counter camera shake takes time, just as autofocus does, but it's so little that you should experience no delays at all when taking photographs. So, you can use stabilization even for subjects that call for the fastest response, such as sports.

- **Use when appropriate.** Sometimes, stabilization produces worse results if used while you're panning. You might want to switch off Anti-Shake when panning or when your camera is mounted on a tripod.
- **Do you need Anti-Shake at all?** Remember that an inexpensive monopod might be able to provide the same additional steadiness as Anti-Shake, and helps keep the camera relatively immobile so you can maintain framing of your subject. If you're out in the field shooting wild animals or flowers and think a tripod isn't practical, try a monopod first.

7

Making Light Work for You

Successful photographers and artists have an intimate understanding of the importance of light in shaping an image. Rembrandt was a master of using light to create moods and reveal the character of his subjects. Artist Thomas Kinkade's official tagline is "Painter of Light." The late Dean Collins, co-founder of Finelight Studios, revolutionized how a whole generation of photographers learned and used lighting. Shortly before I began writing this book, I attended a seminar called "Captivated by the Light," run by photo guru Ed Pierce. It's impossible to underestimate how the use of light adds to—and how misuse can detract from—your photographs.

All forms of visual art use light to shape the finished product. Sculptors don't have control over the light used to illuminate their finished work, so they must create shapes using planes and curved surfaces so that the form envisioned by the artist comes to life from a variety of viewing and lighting angles. Painters, in contrast, have absolute control over both shape and light in their work, as well as the viewing angle, so they can use both the contours of their two-dimensional subjects and the qualities of the "light" they use to illuminate those subjects to evoke the image they want to produce.

Photography is a third form of art. The photographer may have little or no control over the subject (other than posing human subjects) but can often adjust both viewing angle *and* the nature of the light source to create a particular compelling image. The direction and intensity of the light sources create the shapes and textures that we see. The distribution and proportions determine the contrast and tonal values: whether the image is stark or high key, or muted and low in contrast. The colors of the light (because even "white" light has a color balance that the sensor can detect), and how much of those colors the subject reflects or absorbs, paint the hues visible in the image.

As a Pentax K200D photographer, you must learn to be a painter and sculptor of light if you want to move from *taking* a picture to *making* a photograph. This chapter provides an introduction to using the two main types of illumination: *continuous* lighting (such as daylight, incandescent, or fluorescent sources) and the brief, but brilliant snippets of light we call *electronic flash.*

Continuous Illumination versus Electronic Flash

Continuous lighting is exactly what you might think: uninterrupted illumination that is available all the time during a shooting session. Daylight, moonlight, and the artificial lighting encountered both indoors and outdoors count as continuous light sources (although all of them can be "interrupted" by passing clouds, solar eclipses, a blown fuse, or simply by switching a lamp off). Indoor continuous illumination includes both the lights that are there already (such as incandescent lamps or overhead fluorescent lights indoors) and fixtures you supply yourself, including photoflood lamps or reflectors used to bounce existing light onto your subject.

The surge of light we call electronic flash is produced by a burst of photons generated by an electrical charge that is accumulated in a component called a *capacitor* and then directed through a glass tube containing xenon gas, which absorbs the energy and emits the brief flash. Electronic flash is notable because it can be much more intense than continuous lighting, lasts only a brief moment, and can be much more portable than supplementary incandescent sources. It's a light source you can carry with you and use anywhere.

Indeed, your Pentax K200D has a flip-up electronic flash unit built in, as shown in Figure 7.1. But you can also use an external flash, either mounted on the K200D's accessory shoe or used off-camera and linked with a cable or triggered by a slave light (which sets off a flash when it senses the firing of another unit). Studio flash units are electronic flash, too, and aren't limited to "professional" shooters, as there are economical "monolight" (one-piece flash/power supply) units available in the $200 price range. Anyone can buy a couple to store in a closet and use to set up a home studio, or use as supplementary lighting when traveling away from home.

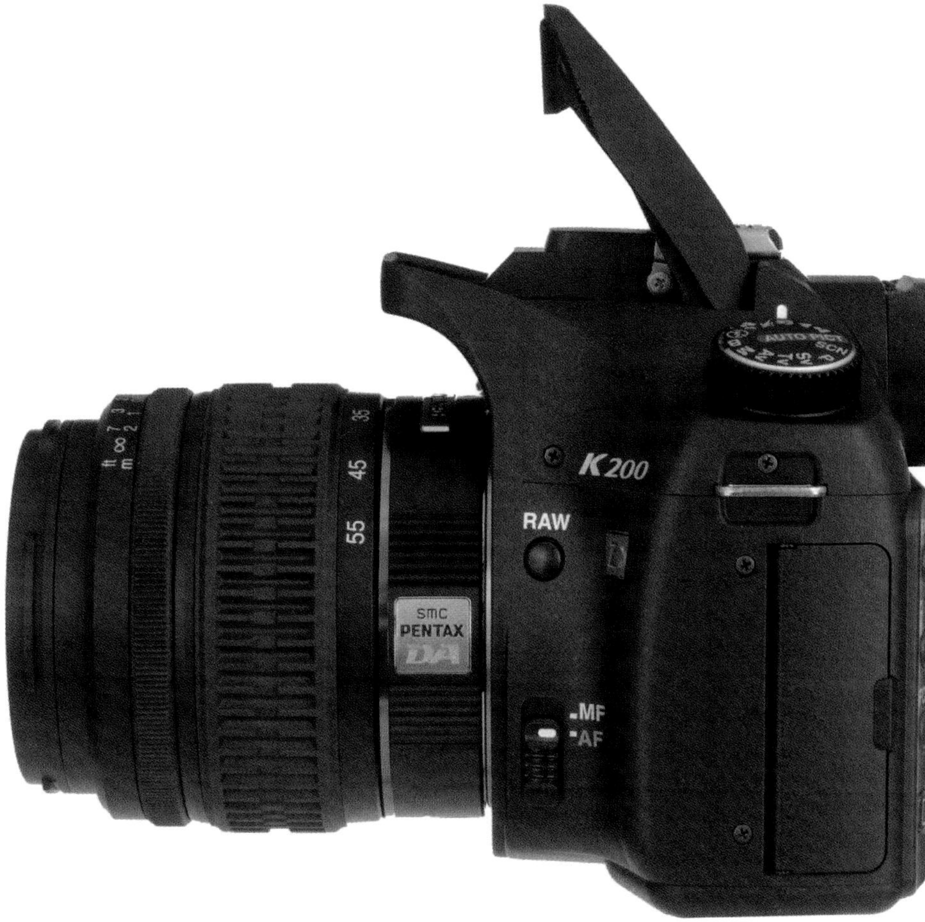

Figure 7.1
One form of light that's always available is the flip-up flash on your Pentax K200D.

There are advantages and disadvantages to each type of illumination. Here's a quick checklist of pros and cons:

- **Lighting preview—Pro: continuous lighting:** With continuous lighting, you always know exactly what kind of lighting effect you're going to get and, if multiple lights are used, how they will interact with each other, as you can see in Figure 7.2. With electronic flash, the general effect you're going to see may be a mystery until you've built some experience, and you may need to review a shot on the LCD, make some adjustments, and then reshoot to get the look you want. (In this sense, a digital camera's review capabilities replace the Polaroid test shots pro photographers relied on in decades past.)
- **Lighting preview—Con: electronic flash:** While some external flash have a modeling light function, your K200D lacks such a capability in its internal flash, and, in any case, this feature is no substitute for continuous illumination, or an always-on modeling lamp like that found in studio flash. As the number of flash units

increases, lighting previews, especially if you want to see the proportions of illumination provided by each flash, grow more complex.

- **Exposure calculation—Pro: continuous lighting:** Your K200D has no problem calculating exposure for continuous lighting, because the illumination remains constant and can be measured through a sensor that interprets the light reaching the viewfinder. The amount of light available just before the exposure will, in almost all cases, be the same amount of light present when the shutter is released. The K200D's Spot metering mode can be used to measure and compare the proportions of light in the highlights and shadows, so you can make an adjustment (such as using more or less fill light) if necessary. You can even use a hand-held light meter to measure continuous light yourself.
- **Exposure calculation—Con: electronic flash:** Electronic flash illumination doesn't exist until the flash fires, and so it can't be measured by the K200D's exposure sensor when the mirror is flipped up during the exposure. Instead, the light must be measured by metering the intensity of a preflash triggered an instant before the main flash, as it is reflected back to the camera and through the lens. An alternative is to use a sensor built into the flash itself and measure reflected light that has not traveled through the lens. If you have a do-it-yourself bent, there are hand-held flash meters, too, including models that measure both flash and continuous light.
- **Evenness of illumination—Pro/con: continuous lighting:** Continuous light sources—daylight, in particular—provide illumination that tends to fill an image completely, lighting up the foreground, background, and your subject almost equally. Shadows do come into play, of course, so you might need to use reflectors or fill-in light sources to even out the illumination further. But, barring objects that block large sections of your image from daylight, the light is spread fairly evenly. Indoors, however, continuous lighting is commonly less evenly distributed. The average living room, for example, has hot spots and dark corners. But on the plus side, you can *see* this uneven illumination and compensate with additional lamps.
- **Evenness of illumination—Con: electronic flash:** Electronic flash units suffer from the effects of their proximity, because of the *inverse square law*, which I'll describe in the next section.
- **Action stopping—Con: continuous lighting:** Action stopping with continuous light sources is completely dependent on the shutter speed you've dialed in on the camera. And the speeds available are dependent on the amount of light available and your ISO sensitivity setting. Outdoors in daylight, there will probably be enough sunlight to let you shoot at 1/1800 second and f/6.3 with a non-grainy sensitivity setting of ISO 400. That's a fairly useful combination of settings if you're not using a super-telephoto with a small maximum aperture. But inside, the reduced illumination quickly has you pushing your Pentax K200D to its limits. For example, if you're shooting indoor sports, there probably won't be enough available light

to allow you to use a 1/2,000th second shutter speed (although I routinely shoot indoor basketball with my K200D at ISO 1600 and 1/500 second at f/4). In many indoor sports situations, you may find yourself limited to 1/500 second or slower.

- **Action stopping—Pro: electronic flash:** When it comes to the ability to freeze moving objects in their tracks, the advantage goes to electronic flash. The brief duration of electronic flash serves as a very high "shutter speed" when the flash is the main or only source of illumination for the photo. Your Pentax K200D's shutter speed may be set for 1/180th second during a flash exposure, but if the flash illumination predominates, the *effective* exposure time will be the 1/1,200 to 1/20,000 second or less duration of the flash, as you can see in Figure 7.3, because the flash unit reduces the amount of light released by cutting short the duration of the flash.

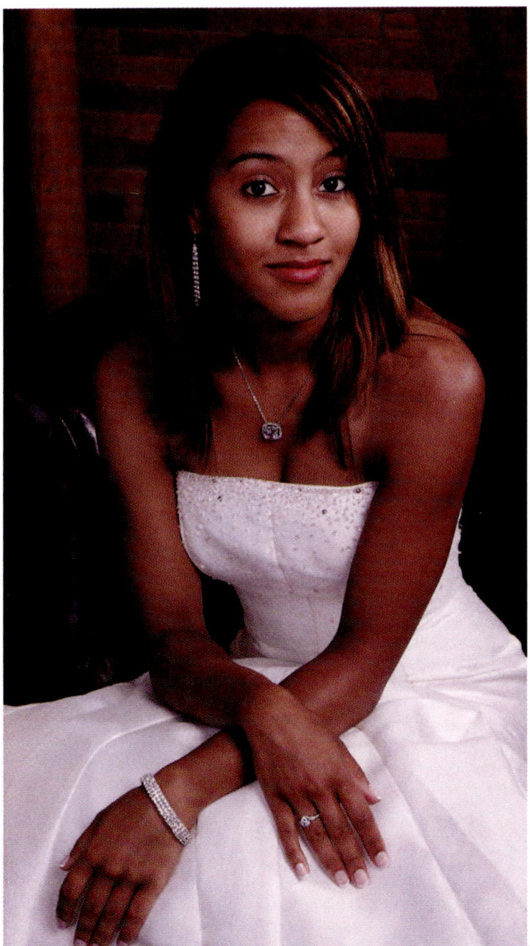

Figure 7.2 Continuous lighting gives you an exact preview of how your illumination will look in the finished photo

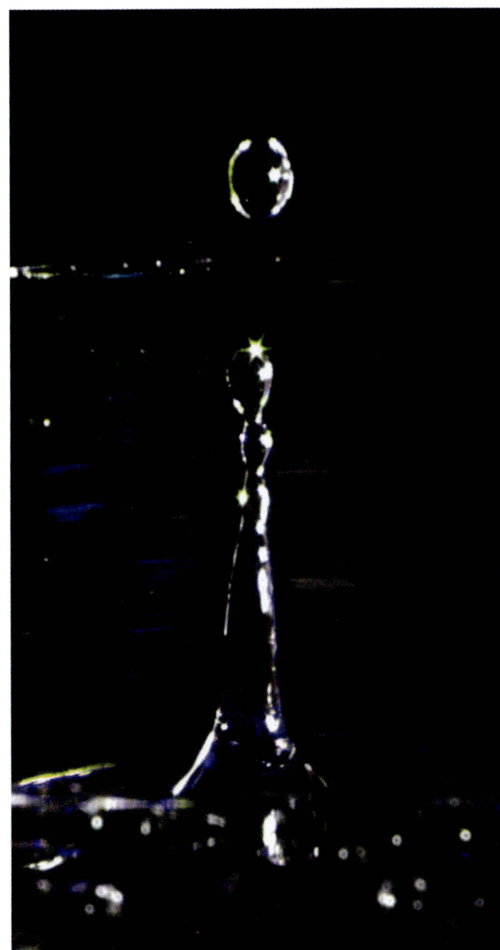

Figure 7.3 Electronic flash can freeze almost any action.

The only fly in the ointment is that, if the ambient light is strong enough, it may produce a secondary, "ghost" exposure, as I'll explain later in this chapter.

- **Cost—Pro: continuous lighting:** Incandescent or fluorescent lamps are generally much less expensive than electronic flash units, which can easily cost several hundred dollars. I've used everything from desktop hi-intensity lamps to reflector flood lights for continuous illumination at very little cost. There are lamps made especially for photographic purposes, too, priced up to $50 or so. Maintenance is economical, too; many incandescent or fluorescents use bulbs that cost only a few dollars.

- **Cost—Con: electronic flash:** Electronic flash units aren't particularly cheap. The lowest-cost dedicated flash designed specifically for the Pentax dSLRs, the Pentax AF-200FG, is about $100. Such units are limited in features, however, and intended for those with entry-level cameras. Plan on spending some money to get the features that a sophisticated electronic flash offers.

- **Flexibility—Con: continuous lighting:** Because incandescent and fluorescent lamps are not as bright as electronic flash, the slower shutter speeds required (see Action stopping, above) mean that you may have to use a tripod more often, especially when shooting portraits. The incandescent variety of continuous lighting gets hot, especially in the studio, and the side effects range from discomfort (for your human models) to disintegration (if you happen to be shooting perishable foods like ice cream). The heat also makes it more difficult to add filtration to incandescent sources.

- **Flexibility—Pro: electronic flash:** Electronic flash's action-freezing power allows you to work without a tripod in the studio (and elsewhere), adding flexibility and speed when choosing angles and positions. Flash units can be easily filtered, and, because the filtration is placed over the light source rather than the lens, you don't need to use high quality filter material. For example, a couple sheets of unexposed, processed Ektachrome film can make a dandy infrared-pass filter for your flash unit. Theatrical lighting gels, which may be too flimsy to use in front of the lens, can be mounted or taped in front of your flash with ease.

Continuous Lighting Basics

While continuous lighting and its effects are generally much easier to visualize and use than electronic flash, there are some factors you need to take into account, particularly the color temperature of the light. (Color temperature concerns aren't exclusive to continuous light sources, of course, but the variations tend to be more extreme and less predictable than those of electronic flash.)

Color temperature, in practical terms, is how "bluish" or how "reddish" the light appears to be to the digital camera's sensor. Indoor illumination is quite warm, comparatively, and appears reddish to the sensor. Daylight, in contrast, seems much bluer to the sensor. Our eyes (our brains, actually) are quite adaptable to these variations, so white objects don't appear to have an orange tinge when viewed indoors, nor do they seem excessively blue outdoors in full daylight. Yet, these color temperature variations are real and the sensor is not fooled. To capture the most accurate colors, we need to take the color temperature into account in setting the color balance (or *white balance*) of the K200D—either automatically using the camera's smarts, or manually, using our own knowledge and experience.

Color temperature can be confusing, because of a seeming contradiction in how color temperatures are named: warmer (more reddish) color temperatures (measured in degrees Kelvin) are the *lower* numbers, while cooler (bluer) color temperatures are *higher* numbers. It might not make sense to say that 3,400K is warmer than 6,000K, but that's the way it is. If it helps, think of a glowing red ember contrasted with a white-hot welder's torch, rather than fire and ice.

The confusion comes from physics. Scientists calculate color temperature from the light emitted by a mythical object called a black body radiator, which absorbs all the radiant energy that strikes it, and reflects none at all. Such a black body not only *absorbs* light perfectly, but it *emits* it perfectly when heated (and since nothing in the universe is perfect, that makes it mythical).

At a particular physical temperature, this imaginary object always emits light of the same wavelength or color. That makes it possible to define color temperature in terms of actual temperature in degrees on the Kelvin scale that scientists use. Incandescent light, for example, typically has a color temperature of 3,200K to 3,400K. Daylight might range from 5,500K to 6,000K. Each type of illumination we use for photography has its own color temperature range—with some cautions. The next sections will summarize everything you need to know about the qualities of these light sources.

Daylight

Daylight is produced by the sun, and so is moonlight (which is just reflected sunlight). Daylight is present, of course, even when you can't see the sun. When sunlight is direct, it can be bright and harsh. If daylight is diffused by clouds, softened by bouncing off objects such as walls or your photo reflectors, or filtered by shade, it can be much dimmer and less contrasty.

Daylight's color temperature can vary quite widely. It is highest (most blue) at noon when the sun is directly overhead, because the light is traveling through a minimum amount of the filtering layer we call the atmosphere. The color temperature at high noon may be 6,000K. At other times of day, the sun is lower in the sky and the particles in

INVERSE SQUARE LAW

The inverse square law affects all light sources—even the sun, but it is most noticeable when the illumination is located fairly close to your subject. That's because this effect is most dramatic when the distance between the light source and the subject is changed by a significant fraction. It was first applied to both gravity and light by Sir Isaac Newton, and dictates that as a light source's distance increases from the subject, the amount of light reaching the subject falls off proportionately to the square of the distance. In plain English, that means that a flash or lamp that's 12 feet away from a subject provides only one-quarter as much illumination as a source that's 6 feet away (rather than half as much). (See Figure 7.4.) This translates into relatively shallow "depth-of-light."

While the inverse square law applies to all types of light, both continuous and electronic flash, some kinds of illumination—such as the sun—are so far away that we never see a significant change in the relative distance. But, if you were able to move the sun an additional 93 million miles from our planet, its illumination would indeed be one-quarter as intense (not half as bright). Of course, in that case, calculating the correct exposure in daylight would not be on the minds of most photographers.

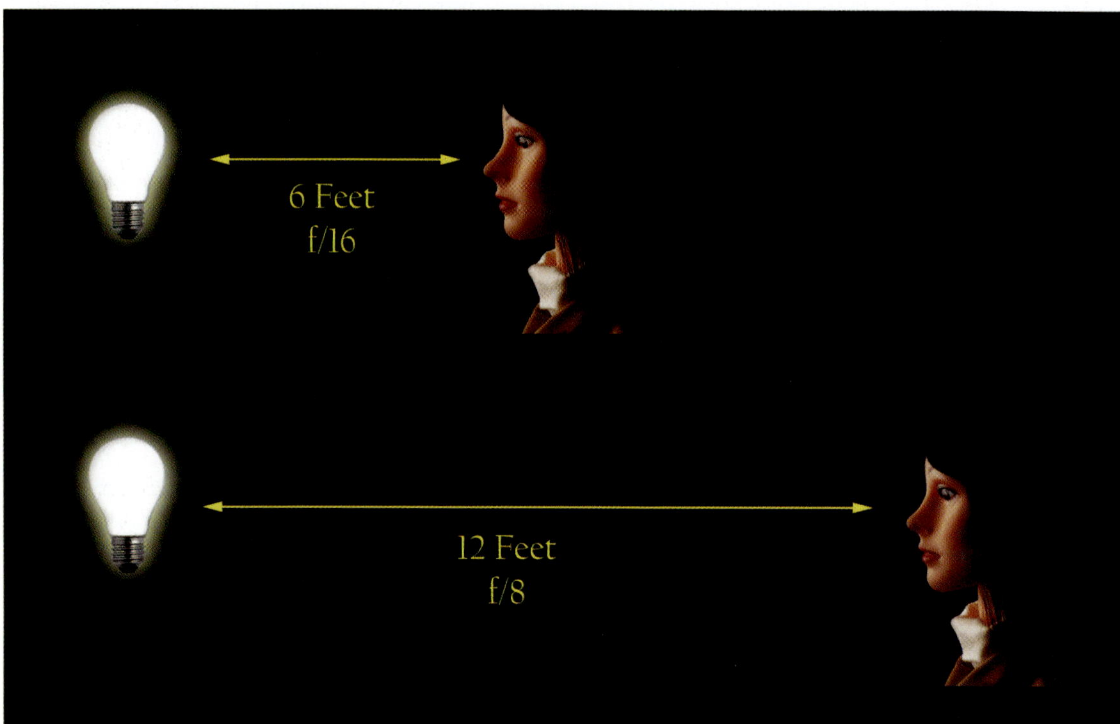

Figure 7.4 A light source that is twice as far away provides only one-quarter as much illumination.

the air provide a filtering effect that warms the illumination to about 5,500K for most of the day. Starting an hour before dusk and for an hour after sunrise, the warm appearance of the sunlight is even visible to our eyes when the color temperature may dip to 4,500K or lower, as shown in Figure 7.5.

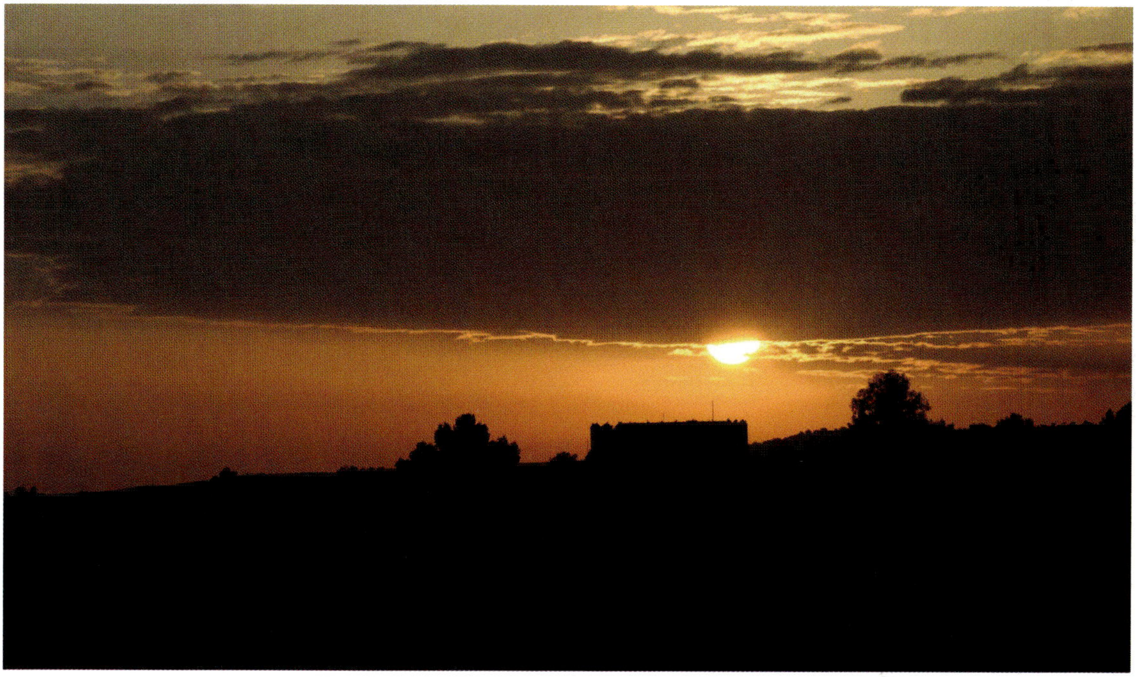

Figure 7.5 At dawn and dusk, the color temperature of daylight may dip as low as 4,500K.

Because you'll be taking so many photos in daylight, you'll want to learn how to use or compensate for the brightness and contrast of sunlight, as well as how to deal with its color temperature. I'll provide some hints later in this chapter.

Incandescent/Tungsten Light

The term incandescent or tungsten illumination is usually applied to the direct descendents of Thomas Edison's original electric lamp. Such lights consist of a glass bulb that contains a vacuum, or is filled with a halogen gas and contains a tungsten filament that is heated by an electrical current, producing photons and heat. Tungsten-halogen lamps are a variation on the basic light bulb, using a more rugged (and longer-lasting) filament that can be heated to a higher temperature, housed in a thicker glass or quartz envelope, and filled with iodine or bromine ("halogen") gases. The higher temperature allows tungsten-halogen (or quartz-halogen/quartz-iodine, depending on their construction) lamps to burn "hotter" and whiter. Although popular for automobile headlamps today, they've also been popular for photographic illumination.

Although incandescent illumination isn't a perfect black body radiator, it's close enough that the color temperature of such lamps can be precisely calculated and used for photography without concerns about color variation (at least, until the very end of the lamp's life).

The other qualities of this type of lighting, such as contrast, are dependent on the distance of the lamp from the subject, type of reflectors used, and other factors that I'll explain later in this chapter.

Fluorescent Light/Other Light Sources

Fluorescent light has some advantages in terms of illumination, but some disadvantages from a photographic standpoint. This type of lamp generates light through an electro-chemical reaction that emits most of its energy as visible light, rather than heat, which is why the bulbs don't get as hot. The type of light produced varies depending on the phosphor coatings and type of gas in the tube. So, the illumination fluorescent bulbs produce can vary widely in its characteristics.

That's not great news for photographers. Different types of lamps have different "color temperatures" that can't be precisely measured in degrees Kelvin, because the light isn't produced by heating. Worse, fluorescent lamps have a discontinuous spectrum of light that can have some colors missing entirely. A particular type of tube can lack certain shades of red or other colors (see Figure 7.6), which is why fluorescent lamps and other alternative technologies such as sodium-vapor illumination can produce ghastly looking human skin tones. Their spectra can lack the reddish tones we associate with healthy skin and emphasize the blues and greens popular in horror movies.

Adjusting White Balance

I showed you how to adjust white balance in Chapter 3, using the K200D's built-in presets and White Balance shift capabilities (there's more on bracketing in Chapter 4, too).

In most cases, however, the Pentax K200D will do a good job of calculating white balance for you, so Auto can be used as your choice most of the time. Use the preset values or set a custom white balance that matches the current shooting conditions when you need to. The only really problematic light sources are likely to be fluorescents. Vendors, such as GE and Sylvania, may actually provide a figure known as the *color rendering index* (or CRI), which is a measure of how accurately a particular light source represents standard colors, using a scale of 0 (some sodium-vapor lamps) to 100 (daylight and most incandescent lamps). Daylight fluorescents and deluxe cool white fluorescents might have a CRI of about 79 to 95, which is perfectly acceptable for most photographic applications. Warm white fluorescents might have a CRI of 55. White deluxe mercury vapor lights are less suitable with a CRI of 45, while low-pressure sodium lamps can vary from CRI 0-18.

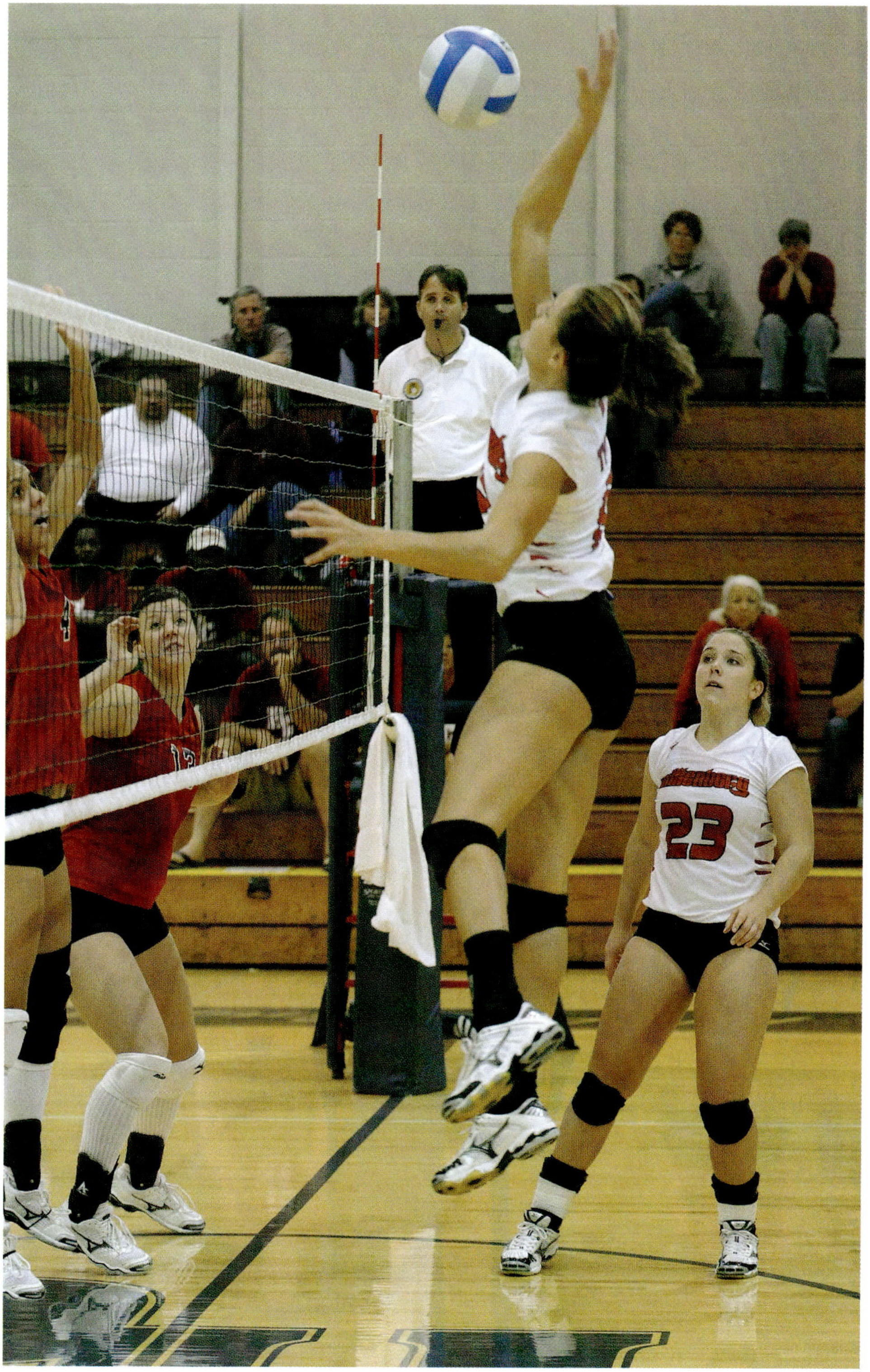

Figure 7.6
The fluorescent lighting in this gym added a distinct greenish cast to the image.

Remember that if you shoot RAW, you can specify the white balance of your image when you import it into Photoshop, Photoshop Elements, or another image editor using your preferred RAW converter. While color-balancing filters that fit on the front of the lens exist, they are primarily useful for film cameras, because film's color balance can't be tweaked as extensively as that of a sensor.

Electronic Flash Basics

Until you delve into the situation deeply enough, it might appear that serious photographers have a love/hate relationship with electronic flash. You'll often hear that flash photography is less natural looking, and that the built-in flash in most cameras should never be used as the primary source of illumination because it provides a harsh, garish look. Indeed, most "pro" cameras don't have a built-in flash at all. Available ("continuous") lighting is praised, and built-in flash photography seems to be roundly denounced.

In truth, however, the bias is against *bad* flash photography. Indeed, flash has become the studio light source of choice for pro photographers, because it's more intense (and its intensity can be varied to order by the photographer), freezes action, frees you from using a tripod (unless you want to use one to lock down a composition), and has a snappy, consistent light quality that matches daylight. (While color balance changes as the flash duration shortens, some Pentax flash units can communicate to the camera the exact white balance provided for that shot.) And even pros will cede that the built-in flash of the Pentax K200D has some important uses as an adjunct to existing light, particularly to fill in dark shadows.

But electronic flash isn't as inherently easy to use as continuous lighting. As I noted earlier, electronic flash units are more expensive, don't show you exactly what the lighting effect will be (unless you use a second source called a *modeling light* for a preview), and the exposure of electronic flash units is more difficult to calculate accurately.

How Electronic Flash Works

The bursts of light we call electronic flash are produced by a flash of photons generated by an electrical charge that is accumulated in a component called a *capacitor* and then directed through a glass tube containing xenon gas, which absorbs the energy and emits the brief flash. For the pop-up flash built into the Pentax K200D, the full burst of light lasts about 1/1,000th second and provides enough illumination to shoot a subject 10 feet away at f/4 using the ISO 100 setting. In a more typical situation, you'd use ISO 200, f/5.6 to f/8 and photograph something 8 to 10 feet away. As you can see, the built-in flash is somewhat limited in range; you'll see why external flash units are often a good idea later in this chapter.

An electronic flash (whether built in or connected to the Pentax K200D through a cable plugged into a hot shoe adapter) is triggered at the instant of exposure, during a period when the sensor is fully exposed by the shutter. As I mentioned earlier in this book, the K200D has a vertically traveling shutter that consists of two curtains. The first curtain opens and moves to the opposite side of the frame, at which point the shutter is completely open. The flash can be triggered at this point (so-called *first-curtain* or *leading curtain sync*), making the flash exposure. Then, after a delay that can vary from 30 seconds to 1/180th second (with the Pentax K200D; other cameras may sync at a faster or slower speed), a second curtain begins moving across the sensor plane, covering up the sensor again. This is the triggering mode the Pentax K200D always uses when you're working with the built-in flash alone.

However, if you are using the Pentax AF-540FGZ or AF-360FGZ external flash units, they offer an additional option (set on the flash itself) called *second-curtain* or *trailing curtain sync*. If you're using the built-in flash in conjunction with one of these external units, and they are set for trailing curtain sync, the built-in flash will fire in that mode, too. In either case, a shutter speed of 1/90th second is the maximum that can be used to take a photo with this sync mode. The next section describes the effects of using leading curtain or trailing curtain sync, and later in this chapter I'll get into more specifics about working with the Pentax built-in flash and optional external flash units.

Ghost Images

The difference might not seem like much, but whether you use leading curtain sync (the basic setting) or trailing curtain sync (an optional setting when using certain flash unit combinations) can make a significant difference to your photograph *if the ambient light in your scene also contributes to the image.* At faster shutter speeds, particularly 1/180th second, there isn't much time for the ambient light to register, unless it is very bright. It's likely that the electronic flash will provide almost all the illumination, so leading curtain sync or trailing curtain sync isn't very important.

However, at slower shutter speeds, or with very bright ambient light levels, there is a significant difference, particularly if your subject is moving, or the camera isn't steady. In any of those situations, the ambient light will register as a second image accompanying the flash exposure, and if there is movement (camera or subject), that additional image will not be in the same place as the flash exposure. It will show as a ghost image and, if the movement is significant enough, as a blurred ghost image trailing in front of or behind your subject in the direction of the movement.

When you're using leading curtain sync, the flash goes off the instant the shutter opens, producing an image of the subject on the sensor. Then, the shutter remains open for an additional period (30 seconds to 1/180th second, as I noted). If your subject is moving, say, towards the right side of the frame, the ghost image produced by the ambient light will produce a blur on the right side of the original subject image, making it look as if your sharp (flash-produced) image is chasing the ghost. For those of us who grew up with lightning-fast objects in cartoons or comic books, which always left a ghost trail *behind them*—that looks unnatural (see Figure 7.7).

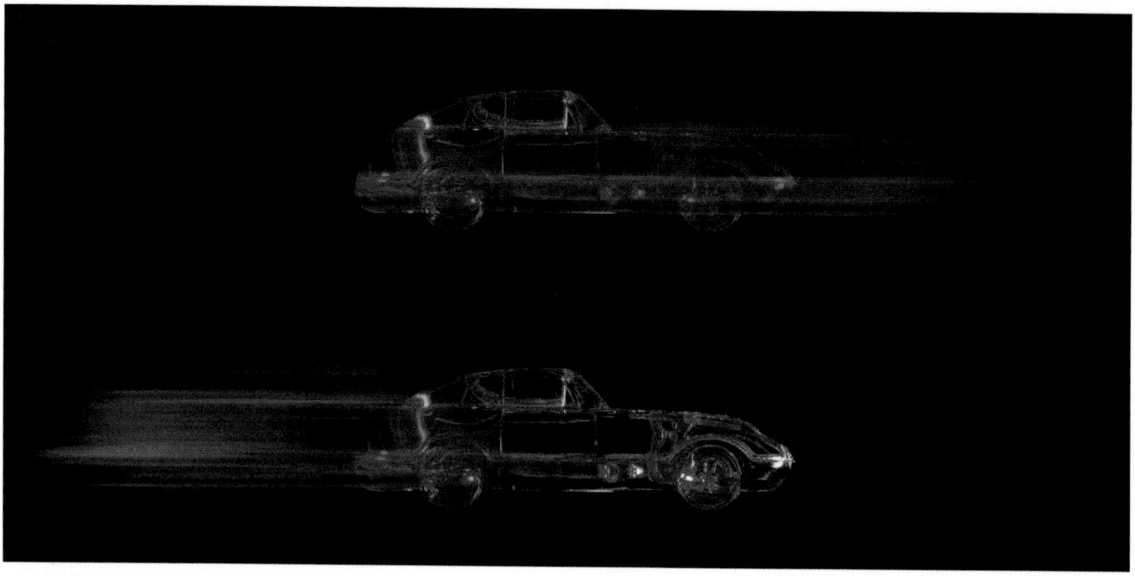

Figure 7.7 Leading curtain sync produces an image that trails in front of the flash exposure (top), while second-curtain sync creates a more "natural looking" trail behind the flash image.

So, Pentax provides trailing curtain sync to remedy the situation when you're using one of the external flash units I listed earlier. In that mode, using a shutter speed of 1/90th second or slower, the shutter opens, as before. The shutter remains open for its designated duration, and the ghost image forms. If your subject moves from the left side of the frame to the right side, the ghost will move from left to right, too. *Then*, about 1.5 milliseconds before the second shutter curtain closes, the flash is triggered, producing a nice, sharp flash image *ahead* of the ghost image. Voilà! We have Speed Racer outrunning his own trailing image.

Triggering the electronic flash only when the shutter is completely open makes a lot of sense if you think about what's going on. To obtain shutter speeds faster than 1/180th second, the K200D exposes only part of the sensor at one time, by starting the second curtain on its journey before the first curtain has completely opened. That effectively provides a briefer exposure as the partially open slit of the shutter passes over the surface of the sensor. If the flash were to fire during the time when the first and second curtains partially obscured the sensor, only the slit that was actually open would be exposed.

Determining Exposure

Calculating the proper exposure for an electronic flash photograph is a bit more complicated than determining the settings by continuous light. The right exposure isn't simply a function of how far away your subject is (which the K200D can figure out based on the autofocus distance that's locked in just prior to taking the picture). Various objects reflect more or less light at the same distance so, obviously, the camera needs to measure the amount of light reflected back and through the lens. Yet, as the flash itself isn't available for measuring until it's triggered, the K200D has nothing to measure.

The solution is to fire the flash twice. The initial shot is a preflash that can be analyzed, then followed by a main flash that's given exactly the calculated intensity needed to provide a correct exposure. As a result, the primary flash may be longer for distant objects and shorter for closer subjects, depending on the required intensity for exposure. This through-the-lens evaluative flash exposure system is called P-TTL, and it operates whenever the pop-up internal flash is used, or you have attached a Pentax dedicated flash unit to the K200D.

Guide Numbers

Guide numbers, usually abbreviated GN, are a way of specifying the power of an electronic flash in a way that can be used to determine the right f/stop to use at a particular shooting distance and ISO setting. In fact, before automatic flash units became prevalent, the GN was actually used to do just that. A GN is usually given as a pair of numbers for both feet and meters that represent the range at ISO 100. For example, the Pentax K200D's built-in flash has a GN of 13/43 (meters/feet) at ISO 100. To calculate the right exposure at that ISO setting, you'd divide the guide number by the distance to arrive at the appropriate f/stop.

Using the K200D's built-in flash as an example, at ISO 100 with its GN of 43, if you wanted to shoot a subject at a distance of 10 feet, you'd use f/4.3 (43 divided by 10; round to f/4 for simplicity's sake). At 8 feet, an f/stop of f/5.4 (round up to f/5.6) would be used. Some quick mental calculations with the GN will give you any particular electronic flash's range. You can easily see that the built-in flash would begin to peter out at about 15 feet, where you'd need an aperture of f/2.8 at ISO 100. Of course, in the real world you'd probably bump the sensitivity up to a setting of ISO 400 so you could use a more practical f/5.6 at that distance.

Today, guide numbers are most useful for comparing the power of various flash units. You don't need to be a math genius to see that an electronic flash with a GN of, say, 148 (like the top-of-the-line Pentax AF-540FGZ) would be *a lot* more powerful than your built-in flash (at ISO 100, you could use f/10 instead of f/2.8 at 15 feet).

Using the Built-In Flash

The Pentax K200D's built-in flash is a handy accessory because it is available as required, without the need to carry an external flash around with you constantly. This section explains how to use the flip-up flash.

Setting a Flash Mode

To select a mode, press the Fn button to produce the Capture Functions screen, and then press the down key to activate the Flash Mode screen. (See Figure 7.8.) Choose the Flash mode with the left/right keys, and dial in any flash exposure compensation (described next) with the e-dial. Press the OK button to confirm your choice. The Flash modes are as follows:

- **Auto Discharge.** In this mode, the K200D measures the available light and the flash pops up automatically if needed. Typical situations include low-light levels, especially when a slow shutter speed that is likely to cause camera shake is called for, or in backlit situations where flash should be used to fill in the shadowed areas. Auto Discharge does not operate when using Exposure Modes (P, Sv, Tv, or Av), but if you're using a Scene/SCN mode other than Sunset, Night Scene, Candlelight, or Museum, you can toggle between Auto Discharge and Flash On mode (described

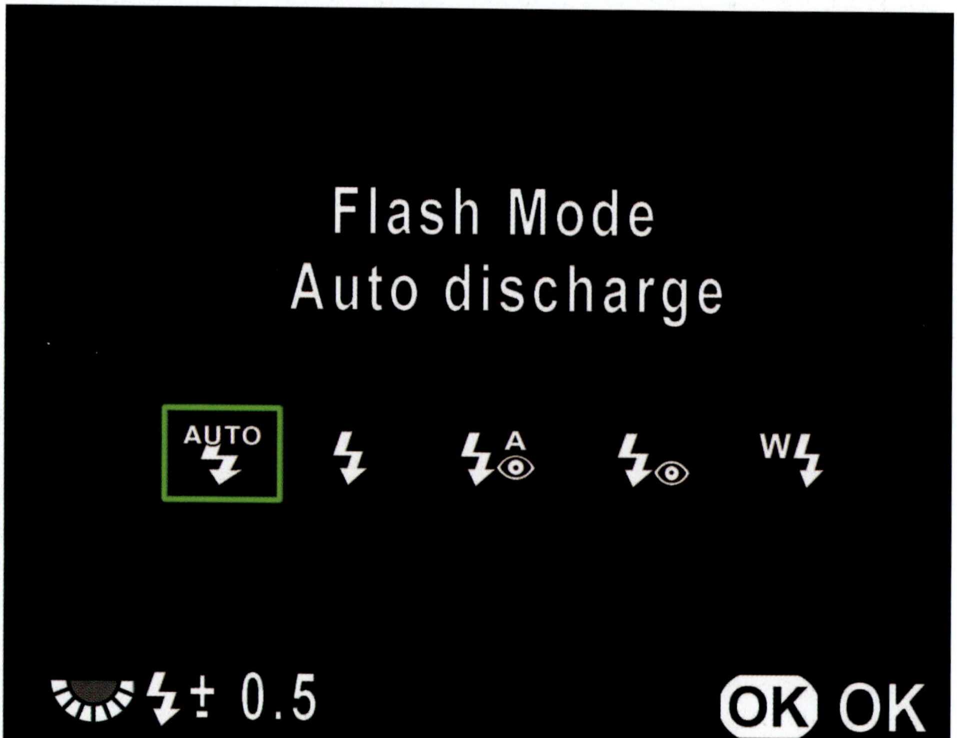

Figure 7.8
Set the Flash mode and any flash exposure compensation using this screen.

next) by pressing the Flash Up button when the flash is elevated. (Flash is disabled for Sunset, Night Scene, Candlelight, and Museum modes.)

Note: The flash may pop up but not flash if the camera decides at the moment of exposure that flash isn't necessary. The flash does not flip up automatically if you're using the infrared remote control (press the Flash Up button in this case to pop up the flash manually).

- **Flash On.** In this mode, the flash discharges when the flash is popped up.
- **Auto Flash+Red-eye.** This is the same as Auto Discharge mode (including toggling between Auto Discharge and Flash On when pressing the Flash Up button when the flash is elevated while using Scene/SCN modes) with the addition of a pre-flash just before the picture is taken. The pre-flash causes the subject's pupils to contract, reducing the possibility of red-eye effects.
- **Flash On+Red-eye.** Combines Flash On behavior with an anti-red-eye pre-flash.
- **Wireless mode.** Allows you to synchronize the Pentax AF-540FGZ or Pentax AF-380FGZ external flash units without using a sync cord. (Described later in this chapter.)

RED-EYE CORRECTION

The best way to truly eliminate red-eye is to raise the flash up off the camera so its illumination approaches the eye from an angle that won't reflect directly back to the retina and into the lens. The extra height of the built-in flash may not be sufficient, however. That alone is a good reason for using an external flash. If you're working with your K200D's built-in flash, your only recourse may be to switch the red-eye reduction flash mode. That causes a pre-burst from the camera's flash to illuminate just before the picture is taken, which may result in your subjects' pupils contracting (see Figure 7.9), decreasing the amount of the red-eye effect. (You may have to ask your subject to look at the lamp to gain maximum effect.)

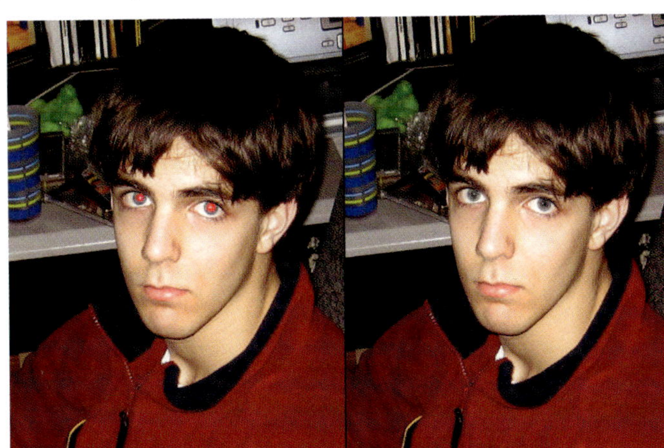

Figure 7.9 Red-eye effects can be reduced by using the K200D's flash modes that include a red-eye pre-flash.

Flash Exposure Modes

The built-in and external electronic flash units operate in conjunction with the Pentax K200D's exposure modes in the following ways:

- **Choosing a shutter speed.** When using the built-in flash, in Tv or M modes you can select any shutter speed equal to or slower than 1/180th second, unless you're using a lens other than one with the DA, D, FA, FA J, FA, or F designation (see Chapter 6 for more information about this alphabet soup). With a non-compliant lens, the shutter speed is locked at 1/180th second. If you happen to set the K200D's shutter to a speed *faster* than 1/180 second, the camera will automatically adjust the shutter speed down to 1/180th second.
- **In Aperture Priority (Av) mode.** You set the aperture, and the camera chooses the shutter speed of 1/180th second or slower. The slowest shutter speed the camera will select depends on the focal length of the lens in use (when you're using a DA, D, FA…etc. lens). Use this setting when you want to allow a slower shutter speed that increases the effect of ambient light on your image (for example, to allow the non-flash-illuminated background to show up in a flash picture). You may want to use the Anti-Shake feature or a tripod to reduce the blur of ambient light at these slower shutter speeds. Combining with slow shutter speeds and flash is called *slow sync*. It's an effect, and not a special sync setting of the camera.
- **In Shutter Priority (Tv) mode.** You set the shutter speed from 1/180th second to 30 seconds, as just described, and the K200D selects the aperture. Using Tv allows you to specify a slower shutter speed, when you want to increase the blurring caused by ambient light. Tv mode also makes it easier to use the slow sync effect. Just set the shutter to a slower speed, and take the picture. In Tv mode, you can also choose a shutter speed *faster* than 1/180th second, for what is called *high-speed sync* (described later in this chapter).
- **In Manual (M) mode.** With the Mode dial set to M, just choose your shutter speed and aperture. Press the Flash Up button, and take the picture. The camera will calculate the correct flash exposure. M mode can be used with high speed sync, too.

Flash Compensation

You can adjust the intensity of the flash relative to the calculated flash exposure using the Flash Compensation controls. Press the Fn button in Capture mode and press the down key to produce the Flash Mode screen. (See Figure 7.8, shown earlier.)Then, rotate the e-dial left or right to adjust the amount of compensation you want, from –2.0 to +1 stops. The compensation increment will be determined by the EV increment of either 1/2 EV or 1/3 EV that you set in CS #1 (EV Steps) option of the Custom Setting menu. To reset the flash compensation to zero while viewing this screen, just press the Green button.

Note that if a particular image requires the maximum output of the flash, any positive EV adjustment you've made will have no effect. Similarly, if a subject is overexposed because it is too close, or you've specified an aperture or ISO setting that is too large, no further negative exposure adjustment can be made.

Using External Electronic Flash

Pentax offers a broad range of accessory electronic flash units for the Pentax K200D. They can be mounted to the flash accessory shoe, or used off-camera with a dedicated cord that plugs into the flash shoe to maintain full communications with the camera for all special features. They range from the Pentax AF-540FGZ, which can correctly expose subjects up to 18.5 feet away at f/8 and ISO 100, to the Pentax AF-200FG, which is good out to 8 feet at f/8 and ISO 100. (You'll get greater ranges at even higher ISO settings, of course.) Units compatible with Pentax's P-TTL flash exposure system are also offered by Metz and Sigma. I'll cover only the key Pentax-brand flashes here.

Pentax AF-540 FGZ

This flagship of the Pentax accessory flash line is the most powerful unit the company offers (at about $320), with a GN of 148 at ISO 100, and an automatic "zoom" flash head that covers the full frame of lenses from 24mm wide angle. (There's a flip-down wide-angle diffuser that spreads the flash to cover a 20mm lens's field of view, too.) These flash coverage figures, supplied by Pentax, refer to a full 24 × 36mm frame, as the company's electronic flashes can also be used with Pentax 35mm film cameras. The AF-540 FGZ (but not the other two Pentax flash units) has a "format" setting with a Digital option that lets you tell the unit to take into account the angle of view difference of the 1.5X sensor "crop."

The exposure system uses the K200D's 16-zone evaluative metering system to calculate the correct flash duration at the designated f/stop. When the Flash mode is set to P-TTL Auto, a pre-flash burst fires as you depress the shutter release down all the way. The pre-flash information confirms subject distance, brightness, contrast, and whether the subject is backlit, using the camera's 16-segment metering sensor. Then, the correct exposure is set.

Powered by economical AA-size batteries, the unit recycles in 0.1 to 6 seconds, and can squeeze 200 flashes from a set of alkaline batteries, 250 with 2500 mAh nickel metal hydride cells, and 350 shots with lithium batteries. The optional TR-III battery pack gives you a pro-level 700 full flashes from each charge.

The AF-540 FGZ (see Figure 7.10) automatically communicates white balance information to your camera, allowing it to adjust WB to match the flash output. If you're using multiple flash units with Pentax's wireless P-TTL system, this model can serve as a master flash that controls the slave units you've set up (more about this later) or function as a slave itself. You have full manual control of flash output (from full power to 1/64th power), even when the unit is being used as a slave. Your K200D's built-in flash can be used to trigger this flash wirelessly.

When working with multiple external flash units, each can be set to a different power level to provide balanced or proportional flash. Pressing the Modeling button produces a continuous one-second burst of light you can use to judge lighting effects. Four transmission channels let you communicate with flash units in different sets. (This capability is especially useful when other Pentax photographers are using these flash units in the same vicinity; as long as you each use a different channel, your flashes won't interfere with each other.)

The AF-540 FGZ is compatible with second/trailing curtain sync (described earlier in this chapter) and high-speed sync (described next). All functions can be controlled from the back panel, shown in Figure 7.11. The hefty (13.4 ounce) unit offers bounce light swivel up to 90 degrees, and rotation 180 degrees to the right and 135 degrees to the

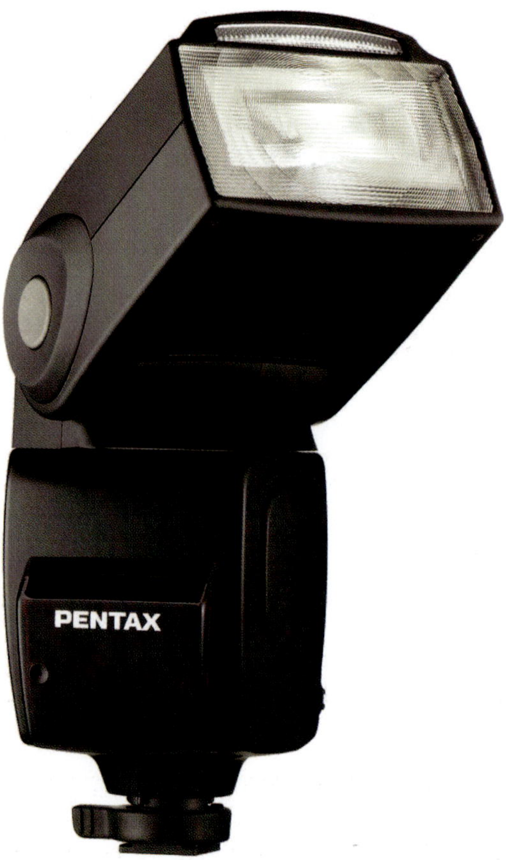

Figure 7.10 The top-of-the-line Pentax AF-540 FGZ electronic flash.

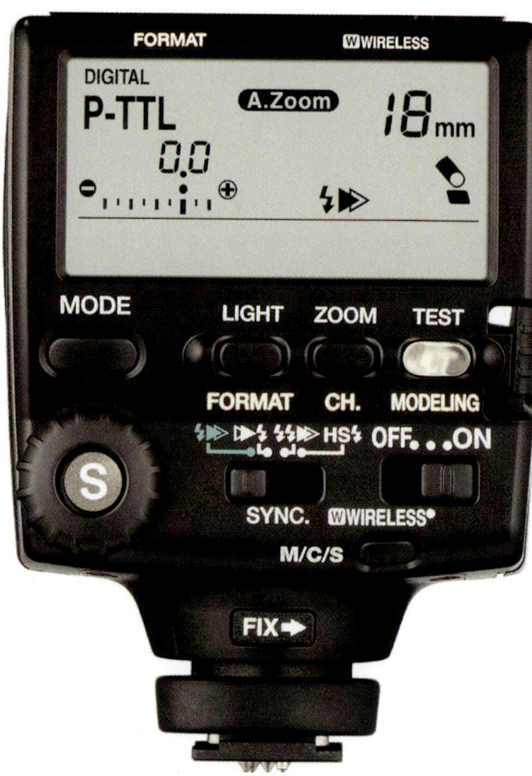

Figure 7.11 All functions can be set from this back-lit LCD panel.

left. It has its own built-in AF assist beam to help your camera focus under low-light conditions, as long as the subject being focused is within a few feet of the camera—the beam is most effective for relatively close objects.

WIRELESS MODE

To use Wireless mode, set the power switch of the external flash unit (either the AF-540 or AF-360) to Wireless. If the flash unit will not be attached to the camera (either with a cable or mounted on the hot shoe), set the unit's Wireless mode to Slave. Set the channel you want to use on the external flash.

Then mount the flash on the K200D's hot shoe, turn the camera on, and press the shutter release halfway. That step sets the built-in flash of the K200D to the same channel you just set on the flash. You can then remove the flash from the camera once the pair of devices have communicated.

Next, set the camera's flash to Wireless mode. Press the Fn button to produce the Capture Functions menu, and press the down key to access the Flash Mode screen. Use the left/right keys to select Wireless, and press OK to confirm your choice.

To use Wireless flash, the camera's Drive mode must not be set to Remote, or the aperture ring on your lens (if present) set to anything except A. (Otherwise, Wireless will be grayed out and not available in the Flash Mode screen.)

If you want the flash to contribute to the exposure (say, for fill flash), use CS #16 in the Custom Setting menu (Flash in Wireless mode) and choose 1. Select 2 instead, and the built-in flash will fire only a pre-flash to trigger the wireless units. It won't fire a full burst or contribute to the exposure.

Pentax AF-360 FGX

The less pricey electronic flash has most of the features of the AF-540, but with less power at a GN of 99. You get automatic zoom coverage for lenses from 24 to 85mm (and 20mm with the flip-down diffuser), wireless control with four channels and variable lighting ratios, along with second/trailing curtain sync and high-speed sync. It can serve as a master flash mounted on the Pentax K200D, or as a slave in Wireless mode, and provides that helpful AF assist beam for low-light conditions. Pressing the Modeling button fires the flash consecutively for about one second, producing a modeling light effect.

However, while the flash head of the AF-360 swivels up and down up to 90 degrees for bounce flash, it doesn't rotate like that of the AF-540, and variable power goes from full power to 1/32 power. This unit sips power a little more frugally than its big brother when using four AA alkaline cells, but squeezes only 160 shots from nickel metal hydroxide batteries, and 300 from lithium cells. While this unit does not have the "format" setting to specify use of a digital camera with a "cropped" sensor, the flash does calculate the difference in angle of view when figuring exposure, using information about the focal length reported by DA, D FA, FA, FA J, or F lenses (check out Chapter 6 again to decipher these designations).

HIGH-SPEED SYNC

Both the AF-540 and AF-360 allow high speed sync, which lets you use electronic flash at a shutter speed greater than 1/180th second. You'll find this capability useful when you want to use a faster shutter speed in bright surroundings, so that the flash can be used as fill for the shadows. Normally, even at ISO 100, at 1/180th second you'd need an aperture of about f/11 for a correct exposure under daylight. That would mean that your fill flash would be effective only out to about 13 feet with the AF-540 and just 9 feet with the AF-360. High-speed sync would let you use 1/400th second at f/8 under full daylight, increasing your fill flash "range" to nearly 19 feet with the AF-540, and 12 feet with the AF-360.

The higher shutter speeds possible with high-speed sync also help reduce the chance of "ghost" images, as described earlier in this chapter.

To use high-speed sync with the Pentax K200D, set the AF-540 or AF-360's Flash sync mode to HS Lighting, and use either Tv or M Exposure modes so that you can select a shutter speed faster than 1/180th second.

Pentax AF-200 FG

Unlike the other two units, this one offers automatic operation only (but with flash EV adjustments of –0.5 and –1 EV), and none of the fancy features of its more expensive siblings. Its 65 guide number is a little beefier than the K200D's built-in flash, making it a good choice as a low-power auxiliary flash unit. It lacks a zoomable flash head and offers fixed coverage equivalent to the field of view of a 28mm full-frame lens, with an adapter provided to cover the field of view (FOV) of a 24mm lens. Weighing just 6.8 ounces without batteries, expect 300 flashes from a set of four AA alkaline batteries.

Most of the other cool features of the more expensive Pentax flash units, including AF assist, high-speed sync, wireless operation, and swivel/rotate orientations are absent. There are three chief advantages of this flash unit. It has slightly more power (GN 65 vs. 43 for the built-in unit), so you can shoot out to 8 feet at f/8 and ISO 100. It is elevated higher than the built-in flash for reduced red-eye effects, and uses its own AA batteries and doesn't draw from your camera's battery like the built-in flash does.

More Advanced Lighting Techniques

As you advance in your Pentax K200D photography, you'll want to learn more sophisticated lighting techniques, using more than just straight-on flash, or using just a single flash unit. Entire books have been written on lighting techniques, and I've written multiple chapters on them in books of my own. I'm going to provide a quick introduction to some of the techniques you should be considering.

Diffusing and Softening the Light

Direct light can be harsh and glaring, especially if you're using the flash built into your camera, or an auxiliary flash mounted in the hot shoe and pointed directly at your subject. The first thing you should do is stop using direct light (unless you're looking for a stark, contrasty appearance as a creative effect). There are a number of simple things you can do with both continuous and flash illumination.

- **Use window light.** Light coming in a window can be soft and flattering, and a good choice for human subjects. Move your subject close enough to the window that its light provides the primary source of illumination. You might want to turn off other lights in the room, particularly to avoid mixing daylight and incandescent light. (See Figure 7.12.)
- **Use fill light.** Your K200D's built-in flash makes a perfect fill-in light for the shadows, brightening inky depths with a kicker of illumination. Any of the three Pentax external flash units can be used for fill, too. (See Figure 7.13.)
- **Bounce the light.** All external electronic flash units mounted on the K200D (except the AF-200 FG) have a swivel that allows them to be pointed up at a ceiling for a bounce light effect. You can also bounce the light off a wall if the flash unit allows it. You'll want the ceiling or wall to be white or have a neutral gray color to avoid a color cast.
- **Use reflectors.** Another way to bounce the light is to use reflectors or umbrellas that you can position yourself to provide a greater degree of control over the quantity and direction of the bounced light. Good reflectors can be pieces of foamboard, Mylar, or a reflective disk held in place by a clamp and stand. Although some expensive umbrellas and reflectors are available, spending a lot isn't necessary. A simple piece of white foamboard does the job beautifully. Umbrellas have the advantage of being compact and foldable, while providing a soft, even kind of light. They're relatively cheap, too, with a good 40-inch umbrella available for as little as $20.
- **Use diffusers.** Sto-Fen and some other vendors offer clip-on diffusers like the one shown in Figures 7.14 and 7.15, that fit over your electronic flash head and provide a soft, flattering light. These add-ons are more portable than umbrellas and other reflectors, yet provide a nice diffuse lighting effect.

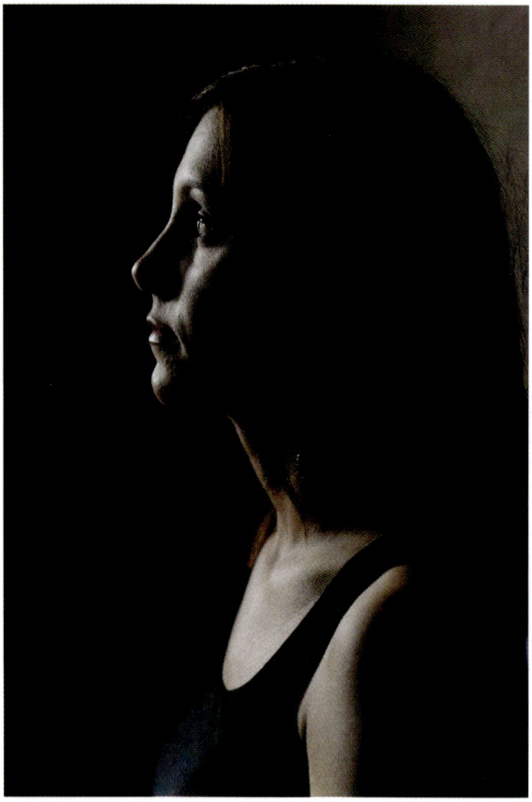

Figure 7.12 Window light makes the perfect diffuse illumination for informal soft-focus portraits like this one.

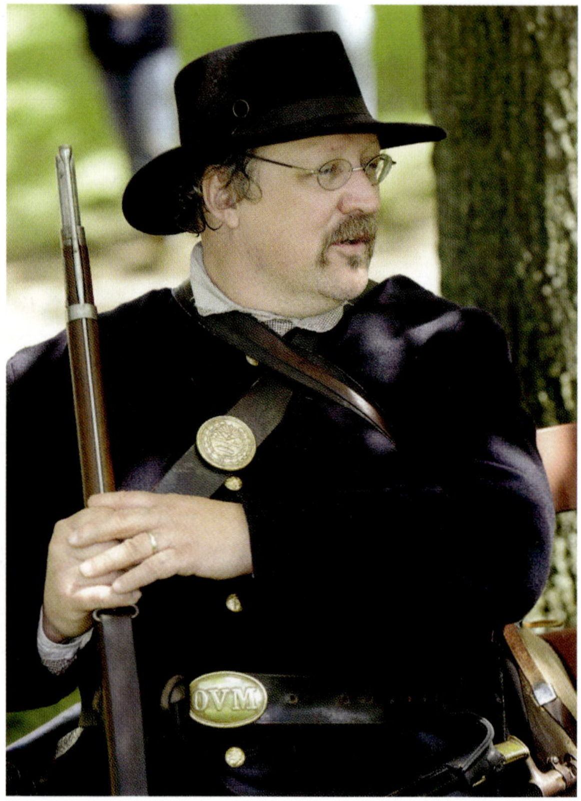

Figure 7.13 Fill flash can lighten up the shadows of photos taken with backlighting.

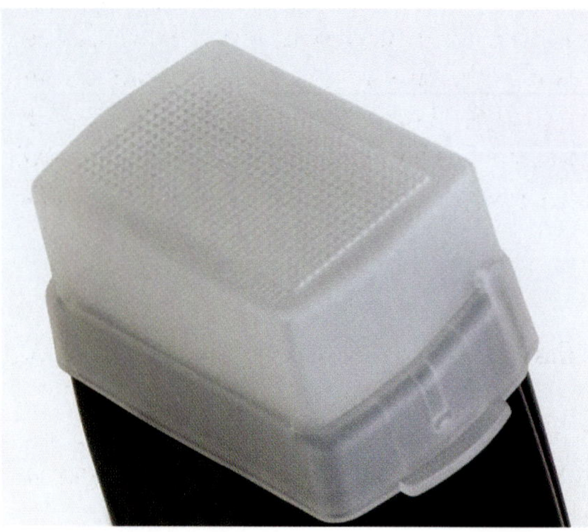

Figure 7.14 The Sto-Fen OmniBounce is a clip-on diffuser that softens the light of an external flash unit.

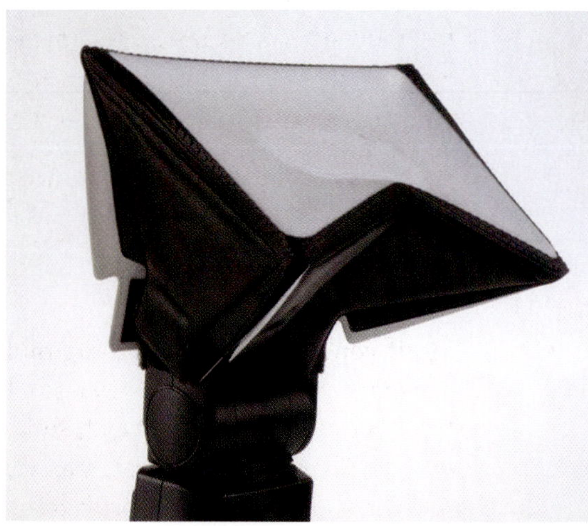

Figure 7.15 Flash-mounted soft boxes use Velcro strips to attach them to third-party flash units (like the one shown) or any Pentax external flash.

Using Multiple Light Sources

Once you gain control over the qualities and effects you get with a single light source, you'll want to graduate to using multiple light sources. Using several lights allows you to shape and mold the illumination of your subjects to provide a variety of effects, from backlighting to side lighting to more formal portrait lighting. You can start simply with several incandescent light sources, bounced off umbrellas or reflectors that you construct. Or you can use more flexible multiple electronic flash setups.

Effective lighting is the one element that differentiates great photography from candid or snapshot shooting. Lighting can make a mundane subject look a little more glamorous. Make subjects appear to be soft when you want a soft look, or bright and sparkly when you want a vivid look, or strong and dramatic if that's what you desire. As you might guess, having control over your lighting means that you probably can't use the lights that are already in the room. You'll need separate, discrete lighting fixtures that can be moved, aimed, brightened, and dimmed on command.

Selecting your lighting gear will depend on the type of photography you do, and the budget you have to support it. It's entirely possible for a beginning K200D photographer to create a basic, inexpensive lighting system capable of delivering high-quality results for a few hundred dollars, just as you can spend megabucks ($1,000 and up) for a sophisticated lighting system.

Basic Flash Setups

If you want to use multiple electronic flash units, the Pentax Speedlites described earlier will serve admirably. The two higher-end models can be used with Pentax's wireless P-TTL feature, which allows you to set up to four separate groups ("channels") of flash units (several flashes can be included in each group) and trigger them using a master flash and the camera. Just set up one master unit (there's a switch on the unit that sets it for master mode) and arrange the compatible slave units around your subject. You can set the relative power of each unit separately, thereby controlling how much of the scene's illumination comes from the main flash, and how much from the auxiliary flash units, which can be used as fill flash, background lights, or, if you're careful, to illuminate the hair of portrait subjects.

Studio Flash

If you're serious about using multiple flash units, a studio flash setup might be more practical. The traditional studio flash is a multi-part unit, consisting of a flash head that mounts on your light stand, and is tethered to an AC (or sometimes battery) power supply. A single power supply can feed two or more flash heads at a time, with separate control over the output of each head.

When they are operating off AC power, studio flash don't have to be frugal with the juice, and are often powerful enough to illuminate very large subjects or to supply lots and lots of light to smaller subjects. The output of such units is measured in watt seconds (ws), so you could purchase a 200ws, 400ws, or 800ws unit, and a power pack to match.

Their advantages include greater power output, much faster recycling, built-in modeling lamps, multiple power levels, and ruggedness that can stand up to transport, because many photographers pack up these kits and tote them around as location lighting rigs. Studio lighting kits can range in price from a few hundred dollars for a set of lights, stands, and reflectors, to thousands for a high-end lighting system complete with all the necessary accessories.

A more practical choice these days is *monolights* (see Figure 7.16), which are "all-in-one" studio lights that sell for about $200-$400. They have the flash tube, modeling light, and power supply built into a single unit that can be mounted on a light stand. Monolights are available in AC-only and battery-pack versions, although an external battery eliminates some of the advantages of having a flash with everything in one unit. They are very portable, because all you need is a case for the monolight itself, plus the stands and other accessories you want to carry along. Because these units are so

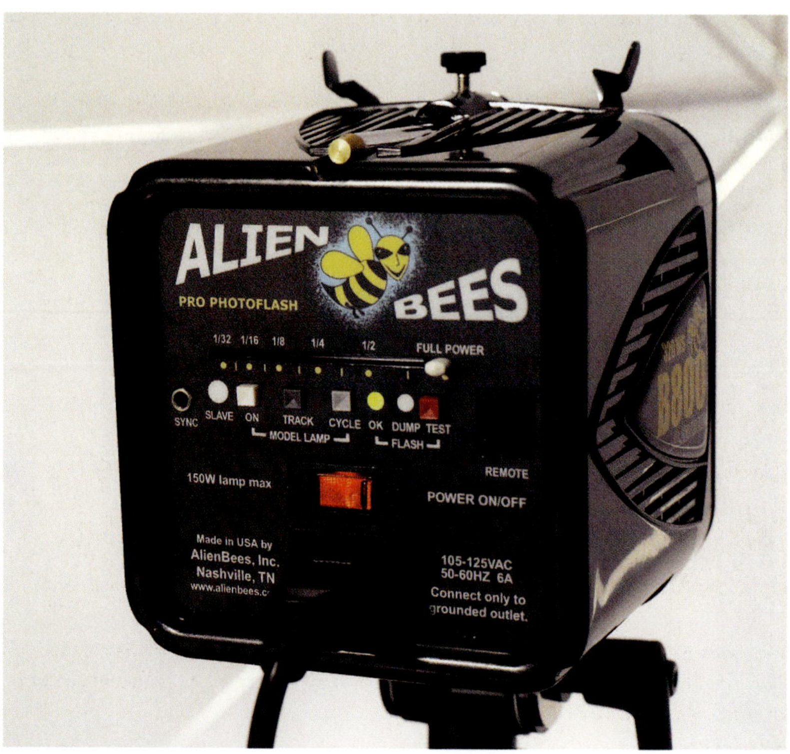

Figure 7.16
All-in-one "monolights" contain flash, power supply, and a modeling light in one compact package (umbrella not included).

popular with photographers who are not full-time professionals, the lower-cost monolights are often designed more for lighter duty than professional studio flash. That doesn't mean they aren't rugged; you'll just need to handle them with a little more care, and, perhaps, not expect them to be used eight hours a day for weeks on end. In most other respects, however, monolights are the equal of traditional studio flash units in terms of fast recycling, built-in modeling lamps, adjustable power, and so forth.

Connecting Multiple Non-Dedicated Units to Your Pentax K200D

Non-dedicated electronic flash units can't use the automated P-TTL features of your Pentax K200D; you'll need to calculate exposure manually, through test shots evaluated on your camera's LCD, or by using an electronic flash meter. Moreover, you don't have to connect them to the accessory shoe on top of the camera. Instead, you can use an adapter in the hot shoe to provide a PC/X connector, and use a shutter speed of 1/60th second or slower.

You should be aware that older electronic flash units sometimes use a triggering voltage that is too much for your K200D to handle. You can actually damage the camera's electronics if the voltage is too high. You won't need to worry about this if you purchase brand new units from Alien Bees, Adorama, or other vendors. But if you must connect an external flash with an unknown triggering voltage, I recommend using a Wein Safe Sync (see Figure 7.17), which isolates the flash's voltage from the camera triggering circuit, and provides a PC/X adapter for plugging in non-dedicated flash units.

Another safe way to connect external cameras is through a radio-control device, such as the transmitter/receiver set shown in Figure 7.18. It piggybacks onto the PC/X adapter

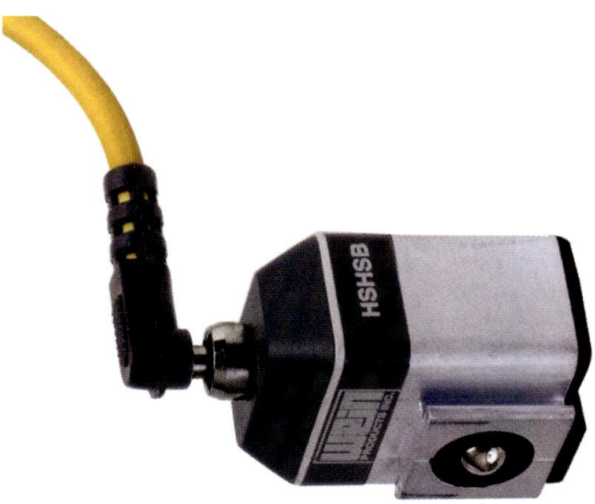

Figure 7.17 A voltage isolator can prevent frying your K200D's flash circuits if you use an older electronic flash, and provides a PC/X connector, which the Pentax K200D lacks.

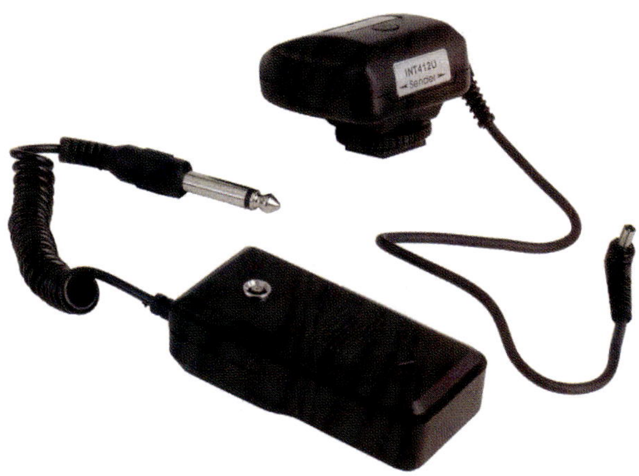

Figure 7.18 A radio-control device frees you from a sync cord tether between your flash and camera.

you've fastened to your hot shoe, and plugs into your adaptor's PC/X connector. It transmits a signal to a matching receiver that's connected to your flash unit. The receiver has both a PC connector of its own as well as a "monoplug" connector (it looks like a headphone plug) that links to a matching port on compatible flash units.

Finally, some flash units have an optical slave trigger built in, or can be fitted with one, so that they fire automatically when another flash, including your camera's built-in unit, fires.

Other Lighting Accessories

Once you start working with light, you'll find there are plenty of useful accessories that can help you. Here are some of the most popular that you might want to consider.

Soft Boxes

Soft boxes are large square or rectangular devices that may resemble a square umbrella with a front cover, and produce a similar lighting effect. They can extend from a few feet square to massive boxes that stand five or six feet tall—virtually a wall of light. With a flash unit or two inside a soft box, you have a very large, semi-directional light source that's very diffuse and very flattering for portraiture and other people photography. (See Figure 7.19.)

Soft boxes are also handy for photographing shiny objects. They not only provide a soft light, but if the box itself happens to reflect in the subject (say you're photographing a chromium toaster), the box will provide an interesting highlight that's indistinct and not distracting.

You can buy soft boxes or make your own. Some lengths of friction-fit plastic pipe and a lot of muslin cut and sewed just so may be all that you need.

Light Stands

Both electronic flash and incandescent lamps can benefit from light stands. These are lightweight, tripod-like devices (but without a swiveling or tilting head) that can be set on the floor, tabletops, or other elevated surfaces and positioned as needed. Light stands should be strong enough to support an external lighting unit, up to and including a relatively heavy flash with soft box or umbrella reflectors. You want the supports to be capable of raising the lights high enough to be effective. Look for light stands capable of extending six to seven feet high. The nine-foot units usually have larger, steadier bases, and extend high enough that you can use them as background supports. You'll be using these stands for a lifetime, so invest in good ones. I bought the light stand shown in Figure 7.20 when I was in college, and I have been using it for decades.

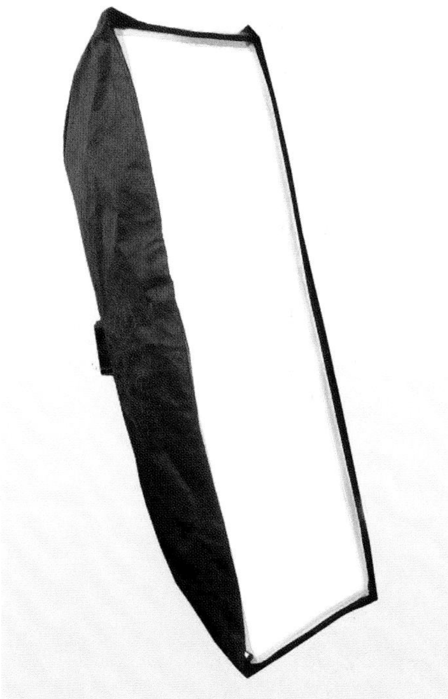

Figure 7.19 Larger soft boxes provide even more diffuse illumination.

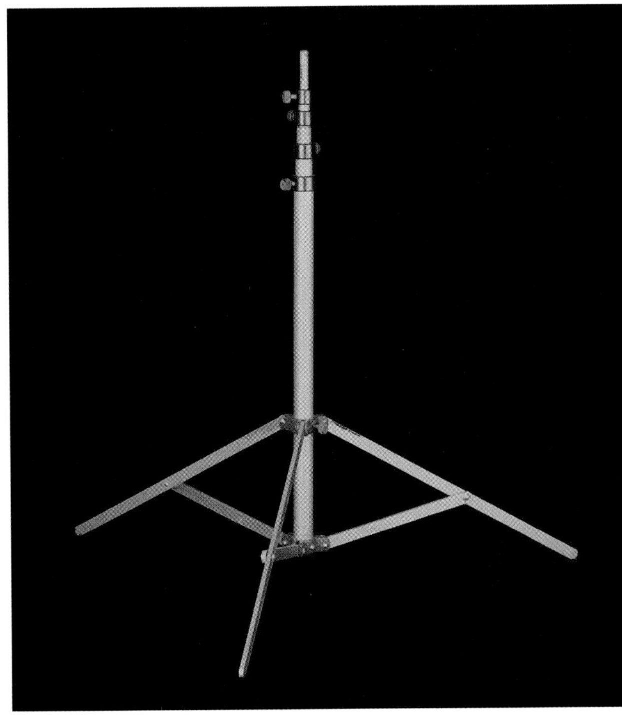

Figure 7.20 Light stands can hold lights, umbrellas, backdrops, and other equipment.

Backgrounds

Backgrounds can be backdrops of cloth, sheets of muslin you've painted yourself using a sponge dipped in paint, rolls of seamless paper, or any other suitable surface your mind can dream up. Backgrounds provide a complementary and non-distracting area behind subjects (especially portraits) and can be lit separately to provide contrast and separation that outlines the subject, or which helps set a mood.

I like to use plain-colored backgrounds for portraits, and white seamless backgrounds for product photography. You can usually construct these yourself from cheap materials and tape them up on the wall behind your subject, or mount them on a pole stretched between a pair of light stands.

Snoots and Barn Doors

These fit over the flash unit and direct the light at your subject. Snoots are excellent for converting a flash unit into a hair light, while barn doors give you enough control over the illumination by opening and closing their flaps that you can use another flash as a background light, with the capability of feathering the light exactly where you want it on the background. Both are shown in Figure 7.21.

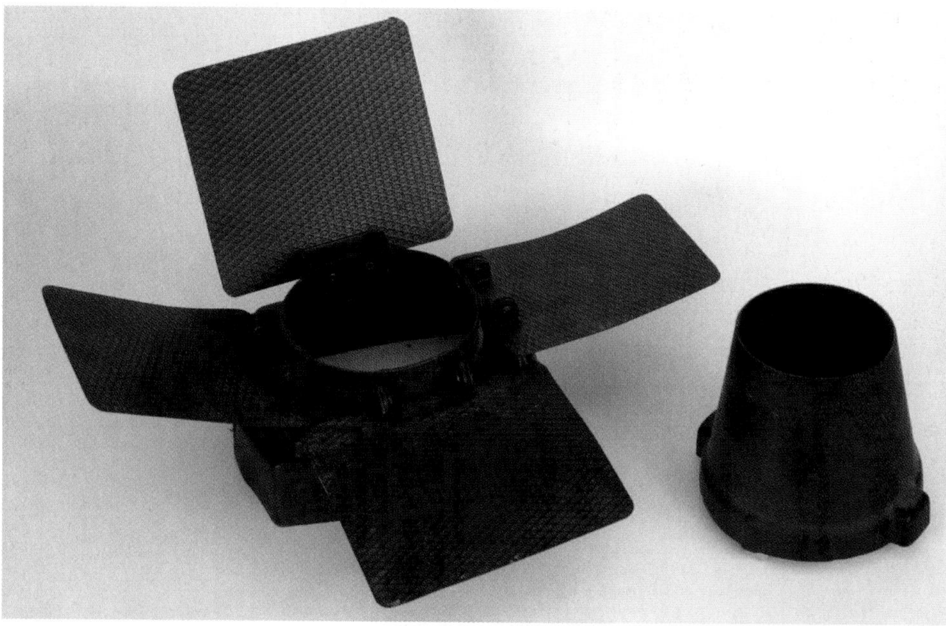

Figure 7.21
Snoots and barn doors allow you to modulate the light from a flash or lamp, and they are especially useful for hair lights and background lights.

8

Downloading and Editing Your Images

Taking the picture is only half the work and, in some cases, only half the fun. After you've captured some great images and have them safely stored on your Pentax K200D's memory card, you'll need to transfer them from your camera and memory card to your computer, where they can be organized, fine-tuned in an image editor, and prepared for web display, printing, or some other final destination.

Fortunately, there are lots of software utilities and applications to help you do all these things. This chapter will introduce you to a few of them.

What's in the Box?

Your Pentax K200D came with software programs on CD for both Windows PCs and Macs. Pop the CD into your computer and install Pentax Photo Browser 3 and Pentax Photo Laboratory 3. Manuals are in the box, so I won't be providing any how-to instructions here.

Pentax Photo Browser 3

This is a simple application for basic viewing, printing, and organizing your images. It's compatible with the JPEG files created in your K200D, as well as RAW files in either the Pentax .PEF or Adobe .DNG formats. You can also work with .BMP, .PCT, .PNG, and .TIF files. These are older formats produced by some image-editing applications.

Photo Browser (see Figure 8.1) displays thumbnails of multiple files in a pane located in the upper-center portion of the application's window. Navigate to the folder containing your images, and select images by clicking them or Ctrl + clicking to select multiple shots (Command + click on the Mac). A larger preview image and information about that photo appears at the bottom of the screen.

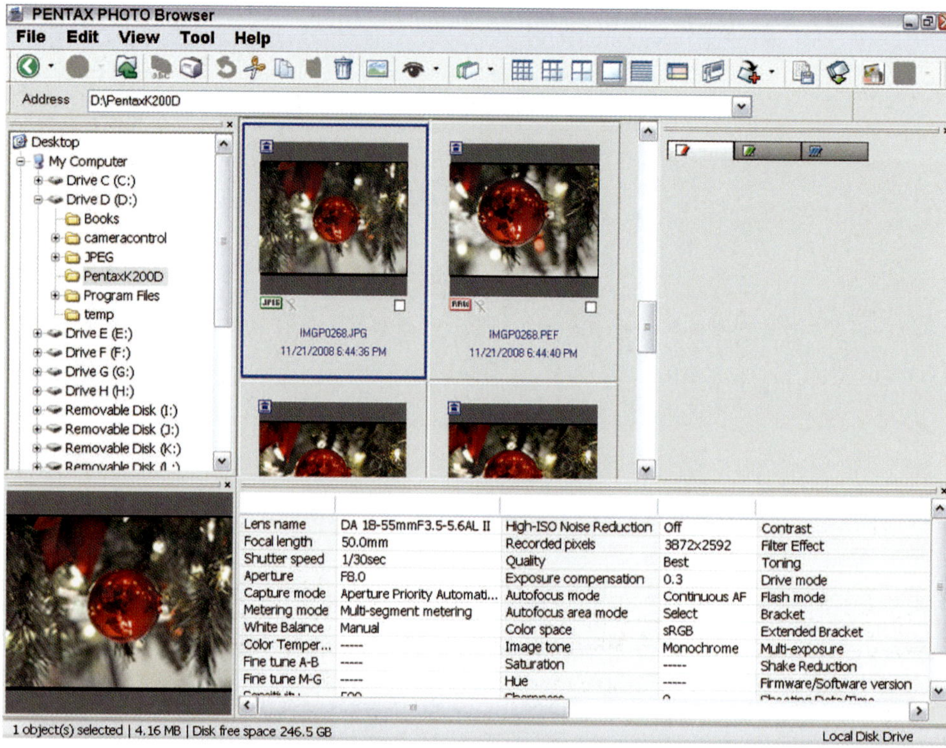

Figure 8.1
The Pentax Photo Browser allows you to view and manage images from your camera.

Double-click an image and it appears in the Main Image View window (see Figure 8.2), which has tools for rotating, cropping, zooming, and an Auto Image Fix option. The latter automatically adjusts the brightness, contrast, and color tone of your image. Your only options are "Strong" or "Slight," which control the degree of changes that are made. The browser's rudimentary image manipulation tools allow you to rotate and print the images, save them under the same or different file names, change the file format, delete unwanted photos, and check or save the image information.

In the Tool menu and toolbar at the top of the screen, you'll get access to Pentax's Easy Transfer utility (described later), and Pentax Photo Laboratory. Choose the latter, and the Laboratory is launched with the images you've selected loaded.

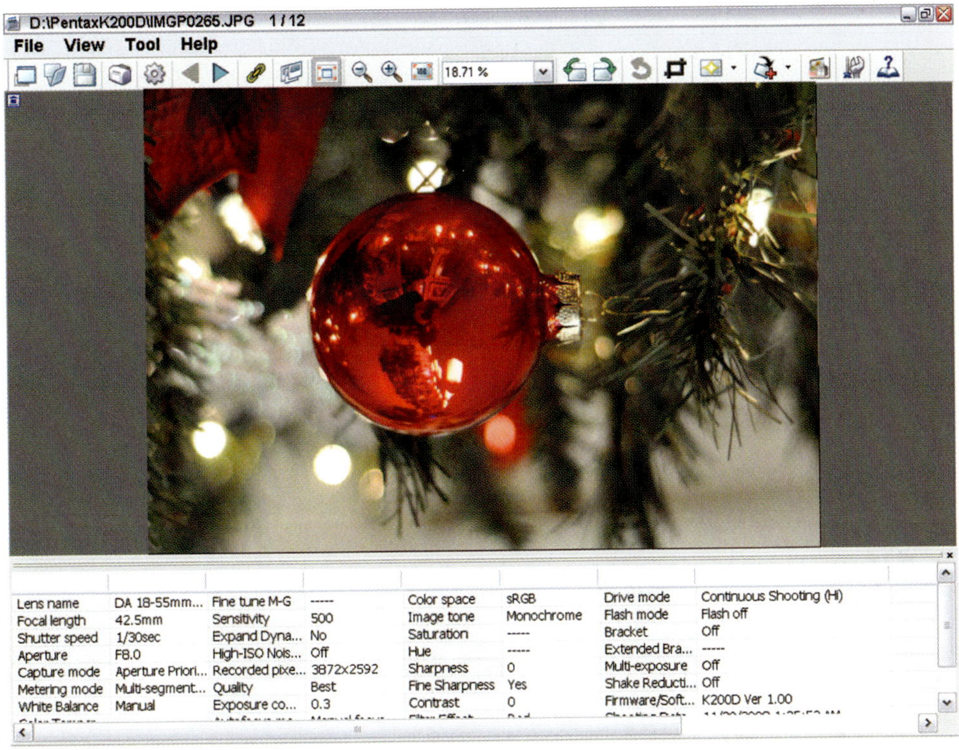

Figure 8.2 The Main Image View window has tools for rotating, cropping, zooming, and a quick fix option.

Tip

Ignore the Pentax Remote Assistant choice in the Tool menu. This is a remote control utility for K200D's "big brother," the Pentax K20D, and it is not installed with your software. It appears as a menu choice, nevertheless, but is not active.

Pentax Photo Laboratory 3

This utility can be accessed directly from Photo Browser, or loaded as a standalone application. (See Figure 8.3.) It's intended for processing PEF and DNG files *created by your Pentax K200D* or another Pentax camera. (It cannot handle DNG files produced by other image-editing applications, or non-Pentax cameras.) Photo Laboratory allows you to convert RAW images to another format, crop them to trim the borders, or resize them to produce a smaller or larger image (in terms of resolution).

While there is a Full Auto Processing mode for quick fixes, you'll find more flexibility in another choice located in the View menu: Custom Processing mode. This mode lets you make selections and set parameters you could have chosen in the camera for a JPEG image, but do it after the photo has already been taken and saved in RAW format. This

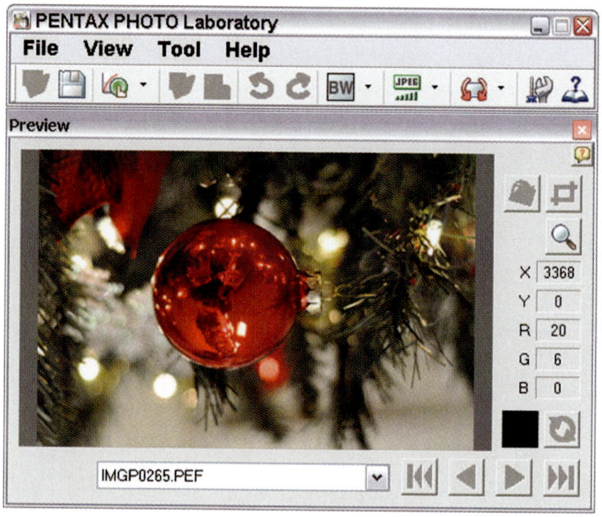

Figure 8.3
Pentax Photo Laboratory can be accessed from Photo Browser or run as a standalone program.

capability is one good reason for shooting RAW: the ability to change your mind about your settings later.

For example, you can choose one of six Image Tone options (Bright, Natural, Portrait, Landscape, Vibrant, and Monochrome), five Picture (Mode Dial Scene) modes (Portrait, Landscape, Macro, Moving Object, and Night Scene), as well as nine Scene (SCN) modes. The available SCN modes are the same as those you can select from the SCN menu: Night Scene, Surf & Snow, Food, Sunset, Kids, Pet, Candlelight, Museum, and Text.

There are also (Figure 8.4) tools for correcting lens aberrations, reducing noise, correcting tonal values, and adjusting white balance. If multiple RAW files are selected, you can apply the same processing settings to an entire batch.

Transferring Your Photos

While it's rewarding to capture some great images and have them ensconced in your camera, eventually you'll be transferring them to your laptop or PC, whether you're using a Windows or Macintosh machine. You have several options for image transfer: direct transfer over a USB cable (manually or using Pentax's Easy Transfer), automated transfer using a card reader and transfer software such as Easy Transfer or Adobe Photoshop Elements Photo Downloader, or manual transfer using drag and drop from a memory card inserted in a card reader.

There are some advantages to transferring photos directly from your Pentax K200D to a computer. The destination computer doesn't need to have a card reader; all it requires

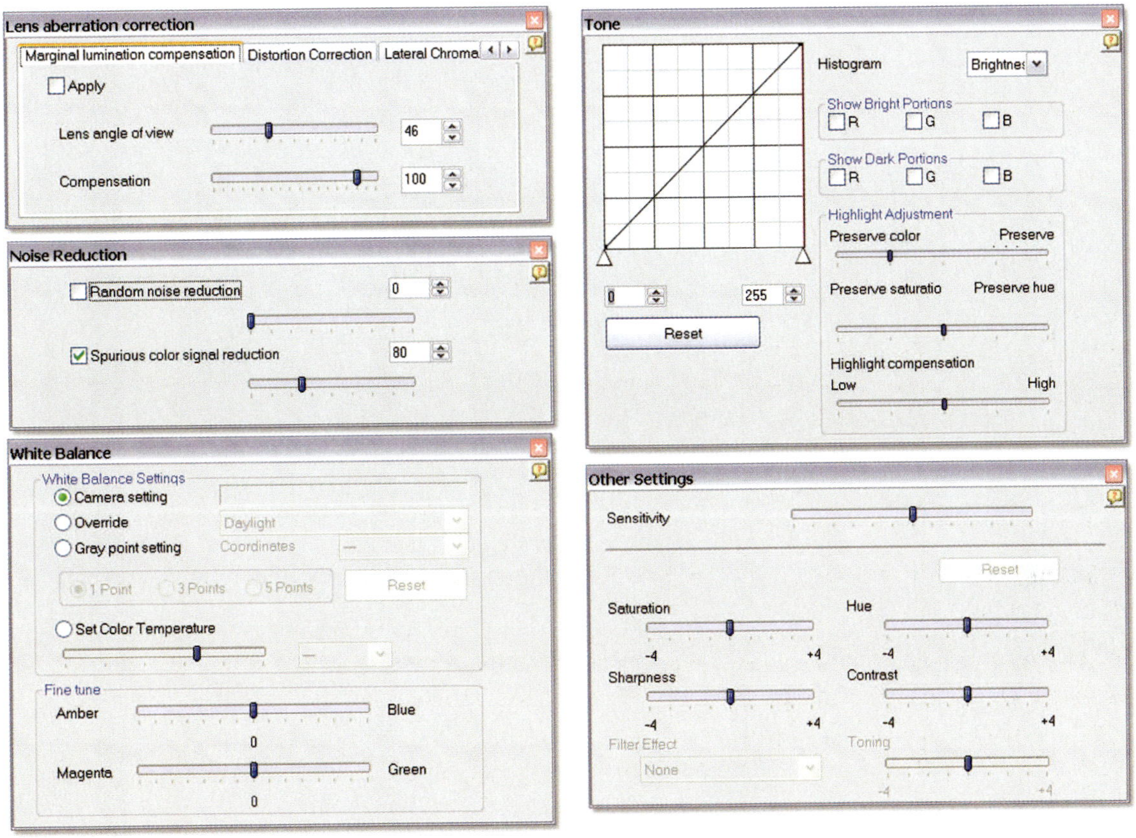

Figure 8.4 Photo Laboratory has dialog boxes for correcting (clockwise from upper left) lens aberrations; tonal values; settings such as hue, saturation, and contrast; white balance; and noise reduction.

is a USB port. So, if you have the USB cable that came with your camera, you can transfer photos to any computer that has the correct utility software (discussed later) installed. However, direct automatic transfer uses your K200D's internal battery power, while removing the card and transferring the photos with a card reader installed on the destination computer does not.

You can also use a memory card reader and software to transfer photos and automate the process using the image-downloading utility built into your computer's operating system (the Windows version is shown in Figure 8.5), Pentax Easy Transfer Utility (see Figure 8.6), Photoshop Elements Photo Downloader, or the downloading program supplied with some other third-party applications. This method is more frugal in its use of your K200D's battery and can be faster if you have a speedy USB 2.0 or FireWire card reader attached to an appropriate port.

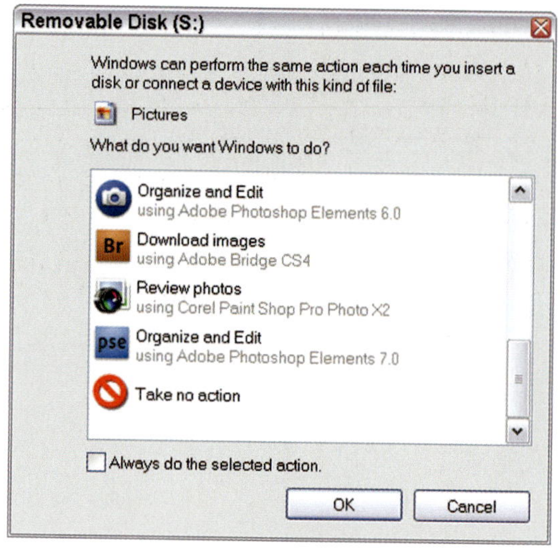

Figure 8.5 Microsoft Windows includes a photo downloading utility.

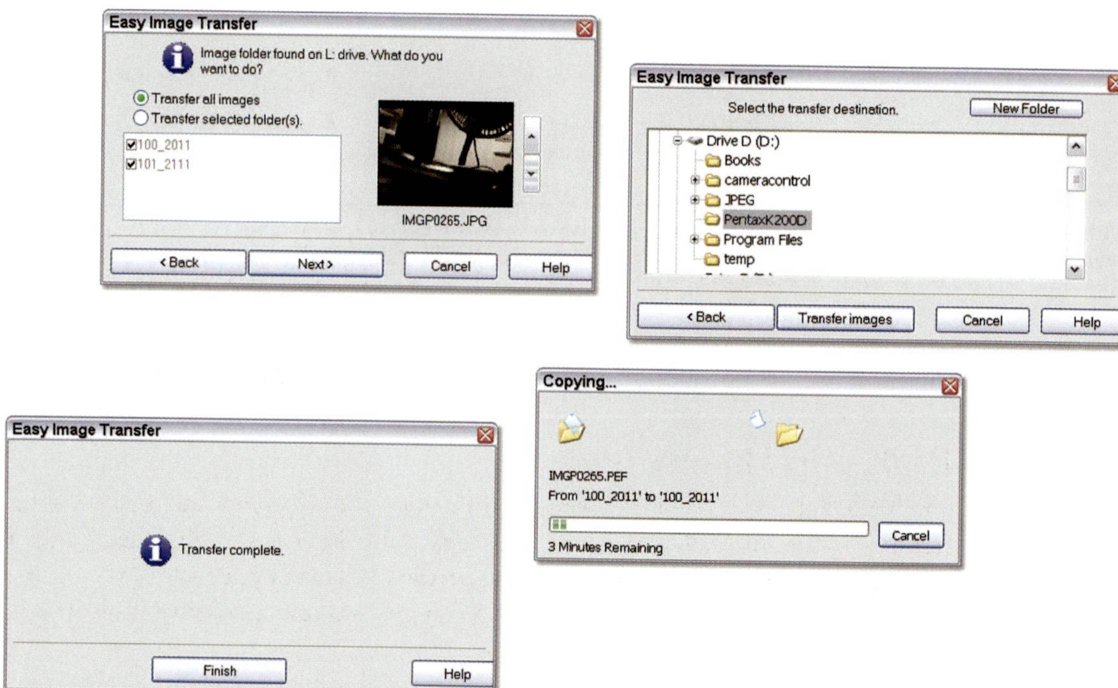

Figure 8.6 Pentax Easy Transfer downloads your photos in just a few steps.

The installed software automatically remains in memory as you work, and it recognizes when a memory card is inserted in your card reader; you don't have to launch it yourself. With Photoshop Elements' Photo Downloader, you can click Get Photos to begin the transfer of all images immediately (see Figure 8.7) or choose Advanced Dialog to produce a dialog box that shows a grid of available images on your card. You can select which images to download from the memory card by marking them with a check. You can choose the photos you want to transfer, plus options such as Automatically Fix Red Eyes. Start the download, and a confirmation dialog box like the one in Figure 8.8 shows the progress.

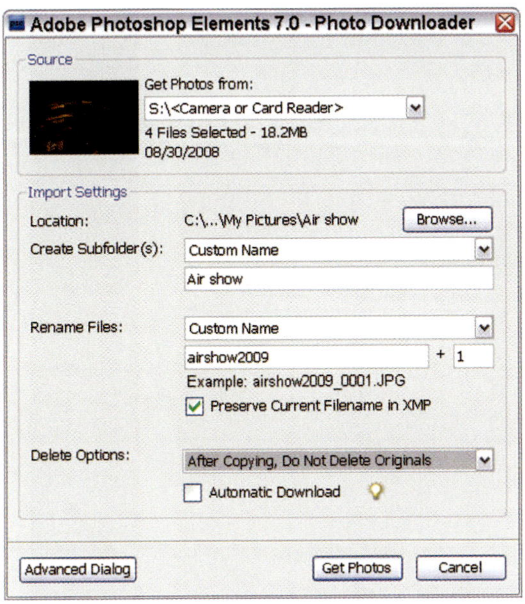

Figure 8.7 Transfer all images with Photoshop Elements' Photo Downloader by clicking Get Photos.

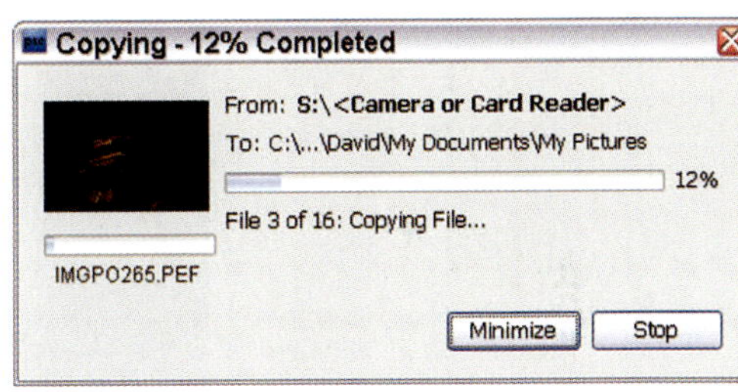

Figure 8.8 The Photo Downloader's confirmation dialog box shows the progress as images are transferred.

Dragging and Dropping

The final way to move photos from your memory card to your computer is the old-fashioned way: manually dragging and dropping the files from one window on your computer to another. The procedure works pretty much the same whether you're using a Mac or a PC, and whether you're using a memory card reader or have connected the K200D to the computer with a USB cable.

1. Remove the memory card from the Pentax K200D and insert it in your memory card reader.
2. Using Windows Explorer, My Computer, or your Mac desktop, open the icon representing the memory card, which appears on your desktop as just another disk drive.

3. Open a second window representing the folder on your computer that you want to use as the destination for the files you are copying or moving.
4. Drag and drop the files from the memory card window to the folder on your computer. You can select individual files, press Ctrl/Command + A to select all the files, or Ctrl/Command + click to select multiple files.

Editing Your Photos

Image manipulation tasks fall into several categories. You might want to fine-tune your images, retouch them, change color balance, composite several images together, and perform other tasks we know as image editing, with a program like Adobe Photoshop, Photoshop Elements, or Corel Photo Paint.

There are specialized tools expressly for tweaking RAW files, ranging from Adobe Camera Raw to PhaseOne's Capture One Pro (C1 Pro). A third type of manipulation is the specialized task of noise reduction, which can be performed within Photoshop, Adobe Camera Raw, or tools like Bibble Professional. There are also specialized tools just for noise reduction, such as Noise Ninja (also included with Bibble) and Neat Image.

Each of these utilities and applications deserves a chapter of its own, so I'm simply going to enumerate some of the most popular image-editing and RAW conversion programs here and tell you a little about what they do.

Image Editors

Image editors are general-purpose photo-editing applications that can do color correction, tonal modifications, retouching, combining of several images into one, and usually include tools for working with RAW files and reducing noise. So, you'll find programs like those listed here good for all-around image manipulation. The leading programs are as follows:

Adobe Photoshop/Photoshop Elements. Photoshop is the serious photographer's number one choice for image editing, and Elements is an excellent option for those who need most of Photoshop's power, but not all of its professional-level features. Unfortunately, Adobe's releases of Elements for the Macintosh tend to lag behind the Windows version. While Elements 6.0 for Windows was introduced about a month after the Pentax K200D, the Macintosh edition wasn't made available until early 2008. Both editors use the latest version of Adobe's Camera Raw plug-in, which makes it easy to adjust things like color space profiles, color depth (either 8 bits or 16 bits per color channel), image resolution, white balance, exposure, shadows, brightness, sharpness, luminance, and noise reduction. One plus with the Adobe products is that they are available in identical versions for both Windows and Macs (eventually!).

Corel Photo Paint. This is the image-editing program that is included in the popular CorelDRAW Graphics suite. Although a Mac version was available in the past, this is primarily a Windows application today. It's a full-featured photo retouching and image-editing program with selection, retouching, and painting tools for manual image manipulations, and it also includes convenient automated commands for a few common tasks, such as red-eye removal. Photo Paint accepts Photoshop plug-ins to expand its assortment of filters and special effects.

Corel Paint Shop Pro. This is a general-purpose Windows-only image editor that has gained a reputation as the "poor man's Photoshop" for providing a substantial portion of Photoshop's capabilities at a fraction of the cost. It includes a nifty set of wizard-like commands that automate common tasks, such as removing red-eye and scratches, as well as filters and effects, which can be expanded with other Photoshop plug-ins.

Macromedia Fireworks. This is the image-editing program for Macs and PCs formerly from Macromedia, and now owned by Adobe, and it is most useful when used with web development and animation software like Dreamweaver and Flash. If you're using your Pentax K200D images on web pages, you'll like this program's capabilities in the web graphics arena, such as banners, image maps, and rollover buttons.

Corel Painter. Here's another image-editing program from Corel for both Mac and Windows. This one's strength is in mimicking natural media, such as charcoal, pastels, and various kinds of paint. Painter includes a basic assortment of tools that you can use to edit existing images, but the program is really designed for artists to use in creating original illustrations. As a photographer, you might prefer another image editor, but if you like to paint on top of your photographic images, nothing else really does the job of Painter.

Corel PhotoImpact. Corel finally brought one of the last remaining non-Adobe image editors into its fold when it acquired PhotoImpact. This is a general-purpose photo-editing program for Windows with a huge assortment of brushes for painting, retouching, and cloning in addition to the usual selection, cropping, and fill tools. If you frequently find yourself performing the same image manipulations on a number of files, you'll appreciate PhotoImpact's batch operations. Using this feature, you can select multiple image files and then apply any one of a long list of filters, enhancements, or auto-process commands to all the selected files.

RAW Utilities

Your software choices for manipulating RAW files are broader than you might think. Camera vendors always supply a utility to read their cameras' own RAW files, but sometimes, particularly with those point-and-shoot cameras that can produce RAW files, the options are fairly limited.

Because in the past digital camera vendors offered RAW converters that weren't very good, there is a lively market for third-party RAW utilities available at extra cost.

The third-party solutions are usually available as standalone applications (often for both Windows and Macintosh platforms), as Photoshop-compatible plug-ins, or both. Because the RAW plug-ins displace Photoshop's own RAW converter, I tend to prefer to use most RAW utilities in standalone mode. That way, if I choose to open a file directly in Photoshop, it automatically opens using Photoshop's fast and easy-to-use Adobe Camera Raw (ACR) plug-in. If I have more time or need the capabilities of another converter, I can load that, open the file, and make my corrections there. Most are able to transfer the processed file directly to Photoshop even if you aren't using plug-in mode.

This section provides a quick overview of the range of RAW file handlers, so you can get a better idea of the kinds of information available with particular applications. I'm going to include both high-end and low-end RAW browsers so you can see just what is available.

IrfanView

At the low (free) end of the price scale is IrfanView, a Windows freeware program you can download at www.irfanview.com. It can read many common RAW photo formats. It's a quick way to view RAW files (just drag and drop to the IrfanView window) and make fast changes to the unprocessed file. You can crop, rotate, or correct your image, and do some cool things like swap the colors around (red for blue, blue for green, and so forth) to create false color pictures.

The price is right, and IrfanView has some valuable capabilities.

Phase One Capture One Pro (C1 Pro)

This premium-priced program does everything, does it well, and does it quickly. If you can't justify the price tag of this professional-level software, there are "lite" versions for serious amateurs and cash-challenged professionals called Capture One dSLR and Capture One dSLR SE.

Aimed at photographers with high-volume needs (that would include school and portrait photographers, as well as busy commercial photographers), C1 Pro is available for both Windows and Mac OS X. Phase One is a leading supplier of megabucks digital camera backs for medium and larger format cameras, so they really understand the needs of photographers.

The latest features include individual noise reduction controls for each image, automatic levels adjustment, a "quick develop" option that allows speedy conversion from RAW to TIFF or JPEG formats, dual-image side-by-side views for comparison purposes, and helpful grids and guides that can be superimposed over an image. Photographers concerned about copyright protection will appreciate the ability to add watermarks to the output images.

Bibble Pro

One of my personal favorites among third-party RAW converters is Bibble Pro, which just came out with a new version as I was writing this book. It supports one of the broadest ranges of RAW file formats available, including NEF files from Nikon D1, D1x/h, D2H, D100; .CRW files from the Canon C30/D60/10D/300D; .CR2 files from newer Canon models; .ORF files from the Olympus E10/E20/E1/C5050/C5060; .DCR files from the Kodak 720x/760/14n; .RAF files from the Fuji S2Pro; .PEF files from Pentax cameras; .MRW files from the Minolta Maxxum; and .TIF from Canon 1D/1DS.

The utility supports lots of different platforms, too. It's available for Windows, Mac OS X, and, believe it or not, Linux.

Bibble works fast because it offers instantaneous previews and real-time feedback as changes are made. That's important when you have to convert many images in a short time (event photographers will know what I am talking about!). Bibble's batch-processing capabilities also let you convert large numbers of files using settings you specify without further intervention.

Its customizable interface lets you organize and edit images quickly and then output them in a variety of formats, including 16-bit TIFF and PNG. You can even create a web gallery from within Bibble. I often find myself disliking the generic file names applied to digital images by cameras, so I really like Bibble's ability to rename batches of files using new names that you specify.

Bibble is fully color managed, which means it can support all the popular color spaces (Adobe sRGB and so forth) and use custom profiles generated by third-party color-management software. There are two editions of Bibble, a Pro version and a Lite version. Because the Pro version is reasonably priced at $129, I don't really see the need to save $60 with the Lite edition, which lacks the top-line's options for tethered shooting, embedding IPTC-compatible captions in images, and can also be used as a Photoshop plug-in (if you prefer not to work with the application in its standalone mode). Bibble Pro now incorporates Noise Ninja technology, so you can get double-duty from this valuable application.

Adobe Photoshop

The latest version of Photoshop includes a built-in RAW plug-in that is compatible with the proprietary formats of a growing number of digital cameras, both new and old. This plug-in also works with Photoshop Elements and can process JPEG images, too.

To open a RAW image in Photoshop, just follow these steps (Elements users can use much the same workflow, although fewer settings are available):

1. Transfer the RAW images from your camera to your computer's hard drive.
2. In Photoshop, choose Open from the File menu, or use Bridge.
3. Select a RAW image file. The Adobe Camera Raw plug-in will pop up, showing a preview of the image, like the one shown in Figure 8.9.

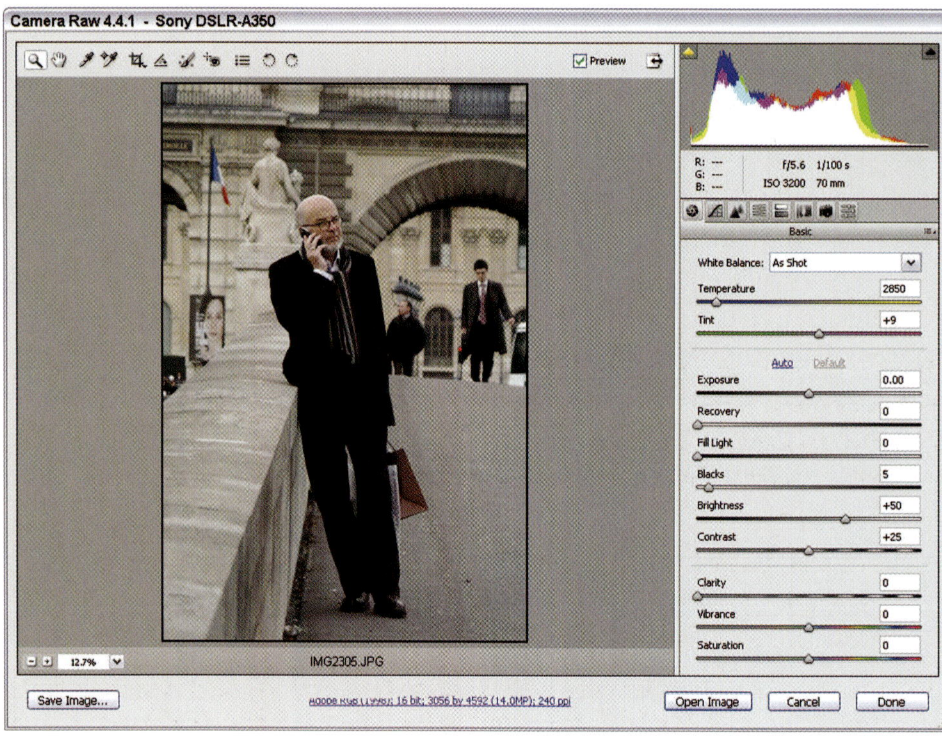

Figure 8.9
The basic ACR dialog box looks like this when processing a single image.

4. If you like, use one of the tools found in the toolbar at the top left of the dialog box. From left to right, they are as follows:
   - **Zoom.** Operates just like the Zoom tool in Photoshop.
   - **Hand.** Use like the Hand tool in Photoshop.
   - **White Balance.** Click an area in the image that should be neutral gray or white to set the white balance quickly.
   - **Color Sampler.** Use to determine the RGB values of areas you click with this eyedropper.
   - **Crop.** Pre-crops the image so that only the portion you specify is imported into Photoshop. This option saves time when you want to work on a section of a large image, and you don't need the entire file.
   - **Straighten.** Drag in the preview image to define what should be a horizontal or vertical line, and ACR will realign the image to straighten it.
   - **Retouch.** Used to heal or clone areas you define.
   - **Red-Eye Removal.** Quickly zap red pupils in your human subjects.
   - **ACR Preferences.** Produces a dialog box of Adobe Camera Raw preferences.
   - **Rotate Counterclockwise.** Rotates counterclockwise in 90-degree increments with a click.
   - **Rotate Clockwise.** Rotates clockwise in 90-degree increments with a click.
5. Using the Basic tab, you can have ACR show you red and blue highlights in the preview that indicate shadow areas that are clipped (too dark to show detail) and light areas that are blown out (too bright). Click the triangles in the upper-left corner of the histogram display (shadow clipping) and upper-right corner (highlight clipping) to toggle these indicators on or off.
6. Also in the Basic tab you can choose white balance, either from the drop-down list or by setting a color temperature and green/magenta color bias (tint) using the sliders.
7. Other sliders are available to control exposure, recovery, fill light, blacks, brightness, contrast, vibrance, and saturation. A check box can be marked to convert the image to grayscale.

8. Make other adjustments (described in more detail below).
9. ACR makes automatic adjustments for you. You can click Default and make the changes for yourself, or click the Auto link (located just above the Exposure slider) to reapply the automatic adjustments after you've made your own modifications.
10. If you've marked more than one image to be opened, the additional images appear in a "filmstrip" at the left side of the screen. You can click on each thumbnail in the filmstrip in turn and apply different settings to each.
11. Click Open Image/Open Image(s) into Photoshop using the settings you've made.

The Basic tab is displayed by default when the ACR dialog box opens, and it includes most of the sliders and controls you'll need to fine-tune your image as you import it into Photoshop. These include:

- **White Balance.** Leave it As Shot or change to a value such as Daylight, Cloudy, Shade, Tungsten, Fluorescent, or Flash. If you like, you can set a custom white balance using the Temperature and Tint sliders.
- **Exposure.** This slider adjusts the overall brightness and darkness of the image.
- **Recovery.** Restores detail in the red, green, and blue color channels.
- **Fill Light.** Reconstructs detail in shadows.
- **Blacks.** Increases the number of tones represented as black in the final image, emphasizing tones in the shadow areas of the image.
- **Brightness.** This slider adjusts the brightness and darkness of an image.
- **Contrast.** Manipulates the contrast of the midtones of your image.
- **Convert to Grayscale.** Mark this box to convert the image to black-and-white.
- **Vibrance.** Prevents over-saturation when enriching the colors of an image.
- **Saturation.** Manipulates the richness of all colors equally, from zero saturation (gray/black, no color) at the –100 setting to double the usual saturation at the +100 setting.

Additional controls are available on the Tone Curve, Detail, HSL/Grayscale, Split Toning, Lens Corrections, Camera Calibration, and Presets tabs, shown in Figure 8.10. The Tone Curve tab can change the tonal values of your image. The Detail tab lets you adjust sharpness, luminance smoothing, and apply color noise reduction. The HSL/Grayscale tab offers controls for adjusting hue, saturation, and lightness and converting an image to black-and-white. Split Toning helps you colorize an image with sepia or cyanotype (blue) shades. The Lens Corrections tab has sliders to adjust for chromatic aberrations and vignetting. The Camera Calibration tab provides a way for calibrating the color corrections made in the Camera Raw plug-in. The Presets tab (not shown) is used to load settings you've stored for reuse.

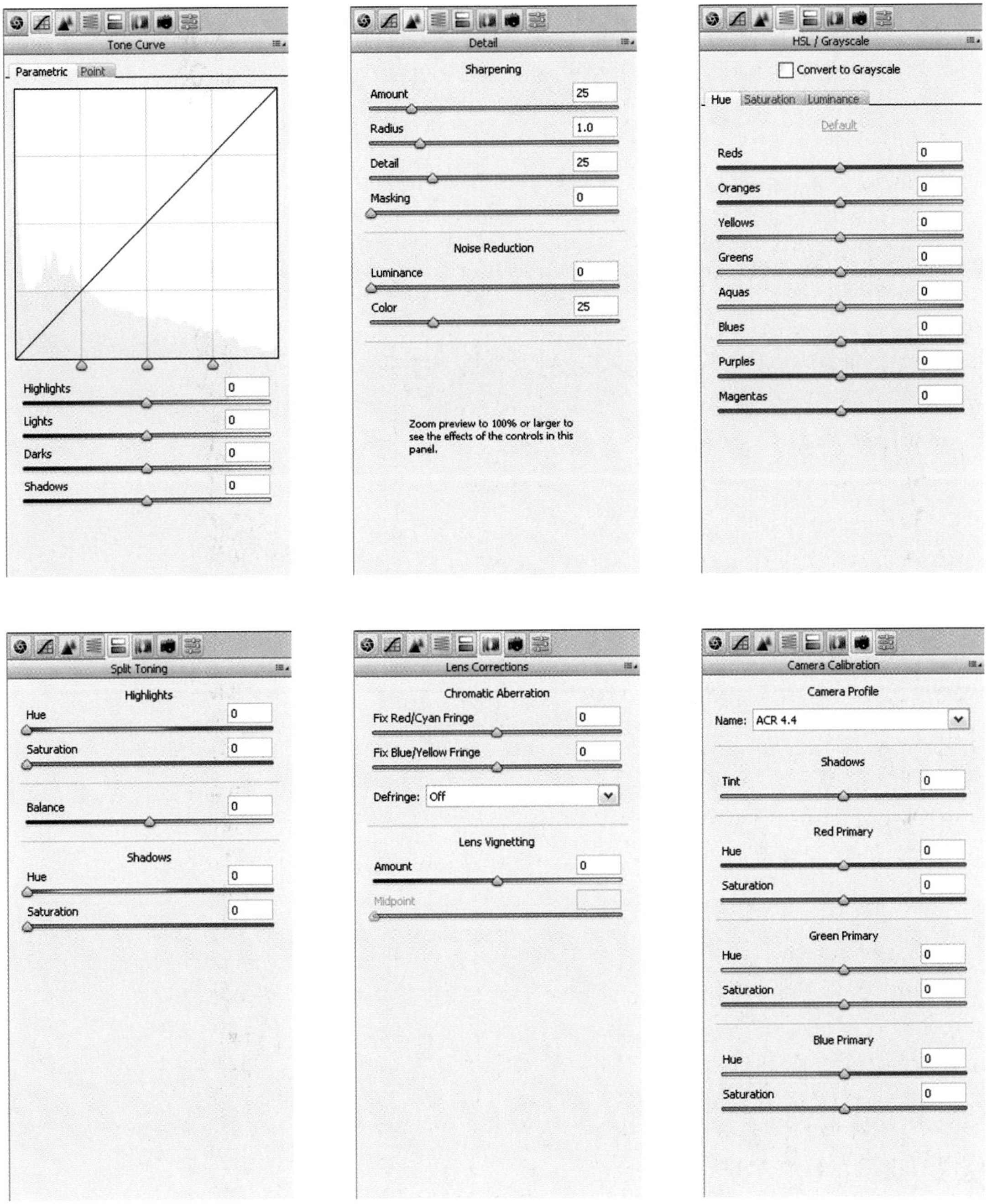

Figure 8.10 More controls are available within the additional tabbed dialog boxes in Adobe Camera Raw.

9

Pentax K200D: Troubleshooting and Prevention

One of the nice things about modern electronic cameras like the Pentax K200D is that they have fewer mechanical moving parts to fail, so they are less likely to "wear out." No film transport mechanism, no wind lever or motor drive, no complicated mechanical linkages from camera to lens to physically stop down the lens aperture. Instead, tiny, reliable motors are built into each lens (and you lose the use of only that lens should something fail), and one of the few major moving parts in the camera itself is a lightweight mirror (its small size compared to the mirrors found in film cameras is one of the advantages of the K200D's 1.5X crop factor) that flips up and down with each shot.

Of course, the camera also has a moving shutter that can fail, but the shutter is built rugged enough that you can expect it to last what I'd estimate to be 100,000 shutter cycles or more. Unless you're shooting sports in continuous mode day in and day out, the shutter on your K200D is likely to last as long as you expect to use the camera.

The only other things on the camera that move are switches, dials, buttons, the flip-up electronic flash, and the door that slides open to allow you to remove and insert the memory card. Unless you're extraordinarily clumsy or unlucky and manage to give your built-in flash a good whack while it is in use, there's not a lot that can go wrong mechanically with your Pentax K200D.

On the other hand, one of the chief drawbacks of modern electronic cameras is that they are modern *electronic* cameras. Your K200D is fully dependent on those four AA-sized batteries. Without them, the camera can't be used. There are numerous other electrical and electronic connections in the camera (many connected to those mechanical switches and dials), and components like the color LCD and top panel status LCD that can potentially fail or suffer damage. The camera also relies on its "operating system," or *firmware*, which can be plagued by bugs that cause unexpected behavior. Luckily, electronic components are generally more reliable and trouble-free, especially when compared to their mechanical counterparts from the pre-electronic film camera days. (Film cameras of the last 10 to 20 years have had almost as many electronic features as digital cameras, but, believe it or not, there were whole generations of film cameras that had *no* electronics or batteries.)

Digital cameras have problems unique to their breed, too; the most troublesome being the need to clean the sensor of dust and grime periodically. This is true even if you use the K200D's Dust Removal sensor shaking feature, described in Chapter 3. The action is loud and vigorous, but does not always remove every speck of dust. This chapter will show you how to diagnose problems, fix some common ills, and, importantly, learn how to avoid them in the future.

Update Your Firmware

As I said, the firmware in your Pentax K200D is the camera's operating system, which handles everything from menu display (including fonts, colors, and the actual entries themselves), what languages are available, and even support for specific devices and features. Upgrading the firmware to a new version makes it possible to add new features while fixing some of the bugs that sneak in. So far, we K200D owners have been lucky, and as I write this there have been no firmware updates available for this camera.

That may be why information on updating firmware is so sparse in the manual that comes with the camera. In fact, the word doesn't even appear within its 268 pages. (I know, because I did a search of the PDF version of the hardcopy manual.)

How can you even tell what version of firmware you have, then? That's easy enough, even if Pentax wants to keep the information a secret. Just hold down the Menu button when you turn the K200D on, and the firmware version appears in the center of the LCD screen. It will say VER: 1.00 if you've never updated your camera's operating system, as shown in Figure 9.1.

Firmware upgrades are used most frequently to fix bugs in the software, and much less frequently to add or enhance features. The exact changes made to the firmware are generally spelled out in the firmware release announcement. You can examine the remedies provided and decide if a given firmware patch is important to you. If not, you can usually safely wait a while before going through the bother of upgrading your firmware—

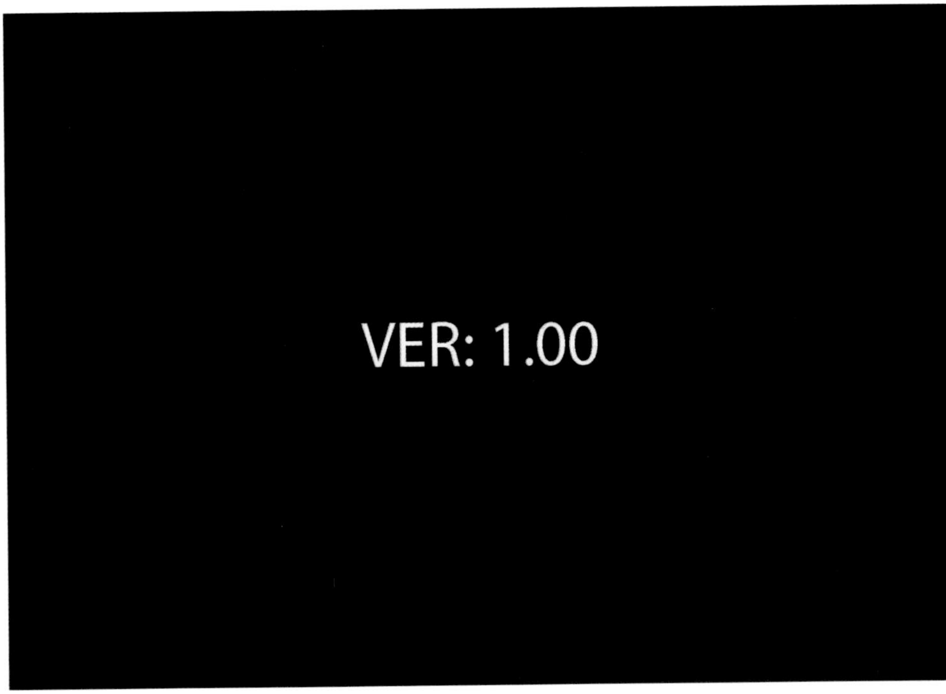

Figure 9.1
Hold down the Menu button when turning on the camera to view the current firmware version.

at least long enough for the early adopters to report whether the bug fixes have introduced new bugs of their own. Each new firmware release incorporates the changes from previous releases, so if you skip a minor upgrade you should have no problems.

Upgrading Your Firmware

If you're computer savvy, you might wonder how your Pentax K200D is able to overwrite its own operating system—that is, how can the existing firmware be used to load the new version on top of itself? It's a little like lifting yourself by reaching down and pulling up on your bootstraps. Not ironically, that's almost exactly what happens: At your command (when you start the upgrade process), the K200D shifts into a special mode in which it is no longer operating from its firmware but, rather, from a small piece of software called a *bootstrap loader*—a separate, protected software program that functions only at startup or when upgrading firmware. The loader's function is to look for firmware to launch or, when directed, to copy new firmware from a memory card to the internal memory space where the old firmware is located. Once the new firmware has replaced the old, you can turn your camera off and then on again, and the updated operating system will be loaded.

The loader software isn't set up to go hunting through your memory card for the firmware file. It looks only in the top or root directory of your card, so that's where you must copy the firmware you download. Once you've determined that a new firmware update is available for your camera and that you want to install it, just follow these steps.

> **WARNING**
>
> Use a fully charged battery or Pentax's optional AC adapter to ensure that you'll have enough power to operate the camera for the entire upgrade. Moreover, you should not turn off the camera while your old firmware is being overwritten. Don't open the memory card door or do anything else that might disrupt operation of the K200D while the firmware is being installed.

1. Download the firmware from Pentax. You'll find it in the Download Service section of the Support & Service portion of Pentax's website. The location of the software has changed in recent weeks, and I can't guarantee where it will be when you buy this book. So, you should do what I did, and Google the term "Pentax firmware" or something similar to find the current link.
2. Download the firmware and place it on your computer's hard drive. The firmware is contained in a self-extracting file for either Windows or Mac OS with a .exe or .zip extension, respectively. Extract the contents, which will include a README.TXT file, and the actual firmware, which will have a name like fw*xxxxxx*.bin (which is the format Pentax has used for previous firmware updates).
3. In your camera, format an SD memory card. Choose Format from the Set-up 1 menu, and initialize the card (make sure you don't have images you want to keep before you do this!).
4. You can copy the upgrade software to the *root* (top) directory of the card either using a memory card reader or by connecting the camera to your computer with a USB cable and copying from your computer directly to the camera.
5. If the camera is on, turn it off.
6. Insert the SD card with the firmware update into the camera and shut the card cover.
7. Turn the camera power on while holding down the Menu button. The message NOW LOADING appears in the LCD, and then changes to PROGRAM UPDATE. The current firmware version and update version will be displayed at the bottom of the LCD.
8. You'll be asked to confirm the update. Use the controller keys to select Yes, and press the OK button.
9. The message UPDATING appears on the LCD, and your firmware will be updated. Under no circumstances turn off the camera until you see the message COMPLETE on the LCD.

10. Turn the camera off and remove the SD card, insert it into your memory card reader, and delete the firmware file before using it again.
11. Turn the camera on while holding down the MENU button to see the firmware version and confirm that the update has been properly made.

Protect Your LCD

The 3-inch color LCD on the back of your Pentax K200D almost seems like a target for banging, scratching, and other abuse. Fortunately, it's quite rugged, and a few errant knocks are unlikely to shatter the protective cover over the LCD, and scratches won't easily mar its surface. However, if you want to be on the safe side, there are a number of protective products you can purchase to keep your LCD safe—and, in some cases, make it a little easier to view. Here's a quick overview of your options.

- **Plastic overlays.** The simplest solution (although not always the cheapest) is to apply a plastic overlay sheet or "skin" cut to fit your LCD. These adhere either by static electricity or through a light adhesive coating that's even less clingy than stick-it notes. You can cut down overlays made for PDAs (although these can be pricey at up to $19.95 for a set of several sheets), or purchase overlays sold specifically for digital cameras. Adorama (www.adorama.com) sells a Zagg ShieldZone invisibleSHIELD LCD screen protector especially for the K200D for about $12.
- **Acrylic shields.** These scratch-resistant acrylic panels, laser cut to fit your camera perfectly, are my choice as the best protection solution, and what I use on my own K200D. At about $6-$10 each, they also happen to be the least expensive option as well. I like the GGS 2.7-inch LCD Protector for the Pentax K200D, available from multiple sources on eBay for less than $10. Similar models from other vendors (like the one shown in Figure 9.2) attach using sticky adhesive that holds the

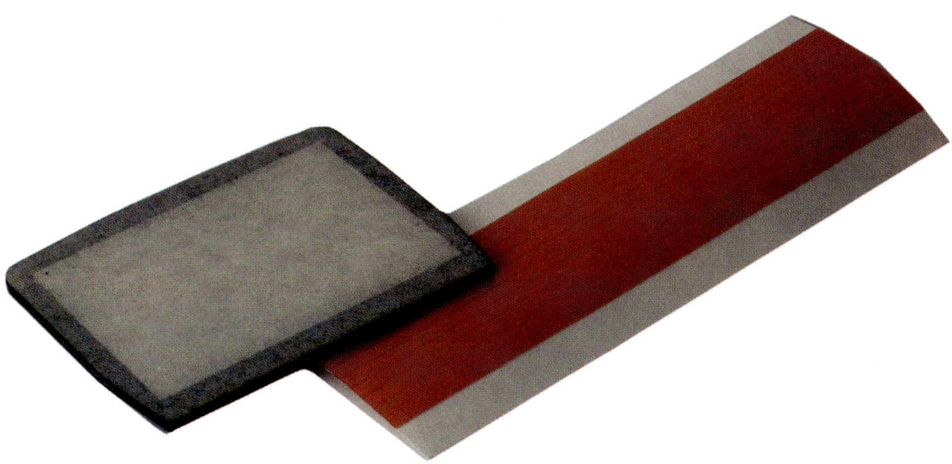

Figure 9.2
A tough acrylic shield, here shown with a piece of plastic containing a set of peel-off sticky strips to help it adhere to the camera, can protect your LCD from scratches.

panel flush and tight, but which allow the acrylic to be pried off and the adhesive removed easily if you want to remove or replace the shield. They don't attenuate your view of the LCD and are non-reflective enough for use under a variety of lighting conditions.

- **Flip-up hoods.** These protectors attach to the back of the camera using an adhesive, and provide a cover that completely shields the LCD, but unfolds to provide a three-sided hood that allows viewing the LCD while minimizing the extraneous light falling on it and reducing contrast. They're sold for about $20 by Delkin (www.delkin.com). A custom model for the K200D is not available, but the Universal 2.7-inch version from Delkin, using the adhesive attachment, is worth a try. It's intended for point-and-shoot cameras with large LCDs, but should attach to the K200D as well. If you want to completely protect your LCD from hard knocks and need to view the screen outdoors in bright sunlight, there is nothing better. However, I have a couple problems with these devices. First, with the cover closed, you can't peek down after taking a shot to see what your image looks like during picture review. You must open the cap each time you want to look at the LCD. Moreover, with the hood unfolded, it's difficult to look through the viewfinder: Don't count on being able to use the viewfinder *and* the LCD at the same time with one of these hoods in place. A better choice might be the HoodLoupe, from Hoodman (www.hoodmanusa.com), which comes with a strap that you wear around the neck, pressing the loupe against the LCD only when you're ready to examine the screen.

Troubleshooting Memory Cards

Sometimes good memory cards go bad. Sometimes good photographers can treat their memory cards badly. It's possible that a memory card that works fine in one camera won't be recognized when inserted into another. In the worst case, you can have a card full of important photos and find that the card seems to be corrupted and you can't access any of them. Don't panic! If these scenarios sound horrific to you, there are lots of things you can do to prevent them from happening, and a variety of remedies available if they do occur. You'll want to take some time—before disaster strikes—to consider your options.

All Your Eggs in One Basket?

The debate about whether it's better to use one large memory card or several smaller ones has been going on since even before there were memory cards. I can remember when computer users wondered whether it was smarter to install a pair of 200MB (not *gigabyte*) hard drives in their computer, or if they should go for one of those newfangled 500MB models. By the same token, a few years ago the user groups were full of proponents who insisted that you ought to use 128MB memory cards rather than the huge 512MB versions. Today, most of the arguments involve 4GB cards versus 2GB cards, and I expect that as prices for 8GB memory cards continue to drop, they'll find their way into the debate as well.

Why all the fuss? Are 4GB memory cards more likely to fail than 2GB cards? Are you risking all your photos if you trust your images to a larger card? Isn't it better to use several smaller cards, so that if one fails you lose only half as many photos? Or, isn't it wiser to put all your photos onto one larger card, because the more cards you use, the better your odds of misplacing or damaging one and losing at least some pictures?

In the end, the "eggs in one basket" argument boils down to statistics, and how you happen to use your K200D. The rationales can go both ways. If you have multiple smaller cards, you do increase your chances of something happening to one of them, so, arguably, you might be boosting the odds of losing some pictures. If all your images are important, the fact that you've lost 100 rather than 200 pictures isn't very comforting.

Also consider that the eggs/basket scenario assumes that the cards that are lost or damaged are always full. It's actually likely that your 4GB card might suffer a mishap when it's less than half full (indeed, it's more likely that a large card won't be completely filled before it's offloaded to a computer), so you really might not lose any more shots with a single 4GB card than with multiple 2GB cards.

If you shoot photojournalist-type pictures, you probably change memory cards when they're less than completely full in order to avoid the need to do so at a crucial moment. (When I shoot sports, my cards rarely reach 80 to 90 percent of capacity before I change them.) Using multiple smaller cards means you have to change them that more often, which can be a real pain when you're taking a lot of photos. As an example, if you use 1GB memory cards with a Pentax K200D and shoot JPEG+RAW, you may get only 45 pictures on the card. That's not much more than the capacity of a 36-exposure roll of film (remember those?). In my book, I prefer keeping all my eggs in one basket, and then making very sure that nothing happens to that basket.

There are only two really good reasons to justify limiting yourself to smaller memory cards when larger ones can be purchased at the same cost per-gigabyte. One of them is when every single picture is precious to you and the loss of any of them would be a disaster. If you're a wedding photographer, for example, and unlikely to be able to restage the nuptials if a memory card goes bad, you'll probably want to shoot no more pictures than you can afford to lose on a single card, and have an assistant ready to copy each card removed from the camera onto a backup hard drive or DVD onsite. To be even more safe, you'd want to alternate cameras or have a second photographer at least partially duplicating your coverage so your shots are distributed over several memory cards simultaneously.

If none of these options are available to you, consider *interleaving* your shots. Say you don't shoot weddings, but you do go on vacation from time to time. Take 50 or so pictures on one card, or whatever number of images might fill about 25 percent of its capacity. Then, replace it with a different card and shoot about 25 percent of that card's available space. Repeat these steps with diligence (you'd have to be determined to go through this inconvenience), and, if you use four or more memory cards you'll find your pictures from each location scattered among the different memory cards. If you lose or damage one, you'll still have *some* pictures from all the various stops on your trip on the other cards. That's more work than I like to do (I usually tote around a portable hard disk and copy the files to the drive as I go), but it's an option.

What Can Go Wrong?

There are lots of things that can go wrong with your memory card, but the ones that aren't caused by human stupidity are statistically very rare. Yes, a memory card's internal bit bin or controller can suddenly fail due to a manufacturing error or some inexplicable event caused by old age. However, if your memory card works for the first week or two that you own it, it should work forever. There's really not a lot that can wear out.

The typical memory card is rated for a Mean Time Between Failures of 1,000,000 hours of use. That's constant use 24/7 for more than 100 years! According to the manufacturers, they are good for 10,000 insertions in your camera, and should be able to retain their data (and that's without an external power source) for something on the order of 11 years. Of course, with the millions of memory cards in use, there are bound to be a few lemons here or there.

Given the reliability of solid-state memory, compared to magnetic memory, though, it's more likely that your memory card problems will stem from something that you do. Although they're not as tiny as the xD cards a few other digital SLRs use, Secure Digital memory cards are still small and easy to misplace if you're not careful. For that reason, it's a good idea to keep them in their original cases or a "card safe" offered by Gepe (www.gepecardsafe.com), Pelican (www.pelican.com), and others. Always placing your memory card in a case can provide protection from the second-most common mishap that befalls memory cards: the common household laundry. If you slip a memory card in a pocket, rather than a case or your camera bag often enough, sooner or later it's going to end up in the washing machine and probably the clothes dryer, too. There are plenty of reports of relieved digital camera owners who've laundered their memory cards and found they still worked fine, but it's not uncommon for such mistreatment to do some damage.

Memory cards can also be stomped on, accidentally bent, dropped into the ocean, chewed by pets, and otherwise rendered unusable in myriad ways. It's also remotely possible to force a card into your K200D's memory card slot incorrectly if you're diligent enough, doing little damage to the card itself, but possibly damaging the camera internally, eliminating its ability to read or write to any memory card. I've never heard of this happening with a camera using SD cards, but don't discount the ingenuity of a determined fumble-fingers.

Or, if the card is formatted in your computer with a memory card reader, your K200D may fail to recognize it. Occasionally, I've found that a memory card used in one camera would fail if used in a different camera (until I reformatted it in Windows, and then again in the camera). Every once in awhile, a card goes completely bad and—seemingly—can't be salvaged.

Another way to lose images is to do commonplace things with your memory card at an inopportune time. If you remove the card from the K200D while the camera is writing images to the card, you'll lose any photos in the buffer and may damage the file structure of the card, making it difficult or impossible to retrieve the other pictures you've taken. The same thing can happen if you remove the memory card from your computer's card reader while the computer is writing to the card (say, to erase files you've already moved to your computer). You can avoid this by *not* using your computer to erase files on a memory card but, instead, always reformatting the card in your K200D before you use it again.

What Can You Do?

Pay attention: If you're having problems, the *first* thing you should do is *stop* using that memory card. Don't take any more pictures. Don't do anything with the card until you've figured out what's wrong. Your second line of defense (your first line is to be sufficiently careful with your cards that you avoid problems in the first place) is to *do no harm* that hasn't already been done. Read the rest of this section and then, if necessary, decide on a course of action (such as using a data recovery service or software described later) before you risk damaging the data on your card further.

Now that you've calmed down, the first thing to check is whether you've actually inserted a card in the camera. It's entirely possible (although not particularly plausible) that you've been snapping away with no memory card to store the pictures to, which can lead to massive disappointment later on. Of course, the No card in the camera message appears on the LCD when the camera is powered up, and it is superimposed on the review image after every shot, but maybe you're inattentive, aren't using Picture Review, or have purchased one of those LCD fold-up hoods mentioned earlier in this chapter.

Things get more exciting when the card itself is put in jeopardy. If you lose a card, there's not a lot you can do other than take a picture of a similar card and print up some Have You Seen This Lost Flash Memory? flyers to post on utility poles all around town.

If all you care about is reusing the card, and have resigned yourself to losing the pictures, try reformatting the card in your camera. You may find that reformatting removes the corrupted data and restores your card to health. Sometimes I've had success reformatting a card in my computer using a memory card reader (this is normally a no-no because your operating system doesn't understand the needs of your K200D), and *then* reformatting again in the camera.

If your memory card is not behaving properly, and you *do* want to recover your images, things get a little more complicated. If your pictures are very valuable, either to you or to others (for example, a wedding), you can always turn to professional data recovery firms. Be prepared to pay hundreds of dollars to get your pictures back, but these pros often do an amazing job. You wouldn't want them working on your memory card on behalf of the police if you'd tried to erase some incriminating pictures. There are many firms of this type, and I've never used them myself, so I can't offer a recommendation. Use a Google search to turn up a ton of them.

THE ULTIMATE IRONY

I recently purchased an 8GB Kingston memory card that was furnished with some nifty OnTrack data recovery software. The first thing I did was format the card to make sure it was OK. Then I hunted around for the free software, only to discover it was preloaded onto the memory card. I was supposed to copy the software to my computer before using the memory card for the first time.

Fortunately, I had the OnTrack software that would reverse my dumb move, so I could retrieve the software. No, wait. I *didn't* have the software I needed to recover the software I erased. I'd reformatted it to oblivion. Chalk this one up as either the ultimate irony or Stupid Author Trick #523.

A more reasonable approach is to try special data recovery software you can install on your computer and use to attempt to resurrect your "lost" images yourself. They may not actually be gone completely. Perhaps your memory card's "table of contents" is jumbled, or only a few pictures are damaged in such a way that your camera and computer can't read some or any of the pictures on the card. Some of the available software was written specifically to reconstruct lost pictures, while other utilities are more general-purpose applications that can be used with any media, including floppy disks and hard disk drives. They have names like OnTrack, Photo Rescue 2, Digital Image Recovery, MediaRecover, Image Recall, and the aptly named Recover My Photos. You'll find a comprehensive list and links, as well as some picture-recovery tips at www.ultimateslr.com/memory-card-recovery.php. Figure 9.3 shows RescuePro, available from SanDisk and often furnished for free with the company's memory cards.

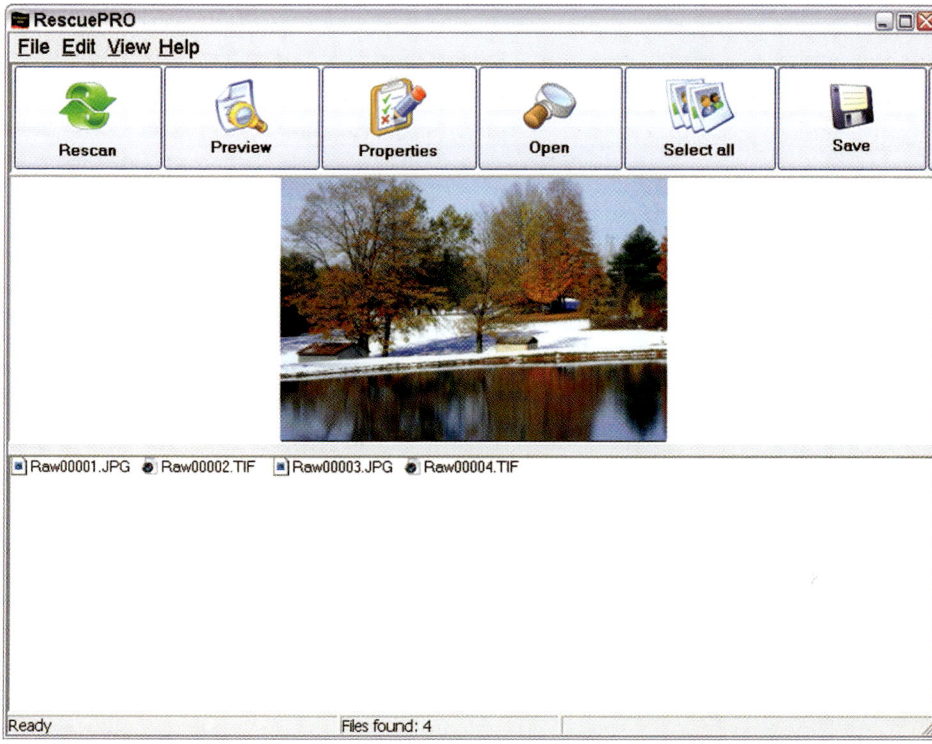

Figure 9.3 Rescue software will seek out recoverable images on your memory cards.

DIMINISHING RETURNS

Usually, once you've recovered any images on a memory card, reformatted it, and returned it to service, it will function reliably for the rest of its useful life. However, if you find a particular card going bad more than once, you'll almost certainly want to stop using it forever. See if you can get it replaced by the manufacturer, if you can, but, in the case of memory card failures, the third time is never the charm.

Clean Your Sensor

There's no avoiding dust. No matter how careful you are, some of it is going to settle on your camera and on the mounts of your lenses, eventually making its way inside your camera to settle in the mirror chamber. As you take photos, the mirror flipping up and down causes the dust to become airborne and eventually make its way past the shutter curtain to come to rest on the anti-aliasing filter atop your sensor. There, dust and particles can show up in every single picture you take at a small enough aperture to bring the foreign matter into sharp focus. No matter how careful you are and how cleanly you work, eventually you will get some of this dust on your camera's sensor.

The Pentax K200D's Dust Removal system, which can be set to shake your sensor every time the camera is fired up, should be your first line of defense. But eventually you'll get some stubborn flecks that can't be dislodged with Dust Removal. You'll want to learn how to manually clean your sensor, as well. I'll provide some tips later in this chapter.

Here are some of the most frequently asked questions about sensor dust issues.

Q. I see tiny specks in my viewfinder. Do I have dust on my sensor?

A. If you see sharp, well-defined specks, they are clinging to the underside of your focus screen and not on your sensor. They have absolutely no effect on your photographs, and are merely annoying or distracting.

Q. I can see dust on my mirror. How can I remove it?

A. Like focus-screen dust, any artifacts that have settled on your mirror won't affect your photos. You can often remove dust on the mirror or focus screen with a bulb air blower, which will loosen it and whisk it away. Stubborn dust on the focus screen can sometimes be gently flicked away with a soft brush designed for cleaning lenses. I don't recommend brushing the mirror or touching it in any way. The mirror is a special front-surface-silvered optical device (unlike conventional mirrors, which are silvered on the back side of a piece of glass or plastic) and can be easily scratched. If you can't blow mirror dust off, it's best to just forget about it. You can't see it in the viewfinder, anyway.

Q. I see a bright spot in the same place in all of my photos. Is that sensor dust?

A. You've probably got either a "hot" pixel or one that is permanently "stuck" due to a defect in the sensor. A hot pixel is one that shows up as a bright spot only during long exposures as the sensor warms. A pixel stuck in the "on" position always appears in the image. Both show up as bright red, green, or blue pixels, usually surrounded by a small cluster of other improperly illuminated pixels, caused by the camera's interpolating the hot or stuck pixel into its surroundings, as shown in Figure 9.4. A stuck pixel can also be permanently dark. Either kind is likely to show up when they contrast with plain, evenly colored areas of your image.

Figure 9.4
A stuck pixel is surrounded by improperly interpolated pixels created by the K200D's demosaicing algorithm.

Finding one or two hot or stuck pixels in your sensor is unfortunately fairly common. They can be "removed" by telling the K200D to ignore them through a simple process called *pixel mapping*. If the bad pixels become bothersome, Pentax can remap your sensor's pixels with a quick trip to a service center.

Bad pixels can also show up on your camera's color LCD panel, but, unless they are abundant, the wisest course is to just ignore them.

Q. I see an irregular out-of-focus blob in the same place in my photos. Is that sensor dust?

A. Yes. Sensor contaminants can take the form of tiny spots, larger blobs, or even curvy lines if they are caused by minuscule fibers that have settled on the sensor. They'll appear out of focus because they aren't actually on the sensor surface but, rather, a fraction of a millimeter above it on the filter that covers the sensor. The smaller the f/stop used, the more in-focus the dust becomes. At large apertures, it may not be visible at all.

Q. I never see any dust on my sensor. What's all the fuss about?

A. Those who never have dust problems with their Pentax K200D fall into one of four categories: those for whom the camera's automatic dust removal features are working well; those who seldom change their lenses and have clean working habits that minimize the amount of dust that invades their cameras in the first place; those who simply don't notice the dust (often because they don't shoot many macro photos or other pictures using the small f/stops that makes dust evident in their images); and those who are very, very lucky.

Identifying and Dealing with Dust

Sensor dust is less of a problem than it might be because it shows up only under certain circumstances. Indeed, you might have dust on your sensor right now and not be aware of it. The dust doesn't actually settle on the sensor itself, but, rather, on a protective filter a very tiny distance above the sensor, subjecting it to the phenomenon of *depth-of-focus*. Depth-of-focus is the distance the focal plane can be moved and still render an object in sharp focus. At f/2.8 to f/5.6 or even smaller, sensor dust, particularly if small, is likely to be outside the range of depth-of-focus and blur into an unnoticeable dot.

However, if you're shooting at f/16 to f/22 or smaller, those dust motes suddenly pop into focus. Forget about trying to spot them by peering directly at your sensor with the shutter open and the lens removed. The period at the end of this sentence, about .33mm in diameter, could block a group of pixels measuring 40 × 40 pixels (160 pixels in all!). Dust spots that are even smaller than that can easily show up in your images if you're shooting large, empty areas that are light colored. Dust motes are most likely to show up in the sky, as in Figure 9.5, or in white backgrounds of your seamless product shots and are less likely to be a problem in images that contain lots of dark areas and detail.

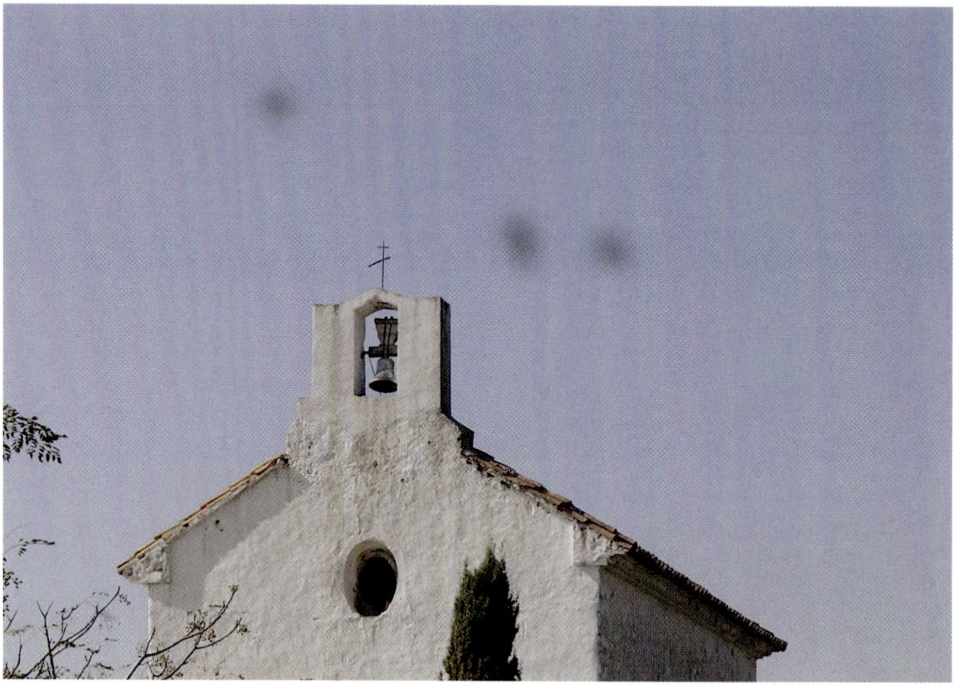

Figure 9.5
Only the dust spots in the sky are apparent in this shot.

To see if you have dust on your sensor, use the K200D's Dust Alert feature, described in Chapter 3. It tends to exaggerate the severity of the dust problem, and it will show you some spots that may not show up in your images. If you want a real-world check, take a few test shots of a plain, blank surface (such as a piece of paper or a cloudless sky) at small f/stops, such as f/22, and a few wide open. Open Photoshop, copy several shots into a single document in separate layers, then flip back and forth between layers to see if any spots you see are present in all layers. You may have to boost contrast and sharpness to make the dust easier to spot.

Avoiding Dust

Of course, the easiest way to protect your sensor from dust is to prevent it from settling on the sensor in the first place. Here are my stock tips for eliminating the problem before it begins.

- **Clean environment.** Avoid working in dusty areas if you can do so. Hah! Serious photographers will take this one with a grain of salt, because it usually makes sense to go where the pictures are. Only a few of us are so paranoid about sensor dust (considering that it is so easily removed) that we'll avoid moderately grimy locations just to protect something that is, when you get down to it, just a tool. If you find a great picture opportunity at a raging fire, during a sandstorm, or while surrounded by dust clouds, you might hesitate to take the picture, but, with a little caution (don't remove your lens in these situations, and clean the camera afterwards!) you can still shoot. However, it still makes sense to store your camera in a clean environment. One place cameras and lenses pick up a lot of dust is inside a camera bag. Clean your bag from time to time, and you can avoid problems.

- **Clean lenses.** There are a few paranoid types that avoid swapping lenses in order to minimize the chance of dust getting inside their cameras. It makes more sense just to use a blower or brush to dust off the rear lens mount of the replacement lens first, so you won't be introducing dust into your camera simply by attaching a new, dusty lens. Do this before you remove the lens from your camera, and then avoid stirring up dust before making the exchange.
- **Work fast.** Minimize the time your camera is lens-less and exposed to dust. That means having your replacement lens ready and dusted off, and a place to set down the old lens as soon as it is removed, so you can quickly attach the new lens.
- **Let gravity help you.** Face the camera downward when the lens is detached so any dust in the mirror box will tend to fall away from the sensor. Turn your back to any breezes, indoor forced air vents, fans, or other sources of dust to minimize infiltration.
- **Protect the lens you just removed.** Once you've attached the new lens, quickly put the end cap on the one you just removed to reduce the dust that might fall on it.
- **Clean out the vestibule.** From time to time, remove the lens while in a relatively dust-free environment and use a blower bulb like the one shown in Figure 9.6 (*not* compressed air or a vacuum hose) to clean out the mirror box area. A blower bulb is generally safer than a can of compressed air, or a strong positive/negative airflow, which can tend to drive dust further into nooks and crannies.

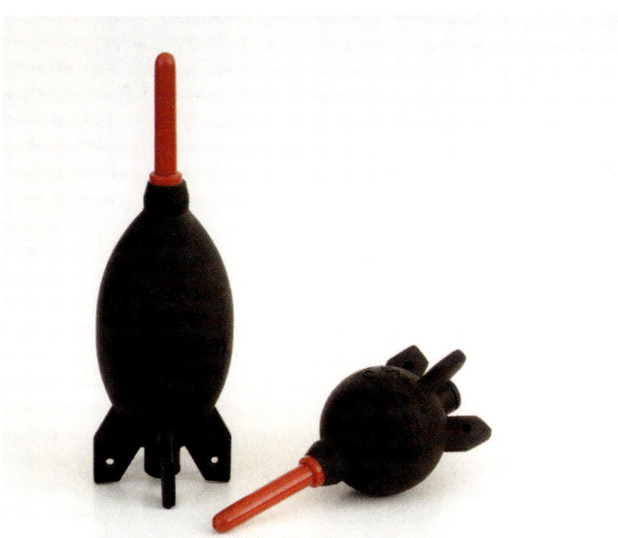

Figure 9.6
Use a robust air bulb like the Giottos Rocket for cleaning your sensor.

- **Be prepared.** If you're embarking on an important shooting session, it's a good idea to clean your sensor *now*, rather than come home with hundreds or thousands of images with dust spots caused by flecks that were sitting on your sensor before you even started. Before I left on my recent trip to Spain, I put both cameras I was taking through a rigid cleaning regimen, figuring they could remain dust-free for a measly 10 days. I even left my bulky blower bulb at home. It was a big mistake, but my intentions were good. I now have a smaller version of the Giottos Rocket Blower, and *that* goes with me everywhere.
- **Clone out existing spots in your image editor.** Photoshop and other editors have a clone tool or healing brush you can use to copy pixels from surrounding areas over the dust spot or dead pixel. This process can be tedious, especially if you have lots of dust spots and/or lots of images to be corrected. The advantage is that this sort of manual fix-it probably will do the least damage to the rest of your photo. Only the cloned pixels will be affected.
- **Use filtration in your image editor.** A semi-smart filter like Photoshop's Dust & Scratches filter can remove dust and other artifacts by selectively blurring areas that the plug-in decides represent dust spots. This method can work well if you have many dust spots, because you won't need to patch them manually. However, any automated method like this has the possibility of blurring areas of your image that you didn't intend to soften.

Sensor Cleaning

Those new to the concept of sensor dust actually hesitate before deciding to clean their camera themselves. Isn't it a better idea to pack up your K200D and send it to a Pentax service center so their crack technical staff can do the job for you? Or, at the very least, shouldn't you let the friendly folks at your local camera store do it?

Of course, if you choose to let someone else clean your sensor, they will be using methods that are more or less identical to the techniques you would use yourself. None of these techniques are difficult, and the only difference between their cleaning and your cleaning is that they might have done it dozens or hundreds of times. If you're careful, you can do just as good a job.

Of course vendors like Pentax won't tell you this, but it's not because they don't trust you. It's not that difficult for a real goofball to mess up their camera by hurrying or taking a shortcut. Perhaps the person uses the "Bulb" method of holding the shutter open and a finger slips, allowing the shutter curtain to close on top of a sensor cleaning brush. Or, someone tries to clean the sensor using masking tape, and ends up with goo all over its surface. If Pentax recommended *any* method that's mildly risky, someone would do it wrong, and then the company would face lawsuits from those who'd contend they did it exactly in the way the vendor suggested, so the ruined camera is not their fault. If you visit Pentax's website, you'll find this recommendation: "If the image sensor needs cleaning, we recommend having it cleaned at a Pentax service center, as it is a very delicate component."

You can see that vendors like Pentax tend to be conservative in their recommendations, and, in doing so, make it seem as if sensor cleaning is more daunting and dangerous than it really is. Some vendors recommend only dust-off cleaning, through the use of reasonably gentle blasts of air, while condemning more serious scrubbing with swabs and cleaning fluids. However, these cleaning kits for the exact types of cleaning they recommended against are for sale in Japan only, where, apparently, your average photographer is more dexterous than those of us in the rest of the world. These kits are similar to those used by official repair staff to clean your sensor if you decide to send your camera in for a dust-up.

As I noted, sensors can be affected by dust particles that are much smaller than you might be able to spot visually. The filters that cover sensors tend to be fairly hard compared to optical glass. Cleaning the 23.5mm × 15.7mm sensor in your Pentax K200D within the tight confines of the mirror box can call for a steady hand and careful touch. If your sensor's filter becomes scratched through inept cleaning, you can't simply remove it yourself and replace it with a new one.

There are four basic kinds of cleaning processes that can be used to remove dusty and sticky stuff that settles on your dSLR's sensor. All of these must be performed with the shutter locked open. I'll describe these methods and provide instructions for locking the shutter later in this section.

- **Air cleaning.** This process involves squirting blasts of air inside your camera with the shutter locked open. This works well for dust that's not clinging stubbornly to your sensor.
- **Brushing.** A soft, very fine brush is passed across the surface of the sensor's filter, dislodging mildly persistent dust particles and sweeping them off the imager.
- **Liquid cleaning.** A soft swab dipped in a cleaning solution such as ethanol is used to wipe the sensor filter, removing more obstinate particles.
- **Tape cleaning.** There are some who get good results by applying a special form of tape to the surface of their sensor. When the tape is peeled off, all the dust goes with it. Supposedly. I'd be remiss if I didn't point out right now that this form of cleaning is somewhat controversial; the other three methods are much more widely accepted. Now that Pentax has equipped the front-sensor filter with a special anti-dust coating, I wouldn't chance damaging that coating by using any kind of adhesive tape.

Placing the Shutter in the Locked and Fully Upright Position for Landing

Make sure you're using a fully charged battery or the optional AC Adapter.

1. Remove the lens from the camera and then turn the camera on.
2. Select Sensor Cleaning from the Set-up menu.
3. Choose Mirror Up from the screen that appears. Press OK.
4. The mirror will flip up and the shutter will open. A message appears on the LCD asking you to turn off the camera to finish. The mirror remains locked in the up position, and the shutter stays open until you turn the camera back on.
5. Use one of the methods described below to remove dust and grime from your sensor. Be careful not to accidentally switch the power back on as you work. If that happens, the shutter may be damaged if it closes onto your cleaning tool.
6. When you're finished, replace your lens, and switch your camera back on.

Air Cleaning

Your first attempts at cleaning your sensor should always involve gentle blasts of air. Many times, you'll be able to dislodge dust spots, which will fall off the sensor and, with luck, out of the mirror box. Attempt one of the other methods only when you've already tried air cleaning and it didn't remove all the dust.

Here are some tips for doing air cleaning:

- **Use a clean, powerful air bulb.** Your best bet is bulb cleaners designed for the job, like the Giottos Rocket shown in Figure 9.6. Smaller bulbs, like those air bulbs with a brush attached sometimes sold for lens cleaning or weak nasal aspirators may not provide sufficient air or a strong enough blast to do much good.
- **Hold the Pentax K200D upside down.** Then look up into the mirror box as you squirt your air blasts, increasing the odds that gravity will help pull the expelled dust downward, away from the sensor. You may have to use some imagination in positioning yourself. (And don't let dust fall into your eye!)
- **Never use air canisters.** The propellant inside these cans can permanently coat your sensor if you tilt the can while spraying. It's not worth taking a chance.
- **Avoid air compressors.** Super-strong blasts of air are likely to force dust under the sensor filter.

Brush Cleaning

If your dust is a little more stubborn and can't be dislodged by air alone, you may want to try a brush, charged with static electricity, which can pick off dust spots by electrical attraction. One good, but expensive, option is the Sensor Brush sold at www.visible-dust.com. A cheaper version can be purchased at www.copperhillimages.com. You need a 16mm version, like the one shown in Figure 9.7, which can be stroked across the long dimension of your K200D's sensor.

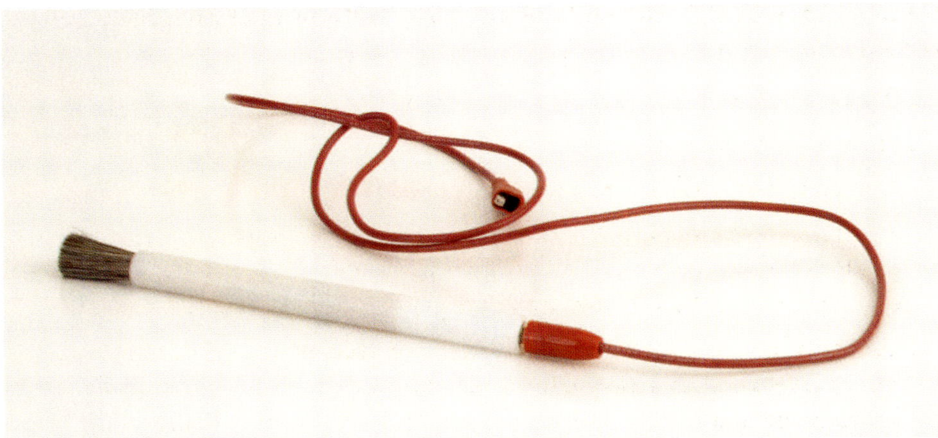

Figure 9.7
A proper brush is required for dusting off your sensor.

Ordinary artist's brushes are much too coarse and stiff and have fibers that are tangled or can come loose and settle on your sensor. A good sensor brush's fibers are resilient and described as "thinner than a human hair." Moreover, the brush has a wooden handle that reduces the risk of static sparks. The brush I use has a grounding cable, as shown in the figure. Check out my *Digital SLR Pro Secrets* book if you want to make a sensor brush (or sensor swabs) yourself.

Brush cleaning is done with a dry brush by gently swiping the surface of the sensor filter with the tip. The dust particles are attracted to the brush particles and cling to them. You should clean the brush with compressed air before and after each use, and store it in an appropriate air-tight container between applications to keep it clean and dust-free. Although these special brushes are expensive, one should last you a long time.

Liquid Cleaning

Unfortunately, you'll often encounter really stubborn dust spots that can't be removed with a blast of air or flick of a brush. These spots may be combined with some grease or a liquid that causes them to stick to the sensor filter's surface. In such cases, liquid cleaning with a swab may be necessary. During my first clumsy attempts to clean my own sensor, I accidentally got my blower bulb tip too close to the sensor, and some sort of deposit from the tip of the bulb ended up on the sensor. I panicked until I discovered that liquid cleaning did a good job of removing whatever it was that took up residence on my sensor.

You can make your own swabs out of pieces of plastic (some use fast food restaurant knives, with the tip cut at an angle to the proper size) covered with a soft cloth or Pec-Pad, as shown in Figures 9.8 and 9.9. However, if you've got the bucks to spend, you can't go wrong with good-quality commercial sensor cleaning swabs, such as those sold by Photographic Solutions, Inc. (www.photosol.com/swabproduct.htm).

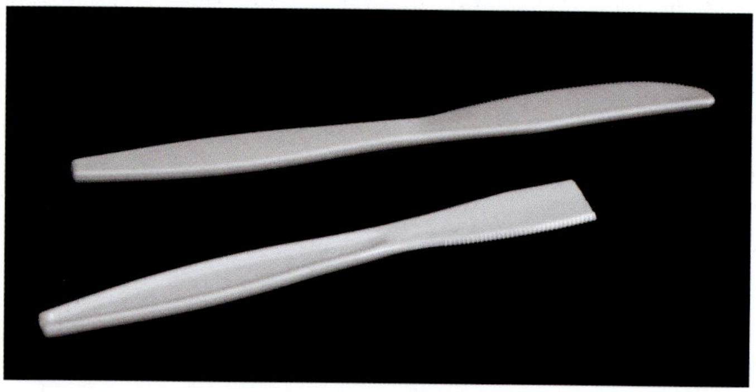

Figure 9.8 You can make your own sensor swab from a plastic knife that's been truncated.

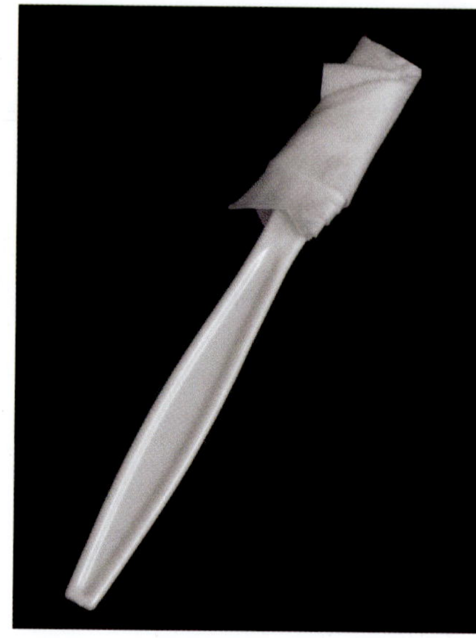

Figure 9.9 Carefully wrap a Pec-Pad around the swab.

You want a sturdy swab that won't bend or break so you can apply gentle pressure to the swab as you wipe the sensor surface. Use the swab with methanol (as pure as you can get it, particularly medical grade; other ingredients can leave a residue), or the Eclipse solution also sold by Photographic Solutions. Eclipse (see Figure 9.10) is actually quite a bit purer than even medical-grade methanol. A couple drops of solution should be enough, unless you have a spot that's extremely difficult to remove. In that case, you may need to use extra solution on the swab to help "soak" the dirt off.

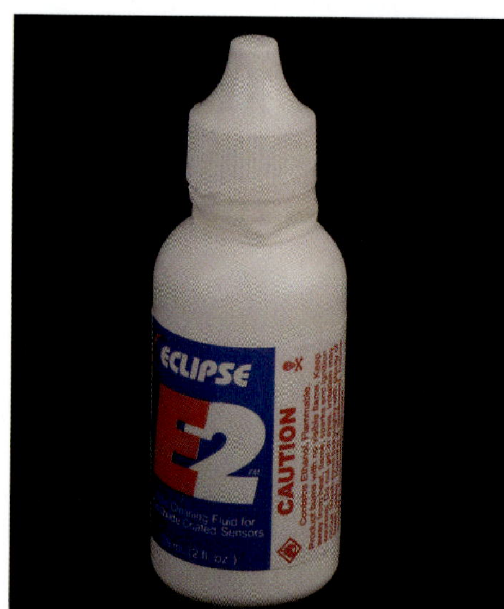

Figure 9.10 Pure Eclipse solution makes the best sensor cleaning liquid.

Once you overcome your nervousness at touching your K200D's sensor, the process is easy. You'll wipe continuously with the swab in one direction, then flip it over and wipe in the other direction. You need to completely wipe the entire surface; otherwise, you may end up depositing the dust you collect at the far end of your stroke. Wipe; don't rub.

If you want a close-up look at your sensor to make sure the dust has been removed, you can pay $50-$100 for a special sensor "microscope" with an illuminator. Or, you can do like I do and work with a plain old Carson MiniBrite PO-25 illuminated 3X magnifier, as seen in Figure 9.11. (Older packaging and ads may call this a 2X magnifier, but it's actually a 3X unit.) It has a built-in LED and, held a few inches from the lens mount with the lens removed from your Pentax, provides a sharp, close-up view of the sensor, with enough contrast to reveal any dust that remains.

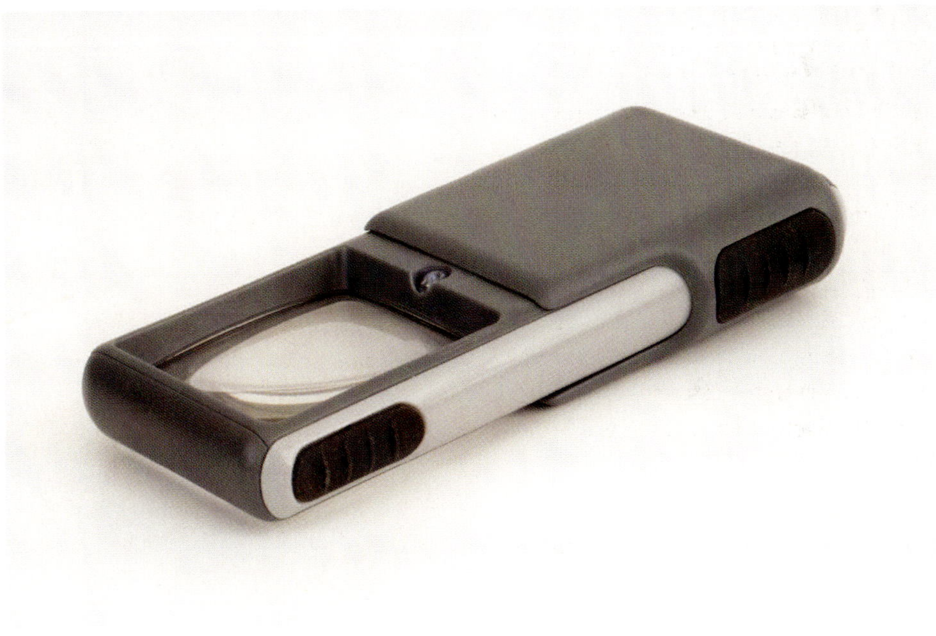

Figure 9.11
An illuminated pocket magnifier, like this one, can help you inspect your sensor.

Tape Cleaning

There are people who absolutely swear by the tape method of sensor cleaning. The concept seems totally wacky, and I have never tried it personally, so I can't say with certainty that it either does or does not work. In the interest of completeness, I'm including it here. I can't give you a recommendation, so if you have problems, please don't blame me. The Pentax K200D hasn't generated any reports of users accidentally damaging the anti-dust coating on the sensor filter using this method, but that doesn't mean it's safe.

Tape cleaning works by applying a layer of Scotch Brand Magic Tape to the sensor. This is a minimally sticky tape that some of the tape cleaning proponents claim contains no adhesive. I did check this out with 3M, and can say that Magic Tape certainly *does* contain an adhesive. The question is whether the adhesive comes off when you peel back the tape, taking any dust spots on your sensor with it. The folks who love this method claim there is no residue. There have been reports from those who don't like the method that residue is left behind. This is all anecdotal evidence, so you're pretty much on your own in making the decision whether to try out the tape cleaning method.

Glossary

Here are some terms you might encounter while reading this book or working with your Pentax K200D.

additive primary colors The red, green, and blue hues, which are used alone or in combinations to create all other colors that you capture with a digital camera, view on a computer monitor, or work with in an image-editing program, such as Photoshop. *See also* CMYK color model.

Adobe RGB One of two color space choices offered by the Pentax K200D. Adobe RGB is an expanded color space useful for commercial and professional printing, and it can reproduce a larger number of colors. You don't need to use this color space if your images will be displayed primarily on your computer screen or output by your personal printer. *See also* sRGB.

ambient lighting Diffuse, non-directional lighting that doesn't appear to come from a specific source but, rather, bounces off walls, ceilings, and other objects in the scene when a picture is taken.

analog/digital converter The electronics built into a camera that convert the analog information captured by the Pentax's sensor into digital bits that can be stored as an image bitmap.

angle of view The area of a scene that a lens can capture, determined by the focal length of the lens. Lenses with a shorter focal length have a wider angle of view than lenses with a longer focal length.

anti-alias A process that smoothes the look of rough edges in images (called *jaggies* or *staircasing*) by adding partially transparent pixels along the boundaries of diagonal lines that are merged into a smoother line by our eyes. *See also* jaggies.

Aperture Priority (Av) A camera setting that allows you to specify the lens opening or f/stop that you want to use, with the camera selecting the required shutter speed automatically based on its light-meter reading. This setting is represented by the abbreviation Av on the Pentax's Mode dial. *See also* Shutter Priority.

artifact A type of noise in an image, or an unintentional image component produced in error by a digital camera during processing, usually caused by the JPEG compression process in digital cameras.

aspect ratio The proportions of an image as printed, displayed on a monitor, or captured by a digital camera. The Pentax K200D camera offers the traditional 3:2 aspect ratio used by most other digital SLRs.

autofocus A camera setting that allows the Pentax K200D to choose the correct focus distance for you, based on the contrast of an image (the image will be at maximum contrast when in sharp focus). The camera can be set for *Single Autofocus (AF.S)*, in which the lens is not focused until the shutter release is partially depressed, or *Continuous Autofocus (AF.C)*, in which the lens refocuses constantly as you frame and reframe the image.

Automatic exposure bracketing Automatic exposure bracketing takes a series of pictures at different exposure increments to improve the chances of producing one picture that is perfectly exposed.

backlighting A lighting effect produced when the main light source is located behind the subject. Backlighting can be used to create a silhouette effect, or to illuminate translucent objects. *See also* front lighting and sidelighting.

barrel distortion A lens defect that causes straight lines at the top or side edges of an image to bow outward into a barrel shape. *See also* pincushion distortion.

blooming An image distortion caused when a photosite in an image sensor has absorbed all the photons it can handle so that additional photons reaching that pixel overflow to affect surrounding pixels, producing unwanted brightness and overexposure around the edges of objects.

blur To soften an image or part of an image by throwing it out of focus, or by allowing it to become soft due to subject or camera motion. Blur can also be applied in an image-editing program.

bokeh A term derived from the Japanese word for blur, which describes the aesthetic qualities of the out-of-focus parts of an image. Some lenses produce "good" bokeh and others offer "bad" bokeh. Some lenses produce uniformly illuminated out-of-focus discs. Others produce a disc that has a bright edge and a dark center, producing a "doughnut" effect, which is the worst from a bokeh standpoint. Lenses that generate a bright center that fades to a darker edge are favored, because their bokeh allows the circle of confusion to blend more smoothly with the surroundings. The bokeh characteristics of a lens are most important when you're using selective focus (say, when shooting a portrait) to deemphasize the background, or when shallow depth-of-field is a given because you're working with a macro lens, with a long telephoto, or with a wide-open aperture. *See also* circle of confusion.

bounce lighting Light bounced off a reflector, including ceiling and walls, to provide a soft, natural-looking light.

buffer The digital camera's internal memory where an image is stored immediately after it is taken until it can be written to the camera's non-volatile (semi-permanent) memory or a memory card.

burst mode The digital camera's equivalent of the film camera's motor drive, used to take multiple shots within a short period of time, each stored in a memory buffer temporarily before writing them to the media. The K200D can shoot 2.8 frames per second in its continuous shooting mode.

calibration A process used to correct for the differences in the output of a printer or monitor when compared to the original image. Once you've calibrated your scanner, monitor, and/or your image editor, the images you see on the screen more closely represent what you'll get from your printer, even though calibration is never perfect.

Camera Raw An Adobe plug-in included with Photoshop and Photoshop Elements that can manipulate the unprocessed images captured by digital cameras, such as the Pentax K200D's .PEF or .DNG files. The latest versions of this module can also work with JPEG and TIFF images.

camera shake Movement of the camera, aggravated by slower shutter speeds, which produces a blurred image, unless countered by the Pentax's Anti-Shake feature.

CCD *See* charge-coupled device (CCD).

Center-Weighted meter A light-measuring device that emphasizes the area in the middle of the frame when calculating the correct exposure for an image. *See also* Spot meter.

charge-coupled device (CCD) A type of solid-state sensor that captures the image used in the Pentax K200D, as well as scanners and other digital cameras.

chromatic aberration An image defect, often seen as green or purple fringing around the edges of an object, caused by a lens failing to focus all colors of a light source at the same point. *See also* fringing.

circle of confusion A term applied to the fuzzy discs produced when a point of light is out of focus. The circle of confusion is not a fixed size. The viewing distance and amount of enlargement of the image determine whether we see a particular spot on the image as a point or as a disc. *See also* bokeh.

close-up lens A lens add-on that allows you to take pictures at a distance that is less than the closest-focusing distance of the lens alone.

CMOS *See* complementary metal-oxide semiconductor (CMOS).

CMYK color model A way of defining all possible colors in percentages of cyan, magenta, yellow, and frequently, black. (K represents black, to differentiate it from blue in the RGB color model.) Black is added to improve rendition of shadow detail. CMYK is commonly used for printing (both on press and with your inkjet or laser color printer).

color correction Changing the relative amounts of color in an image to produce a desired effect, typically a more accurate representation of those colors. Color correction can fix faulty color balance in the original image, or compensate for the deficiencies of the inks used to reproduce the image.

complementary metal-oxide semiconductor (CMOS) A method for manufacturing a type of solid-state sensor that captures the image, used in scanners and digital cameras such as those from Pentax, such as the K200D's stablemate, the Pentax K20D.

compression Reducing the size of a file by encoding using fewer bits of information to represent the original. Some compression schemes, such as JPEG, operate by discarding some image information, while others, such as RAW, preserve all the detail in the original, discarding only redundant data.

Continuous Autofocus (AF.C) An automatic focusing setting in which the camera constantly refocuses the image as you frame the picture. This setting is often the best choice for moving subjects.

contrast The range between the lightest and darkest tones in an image. A high-contrast image is one in which the shades fall at the extremes of the range between white and black. In a low-contrast image, the tones are closer together.

dedicated flash An electronic flash unit, such as the Pentax AF-560 FGZ, designed to work with the automatic exposure features of a specific camera.

depth-of-field A distance range in a photograph in which all included portions of an image are at least acceptably sharp.

diaphragm An adjustable component, similar to the iris in the human eye, which can open and close to provide specific-sized lens openings, or f/stops, and thus control the amount of light reaching the sensor or film.

diffuse lighting Soft, low-contrast lighting.

digital processing chip A solid-state device found in digital cameras that's in charge of applying the image algorithms to the raw picture data prior to storage on the memory card.

diopter A value used to represent the magnification power of a lens, calculated as the reciprocal of a lens's focal length (in meters). Diopters are most often used to represent the optical correction used in a viewfinder to adjust for limitations of the photographer's eyesight, and to describe the magnification of a close-up lens attachment.

equivalent focal length A digital camera's focal length translated into the corresponding values for a 35mm film camera. This value can be calculated for lenses used with the Pentax K200D by multiplying by 1.5.

evaluative metering A system of exposure calculation that looks at many different segments of an image to determine the brightest and darkest portions. The Pentax K200D uses this system when you select the Multi-Segment metering mode.

exchangeable image file format (Exif) Developed to standardize the exchange of image data between hardware devices and software. A variation on JPEG, Exif is used by most digital cameras, and includes information such as the date and time a photo was taken, the camera settings, resolution, amount of compression, and other data.

Exif *See* exchangeable image file format (Exif).

exposure The amount of light allowed to reach the film or sensor, determined by the intensity of the light, the amount admitted by the iris of the lens, the sensitivity of the sensor, and the length of time determined by the shutter speed.

exposure values (EV) EV settings are a way of adding or decreasing exposure without the need to reference f/stops or shutter speeds. For example, if you tell your camera to add +1EV, it will provide twice as much exposure by using a larger f/stop, slower shutter speed, or both.

fill lighting In photography, lighting used to illuminate shadows. Reflectors or additional incandescent lighting or electronic flash can be used to brighten shadows. One common outdoors technique is to use the camera's flash as a fill.

filter In photography, a device that fits over the lens, changing the light in some way. In image editing, a feature that changes the pixels in an image to produce blurring, sharpening, and other special effects. Adobe Photoshop includes several interesting filter effects, including Lens Blur and Photo Filters.

flash sync The timing mechanism that ensures that an internal or external electronic flash fires at the correct time during the exposure cycle. A digital SLR's flash sync speed is the highest shutter speed that can be used with flash, ordinarily 1/180th of a second with the Pentax K200D. *See also* front-curtain sync and rear-curtain sync.

focal length The distance between the film and the optical center of the lens when the lens is focused on infinity, usually measured in millimeters.

focus tracking The ability of the automatic focus feature of a camera to change focus as the distance between the subject and the camera changes. One type of focus tracking is *predictive,* in which the mechanism anticipates the motion of the object being focused on, and adjusts the focus to suit.

format To erase a memory card and prepare it to accept files.

fringing A chromatic aberration that produces fringes of color around the edges of subjects, caused by a lens's inability to focus the various wavelengths of light onto the same spot. Purple fringing is especially troublesome with backlit images.

front-curtain sync (first-curtain sync/leading curtain sync) The default kind of electronic flash synchronization technique, originally associated with focal plane shutters, which consists of a traveling set of curtains, including a *front curtain*, which opens to reveal the film or sensor, and a *rear curtain* , which follows at a distance determined by shutter speed to conceal the film or sensor at the conclusion of the exposure. For a flash picture to be taken, the entire sensor must be exposed at one time to the brief flash exposure, so the image is exposed after the front curtain has reached the other side of the focal plane, but before the rear curtain begins to move. Front-curtain sync causes the flash to fire at the beginning of this period when the shutter is completely open, in the instant that the first curtain of the focal plane shutter finishes its movement across the film or sensor plane. With slow shutter speeds, this feature can create a blur effect from the ambient light, showing as patterns that follow a moving subject with the subject shown sharply frozen at the beginning of the blur trail. *See also* rear-curtain sync.

front lighting Illumination that comes from the direction of the camera. *See also* backlighting and sidelighting.

f/stop The relative size of the lens aperture, which helps determine both exposure and depth-of-field. The larger the f/stop number, the smaller the lens opening created.

graduated filter A lens attachment with variable density or color from one edge to another. A graduated neutral density filter, for example, can be oriented so the neutral density portion is concentrated at the top of the lens's view with the less dense or clear portion at the bottom, thus reducing the amount of light from a very bright sky while not interfering with the exposure of the landscape in the foreground. Graduated filters can also be split into several color sections to provide a color gradient between portions of the image.

gray card A piece of cardboard or other material with a standardized 18-percent reflectance. Gray cards can be used as a reference for determining correct exposure or for setting white balance.

high contrast A wide range of density in a print, negative, or other image.

highlights The brightest parts of an image containing detail.

histogram A kind of chart showing the relationship of tones in an image using a series of 256 vertical bars, one for each brightness level. A histogram chart, such as the one the Pentax K200D can display during picture review, typically looks like a curve with one or more slopes and peaks, depending on how many highlight, midtone, and shadow tones are present in the image. The K200D can also display separate histograms for brightness, as well as the red, green, and blue channels of an image.

hot shoe A mount on top of a camera used to hold an electronic flash, while providing an electrical connection between the flash and the camera.

hyperfocal distance A point of focus where everything from half that distance to infinity appears to be acceptably sharp. For example, if your lens has a hyperfocal distance of four feet, everything from two feet to infinity would be sharp. The hyperfocal distance varies by the lens and the aperture in use. If you know you'll be making a grab shot without warning, sometimes it is useful to turn off your camera's automatic focus, and set the lens to infinity, or, better yet, the hyperfocal distance. Then, you can snap off a quick picture without having to wait for the lag that occurs with most digital cameras as their autofocus locks in.

image rotation A feature that senses whether a picture was taken in horizontal or vertical orientation. That information is embedded in the picture file so that the camera and compatible software applications can automatically display the image in the correct orientation.

image stabilization A technology that compensates for camera shake, which, in Pentax's Anti-Shake implementation, is achieved by adjusting the position of the camera sensor. Some other vendors, such as Nikon and Canon, move the lens elements in response to movements of the camera (which means that the feature is available only with lenses designed to provide it).

incident light Light falling on a surface.

International Organization for Standardization (ISO) A governing body that provides standards used to represent film speed, or the equivalent sensitivity of a digital camera's sensor. Digital camera sensitivity is expressed in ISO settings.

interpolation A technique digital cameras, scanners, and image editors use to create new pixels required whenever you resize or change the resolution of an image based on the values of surrounding pixels. Devices such as scanners and digital cameras can also use interpolation to create pixels in addition to those actually captured, thereby increasing the apparent resolution or color information in an image.

ISO *See* International Organization for Standardization (ISO).

jaggies Staircasing effect of lines that are not perfectly horizontal or vertical, caused by pixels that are too large to represent the line accurately. *See also* anti-alias.

JPEG A file "lossy" format (short for Joint Photographic Experts Group) that supports 24-bit color and reduces file sizes by selectively discarding image data. Digital cameras generally use JPEG compression to pack more images onto memory cards. You can select how much compression is used (and, therefore, how much information is thrown away). *See also* RAW.

Kelvin (K) A unit of measure based on the absolute temperature scale in which absolute zero is zero; it's used to describe the color of continuous-spectrum light sources and applied when setting white balance. For example, daylight has a color temperature of about 5,500K, and a tungsten lamp has a temperature of about 3,400K.

lag time The interval between when the shutter is pressed and when the picture is actually taken. During that span, the camera may be automatically focusing and calculating exposure. With digital SLRs like the Pentax K200D, lag time is generally very short; with some non-dSLRs, the elapsed time easily can be one second or more.

latitude The range of camera exposures that produces acceptable images with a particular digital sensor or film.

lens flare A feature of conventional photography that is both a bane and a creative outlet. It is an effect produced by the reflection of light internally among elements of an optical lens. Bright light sources within or just outside the field of view cause lens flare. Flare can be reduced by the use of coatings on the lens elements or with the use of lens hoods. Photographers sometimes use the effect as a creative technique, and Photoshop includes a filter that lets you add lens flare at your whim.

lighting ratio The proportional relationship between the amount of light falling on the subject from the main light and other lights, expressed in a ratio, such as 3:1.

lossless compression An image-compression scheme, such as TIFF, that preserves all image detail. When the image is decompressed, it is identical to the original version.

lossy compression An image-compression scheme, such as JPEG, that creates smaller files by discarding image information, which can affect image quality.

macro lens A lens that provides continuous focusing from infinity to extreme close-ups, often to a reproduction ratio of 1:2 (half life-size) or 1:1 (life-size).

maximum burst The number of frames that can be exposed at the current settings until the buffer fills.

midtones Parts of an image with tones of an intermediate value, usually in the 25 to 75 percent brightness range. Many image-editing features allow you to manipulate midtones independently from the highlights and shadows.

mirror lock-up The ability of the K200D to flip up its mirror to allow access to the sensor for cleaning.

neutral color A color in which red, green, and blue are present in equal amounts, producing a gray.

neutral density filter A gray camera filter reduces the amount of light entering the camera without affecting the colors.

noise In an image, pixels with randomly distributed color values. Visual noise in digital photographs tends to be the product of low-light conditions and long exposures, particularly when you've set your camera to a high ISO.

noise reduction A technology used to cut down on the amount of random information in a digital picture, usually caused by long exposures and/or increased sensitivity ratings.

normal lens A lens that makes the image in a photograph appear in a perspective that is like that of the original scene, typically with a field of view of roughly 45 degrees.

overexposure A condition in which too much light reaches the film or sensor, producing a dense negative or a very bright/light print, slide, or digital image.

pincushion distortion A type of lens distortion in which lines at the top and side edges of an image are bent inward, producing an effect that looks like a pincushion. *See also* barrel distortion.

polarizing filter A filter that forces light, which normally vibrates in all directions, to vibrate only in a single plane, reducing or removing the specular reflections from the surface of objects.

RAW An image file format, such as the PEF and DNG formats in the Pentax K200D, which includes all the unprocessed information captured by the camera after conversion to digital form. RAW files are very large compared to JPEG files and must be processed by a special program such as Pentax Photo Laboratory, or Adobe's Camera RAW filter after being downloaded from the camera.

rear-curtain sync (second-curtain sync/trailing curtain sync) An optional kind of electronic flash synchronization technique, originally associated with focal plane shutters, which consists of a traveling set of curtains, including a *front (first) curtain* (which opens to reveal the film or sensor) and a *rear (second) curtain* (which follows at a distance determined by shutter speed to conceal the film or sensor at the conclusion of the exposure). For a flash picture to be taken, the entire sensor must be exposed at one time to the brief flash exposure, so the image is exposed after the front curtain has reached the other side of the focal plane, but before the rear curtain begins to move. Rear-curtain sync causes the flash to fire at the end of the exposure, a fraction of an instant before the second or rear curtain of the focal plane shutter begins to move. With slow shutter speeds, this feature can create a blur effect from the ambient light, showing as patterns that follow a moving subject with the subject shown sharply frozen at the end of the blur trail. If you were shooting a photo of The Flash, the superhero would appear sharp, with a ghostly trail behind him. *See also* front-curtain sync (first-curtain sync).

red-eye An effect from flash photography that appears to make a person's eyes glow red, or an animal's yellow or green. It's caused by light bouncing from the retina of the eye and is most pronounced in dim illumination (when the irises are wide open) and when the electronic flash is close to the lens and, therefore, prone to reflect directly back. Image editors can fix red-eye through cloning other pixels over the offending red or orange ones.

RGB color A color model that represents the three colors—red, green, and blue—used by devices such as scanners or monitors to reproduce color. Photoshop works in RGB mode by default, and even displays CMYK images by converting them to RGB.

saturation The purity of color; the amount by which a pure color is diluted with white or gray.

selective focus Choosing a lens opening that produces a shallow depth-of-field and focusing carefully on the subject that you want to appear sharp. Usually this is used to isolate a subject in portraits, close-ups, and other types of images, by causing most other elements in the scene to be blurred.

self-timer A mechanism that delays the opening of the shutter for some seconds after the release has been operated.

sensitivity A measure of the degree of response of a film or sensor to light, measured using the ISO setting.

Sensitivity Priority (Sv) An exposure mode, represented by the letters Sv on the Pentax's Mode dial, in which you set the ISO desired, and the camera determines the appropriate f/stop and shutter speed. *See also* Aperture Priority.

shadow The darkest part of an image, represented on a digital image by pixels with low numeric values.

sharpening Increasing the apparent sharpness of an image by boosting the contrast between adjacent pixels that form an edge.

shutter In a conventional film camera, the shutter is a mechanism consisting of blades, a curtain, a plate, or some other movable cover that controls the time during which light reaches the film. Digital cameras may use actual mechanical shutters for the slower shutter speeds (less than 1/160th second) and an electronic shutter for higher speeds.

Shutter Priority (Tv) An exposure mode, represented by the letters Tv on the Pentax's Mode dial, in which you set the shutter speed and the camera determines the appropriate f/stop. *See also* Aperture Priority.

sidelighting Applying illumination from the left or right sides of the camera. *See also* backlighting and front lighting.

slave unit An accessory flash unit that supplements the main flash, usually triggered electronically when the slave senses the light output by the main unit, or through radio waves.

slow sync An electronic flash synchronizing method that uses a slow shutter speed so that ambient light is recorded by the camera in addition to the electronic flash illumination. This allows the background to receive more exposure for a more realistic effect.

specular highlight Bright spots in an image caused by reflection of light sources.

Spot meter An exposure system that concentrates on a small area in the image, represented by the circle in the center of the Pentax's viewfinder. *See also* Center-Weighted meter.

sRGB One of two color space choices available with the Pentax K200D. The sRGB setting is recommended for images that will be output locally on the user's own printer or which are sent to a photofinisher, as this color space matches that of the typical printer and a properly calibrated monitor fairly closely. *See also* Adobe RGB.

subtractive primary colors Cyan, magenta, and yellow, which are the printing inks that theoretically absorb all color and produce black. In practice, however, they generate a muddy brown, so black is added to preserve detail (especially in shadows). The combination of the three colors and black is referred to as CMYK. (K represents black, to differentiate it from blue in the RGB model.)

through-the-lens (TTL) A system of providing viewing and exposure calculation through the actual lens taking the picture.

time exposure A picture taken by leaving the shutter open for a long period, usually more than one second. The camera is generally locked down with a tripod to prevent blur during the long exposure.

tungsten light Light from ordinary room lamps and ceiling fixtures, as opposed to fluorescent illumination.

underexposure A condition in which too little light reaches the film or sensor, producing a thin negative, a dark slide, a muddy-looking print, or a dark digital image.

unsharp masking The process for increasing the contrast between adjacent pixels in an image, increasing sharpness, especially around edges.

vignetting Dark corners of an image, often produced by using a lens hood that is too small for the field of view, a lens that does not completely fill the image frame, or generated artificially using image-editing techniques for artistic purposes.

white balance The adjustment of a digital camera to the color temperature of the light source. Interior illumination is relatively red; outdoor light is relatively blue. Digital cameras like the K200D set correct white balance automatically or let you do it through menus. Image editors can often do some color correction of images that were exposed using the wrong white balance setting, especially when working with RAW files that contain the information originally captured by the camera before white balance was applied.

Index

A

B

C

E

F

G

H

I

J

Q

R

U

V

W

X

Y

Z